THE METHUEN DRAMA
GUIDE TO CON[T]
IRISH PLAYWRI

Martin Middeke holds the Chair of English Literature at the University of Augsburg. He read English, German and Philosophy at the Universities of Paderborn and Reading, was a post-doctorate Fulbright scholar at New York University, and in 2008 and 2009 taught as Visiting Professor at the University of Johannesburg. His major fields of research are Literary Theory, Nineteenth-Century English Fiction, Samuel Beckett, and Contemporary British and Irish Fiction and Drama. He is Co-Editor of *Anglia* and General Editor of the CDE book series. His publications include *Stephen Poliakoff* (1994) and two studies on the aesthetics of time-consciousness in the novel (*Zeit und Roman*, 2002; *Die Kunst der gelebten Zeit*, 2004). Book-length publications which he (co-)edited include *Anthropological Perspectives* (1998); *Biofictions* (1999); *Self-Reflexivity in Literature* (2005); *Drama and/after Postmodernism* (2007); and *Literature and Circularity* (2009). Forthcoming in 2010 is a book project on *Melancholia as a Central Discourse in English Literary and Cultural History*.

Peter Paul Schnierer read English, German, Political Sciences and Philosophy at the universities of London, Greenwich and Tübingen. He has taught full time at the universities of Greenwich, Buckingham, Tübingen, Northern Arizona, Maryland and Vienna, and he currently holds the Chair of English Literature at the University of Heidelberg. His research interests include modern drama, Irish literature, literary hypertexts and the Gothic tradition. His publications on contemporary English drama include two books (*Rekonventionalisierung im englischen Drama 1980–1990*, 1994; and *Modernes englisches Drama und Theater seit 1945: Eine Einführung*, 1997), one edited collection (*Contemporary Drama in English: Beyond the Mainstream*, 1997) and one collection co-edited with Ellen Redling (*Non-Standard Forms of Contemporary Drama and Theatre*, 2008). He has also published a monograph on literary demonisation since the Renaissance.

THE METHUEN DRAMA GUIDE TO CONTEMPORARY IRISH PLAYWRIGHTS

Edited and with an introduction by Martin Middeke and Peter Paul Schnierer

Methuen Drama

Methuen Drama

1 3 5 7 9 10 8 6 4 2

First published in Great Britain in 2010 by Methuen Drama

Methuen Drama
A & C Black Publishers Limited
36 Soho Square
London W1D 3QY
www.methuendrama.com

Copyright © 2010 by Martin Middeke and Peter Paul Schnierer

The rights of the editors to be identified as the editors of these works have been
asserted by them in accordance with the Copyright, Design and Patents Act, 1988

ISBN 978 1 408 11346 2

A CIP catalogue record for this book is available from the British Library

Typeset by SX Composing DTP, Rayleigh, Essex
Printed and bound in Great Britain by Martins the Printers, Berwick-upon-Tweed

CONTENTS

INTRODUCTION

Martin Middeke and Peter Paul Schnierer

Unlike the literary genres of narrative fiction and poetry, drama and its constitutive categories of dialogue, interaction and immediacy in performance have by definition always had a close affinity to the structures of the particular society they reflect. This very notably applies to Ireland because, undoubtedly, it was the genre of drama and the Irish National Theatre movement that created a national identity for a colonised nation.[1] However, the status of Irish drama and its relationship to the British dramatic scene has been in a constant state of flux.

At the beginning of the twentieth century Lady Gregory, William Butler Yeats, John Millington Synge, Sean O'Casey and a host of other writers sought to put their talents to the cause of national emancipation and anti-imperialist struggle. With the emergence of a consciously Irish dramatic scene in Ireland itself, which inevitably reflected aspects of *Irish* society specifically, the intermingling of British and Irish dramatic talent of earlier years decreased. Over time, however, this movement lost its force; for example, O'Casey emigrated to England and Beckett went straight to France. And yet, despite the gradual dissolution of the Irish National Theatre movement, Irish and British drama remained shaped by the conditions and structures of the respective societies.

In the last two decades, however, the gap between what is recognisably Irish and British drama has narrowed. This rapprochement is a result of two major political and economic upheavals that provided a fundamental change in Irish society and resulted in its more globalised structure becoming more like that of Britain again. At the end of the 1980s, Ireland saw the start of an economic miracle in industry, trade, tourism, public services, and especially in information technologies, which transformed Ireland into one of the most globalised countries in the world within a decade. Economic growth (up to ten per cent each year), low unemployment, taxes and inflation rates, along with a huge potential of well-trained young people eager to enter the labour market all resulted in Ireland attracting foreign investment. During this time, Ireland also underwent a political transformation after years of conflict and division. In the early- and mid-1990s the peace process in Northern Ireland gained momentum, having come a long way from the Sunningdale Agreement of 1973, the terrible hunger strikes of the early 1980s, the Anglo-Irish Agreement of 1985 and the IRA agreeing to a ceasefire in 1994. This was consolidated in 1998 by the Good Friday Agreement, which set the basis for a government consisting of parties from both sides of the political divide.

This period of economic growth and increasing political stability has been accompanied by a radical reshaping of Irish identity as a new Ireland has emerged. This has included a host of progressive changes, such as: the peace process, economic boom, new social legislation, the growing force of feminism and a (necessary) redefinition of mores, identities and gender-roles, and the election of two female Presidents. At the same time, Irish society has been fractured by Church scandals, an increasing crime rate and growing lawlessness and alienation. Finally, there has been a slackening of the inclination towards including Britain in the evaluation of Irish identity.

Irish society and Irish drama are in serious transition and even though not every writer covered in this survey can be said to transcend national issues or even stereotypes, a product of this is that many writers are now equally at home in Dublin, Galway, London or what is still called the Irish diaspora. We are witnessing at the moment a period of accelerated Irish history and an accumulation of identities that have radically changed the structures of Irish society, albeit, for better or worse, in an often precarious way:

> Economic growth means that Ireland now seems in many ways indistinguishable from other countries in the West, prompting a growing sense of uncertainty about national identity: 'we' may be wealthier, but it's not clear what the

word 'we' refers to any more. As peace takes root in Northern Ireland, other divisions are becoming apparent throughout the island – in terms of class, gender, race and other characteristics. Perhaps most importantly, there is a growing fear that the country is developing a strange form of collective amnesia, a reluctance to acknowledge that its history is dominated by failure: by mass emigration, military defeat, economic stagnation and underdevelopment. So as we move into the second decade of this century, Ireland is faced with difficult questions. How can we reconcile the memory of that troubled past with the desire to enjoy an apparently successful present? And if we let go of our histories, will we still remember who we are?[2]

Inevitably, the social and political shifts that surround contemporary Irish playwrights have had an impact on their writing, and the intersection between post-colonial and post-modern influences has been channelled into elaborate aesthetic structures, which have cast doubts on and, ultimately, seared such forms as the peasant play, the religious play, the family play or the history play in their respective Irish incarnations.

Our collection introduces twenty-five representative playwrights of contemporary Irish drama. The chapters are written by a team of internationally renowned specialists from the Republic of Ireland, Northern Ireland, England, Scotland and Germany. Each chapter has a four-part structure: an introduction, including a short biographical sketch of each playwright; a survey and concise analysis of the published plays of the respective author in chronological order; summarising statements on central topics and aesthetic techniques and comments on existing critical reception and the position of the playwright in the discourse of contemporary Irish theatre; and, finally, a bibliography of primary texts and a selected list of critical material. For those playwrights with an exceedingly high output over decades, the survey and analysis section has been limited to what seemed the most important works.

The twenty-five chapters in this volume discuss a total of 190 plays in detail – an abundant corpus constituting a heuristically valuable starting point of an analysis of the state of affairs in contemporary Irish drama. Many more intertextual sources are mentioned and referred to as sources underlying the respective work at issue. The plays under scrutiny span 1959 – John B. Keane's *Sive* – to the present.[3] More than half of the plays discussed in this volume were written in the last decade of the twentieth and first decade of the twenty-first century, thus presenting a body of work hitherto unprecedented in critical analysis of contemporary Irish drama. Christopher Murray's 1996 prognosis that 'the last great period of Irish drama has just come to an end, and we seem to have entered a quietist, minimalist phase'[4] has not quite proved true.

Surveying the twenty-five chapters, major thematic and aesthetic directions and trends stand out. The themes of exile and emigration can still be traced from Friel's *Philadelphia, Here I Come!* to Enda Walsh's *The Walworth Farce* even though, historically speaking, Ireland has witnessed 'a decade in which it has begun to attract substantial numbers of immigrants.'[5] Exile and return, memory and loss, and displacement and dispossession are, however, still important topics on the contemporary Irish stage. Likewise, the relationship between the past and the present remains both an important thematic and structural constituent of Irish drama. Stories, story-telling, memories and conjurations of the past abound in the plays. The historical consciousness and, even more generally, the concept of history ensuing from this turning to the past range between 'a suffering from "historyalis"', that is, '"stuckness in the past"'[6], a melancholy death-consciousness, to more moderate, revisionist representations of the past which seek to find an unstable equilibrium between remembering and forgetting. On the surface of contemporary Irish drama the nostalgic reverence for the olden days (to be found in writers such as John B. Keane) gives way more and more to a debunking of the idea of a glorious past or of the superficial desire for heroic versions of the past and a melancholy sense of loss (of youth, of life, of future). Writers such as Sebastian Barry confront and see through the ways individual, cultural or collective memories are constructed or suppressed in a thoroughly liberating way. At the same time – and somewhat surprisingly – plays such as Barry's *Tales of Ballycumber* (2009) still reveal a fascination for ghosts and, thus, still seem to be replete with that particularly Irish sense of historical and moral paralysis that James Joyce had diagnosed in *Dubliners* almost a hundred years ago. Beyond that, however, the last two decades have seen a growing number of truly iconoclastic reckonings with the past and past traditions, for instance, in the works of Marina Carr, Martin McDonagh and Owen McCafferty.

Another major topic of contemporary Irish drama is, in Lyotardian terminology, the collapse or interrogation of the grand narratives of 'history', 'religion', 'nation', 'progress', 'community' and the rigorous questioning of private and public institutions ('family', 'home', 'church') and of the concept of individual as well as social and national 'identity.' Tom Murphy's work springs to mind with its portrayal of families broken by violence, cruelty and the inability to communicate. Murphy's work also paradigmatically corroborates the sense of private and social homelessness that is omnipresent in contemporary Irish drama.

Again and again, plays confront Ireland's (post-colonial) past by turning to the insecurity of national identity. The mythical surface of the Irish island idyll is hollowed out by homophobia and almost atavistic violence. How central this idea is to contemporary Irish drama becomes clear if one keeps in mind that we encounter such de-mythologising – the prototype of which of course is Synge – in Brian Friel's *The Gentle Island* and, twenty-five years later, in Martin McDonagh. McDonagh's *The Lieutenant of Inishmore* (2001) is perhaps the harshest deconstruction of de Valera's vision of

> a land whose countryside would be bright with cosy homesteads, whose fields and villages would be joyous with the sounds of industry, with the romping of sturdy children, the contests of athletic youths, the laughter of comely maidens; whose firesides would be forums for the wisdom of old age.[7]

McDonagh adapts de Valera's characteristic style but distorts it into 'an Ireland free. Free for kids to run and play. Free for fellas and lasses to dance and sing. Free for cats to roam about without being clanked in the brains with a handgun.'[8] McDonagh's deconstruction, although London-Irish in origin, is well in accordance with the life and the feelings of many Irish of the younger generation because it unmasks de Valera's vision as phantasmagoria that never existed in the first place.[9]

Contemporary Irish playwrights – most notably perhaps Marina Carr, Sebastian Barry, Dermot Bolger, Brian Friel, Tom Murphy, Marie Jones, Christina Reid, Graham Reid and Enda Walsh – have reflected on the fractured state of the family or the concept of home. Such fragmentation often appears as veritable death-in-life situations of paralysis, lost chances and psychological entrapment. In this context, instances of emotional or psychological, physical and structural violence are all-pervasive on the contemporary Irish stage. Again and again, violence is often presented as an effect of Celtic Tiger (self-)alienation. The revolt against a neo-liberal society in many contemporary Irish plays and their portrayal of fragmented social mores thoroughly oppose the unwillingness of the Irish establishment to distribute the new wealth in a just way, while at the same time the new liberties won by the economic boom are thoroughly enjoyed.

Another common characteristic of contemporary Irish drama is a peremptory concern with feminist issues. The battle of sexes and the complexities of interrelationships between men and women are ubiquitous in Irish drama. Not only have women playwrights such as Emma Donoghue, Anne Devlin, Marina Carr, Christina Reid and Marie Jones established gender as a key aspect of human identity, the gender struggles inherent in many contemporary Irish plays have contributed to a thorough re-mapping of the boundaries of gender regulation and gender stereotypes. In particular, the aspect of gender performativity has unmasked gender as an arbitrary gesture and its construction very often as a traumatic instance of patriarchal (self-)fashioning. Irish feminist writing has deconstructed the 'male gaze', the marginalisation of women in history, traditional and conventional concepts of wifehood, and motherhood or pregnancy, and has introduced new aspects of male and female homosexuality. An increasing number of plays and playwrights (McCafferty, McPherson, Roche) have also turned to issues around the construction of masculinities (fatherhood etc.) and the ensuing anxieties involved in the inability to find an expression of men's identity in an increasingly 'fatherless' society.

For decades the political crisis in Northern Ireland, the Troubles and, since the mid-1990s, the peace process have been a prevalent subject which has made its appearance in various facets and forms. Contemporary Irish drama reveals this problem as still pending. Multiple views of the obsessive interrogation of the Irish–British relationship include the experience of women surviving the political crisis addressed, for instance, by Anne Devlin. Owen McCafferty has mapped out the sectarian geography of Belfast; Gary Mitchell questions the presuppositions of violent loyalism, and his work constitutes a veritable threat to organisations responsible for so-called pro-state terrorism; Martin Lynch sets out to portray the every-day struggle of ordinary people trying to survive their impoverished living conditions. In 1980 Brian Friel's *Translations* focused on the failure of communication between the coloniser and the colonised. Again and again, analogies have been drawn between terrorist violence and mental dispositions of the terrorist and sectarian mindset. Graham Reid, for instance, presents sexual and political repression and exploitation as interrelated. Such pessimistic views stand next to more optimistic visions, such as Stewart Parker's, of the theatre as a means of reconciling Catholics and Protestants in the North.

A brief look at the formal and stylistic features of contemporary Irish drama presents a similarly heterogeneous picture. Inasmuch as Ireland began to be multi-ethnic and multi-racial during and after the economic boom of the 1990s, the aesthetics of the contemporary Irish stage, which for such a long time had been 'text-based, formally conservative, dominated by author rather than the director, designer or acting company'[10] gradually also incorporated ensemble-scripted and often site- and company-specific plays. Generally speaking, the distinction that Irish drama is oscillating between tradition and innovation, between realistic and experimental avant-garde aesthetics, as Christopher Murray pointed out, is still valid.[11] If realism is characterised by a mimetic frame of reference towards life, by eventful and causally interrelated linear plotlines, by psychological authenticity, by heteroreferentiality and by the attempt to create an unbroken impression the events might have happened just the way they are presented on stage, even the more traditional examples of contemporary Irish drama seem to be characterised by a rather heightened realism. Beyond that, statements on the aesthetics of contemporary Irish playwrights are complicated because many playwrights with long careers and an extensive list of plays have evolved various phases of stylistic development. Brian Friel is a case in point: his early and later work differs considerably because the latter much more consciously turns to formal experiment and metatheatricality. Tom Murphy's work has always been heightened by mythic dimensions. Graham Reid, whose works are tied so much to the realistic setting of the Troubles and whose concerns are so ostensibly directed at those religious, political, social and psychological factors which have – quite realistically – determined the conflict is, at the same time, heightened by a dignified symbolism. The same is true for the melodrama in John B. Keane, the self-conscious appropriation of music-hall elements in Stewart Parker, or Billy Roche's symbolic heightening of the local. On the one hand, the stage realism of these plays aims at a portrayal of the daily struggle of ordinary people; on the other hand, the stage imagery goes beyond the social realism of kitchen sink dramaturgy in quite a poetic way.

Similarly in this vein, many contemporary Irish plays provide evidence of an aesthetics of moderate experiment. The urban character of Thomas Kilroy's plays and their satiric eye on Irish society have always been characterised by the challenging of both form and language. Frank McGuinness, for instance, fuses the tragic and the comic, the real and the surreal and hence makes his stylistic register shift from ostensive realism in plays such as *The Factory Girls* to much more psychological nightmare visions in *Innocence*. These moderate experiments imply different stances towards authenticity. In Dermot Bolger's psychic realism, for instance, we encounter memories, soliloquies and real and imagined characters from past and present. The lyrically heightened realism of Sebastian Barry springs to mind, likewise Gary Mitchell's dramaturgy of casting single glimpses at particular surroundings. Despite many realist settings there have been various experiments with chronology and the linear structure of the plotlines. In this context Martin McDonagh's Leenane Trilogy must be mentioned, but so should Billy Roche's oscillating time schemes dissolving the idea of linearity development and closure, Marina Carr's nightmarish visions, Christina Reid's attempts at creating panoramic portrayals of different generations, the non-chronological scenic snapshots taken from retrospective in Bolger's *The Lament for Arthur Cleary*, or the looped time-structure in plays by Emma Donoghue.

Storytelling brings a narrative element to dramatic structure diverting action on stage entirely into the realm of the imagination and the imaginary. Storytelling and its implicit juxtaposition of present and past turn drama into an intricate time machine of memory, forgetting and imagination. Murphy's groundbreaking *Bailegangaire* self consciously draws on the Irish history of storytelling in much the same way as does Martin McDonagh's *The Pillowman*, although the latter does so in a much more autoreflexive, metafictional way. However, both plays accentuate via storytelling that any concept of personal, local and national identity is based upon the ability to have access to and a grip on one's history, or one's story, which, again, is intertwined with other stories. Conor McPherson's *The Weir* is another example of the prevalence of storytelling in contemporary Irish drama, although it constitutes a rather conventional play which only goes some ways towards deconstructing its well-established naturalistic setting by blending the traditional sources with contemporary issues. Thus, the setting of the Irish pub in the remote West notably aims at universal issues beyond its Irish roots; it nevertheless means a kind of displace-ment for audiences around the world which felt attracted to the play: 'Ireland in the Irish play is a world elsewhere.'[12] In a much more radical, violent and aesthetically daring way, Enda Walsh has emphasised the importance (as well as the performativity) of an existing (hi-)story for the construction of personal identity in Dinny's unforgettably shocking performance of the family history in Cork in *The Walworth Farce*. Walsh's plays are thoroughly set in realistic surroundings but the self-conscious use of performance and perfor-mative aspects of language both in *The Walworth Farce* and also in his earlier *Disco Pigs* aim at transcending the realistic or naturalistic framework.

Walsh's work, in unison with earlier plays by Tom Mac Intyre or by Walsh's contemporaries Marina Carr, Mark O'Rowe, Martin McDonagh and Owen McCafferty, embodies that branch of contemporary Irish drama which distinguishes itself by establishing the freedom for radical experiment and the metadramatic turn to aesthetic hybridisation. Ensuing stylistic features include the fragmentation of language, and self-reflexive modes such as parody, travesty and pastiche. In Marina Carr's drama we encounter avant-garde frescoes of the skull that explore dream states and subconscious layers of the psyche. Very similar to developments in contemporary fiction, plays by women playwrights especially have departed from the (paternalistic) fetters of the realist tradition. The idea of a gendered language pays attention to the interrelatedness of body and language in the attainment of subjectivity. Marina Carr's stage imagery is replete with violent images of incest, child abuse, and physical and emotional brutality. This predilection for often ritualised, graphic yet thoroughly sublime stage violence is also to be found in O'Rowe, McDonagh and McCafferty, thereby connecting these playwrights and, in consequence, much of Irish avant-garde drama today, to aesthetic trends in Britain (such as In-Yer-Face theatre) and on the European continent (such as post-dramatic theatre and drama). Carr's experimental hybrids mix elements from folk-tale, memory and indi-vidual desire; Anne Devlin's plays juxtapose naturalism and surrealism; Martin McDonagh's work reveals a fascination with the carnivalesque, the grotesque, the paradox, in which the realistic fact metadramatically and self-consciously turns into artefact. At issue here is the plurality of fractured selves, which are articulated through emotional, spiritual and psychic images, voices and individual experience. In this post-modern way, the very hybridity of aesthetic forms stays abreast of the changes in Irish experience and its much more globalised vision and interconnectedness.[13] Contemporary Irish drama with its globalised perspective reflects upon and casts doubts on notions of authenticity which have not been challenged for a long time. These are no longer plays of national but rather of cultural imagination because they increasingly and visibly foster mistrust against any idea of totalising systems of thought in order to establish new and vital avenues into an open future.

In conclusion, on the way to a post-Troubles and post-Celtic Tiger condition both Irish society and contemporary Irish drama stand in a liminal zone, a zone of transition. According to the anthropologist Victor Turner such liminality can be understood as 'a fructile chaos, a fertile nothingness, a storehouse of possibilities.'[14] Commenting on the more experimental threads in contemporary Irish drama and their development in the last two decades of the twentieth and the first decade of the twenty-first century, Nicholas Grene stated that the Irish 'will become a "truly postcolonial society" when we are liberated from the need to express the essence of Ireland or even "varieties of Irishness" on stage.'[15] The following twenty-five chapters of our guide to contemporary Irish drama will provide abounding evidence of the fact that Irish drama has lost neither its zeal and edge nor its productivity and individual face in the context of a more and more globalised, late-capitalist world. Thus, in 'striving after new forms and anticipating postliminal existence'[16], contemporary Irish drama and the Irish nation of the twenty-first century are well on their way.

Martin Middeke and Peter Paul Schnierer

Augsburg and Heidelberg, January 2010

Bibliography

Grene, Nicholas, *The Politics of Irish Drama. Plays in Context from Boucicault to Friel* (Cambridge: CUP, 1999).

Grene, Nicholas, 'Contemporary Irish Theatre – The Way We Live Now,' in Werner Huber and Margarete Rubik (eds) *Staging Multiculturality*. Contemporary Drama in English, vol. 16 (Trier: WVT, 2010) [forthcoming].

Hughes, Declan, 'Who the Hell Do We Think We Still Are? Reflections on Irish Theatre and Identity', in Eamonn Jordan, *Theatre Stuff: Critical Essays on Contemporary Irish*

Theatre (Dublin: Carysfort Press, 2000), pp. 8–15.

Jordan, Eamonn, 'Introduction', *Theatre Stuff: Critical Essays on Contemporary Irish Theatre* (Dublin: Carysfort Press, 2000), pp. xi–xlviii.

Lonergan, Patrick, *Theatre and Globalization: Irish Drama in the Celtic Tiger Era* (Basingstoke: Palgrave MacMillan, 2009).

Lonergan, Patrick, 'Introduction', *The Methuen Drama Anthology of Irish Plays* (London: Methuen Drama, 2008), pp. vii–xv.

Murray, Christopher, 'The State of Play: Irish Theatre in the 'Nineties', Eberhard Bort (ed.) *The State of Play: Irish Theatre in the 'Nineties* (Trier: WVT), 1996), pp. 9–23.

Murray, Christopher, *Twentieth-Century Irish Drama. Mirror up to Nation* (New York: Syracuse UP, 2000).

Richards, Shaun, 'Plays of (ever) changing Ireland', in Shaun Richards (ed.) *The Cambridge Companion to Twentieth-Century Irish Drama* (Cambridge: CUP, 2004), p. 1–17.

Roche, Anthony, *Contemporary Irish Drama. From Beckett to McGuinness* (Dublin: Gill and Macmillan, 1994) [revised edition: Basingstoke: Palgrave Macmillan, 2009].

Turner, Victor, 'Are there Universals of Performance in Myth, Ritual, and Drama?', in Richard Schechner and Willa Appel (eds.) *By Means of Performance: Intercultural Studies of Theatre and Ritual* (Cambridge: CUP, 1995), pp. 8–18.

Notes

1. Nicholas Grene, *The Politics of Irish Drama. Plays in Context from Boucicault to Friel* (Cambridge: CUP, 1999), p. 1; see also Murray, *Twentieth-Century Irish Drama. Mirror up to Nation* (New York: Syracuse UP, 2000), p. 3., and Richards, op. cit., p. 1.

2. Patrick Lonergan, 'Introduction', *The Methuen Drama Anthology of Irish Plays* (London: Methuen Drama, 2008), p. vii.

3. As is well-known, Richard Pine settled on September 28, 1964 – the day when Friel's *Philadephia, Here I Come!* was premiered – as the starting point of contemporary Irish drama. See Anthony Roche, *Contemporary Irish Drama. From Beckett to McGuinness* (Dublin: Gill and Macmillan, 1994) [revised edition: Basingstoke: Palgrave Macmillan, 2009] , pp. 2–3.

4. Christopher Murray, 'The State of Play: Irish Theatre in the 'Nineties', op. cit., p. 11.

5. Nicholas Grene, 'Contemporary Irish Theatre,' [forthcoming].

6. Ibid.

7. St Patrick's Day speech made by Taoiseach of Ireland Éamon de Valera on Raidió Éireann on 17 March 1943.

8. Martin McDonagh, *The Lieutenant of Inishmore* (London: Methuen Drama, 2001), p. 60.

9. See Richards, op. cit., pp. 6–7.

10. Ibid.

11. See Murray, *Twentieth-Century Irish Drama.*
12. Grene, *The Politics of Irish Drama*, p. 262.
13. For an extensive study of such interconnectedness see Patrick Lonergan's groundbreaking study *Theatre and Globalization.* In this context, Shaun Richards certainly has a point when he argues that Ireland and Irish drama have been in constant change ever since the Irish Revival and that 'change' itself, therefore, is no exclusive Celtic Tiger phenomenon. In the face of the dramatic historical, economic and political landslide in Ireland in the 1990s and especially in the context of globalisation, however, Richards's contention that the 'iconoclastic urge' of writers such as Carr or McDonagh and their aesthetic impact was not actually 'a still critical necessity' and rather served 'to reinforce the centrality of the images it seeks to displace' seems a misjudgment. See Richards, op. cit., p. 9. Eamonn Jordan poignantly postulated in his preface to *Theatre Stuff* that 'change is fundamental to a dramatic practice and the challenge facing all of our present dramatists is to match and map the experiences, confidences and demands of a changing society.' Jordan, op. cit., xv. In the same collection of essays, Declan Hughes rails against a spirit of nostalgia and that people still need to be shaken out of the satisfaction of 'being Irish with themselves' (see Hughes, op. cit.). Carr's and McDonagh's iconoclasms, hence, have a thoroughly liberating function in the process of thwarting the 'fetishisation of authentication' as 'a dangerous cul-de-sac.' (Jordan, op. cit., xvi).
14. Turner, op. cit., pp. 16–17.
15. Grene, 'Contemporary Irish Theatre – The Way We Live Now' [forthcoming].
16. Turner, op. cit., pp. 16–17.

1 SEBASTIAN BARRY

Jürgen Wehrmann

Boss Grady's Boys; *Prayers of Sherkin*; *White Woman Street*; *The Only True History of Lizzie Finn*; *The Steward of Christendom*; *Our Lady of Sligo*; *Hinterland*; *Whistling Psyche*; *The Pride of Parnell Street*; *Dallas Sweetman*

Introduction

Sebastian Barry was born on 5 July 1955 in Dublin. Since his mother was the well-known actress Joan O'Hara, the Abbey Theatre formed an important background to his childhood, and already by the early 1960s he had watched such Irish classics as *Cathleen ni Houlihan* with his mother in the leading role. His first novel, *Macker's Garden*, and his first collection of poetry, *The Water-Colourist*, came out in 1982. Before his breakthrough in the theatre, he published another collection of poetry, a book for children and increasingly experimental prose. Barry is one of the very few Irish dramatists who have also been recognised as eminent poets and novelists: none of his plays but several of his poems were included in the *Field Day Anthology of Irish Writing*, and his two latest novels, *The Long Long Way* (2005) and *The Secret Scripture* (2008), were shortlisted for the Booker Prize. Although he had written some unpublished plays before, one of which, the monologue *The Pentagonal Dream*, had been staged in 1986, Barry looks at conceiving *Boss Grady's Boys* and its acceptance at the Abbey as the decisive departure in his life – both aesthetically and privately: the success of this and his later plays allowed him to start a family with actress Alison Deegan in 1992.

Since 1988, Barry's prose and poetry have been closely connected to his series of plays about his family. While some of the poems in *Fanny Hawke Goes to the Mainland Forever* (1988) encapsulate the plot and imagery of later plays, *Annie Dunne* (2002) and *The Long Long Way* can be considered, respectively, as sequel and prequel to *The Steward of Christendom* (1995).

The Plays

Boss Grady's Boys (1988)

Sebastian Barry's first published play, *Boss Grady's Boys*, is set in the 1950s and deals with two brothers – bachelors in their sixties and seventies respectively – who live together on a small farm in the south west of Ireland. Rather than depicting their hard everyday life realistically, the drama focuses on the brothers' dreams and memories in an anti-mimetic theatrical style, which blurs the boundaries between past and present, dreaming and waking, reality and fantasy, and even self and other. To their father, Mick and Josey indeed seemed to embody two different, conflicting parts of himself:[1] since the elder brother, Josey, who might be slightly mentally handicapped, easily gets lost in his dreams, feelings and sensual perceptions, Mick has adopted the role of the rational, practical and responsible one. In contrast to the traditional Irish peasant play, the myths that feed Josey's fantasies are not derived from an old oral tradition but from Hollywood. Mick once believed in the promise of the Irish revolution to improve the miserable situation of subsistence farmers such as Josey and himself and to make them belong. As this promise has never been fulfilled, the disillusioned Mick accuses Irish nationalism of hypocritically using the rural west as the image of a 'true' Ireland while marginalising it at the same time (p. 21). Despite the lyrical language and the emphasis on the loving and caring relationship between the brothers, there is a strong undercurrent of violence in the play, comprising allusions to political killings and torture, Boss Grady's threats of domestic violence (p. 19) and the possibility of sexual violence as a reaction to suppression and frustration. Both Mick and Josey are haunted by the memory or fantasy of a neglected girl that Josey might have raped and who probably drowned herself afterwards (p. 29, pp. 36–8, p. 45f.).

Prayers of Sherkin (1990)

Prayers of Sherkin is the improbable love story of Patrick Kirwan, a Catholic lithographer from Cork, and Fanny Hawke, one of the last descendants of a millenarian community on Sherkin Island that forbids intermarriage with other denominations. Set in the 1890s, the play surprises with the absence of any open conflict between the various religious groups or the two generations of the millenarian community. Instead, a complex local symbiosis is represented, based on economic exchange but also characterised by mutual respect and esteem: John Hawke, Fanny's father, makes candles from the wax provided by nuns living on the mainland. Thus, John Hawke is proud of illuminating the town; light and darkness are the central metaphors of this drama, structuring both the dialogue and the stage directions. Fanny decides to leave her family after the intervention of Matt Purdy, the founder of her community, appearing in the play as a ghost and acting throughout as a narrator who describes the beginnings of the group. In a literature abundant in ghosts that symbolise a relentless repetition of the past in the present, Matt Purdy's sending Fanny 'into a century of unlucky stars' (p. 106) can be understood as the allegory of an alternative, liberating potential of the past. *Prayers of Sherkin* is the first of Barry's plays on distant and often almost forgotten members of his family.

White Woman Street (1991)

In *White Woman Street*, an Irish emigrant and veteran of the Indian Wars faces the closing of the American frontier at Easter 1916. Trooper O'Hara is the boss of a strange, multicultural gang of outlaws, consisting of an Englishman, a former Amish, a man from Brooklyn of Chinese and Russian parentage, and an African-American from Tennessee. In order to obtain the means to return to Ireland, O'Hara persuades his men to raid a gold train near the little town White Woman Street in Ohio. Yet White Woman Street was also the scene of a traumatic experience of his. The town was named after a famous prostitute, the 'only white woman for five hundred miles of

3

wilderness' (p. 147), to whom Trooper O'Hara once went. He found out that the woman in the dark bedroom was actually not white at all but a very young Native American girl. After he had slept with her, she cut her throat before his eyes. By confessing this story to the former Amish Mo, O'Hara approaches a moment of forgiveness. The train robbery, however, fails, and Trooper O'Hara is killed.

Despite being widely neglected by literary criticism, *White Woman Street* might be Barry's most complete realisation of the potential of poetic drama: complex, multifaceted imagery pervades the play and exploits all the sign systems of theatre. Such a poetic theatricality conflicts with the audience's expectations of the Western genre, dominated by American films. Parallel to this intermedial dialogue, the American and Irish national narratives are superimposed in the story of the 'white woman', varying and criticising both the Irish myth of sovereignty and the American frontier myth.

The Only True History of Lizzie Finn (1995)

Although references to the theatre and other arts, especially to films, can be found in almost every one of Barry's plays, *The Only True History of Lizzie Finn* is his only drama with a professional performer as protagonist and contains the most explicit and extensive metadramatic reflections among his works to date. Lizzie Finn has already been touring the music halls of Great Britain as a dancer and singer for many years, when she meets Robert Gibson, a shell-shocked ex-soldier, who has just lost his three brothers in the Boer War. They fall in love, and Lizzie agrees to marry Robert and return to Kerry with him, where both grew up. In Ireland, however, Lizzie, the daughter of Presbyterian travellers, learns that Robert belongs to the Anglo-Irish Ascendancy, whose members, most prominently Robert's mother Lady Gibson, welcome his new wife only reluctantly. When Robert tells his Ascendancy neighbours that he changed sides during the Boer War and fought in the nationalist Irish Brigade for the Boers, even his mother is shunned. Already suffering from her diminished wealth and status in the wake of the land reforms, Lady Gibson cannot cope with this isolation and drowns herself. Robert and Lizzie decide to leave the family seat on its eroding cliff to the sea, which symbolises the powers of change in the play. They start a new life in Cork, where a music hall is about to be opened.

In *The Only True History of Lizzie Finn*, theatre is celebrated as transcending social differences as well as spatial and temporal distances. By focusing on music halls and the spectacles of Buffalo Bill's Wild West Show, the play rejects any distinctions between high and low art, which could impose the hierarchy of social stratification on artistic expression and reception. Buffalo Bill in particular epitomises the transforming power of performance in the play, its ability to create new identities and to open up new free spaces: during the last dialogue between Lizzie and her husband, the south west of Ireland is turned into a Wild West.

The Steward of Christendom (1995)

The Steward of Christendom looks at the Irish revolution from a provocatively unfamiliar angle: through the memory of Thomas Dunne, a Catholic unionist and formerly chief superintendent of the Dublin Metropolitan Police, who faces madness and oblivion in a county home for the insane at the time of action, in 1932. For Dunne and his daughters, the establishment of the Irish nation state meant the destruction of Ireland as they knew and loved it. Since Dunne has difficulties in distinguishing past and present, the play moves between scenically depicted memories and the harsh reality of the county home. This institution might be seen as an instrument of the new state's exclusion and disciplining of groups and historical narratives that cannot be contained in national identity and remembrance. At the same time, Dunne's brutal treatment by the orderly Smith mirrors the baton charge during the Dublin lock-out, for which Dunne was responsible and during which several people died. Both are instances of the sheepdog attacking the sheep, as in the childhood memory that concludes the play. Dunne only feels guilty towards his son Willie, whom he sent to his death in the First World War, and towards his maiden daughter Annie, slightly disfigured by a bowed back, whom he abandoned by his retreat into madness. Yet although Dunne never

5

accepts his political guilt, the play does not justify his actions nor adopt his political position; it is not revisionist in the sense of simply reversing the nationalist evaluation of events, as some critics have maintained.[2] Instead, it allows us a glimpse of the complexity of history and of the workings of historical consciousness.

Our Lady of Sligo (1998)

Of Barry's series of plays on his family, *Our Lady of Sligo* is the one that comes closest to tackling his own lifetime: it is set in 1953 and deals with the last days of his grandmother in a Dublin hospital, the end of a life in the hell of alcoholism. Mai O'Hara and her husband belong to a Catholic elite that intended to gain Irish autonomy by constitutional means *within* the British Empire and whose expectations have been frustrated in the aftermath of the Irish revolution. Whereas merely a few scraps of information provided by family legends or historical documents inspired the earlier plays, in the case of *Our Lady of Sligo*, eye witnesses, most importantly the author's mother, and much more material were available. As to form, *Our Lady of Sligo* is quite similar to its predecessor: it is a memory play like *The Steward of Christendom*, a montage between scenes set in a confined present and scenes staging key episodes of the protagonist's life, but *Our Lady of Sligo* contains a few more monologues in which characters relate the past or are transported into it. The closeness of the plot to the author, while accounting for the play's emotional power, is arguably also responsible for the lack of masterly coherence of form and imagery which distinguishes Barry's best plays.

Hinterland (2002)

The production of *Hinterland* at the Abbey brought Barry his own minor scandal – undoubtedly an honour in the context of the Irish dramatic tradition, even if the protest was articulated verbally in reviews and TV shows instead of physically in the theatre as in the time of Synge and O'Casey. Obviously, Barry's protagonist Johnny Silvester and the plot of his play resemble Charles Haughey and his story in many respects: like Haughey, Silvester was once a very charismatic and immensely popular politician who, after a brilliant career, became Taioseach, the Irish head of government, but had to resign after being charged with corruption on an enormous scale. Also like Haughey, Silvester betrayed his wife for decades with a journalist, who later wrote about this affair in minute detail. Because *Hinterland* seemed to focus on the private man rather than on the politician, Barry, by a surprisingly broad public consensus, was accused of exploiting Haughey's life story in a sensationalist manner. Since then, attempts have been made to defend the play as using Haughey as a metaphor for 'a private ache' of Barry's: his highly problematic relationship to his father.[3] Yet such an interpretation cuts off the political dimension of the play, which is concerned with the interdependence of the public and the private as created by, among other factors, the very voyeurism with which Barry was charged. In order to be politically successful, Silvester became an actor whose public role has infected and destroyed all real intimacy: while posing as a family man and the father of the nation, he neglected his son and treated his wife 'like a minor ministry' in his government (p. 26). During his beleaguered retirement, when the play is set, Silvester lacks the private language to reach anybody. At the same time, his wife explains his political failure by his failure as a father and husband: with this existential core, he also lost moral fibre and responsibility (p. 25). *Hinterland* differs from Barry's other plays in its realistic and often witty dialogue as well as some farcical elements. However, its form and subject matter – an analytic structure with a protagonist trying to cope with his past in present confinement and disgrace – are much closer to his former successes *The Steward of Christendom* and *Our Lady of Sligo* than most critics realised. *Hinterland* is most significantly set apart by a protagonist condemned by a *present* political consensus instead of a past one; in several passages, Barry attempts to depict Silvester as sympathetically as he did Thomas Dunne.

Whistling Psyche (2004)

In *Whistling Psyche*, two dead historical figures meet: Florence Nightingale and the more obscure Dr James Miranda Barry who, like Nightingale, committed herself to the reform of hospitals and, much more radically, transgressed gender barriers by cross-dressing as a man throughout her life. Ignoring Nightingale and her attempts to communicate with him, Dr Barry is at first completely absorbed in her/his memories. Yet associative, introspective monologues develop into narratives addressed to each other and, finally, into a dialogue that culminates in a mutual recognition and the hope of some redemption. Dr Barry, a descendant of an impoverished Ascendancy family, is driven by her childhood experiences of widespread hunger and suffering in early-nineteenth-century Ireland. Thus, she sees 'version[s]' and 'palimpsest[s]' of Ireland (p. 15) everywhere. As an officer in the British Army, however, her identification with the victims of imperialism remains highly problematic. Dr Barry's global extrapolation of the Irish experience resembles the way in which Mary Robinson, during her presidency in the 1990s, compared the Great Famine to humanitarian catastrophes in Africa at the turn from the twentieth to the twenty-first century.

The Pride of Parnell Street (2007)

The Pride of Parnell Street, the first play by Barry for almost ten years to enjoy some popular success in Ireland, is set on the eve of the new millennium, when a man and a woman from the margins of Irish society look back at the boom decade that turned Ireland into the 'Celtic Tiger'. In 1990, Joe and Janet enthusiastically followed the progress of the Irish football team at the World Cup. But as the Irish team crashed out, Joe, a petty criminal who had never been able to find a real job, realised that people like him had never truly participated in the team's success:

> When the Irish team lost, the lads suddenly knew what was what. When the Irish team were winning they could pretend they were winning, but when they lost, they knew they were losers too – had never been winners in the first place. (p. 14f.)

On the night of the match, Joe horribly beat up Janet, thus destroying their family for ever. Whereas Janet has succeeded in breaking free from Joe, bringing up their children on her own and seizing some of the chances that the economic boom has been offering, Joe's life since the separation has been a steady decline: he became a drug addict and was convicted for brutally robbing two French tourists. After serving five years, he successfully underwent treatment against drug addiction – only to find that he had contracted HIV while waiting for a place in the programme. In hospital and about to die, Joe is visited by Janet, and he, who has always tried to make her come back to him, learns by some little signs that she is still in love with him.

It is obvious in *The Pride of Parnell Street* that the neoliberal society of the emerging Celtic Tiger significantly contributes to Joe's downfall: as the lack of opportunity and the depressing poverty of the late 1980s set the scene for Joe's violent outburst, the unwillingness of the Irish establishment to spend sufficient amounts of the new wealth on the people left behind by the boom seals his fate in the 1990s. At the same time, the play shows that Joe's quest for forgiveness is successful only because he accepts full responsibility for his actions.

Dallas Sweetman (2008)

There is a probably fictitious anecdote that Henry VIII ordered Thomas Becket from his tomb in Canterbury Cathedral and put him on trial for treason and heresy. When Barry was asked to write a play in order to revive the tradition of staging new plays at Canterbury Cathedral, he created both the form and the content of his commissioned work, *Dallas Sweetman*, around that story. Like Thomas Becket in the anecdote, the protagonist Dallas Sweetman, servant to an Old English gentry family during the Elizabethan conquest of Ireland, is called from his grave centuries after his death and confronted with accusations. His master's second wife, Mrs Reddan, charges him with the rape of his master's daughter, the murder of that daughter's husband and, not least, the betrayal of the Old English loyalty to the Catholic Church. In order to defend himself, Dallas tells his story to the audience, occasionally corrected or supplemented by Mrs Reddan and his master's daughter, Lucinda. Some of the scenes are depicted on stage, though at the same time marked as 'the theatre of Dallas' inner eye' (p. 23). The complex, conflicting accounts evoke the difficult situation of the Old English during the Elizabethan Age: having settled in Ireland in the wake of the medieval Anglo-Norman invasion, the Old English attempted to be loyal to both the English monarchy and the Catholic Church. Dallas identifies with his master's struggle to uphold the Old English way of living, but is even more driven by his love for Lucinda and the need to regain the social position his father lost. At the end of the play Dallas admits that he killed Lucinda's husband when she fell in love with a Protestant minister and married him, adopting his faith. Mrs Reddan, surprisingly, withdraws her charge, and even Lucinda forgives him in a strange scene that cannot be confidently placed in the Elizabethan past or the ghostly present of the play. *Dallas Sweetman* underlines Barry's pluralist approach to Irish history: while Brian Friel's *Making History* (1988) and Frank McGuinness's *Mutabilitie* (1997) depict Elizabethan Irish history as the clash between two civilisations, one English, the other Irish, Barry characteristically focuses on a lost culture in Ireland which resists any national classifications.

Summary

Despite his almost simultaneous successes, Barry does not really belong to the wave of new, young writers such as Marina Carr, Conor McPherson and Martin McDonagh who have dominated Irish drama from the mid-1990s onwards. Barry significantly differs from this group as to age, themes and aesthetics. Rather, his early career in the 1980s began at the margins of the so-called 'Dublin Renaissance', which paved the way to moving the centre of creativity or, at least, of critical attention from the North to the South during the last decade of the twentieth century.[4] Barry was, at this stage, interested in establishing a uniquely Southern literature distanced from the main concerns of Northern drama: the Troubles and Irish history. In the introduction to his anthology of young Southern poets, *The Inherited*

Boundaries (1986), Barry argued that the Republic had to find its own literary expression, while, at the same time, pleading for a radical cultural pluralism within the country.[5] To him, one major obstacle to the development of such a pluralism was a nostalgic attitude towards the past, a 'philosophy of cultural back-track'. 'History' should be replaced by 'topography': '[T]his is a first if fragmentary map to a new country. Everything has been dismissed except what each poet sees around him.'[6] The parallels to statements of writers such as McPherson or Declan Hughes ten and more years later are obvious.[7]

Nevertheless, Barry soon started to continue the tradition of the Irish history play in his own innovative way — against the general trend he had wished for in the 1980s. Writing *Boss Grady's Boys* and having it accepted by the Abbey appears to have been an important shift in Barry's development as a writer. In an interview published a couple of years ago, he describes the experience as 'liberating':

> I could see that here was an arena where you were actually dependent on people responding, which was against my idea of modernism where you're meant to keep the audience or the readership at a bit of a remove.[8]

For Barry, theatre seems to have been an escape from his late-modernist ideals of authorial control and from the notion that a work of art should be a self-contained totality encapsulating a specific moment of history: Barry understands writing for the theatre as a 'surrender' – less to the director, the actors or the audience than to the characters, to the echoes of once actually existing people in his mind.[9] He no longer perceives his plays as 'literary constructs' but as acts 'done for personal reasons of survival' that uncontrollably interact with a wider context.[10] Thus, Barry has given up writing manifestos or criticism and no longer believes in programmes for art.[11] This might be why he can confess to having 'no real relationship with the adjective "postcolonial", or "postmodern"', while admitting: 'Maybe this is truly postcolonial and postmodern.'[12]

At the same time, writing is no purely intuitive activity for Barry. Having finished *Boss Grady's Boys*, he found an autobiographical subtext about his relationship to his brother in the play and decided to create a series on members of his family 'who had become enshrouded in silences of various kinds and for different reasons'.[13] According to Barry, the primary aim of this project was to understand the fractured state of his family. That these people also belong to various groups marginalised or excluded by narrow definitions of 'Irishness' endowed the plays with a political significance seemingly not intended at the beginning.[14] Still, the critique of Irish nationalism and the plea for pluralisation implied in these plays correspond to Barry's reflections in *The Inherited Boundaries*. The diagnosis has remained the same, even though the means of thematising the problems have changed: when historical memories degenerate to 'mythologised propagandas' that can no longer orientate the present,[15] the past need not be rejected completely. Another possible way of coping with that crisis is to imagine alternative histories. Despite being not explicitly about Barry's family, *Boss Grady's Boys* and *Hinterland* are regarded as part of the series by him. *Hinterland* was envisaged as a transition to a new series on contemporary Ireland.[16]

Barry's dramatic works have been described as a 'long, vigorous negotiation between the narrative and dramatic demands of theatre and the lyrical impulses of the poetic voice'.[17] Such a summary of Barry's career suffers from a concept of the theatrical derived from the long dominance of the realistic paradigm on the British and Irish stage, which equates theatre with action and narrative and thus ultimately necessitates either a dismissive or an apologetic treatment of poetic drama and theatre. In contrast, German and American critics of modernist and contemporary theatre have maintained the importance of a 'poeticisation' of theatre in overcoming the crisis of traditional drama and the limitations of nineteenth-century realism. For William Worthen, fully developed poetic theatre replicates the complexity of the poetic text by distributing its dense rhetoric over all the sign systems of theatre.[18] Such an integrated poetry of the stage can be found in Barry's early plays in particular, for example when the complex imagery of the play culminates in one last stage image such as Fanny's crossing to the mainland in *Prayers of Sherkin* (p. 118f.) or the pursuit of the gold train by Trooper O'Hara's gang in *White Woman Street* (p. 165f.).

In the wake of this friendship Barry, too, has been characterised as a revisionist. Elizabeth Butler Cullingford explicitly adopts the charge that especially critics associated with the Field Day Theatre Company levelled against historians such as Foster:

> Barry borrows the rhetoric of silencing from radical critics and appropriates it for conservative ends: his desire to give voice to the historically occluded native collaborator [Thomas Dunne in *The Steward of Christendom*] is a literary extension of the project of historical revisionism.[19]

Some critics react to such a narrow identification of Barry's works with a political agenda by focusing on a 'spiritual' or 'humanist' dimension that is supposed to be more central to the plays than political or historical concerns. This development uncannily seems to repeat the tendency of some criticism of Brian Friel and his play *Translations* (1980) in the 1980s and early 1990s. After Field Day had declared *Translations* the key to their cultural project, revisionists such as Edna Longley illustrated their arguments against Field Day with dismissive criticisms of Friel's play, so that a third group felt they had a mission to rescue the dramatist and his works from their entanglement: they interpreted him as 'an anti-historical and anti-political writer', 'in flight from [politics and history]'.[20] Thus, the polarisation of Irish studies is in danger of continuously generating narrowly political or unpolitical readings.

Other critics have argued that Barry is less interested in telling alternative narratives than in reflecting on the ways historical memories are constructed or suppressed.[21] Scott T. Cummings proposes an interesting interpretation that integrates both the historical and spiritual concerns of Barry's plays: he considers them as representative of a general 'millennial urge' in the Republic of Ireland during the 1990s. After more than twenty years of conflict, many, particularly in the South, wished for bringing nationalist history to an end:

> The plays insinuate a national eschatology, not the end of the Irish state but the end of the beginning of the Irish state – that

is, the period encompassing the birth of a nation and a subsequent, insistent nationalism which takes precedence over less patriotic concerns.[22]

The criticism apparently implied is that Barry's plays share a Southern tendency to replace the nationalist grand narrative with one of modernisation and enlightenment, in which overcoming nationalism is the decisive step. Indeed, Francis Fukuyama's thesis that the worldwide spread of market economy and liberal democracy and the global increase of wealth and security supposedly caused by it led to the end of history appeared to be more convincing in the emerging Celtic Tiger than in other regions of the world at the time.[23]

Yet, as Fintan O'Toole has pointed out, texts such as *Prayers of Sherkin* and *White Woman Street* can be considered as critical elegies on the failure of all utopias and grand narratives.[24] It is significant that Barry's protagonists are usually the people left behind who cannot keep up with the speed of change, as the outlaws in *White Woman Street* are no match for the gold train. History has become an inhuman invincible force, which can hardly be interfered with but only interpreted, dreamt about and symbolically expressed – the poetic form might also be understood as a consequence of this fundamental insight. At the same time, Barry's characters are fascinated by the promise of freedom, of permanent departure implied in the frontier myth. The fantasies of the American West inspire them, help them to imagine radical alternatives, to write their own little narratives and invent their own lives.[25]

Barry has increasingly experimented with post-epic narration, a usage of storytelling that does not aim for alienation but creates intense relationships between narrator and story on the one hand and narrator and audience on the other. Most of Barry's plays are memory plays, but from *Fred and Jane* onwards the act of remembering and telling has almost completely replaced the scenic action. While in earlier texts characters generally talk to themselves when expressing their thoughts and memories in monologues, the audience is often directly addressed in Barry's most recent plays. Academic criticism has hardly begun to explore these new developments.

Maybe the most promising approach that presents itself after the performance of *Dallas Sweetman* in particular is to link the dramaturgy of the latest plays to a dimension of Barry's dramatic work that might be called sacred, religious or metaphysical. David Cregan uses Victor Turner's concept of the liminal and the rite of passage in order to describe Barry's plays. At least in the most recent plays, however, the most important reference to cultural performances is to making and hearing confessions. When Dallas Sweetman awakes, he thinks the Last Judgment has come and asks, 'Is it God calls me, in God's great house?' (p. 11). In the face of the transitoriness of human life and man's creations, Dr Barry expresses her belief in *Whistling Psyche* that:

> every man's story is the whisper of God. [. . .] God takes each and every one and makes him new, returns him to the crisp clear lines of the original mould, relieves him of his heavy sins, and in His wise mercy lets him go into that strange eternity where there is no earthly story and no human song. (p. 60)

Since God does not answer, Barry's works suggest that the writer and the audience should make the quixotic attempt to act as God's substitute, to re-create the dead as fully as possible and include them in their fragile memories. The plays grant the excluded, the forgotten and the guilty at least an imaginary opportunity for confessions, but at the same time they question the present's right to judge the past or even to forgive: forgiveness, in Barry's plays, remains in the hands of the victims and of God – if he exists.

Primary Sources

Works by Sebastian Barry

Boss Grady's Boys (Dublin: Raven Arts, 1989).
Dallas Sweetman (London: Faber and Faber, 2008).
Hinterland (London: Faber and Faber, 2002).

The Only True History of Lizzie Finn in: Three Plays by Sebastian Barry (London: Methuen Drama, 1995).

Our Lady of Sligo (London: Methuen, 1998).

Plays 1: Boss Grady's Boys; Prayers of Sherkin; White Woman Street; The Only True History of Lizzie Finn; The Steward of Christendom (London: Methuen, 1997).

Prayers of Sherkin (London: Methuen Drama, 1991).

The Pride of Parnell Street (London: Faber and Faber, 2007).

The Steward of Christendom (London: Methuen Drama, 1995).

Whistling Psyche (London: Faber and Faber, 2004).

White Woman Street in: *Three Plays by Sebastian Barry* (London: Methuen Drama, 1995).

Secondary Sources

Achilles, Jochen, '"Homesick for Abroad": The Transition from National to Cultural Identity in Contemporary Irish Drama', *Modern Drama*, Vol. 38 (1995), pp. 435–49.

Barry, Sebastian, 'Author's Note', *Our Lady of Sligo* (London: Methuen, 1998), n. pag.

—, 'Introduction: The History and Topography of Nowhere', in Sebastian Barry (ed.), *The Inherited Boundaries: Younger Poets of the Republic of Ireland* (Portlaoise: The Dolmen Press, 1986), pp. 13–29.

—, 'Preface', in his *Plays 1: Boss Grady's Boys; Prayers of Sherkin; White Woman Street; The Only True History of Lizzie Finn; The Steward of Christendom* (London: Methuen, 1997), pp. xv–xviii.

Bertha, Csilla, '"A Haunted Group of Plays": The Drama of Sebastian Barry', in Jürgen Kamm (ed.), *Twentieth-Century Theatre and Drama in English: Festschrift for Heinz Kosok on the Occasion of His 65th Birthday* (Trier: Wissenschaftlicher Verlag Trier, 1999), pp. 527–44.

Biggs, Murray, 'Rhetoric and Silence in Six Plays by Sebastian Barry', *The Princeton University Library Chronicle*, Vol. 68 (2006/7), pp. 649–70.

Coulter, Colin and Steve Coleman (eds), *The End of Irish History? Critical Reflections on the Celtic Tiger* (Manchester: Manchester UP, 2003).

Cregan, David, ' "Everyman's Story is the Whisper of God": Sacred and Secular in Barry's Dramaturgy', in Christina Hunt Mahoney (ed.), *Out of History: Essays on the Writings of Sebastian Barry* (Dublin: Carysfort Press, 2006), pp. 61–79.

Cullingford, Elizabeth, 'Colonial Policing: *The Steward of Christendom* and *The Whereabouts of Eneas McNulty*', *Eire-Ireland, Éire-Ireland: A Journal of Irish Studies*, Vol. 39, Nos 3–4 (2004), pp. 11–37.

Cummings, Scott T., 'The End of History: The Millennial Urge in the Plays of Sebastian Barry', in Stephen Watt, Eillen Morgan and Shakir Mustafa (eds), *A Century of Irish Drama: Widening the Stage* (Bloomington,: Indiana UP, 2000), pp. 291–302.

Dumay, Emile, 'La politique au théâtre: nouvelles approches en Irlande', *Etudes irlandaises*,

Vol. 31 (2006), pp. 37–49.

FitzGibbon, Ger, 'Sebastian Barry in Conversation with Ger FitzGibbon', in Eamonn Jordan, Ger FitzGibbon and Lilian Chambers (eds), *Theatre Talk: Conversations with Irish Theatre Practitioners* (Dublin: Carysfort Press, 2001), pp. 16–28.

—, 'The Poetic Theatre of Sebastian Barry', in Eamonn Jordan (ed.), *Theatre Stuff: Critical Essay on Contemporary Irish Theatre* (Dublin: Carysfort Press, 2000), pp. 224–35.

Gleitman, Claire, '"In the Dark Margins of Things": *Whistling Psyche* and the Illness of Empire', in Christina Hunt Mahoney (ed.), *Out of History: Essays on the Writings of Sebastian Barry* (Dublin: Carysfort Press, 2006), pp. 209–27.

—, 'Reconstructing History in the Irish History Play', in Shaun Richards (ed.), *The Cambridge Companion to Twentieth-Century Drama* (Cambridge: Cambridge UP, 2004), pp. 218–30.

Hughes, Declan, 'Who the Hell Do We Think We Still are? Reflections on Irish Theatre and Identity', *Theatre Stuff: Essays on Contemporary Irish Theatre* (Dublin: Carysfort Press, 2000), pp. 8–15.

Kurdi, Maria, '"Really All Danger". An Interview with Sebastian Barry', *New Hibernia Review*, Vol. 8, No. 1 (2004), pp. 41–54.

Mahoney, Christina Hunt, 'Children of the Light Amid the "Risky Dancers": Barry's Naïfs and the Poetry of Humanism', in Christina Hunt Mahoney (ed.), *Out of History: Essays on the Writings of Sebastian Barry* (Dublin: Carysfort Press, 2006), pp. 83–98.

McCarthy, Conor, *Modernisation, Crisis and Culture in Ireland 1969–1992* (Dublin: Four Courts Press, 2000).

O'Toole, Fintan, 'Introduction: A True History of Lies', *Plays 1: Boss Grady's Boys; Prayers of Sherkin; White Woman Street; The Only True History of Lizzie Finn; The Steward of Christendom* (London: Methuen, 1997), pp. vii–xiv.

—, 'Marking Time: From *Making History* to *Dancing at Lughnasa*', in Alan J. Peacock (ed.), *The Achievement of Brian Friel* (Gerrards Cross: Colin Smythe, 1993), pp. 202–14.

Roche, Anthony, 'Redressing the Irish Theatrical Landscape: Sebastian Barry's *The Only True History Of Lizzie Finn*', in Christina Hunt Mahoney (ed.), *Out of History: Essays on the Writings of Sebastian Barry* (Dublin: Carysfort Press, 2006), pp. 147–65.

Tóibín, Colm, '*Hinterland*: The Public Becomes Private', in Christina Hunt Mahoney (ed.), *Out of History: Essays on the Writings of Sebastian Barry* (Dublin: Carysfort Press, 2006), pp. 199–207.

Wehrmann, Jürgen, 'Revising the Nation: Globalisation and Fragmentation of Irish History in Sebastian Barry's Plays', in Jochen Achilles, Ina Bergmann and Birgit Däwes (eds), *Global Challenges and Regional Responses in Contemporary Drama in English: Papers Given on the Occasion of the Eleventh Annual Conference of the German Society for Contemporary Theatre and Drama in English* (Trier: Wissenschaftlicher Verlag Trier, 2003).

—, 'Irish Tradition or Postdramatic Innovation? Storytelling in Contemporary Irish Plays', *ZAA: Zeitschrift für Anglistik und Amerikanistik*, Vol. 52 (2004), pp. 243–56.

Worthen, William B., *Modern Drama and the Rhetoric of Theater* (Berkeley, CA: University of California Press, 1992).

Notes

1. Sebastian Barry, *Plays 1*, p. 19.
2. Cf. Elizabeth Cullingford, 'Colonial Policing: *The Steward of Christendom* and *The Whereabouts of Eneas McNulty*', p. 14.
3. Colm Tóibín, '*Hinterland*: The Public Becomes Private', p. 207.
4. Compare Conor McCarthy, *Modernisation, Crisis and Culture in Ireland 1969–1992*, pp. 135–64.
5. Sebastian Barry, 'Introduction: The History and Topography of Nowhere', *The Inherited Boundaries: Younger Poets of the Republic of Ireland*, p. 16f.
6. Ibid., p. 17f.
7. Compare Declan Hughes, 'Who the Hell Do We Think We Still are? Reflections on Irish Theatre and Identity'.
8. Ger FitzGibbon, 'Sebastian Barry in Conversation with Ger FitzGibbon', p. 17.
9. Ibid., p. 19.
10. Ibid., p. 17.
11. Interview with the author.
12. Maria Kurdi, ' "Really All Danger": An Interview with Sebastian Barry', p. 43.
13. Ibid., p. 42.
14. Ibid.
15. Barry, 'Introduction', op. cit., p. 16.
16. Kurdi, op. cit., p. 50.
17. Ger FitzGibbon, 'The Poetic Theatre of Sebastian Barry', p. 234.
18. William B. Worthen, *Modern Drama and the Rhetoric of Theater*, pp. 100–2.
19. Cullingford, op. cit., p. 12.
20. Fintan O'Toole, 'Marking Time: From *Making History* to *Dancing at Lughnasa*', p. 205.
21. Claire Gleitman, 'Reconstructing History in the Irish History Play', p. 219.
22. Scott T. Cummings, 'The End of History: The Millennial Urge in the Plays of Sebastian Barry', p. 295.
23. Compare Colin Coulter, *The End of Irish History? Critical Reflections on the Celtic Tiger*.
24. Fintan O'Toole, 'Introduction: A True History of Lies', in Barry, *Plays 1*, p. x.
25. Compare Jürgen Wehrmann, 'Revising the Nation: Globalisation and Fragmentation of Irish History in Sebastian Barry's Plays'.

2 DERMOT BOLGER

Christina Wald

The Lament for Arthur Cleary; Blinded by the Light; In High Germany; The Holy Ground; One Last White Horse; April Bright; The Passion of Jerome; From These Green Heights

Introduction

Dermot Bolger (born 1959) is an extraordinarily prolific and versatile writer, editor and publisher. As a novelist, he gained prominence with *Nightshift* (1985) and the bestselling *The Journey Home* (1990). The popular book project *Finbar's Hotel* (1997), to which seven Irish writers contributed chapters about the events of one night in a Dublin hotel, as well as its sequel *Ladies' Night at Finbar's* (1999) by women authors, were commissioned by Bolger. Bolger has had a seat on the Arts Council of Ireland for several years and lives and works in Dublin.

His dramatic work, beyond the plays discussed below, includes a free adaptation of Joyce's *Ulysses* for the theatre, entitled *A Dublin Bloom* (1994), television and radio plays and a number of (as yet) unpublished stage plays, for instance the one-act play *Consenting Adults* (2000) and the monologue '. . . scuffed shoes' (2005).

The Plays

The Lament for Arthur Cleary (1989)

Bolger's debut play *The Lament for Arthur Cleary* began as a poem, in which Bolger adapted the eighteenth-century Gaelic elegy, 'Caoineadh Airt Uí Laoghaire', written by Eileen O'Connell for her husband.

Bolger transposes the setting to the Dublin of the 1980s, inventing a new identity for Arthur Cleary.

Both the subject matter and the aesthetics of *The Lament for Arthur Cleary* prefigure many of Bolger's later plays. The play focuses on the question of belonging, exploring how far the feeling of being at 'home' is and has to be connected to a particular place – in this case, to Dublin. Arthur, a thirty-five-year-old unskilled worker, returns to Dublin after having worked on the continent for fifteen years. He falls in love with Kathy, an eighteen-year-old girl who dreams of leaving Ireland to live a better life elsewhere. A politician's speech in the play places Arthur's past in the Irish diaspora and Kathy's wish to emigrate in the larger political and economic context, when it praises Ireland's best-exported 'articles': 'Young people are to Ireland what champagne is to France!' (p. 6). The play explores the considerable problems that arise when these workers are 're-imported'. Arthur is deeply disturbed by the enormous differences between the Dublin to which he comes back and the city he once left, which he has transformed into an idealised, immobile image of his 'home', of 'something to come home to that would never change' (p. 27). He tries to map his imaginary Dublin on to the material city, unable to accept the fact that not only its architecture, but also its inhabitants and social structure have changed. Since Arthur does not obey the rules of the newly developed criminal subculture, he is killed.[1]

The play is told in retrospect, partly as Kathy's lament for her dead beloved (which she recites in verse form) and partly from the perspective of Arthur's ghost. The attempts of the two characters to come to terms with their past are presented in an open dramatic form that could be characterised as an experimental memory play. *The Lament for Arthur Cleary* is structured in two acts without further division into scenes, but presents a variety of scenic snapshots which are established by means of music changes, sound effects, lighting and acting. The action shifts from the present to various situations set in the past (Kathy and Arthur's love story, Arthur abroad, Kathy's childhood), which are replayed in an associative rather than causal or chronological order and also include dream and nightmare scenarios. The play ends several years after its beginning, at a time when Kathy has overcome Arthur's death and emigrated to 'Europe . . . the future . . . her children' (p. 67). In the play's final image, Arthur's ghost learns to let go of his obsessive memories and is released.

The theatrical realisation requires skilled transitions between the snapshots and versatile actors who switch their roles onstage in a Brechtian manner (for example by the use of masks) to play a variety of stock characters whom Kathy and Arthur encounter and who create a mosaic of Dublin life. Since new characters keep emerging in this way, since the scenic snapshots are not chronologically or causally ordered and since their quality (actual, remembered, imagined or dreamt) is not classified, audiences are put in a position similar to that of the protagonist, who tries to make sense of a world that is unfamiliar to him. Therefore, they might share Arthur's feeling, '[s]ometimes . . . it frightens me . . . you know like in a dream . . . the sequence doesn't make sense . . .' (p. 49). In this way, the play conveys the subjective perception of the protagonists and their inner realities rather than an external, 'objective' reality. This aesthetics of radical psychic realism has become typical of Bolger's dramatic style and has sometimes made the reception of his plays difficult. Despite the bleak topics of the play, the tone is not only dreamy and elegiac, but also interspersed with comedy, a combination that has become characteristic of Bolger's oeuvre. Bolger's second play, *Blinded by the Light*, highlights the comic; it remains, so far, the only play which the author himself straightforwardly classified as 'comedy'.

Blinded by the Light (1990)

Blinded by the Light was first staged by the Abbey Theatre on its Peacock stage, directed by Caroline FitzGerald. The two-act comedy is divided into scenes and progresses in chronological order, covering a period of several weeks. It depicts the experiences of Mick, a young Dubliner, into whose untidy bed-sit a number of other characters intrude, thus keeping Mick from smoking joints and reading his stolen library books: Mick's girlfriend-to-be, Siobhan, his neighbours and two Mormons determined to convert Mick, which Mick's landlord tries to prevent with the help of his friends from the Legion of Mary. Mick, entirely uninterested in religious matters, tries to convince the insistent Mormons that he is 'not convertible' and no 'Mormon material' (p. 165), taking measures such as boasting about his alleged sexual adventures with three under-age sisters and dressing up in women's underwear. Since Siobhan accidentally learns about this and initially takes it at face value, a number of comic misunderstandings occur.

At the end of the first act, Mick's neighbours hide an ominous parcel in his flat, which he clandestinely opens to find the head of the Irish saint Oliver Plunkett, the remains of Ireland's first beatified martyr. To Mick's surprise and dismay, the head begins to speak to him, constantly switching from old-fashioned preaching to a light, cynical conversational tone. As it turns out, Mick's neighbours kidnapped the relic from Saint Peter's Church in Drogheda to blackmail the Church. The play's second act focuses on the emerging relationship between Mick and 'the Head': Mick initially regards him as a horrific drug-induced hallucination, but soon grows to treasure his company and learns that the Head is an 'impostor' (p. 186) called George MacSpracken, a man executed the same day and mistaken for Saint Oliver. As a result of his encounters with various people throughout the centuries, he has become, among other things, a Communist and passionate poker player. Since the Head yearns for 'Oblivion' and 'Peace' (p. 185), tired by centuries of exhibition and lack of communication, Mick pretends to his neighbours to have burnt the head, and in the play's final image, Mick and the Head merrily watch TV together.

In a light-hearted manner, the play touches on a number of issues which Bolger treats more seriously in his other plays, such as drug abuse, the grip of the past on the present, the sense of being haunted, and the issues of ghosts and of a supernatural afterlife. It mocks religious zealotry with the comic stock characters of the Mormons as well as with the missionaries of the Legion of Mary and reinforces its comic critique of the Catholic Church by revealing the precious relic as a fraud and by recounting George's disillusioning experiences with the Church.

In High Germany (1990)

Largely complying with the conventions of stage realism, the one-act monologue captures Eoin, a passionate Irish soccer fan in his early thirties, who lives in Hamburg, in a critical moment of his life: he returns from the 1988 European Championship, in which Ireland, participating in the championship for the first time, amazingly beat England in this 'Brit sport' (p. 80), but finally lost against the Netherlands. Eoin recounts decisive experiences from not only this championship, but also his childhood and adolescence in Ireland and his life in the Irish diaspora since. His monologue oscillates between the narration of past events (and reflections about their impact on his present situation) and the re-enactment of scenes, in which he imitates the voices and accents of other characters.

The play interconnects Eoin's personal coming-of-age story with that of Irish soccer and of Ireland itself. Eoin was brought up in the belief that he belonged to a 'chosen generation' expected to make up for centuries of oppression, colonisation and deprivation, and to be 'the generation which would make sense of the last seven hundred years' (p. 85). As a teenager, Eoin found an expression of this new national pride in the Irish soccer team, which became increasingly successful, but he soon had to accept that the Irish soccer team recruited expatriate players whose 'new faces and accents to be suspicious of' did not fit his purist 'vision of Ireland' (p. 88). Once Eoin himself was forced to work abroad in Germany, the ritualised attendance of soccer matches became a means to reunite with the Irish community. During the match against the Netherlands Eoin realises that he feels much more at home in foreign stadiums among the diasporic Irish fan community cheering for a hybrid team of Irish players than in Dublin itself:

> even if we went back [to Dublin] and they hadn't changed then we would have. [. . . N]ow when we said 'us' we weren't thinking of those Dublin bars any more, but the scattered army of emigrants. (p. 90)

Eoin develops a sense of Irish diaspora which does not, as in Arthur Cleary's case, presuppose a recuperating return to the home country, but acknowledges the hybrid, intermediate, processual state which critics have termed the '"post-modern" version of diaspora'.[2] His growing awareness of an Irish diaspora and his positive attitude towards this community epitomises a development within Irish society at large, which likewise began to value the large group of (formerly) Irish people living abroad.

While Eoin thus emancipates himself from a particular version of Irish nationalism, he does not depart from nationalism as such. Nor does he abandon his patriarchal upbringing. On the contrary, once he learns that his German girlfriend Frieda is pregnant, he imagines a patriarchal passing on of a national tradition. Being convinced that he will have a son who will replicate him, Eoin asserts, 'I [. . .] finally [. . .] found the only Ireland whose name I can sing [. . .]. And the only Ireland I can pass on to the son who will carry my name and features in a foreign land' (p. 97).

The Holy Ground (1990)

Bolger's second one-act monologue was first staged in tandem with *In High Germany* at the Gate Theatre under the direction of David Byrne. Together, these plays offer two complementary perspectives on Irish identity: in *The Holy Ground*, a woman in her late fifties rather than a young man reflects on her life, which was troubled not by the opening up of possibilities through emigration but by the cruel narrowing down of chances in a section of Irish society that drastically oppresses and marginalises women, in particular women who are not mothers. The monologue is set in a living room in Drumcondra, a suburb of north Dublin. On the day of her husband's funeral, Monica clears the flat of his personal belongings, reflecting on their common past. Like Eoin, she imitates the voices and accents of the people she remembers, particularly of her husband Myles, sometimes also re-playing situations from the past. The play soon signals that Monica is not the mournful widow one might expect: 'Grief, that's what they were looking for. Me to play my part, a public tear at the church or graveside' (p. 104). On the contrary, she experiences Myles's death as the liberation from a prison-like marriage – as a liberation, however, that came too late for Monica to start a new life.

Monica recounts their relationship from the happy early days of courtship in the 1950s and gradually reveals how seriously their marriage deteriorated when it turned out that they could not have children. Myles responded to his infertility with a hatred of all sexual matters and grew into a reactionary Catholic activist who fought against changes in his personal life and in Irish society, in particular against the pill, divorce, pornography and abortion. Since Myles strictly and jealously confined Monica to their home, she clung to the dream of a family, all she 'had ever been taught to dream of' (p. 114), by pretending to have two children for company in her lonely domestic life. When Myles increasingly humiliated his wife and taunted her for her insanity, Monica imagined the murder of her children. Since she could conceive of no other way to terminate her utter loneliness, she set out to kill Myles as well by slowly poisoning him:

> I killed for companionship, can you understand? Those rough women in prison, they didn't frighten me any longer. Four of us crammed into a cell, at least they would have to talk to me. (p. 122)

Ironically, after Myles's death, Monica learns that she prolonged rather than terminated his life, since the rat poison delayed the clotting in his blood from which he eventually died.

In contrast to the conciliatory endings of the earlier plays, *The Holy Ground* ends on a pessimistic and fatalistic note. The final words of Monica's monologue, addressed to Myles, show that she feels unable to begin a new life and even has lost hope of a more comforting spiritual afterlife:

> I tried to pray but nothing would come. You've stolen my youth and left me barren, you've stolen my gaiety and gave me shame, and when I die I will die unmourned. But I could

forgive you [. . .] everything except that . . . seated there at the right hand of God, you had stolen my Christ away from me. (p. 125)

Here, as in many of Bolger's plays, the protagonist's personal story is interlinked with the country's development at large. *The Holy Ground* reflects on the suffocating, repressive impact of radical Catholicism and, through the defeat of Myles's campaign against divorce and through his death, on the decline of this influence,[3] while at the same time it raises the question whether the liberation from the strict rules of the Catholic Church necessarily entails the abandonment of the Christian faith. On a metaphorical level, the deconstruction of motherhood and the assertion of (unsatisfied) female sexual desire in the play can be regarded as a critical, post-colonial and post-nationalist comment on the 'Mother Ireland', which has been feminised in colonialist and desexualised in nationalist discourse.[4]

One Last White Horse (1991)

Bolger's darkest play to date most radically stages his aesthetics of psychic realism. Being 'set in the head of a young man', Eddie, its action follows 'the logic of the dreamer' (p. 147) and requires surreal, abstract scenery devoid of realistic detail. The play's action unfolds as an associative and non-chronological blending of Eddie's nightmares, memories, soliloquies and encounters with figures, both real and imagined, from his past and his present life in Dublin in the mid-1980s. Eddie's early childhood trauma of witnessing the violent death of his mother in a car crash, or possibly even a prior, seemingly trivial, betrayal by his mother left him deeply damaged (p. 155). As Eddie himself concludes towards the end of the play, he has 'a hole in his heart': 'Long ago something was torn out of me, I don't even know what, [. . .] making me never really belong anywhere, never at ease' (p. 198). Searching for a compensation for this loss, Eddie had to experience ever-new losses: the death of his beloved elder brother, the loss of his job, the decline of his masculine self-esteem as the family provider. Like many Dubliners in this play, he seeks comfort in drugs and even robs his child daughter of her scarce savings to satisfy his addiction. At the end of the play (just as, due to the circular, associative dream structure, at its beginning), Eddie is homeless, without family relations, desperate for heroin and cursed by an old man whom he killed accidentally. Having injected himself with air, he envisions his entry into hell but also imagines meeting his mother again.

An enigmatic figure called 'Horse', who wears a shroud-like white robe, is introduced as a personification of heroin (p. 148); accordingly, her recurrent line is 'I have stilled your body, but even I may not control your dreams' (p. 150, see also p. 190). Drug addiction has become the sad fulfilment of Eddie's childhood dreams of domesticating a wild, white mare – a soothing fantasy of belonging, safety and unconditional trust (pp. 191, 203) Accordingly, the eponymous Horse plays several characters who might have provided this sense of belonging for Eddie: his mother, his daughter, a lover. *One Last White Horse* thus combines the fatal consequences of unemployment and drug abuse with a psychological exploration of a primal human need for home.

April Bright (1995)

Byrne directed the first production of *April Bright* at the Peacock. Set in an empty house in Dublin, the play intertwines two stories of families, set in the 1940s (with one scene in the 1970s) and the 1990s. Typically, the two-act play is not divided into scenes but develops in a continuous motion, with both strands of action taking place concurrently. An initially mysterious figure named The Caller mediates between the two levels of action: she unexpectedly visits a young couple, Anna and Sean, when they move into their newly acquired house where they plan to raise their as yet unborn child. As it turns out, The Caller alias Rosie Bright was born in the same house. The scenes set in the 1940s spring from her memories, which recall not only merry scenes of family life, but also the painful loss of her sister April, who died of tuberculosis in her teenage years.

Since the play's action conforms to the psychic reality of The

Caller, for whom her recollections are as vivid as the present-day events, Bolger's memory play again departs from stage realism by presenting real and remembered events in the same theatrical fashion. The double time frame generates ambiguity and dramatic irony for audiences, since Anna and Sean are oblivious of Rosie's memories but at some points seem to react to the presence of the Bright family or to comment on their actions. Likewise, the Bright family at some moments seem to anticipate the presence of the future inhabitants. Bolger describes this effect as a mutual 'unconscious haunting' of the two families (p. 7). A sense of mutual haunting applies also to the desires and fears of the characters: while the family life of the Brights is initially portrayed as happy, April's illness and her eventual death leave them in utter despair and isolation. Conversely, the relationship of Anna and Sean, which is heavily strained by their 'bad memories' (p. 15) of two miscarriages and their fear of losing their third child as well, improves towards the end of the play, so that the play ends on a hopeful and cheerful note, in the expectancy of their 'precious child to come' (p. 120).

April Bright revisits central issues raised in *The Holy Ground*, such as the importance of (unborn) children and the decreasing influence of the Church in shaping family values. Although the play demonstrates how much has changed since the 1940s, it also highlights the persistent social expectancy that women become mothers and their sense of failure when they are unable to do so. The play's ending seems to advocate an almost Freudian *working through*, that is, an acknowledgement of the past that helps to leave its painful and paralysing aspects behind. In the play's final image, April cradles her doll and envisions a happy future as mother (which she will never have, as she already knows), while Anna simultaneously talks to her unborn child and dreams of 'all the happiness that [. . .] [it] will bring' (p. 120). This sentimental ending corresponds to The Caller's earlier comments that projected Anna's baby as a redeemer figure that is able to make up for all past suffering.

The Passion of Jerome (1999)

Bolger's subsequent play, *The Passion of Jerome*, could be read as a sequel to *April Bright*, as it extends the play's sense of haunting and explores the devastating consequences which the loss of such a child as-redeemer can have. Its ambiguous title encapsulates two important issues of the play. Beginning as the story of Jerome, a successful, married businessman in his late thirties who has a passionate sexual affair with his young colleague Clara, the play develops into a story of suffering modelled on the Passion of Christ.

The play is clearly structured in two acts with seven scenes each, features realistic settings and adheres to a chronological time structure. This unusual agreement with stage realism offers a foil which allows Bolger to explore once again the borders of what we commonly accept as real. Jerome, whom his environment perceives as an unusually efficient and rational man – in his brother's words, 'Jerome the perfect, with an invoice book for a brain' (p. 14) – is confronted with events that suggest the existence of an uncontrollable metaphysical power. The play is set in a Ballymun flat which Jerome uses to meet his lover and which is said to be haunted by the ghost of a teenage boy who committed suicide after having lost his parents. When Jerome falls asleep, audiences see the silhouette of the young boy, hanging by the neck from a rope. A bag of nails and a hammer fall down from the top of a packing case and Jerome awakes in agony, each of his hands pierced. Despite medical treatment, the wounds keep reopening, fitting Jerome's recurrent dreams and visions of the young boy asking him 'to play Jesus' for him (p. 30).

Jerome's visions have religious sources as well as psychic motives: he has repressed the grief caused by the death of his baby daughter (with the telling name 'Felicity') as well as by the subsequent childlessness and unhappiness in his marriage. While Jerome's (Protestant) wife became angry with a God figure she still believes in but detests, Jerome (a Catholic) abandoned faith altogether. He claims, 'God should be like the measles, a short childhood illness we can't get twice. He went out with black and white TV' (p. 35). He rather believes in his 'own eyes . . . logic . . . reason' (p. 29). This attitude is opposed to that of

Rita, an inhabitant of Ballymun, whose granddaughter is in danger of dying from lung failure as Jerome's child did. Rita clings to her faith, accepting that 'God works in ways we can't understand' (p. 56). Her response to the issue of theodicy is her belief that 'God makes nobody suffer needlessly' (p. 56) – accordingly, she sees Jerome as a redeemer figure whose pain might save her granddaughter. Jerome eventually blesses her granddaughter with his blood and prays to God, asking him to transfer her suffering on to him. The child dies nevertheless, but shortly before her death she has a dream of a man with stigmata who releases her from her pain – at the same moment that Jerome is beaten and humiliated by three thugs in his brother's flat. Thus, the play does not validate the hope for a Catholic miracle (in which even the local priest no longer believes), but proposes a broader under-standing of reality than allowed for by logic and reason. It suggests the existence of (possibly just psychically projected) supernatural forces which cannot neatly be classified as Catholic or Christian, but which are expressed in Christian imagery and stories. *The Passion of Jerome* thus offers one answer to the question raised at the ending of *The Holy Ground*, namely if and in which forms religious faith and spirituality are possible in a largely secularised world.

The play's ending itself adheres to the plot line of Christ's Passion and Resurrection; after having lost his former life (his wife, his lover, his job, his house) and after having been tortured, Jerome awakes from the (psychically and spiritually) dead and begins an afterlife that he perceives as more genuine. Bolger's subsequent play is likewise concerned with the intertwining of family histories as well as with the 'spiritual' history of a building, namely the very Ballymun Towers where Jerome encounters the poltergeist.

From These Green Heights (2004)

Spanning the years 1966 to 2004, *From These Green Heights* gazes back at the history of the Ballymun Towers, which represents the hopes and defeats of three generations of Dubliners: originally planned as a landmark site of modern living, the towers were soon abandoned by local politics. Since the flats increasingly accommodated the unemployed, the poor and drug addicts, the towers became instead an epitome of social stigma and urban decay. Despite attempts by the inhabitants to rehabilitate the area, the towers were eventually demolished. Bolger initially composed a 'Ballymun Incantation' (reprinted in the play text), which was recited by actors and local people as the centrepiece of a public wake on the eve of the destruction of the first tower in summer 2004.

The play negotiates questions of belonging in terms of kin structures, the local community and, occasionally, the macro level of nation. The basic plot line is delivered in scenic snapshots in a non-linear order. All eight actors are permanently onstage, with those not involved in the action observing, and the presentation of characters does not distinguish between the living and the dead. The tone of the play is dreamy and at times mournful, but this atmosphere is interspersed with elements of dark humour that allow for comic relief. The first scenic snapshots interlock the arrival of five-year-old Dessie with his parents, full of hope and expectation, with the departure of Dessie, Marie and their daughter Tara thirty-eight years later. In a powerful stage image, the families pack and unpack the same suitcase. The play's action unfolds the development between these two moments and connects the life cycle of the Ballymun Towers to developments within Irish society – initially, the Towers are constructed as a shelter that has religious overtones of 'the Promised Land' (p. 4), which is 'halfway to paradise' (p. 10) and offers a valid alternative to the 'exodus' abroad. However, all characters (except Dessie) increasingly come to see this 'halfway' state as a deficient 'halfway Limbo' (p. 19), in which they are stuck due to unemployment and social stigma. The only respect in which Ballymun proves to be the gate to heaven is that it becomes a place of dying. After having depicted the difficulties that the characters had in abandoning old and in adapting to new homes, the play closes with a monologue by the youngest character, Tara, who looks forward to her new room, which she will, she is sure, 'be able to call [. . .] home' (p. 102). This ending on a hopeful and future-oriented note suggests that a new Irish generation, in times of a thriving Irish economy, will more easily be able to transport their notion of home by constructing new homes within Ireland itself. This upbeat ending is undercut again by *The Townlands of Brazil*, a sequel that also chronicles the history of the Ballymun Towers, focusing on the lives of the new immigrant workers whom the rapid economic growth brought to Ireland. The second act in particular shows the xenophobia, poverty and loneliness from which the guest workers suffer, among them Eileen's son Michael.

Summary

The central motif of Bolger's dramatic oeuvre is the quest for a 'home': the characters search for a sense of home in love relationships, in their family, in a particular house or city, in Ireland as a territory and in Ireland as a community that transcends the borders of Irish territory. Bolger's plays depict both the soothing, strengthening impact of experiencing a sense of home and the tormenting, deadening effect of clinging to a vision of home that cannot be achieved. Related thematic concerns are the fear of change and the simultaneous need to feel being on a journey, the crisis of masculinity in the face of unemployment and women's emancipation, the pain of (social) stigma and the loss of trust in the Catholic Church but, at the same time, the persistent need for faith and spirituality. The grip which the past can have on the present is visualised in many of Bolger's plays by the presence of ghosts. Bolger's plays reflect the significant change in Ireland that has taken place in the two decades after the first production of *The Lament for Arthur Cleary*. As a result of the exceptionally fast economic development of the 'Celtic Tiger', Irish emigration is no longer a pressing topic. Instead, the growing division between the exceptionally rich and the poor, among them immigrants, as well as the spiritual emptiness despite material well-being, have become relevant.

Given Bolger's enormous productivity and popularity, the academic reception of his plays has been relatively scarce. Critics disagree about the ideological implications of his preoccupation with notions of home. Christopher Murray and Declan Kiberd consider Bolger an 'outspoken conservative' and label his work nostalgia for lost, better times, 'a golden age, somewhere in the 1950s before he was born, when stability, poverty and happiness went nostalgically together. His plays are a lament for this lost paradise.'[5] The majority of critical assessments of Bolger's dramatic oeuvre, however, argue that Bolger on the contrary invites audiences to let go of such idealised versions of the individual and national past, 'while advocating nomadic subjectivities in their stead'.[6] Since Bolger's plays highlight the constant search of all characters, often through the metaphors of a journey and of moving house, they support a processual notion of personal and national identity. They demonstrate the debilitating impact of fossilised identities which draw on the past as the only directive for the future, perhaps most powerfully in his debut play *The Lament for Arthur Cleary*, which is generally regarded as Bolger's 'masterpiece so far'.[7]

Vic Merriman argues that Bolger's debut play is typical of a shift in Irish drama away from nationalist and neocolonial tropes. Rather than defining Ireland against the 'despised other' of the 'colonising overlord',[8] Irish plays begin to tackle the inequalities and exclusions within Irish society and give a voice to marginalised groups. Frequently set in the working-class suburbs of Dublin that are afflicted by unemployment, poverty and criminality, Bolger's plays innovatively explore a 'virgin territory' for Irish literature,[9] in which the 'rural melancholia familiar on Irish stages gives way to urban anger'.[10]

Bolger has created an individual dramatic form of the memory play that radicalises psychic realism and integrates poetic devices. All the plays except Bolger's only comedy, *Blinded by the Light*, privilege the internal, subjective realities of the protagonists over external, 'objective' reality. Since the plays are indebted to the thoughts, perceptions and imagination of their characters rather than to rules of verisimilitude and probability, they dissolve linear and causal time structures, blend different settings and do not differentiate between the living and the dead. Aspects of Bolger's dramatic style are shared by contemporary Irish playwrights such as Sebastian Barry and Marina Carr, perhaps most prominently the presence of ghosts (especially those of lost children) and imaginary figures, which not only connect past and present, life and death, but are also 'symbols of incompletion'[11] and of loss.[12]

Relinquishing 'a naturalistic theatre of recognition',[13] Bolger's psychic realism invites audiences to participate in alternative views of reality, be it the looking back of the dead and socially marginalised (in *The Lament for Arthur Cleary* and *Walking the Road*), the hallucinations of a desperate character addicted to heroin (in *One Last White Horse*), the sudden supernatural visions of a highly rational businessman (in *The Passion of Jerome*), or the history of a stigmatised building complex and its inhabitants (in the Ballymun trilogy). Bolger himself perceives his creation of a 'theatre of evocation' as an obstacle in the reception, marketing and 'mainstreaming' of his plays and is unsure whether there is 'necessarily a place in Irish theatre for me'.[14]

Primary Sources

Works by Dermot Bolger

Plays 1 [*The Lament for Arthur Cleary; Blinded by the Light; In High Germany; The Holy Ground*] (London: Methuen, 2000).

One Last White Horse, in *A Dublin Quartet* (London: Penguin, 1992), pp. 144–203.

April Bright, in *April Bright and Blinded by the Light: Two Plays* (Dublin: New Island Books, 1997), pp. 6–120.

The Passion of Jerome (London: Methuen, 1999).

From These Green Heights (Dublin: New Island, 2005).

Walking the Road (Dublin: New Island, 2007).

The Townlands of Brazil (Dublin: New Island, 2009).

The Consequences of Lightning (Dublin: New Island, 2009).

Secondary Sources

Aragay, Mireira, 'Reading Dermot Bolger's *The Holy Ground*: National Identity, Gender and Sexuality in Post-Colonial Ireland', *Links & Letters*, Vol. 4 (1997), pp. 53–64.

Bolger, Dermot, 'Author's Note', in his *A Dublin Quartet* (London: Penguin, 1992), pp. ix–x.

—, 'Dermot Bolger in Conversation with Jim O'Hanlon', in Lilian Chambers *et al.* (eds), *Theatre Talk: Voices of Irish Theatre Practitioners* (Dublin: Carysfort Press, 2001).

—, 'Interview with Dermot Bolger' by Mária Kurdi, *Etudes Irlandaises*, Vol. 28, No. 1 (2003), pp. 7–22.

Bort, Eberhard, '"Come on You Boys in Green": Irish Football, Irish Theatre, and the

"Irish Diaspora"', in Eberhard Bort (ed.), *The State of Play: Irish Theatre in the Nineties* (Trier: Wissenschaftlicher Verlag Trier, 1996), pp. 88–103.

Grant, David, 'Introduction', in his *The Crack in the Emerald: New Irish Plays* (London: Nick Hern Books, 1990), pp. vii–xiv.

Hickman, Mary J., 'Migration and Diaspora', in Joe Cleary and Claire Connolly (eds), *The Cambridge Companion to Modern Irish Culture* (Cambridge: Cambridge UP, 2005), pp. 117–36.

Jordan, Eamonn, 'Introduction', in Eamonn Jordan (ed.), *Theatre Stuff: Critical Essays on Contemporary Irish Theatre* (Dublin: Carysfort Press, 2000), pp. xi–xliii.

Kiberd, Declan, *Inventing Ireland: The Literature of the Modern Nation* (London: Vintage, 1996).

Llewellyn-Jones, Margaret, *Contemporary Irish Drama and Cultural Identity* (Bristol: Intellect Books, 2000).

Merriman, Vic, 'Centring the Wanderer', *Irish University Review*, Vol. 27, No. 1 (1997), pp. 166–81.

Murphy, Paul, 'Inside the Immigrant Mind: Nostalgic versus Nomadic Subjectivities in Late Twentieth-Century Irish Drama', *Australasian Drama Studies*, Vol. 43 (2003), pp. 128–47.

Murphy, Paula, 'From Ballymun to Brazil: Bolger's Postmodern Ireland', in Eamon Maher *et al.* (eds), *Modernity and Postmodernity in a Franco-Irish Context* (Frankfurt am Main: Peter Lang, 2008), pp. 161–78.

Murray, Christopher, 'The State of Play: Irish Theatre in the Nineties', in Eberhard Bort (ed.), *The State of Play: Irish Theatre in the Nineties* (Trier: Wissenschaftlicher Verlag Trier, 1996), pp. 9–23.

O'Toole, Fintan, 'Introduction: On the Frontier', in *Dermot Bolger: Plays: 1* (London: Methuen, 2000), pp. ix–xlv.

—, 'Irish Theatre: The State of the Art', in Eamonn Jordan (ed.), *Theatre Stuff: Critical Essays on Contemporary Irish Theatre* (Dublin: Carysfort Press, 2000), pp. 47–58.

Pelletier, Martine, 'Dermot Bolger's Drama', in Eamonn Jordan (ed.), *Theatre Stuff: Critical Essays on Contemporary Irish Theatre* (Dublin: Carysfort Press, 2000), pp. 249–56.

Wroe, Nichola, 'Always Make Sure You Offend: Dermot Bolger Tells Nicholas Wroe About Helping Irish Writing Grow Up', *Guardian*, 4 March 2000, <http://books.guardian.co.uk/ departments/ generalfiction/story/0,,143005,00.html>.

Notes

1. Margaret Llewellyn-Jones considers Arthur a positive male role model who offers an alternative version of male heroism in a rough urban context (Margaret Llewellyn-Jones, *Contemporary Irish Drama*, p. 105).

2. Mary J. Hickman, 'Migration and Diaspora', p. 119.

3. See Eberhard Bort, 'Come on You Boys in Green', p. 94.

4. See Mireira Aragay, 'Reading Dermot Bolger's *The Holy Ground*'.

5. Christopher Murray, 'The State of Play', p. 15. See also Declan Kiberd, *Inventing Ireland*, pp. 609–10.

6. Paul Murphy, 'Inside the Immigrant Mind', p. 1359. See also Fintan O'Toole, 'Introduction: On the Frontier', and Paula Murphy, 'From Ballymun to Brazil'.

7. Martine Pelletier, 'Dermot Bolger's Drama', p. 250.

8. Vic Merriman, 'Centring the Wanderer', p. 166.

9. O'Toole, op. cit.

10. David Grant, 'Introduction'.

11. Pelletier, op. cit., p. 253.

12. See Eamonn Jordan, 'Introduction', pp. xxxviii–xxxix on ghost characters and dead children in contemporary Irish drama.

13. O'Toole, 'Irish Theatre: The State of the Art', p. 57.

14. Dermot Bolger, 'Dermot Bolger in Conversation', p. 41.

3 MARINA CARR

Aleks Sierz

The Mai; Portia Coughlan; By the Bog of Cats . . .; On Raftery's Hill; Ariel; Woman and Scarecrow

Introduction

The drama of playwright Marina Carr has been described as 'characterized by the expression, in richly scabrous language, of unhappy personal relationships in a comparatively wealthy new society only one generation removed from peasant culture'.[1] If this gives an immediate impression of the social context of her work, it doesn't do justice to its richness of theatrical experimentation, and especially the way that Carr weaves mythological material into the texture of her stories. Over the past two decades, she has built up a remarkable body of work, and is now widely appreciated as 'one of the most powerful, haunting voices on the contemporary Irish stage'.[2]

Carr was born in Dublin on 17 November 1964 and grew up in County Offaly. Her father was a playwright and novelist, her mother a primary school teacher; they had six children. In her 'Introduction' to *Plays One*, she describes the melodramas the children created: 'We loved the havoc, the badness, the blood spillage, but loved equally restoring some sort of botched order and harmony' (p. x). When Carr went to University College Dublin, she joined the Drama Society, and completed her first play, *Ullaloo*. In 1987, she graduated with a degree in English and Philosophy, and started an MA on Samuel Beckett. In 1989, *Ullaloo* was given a rehearsed reading at the Dublin Theatre Festival and her follow-up, *Low in the Dark*, was staged at the Project Arts Centre, Dublin. The next year, *The Deer's Surrender* was put on at the Andrews Lane Theatre, Dublin. In 1991, *Ullaloo* was given a full production at the Abbey Theatre's Peacock space, and *This Love*

Thing was staged in Dublin and Belfast. Then the Abbey commissioned Carr to write *The Mai*, which was her breakthrough, performed at the Peacock in October 1994. It won the Dublin Theatre Festival's Best New Irish Play award and, after a visit to the Tron theatre, Glasgow, was revived at the Abbey the following year. In 1996, Carr was writer-in-residence at the Abbey and her *Portia Coughlan* opened at the Peacock in March and then transferred to the Royal Court in London. In October 1998, *By the Bog of Cats . . .* was first produced at the Abbey as part of the Dublin Theatre Festival, winning the Irish Times/ESB Award for Best New Play. In 2000, *On Raftery's Hill* was commissioned by the Druid Theatre Company, and *Ariel* was produced by the Abbey in 2002. In the following year, *Meat and Salt* was a one-act play for young people staged at the Peacock. In November 2004, *By the Bog of Cats . . .* was revived at the Wyndhams Theatre in London's West End, and, in June 2006, *Woman and Scarecrow* premiered at the Royal Court.

The Plays

Carr's early work was influenced by Beckett and the Theatre of the Absurd. *Ullaloo*, *The Deer's Surrender* and *This Love Thing* have not been published but Christopher Fitz-Simon writes that *Ullaloo* 'revealed a highly original talent waiting to be released from Beckettian thrall'.[3] Carr's official career starts with *Low in the Dark*, written in collaboration with the actors of the Crooked Sixpence company.[4] Set on a stage split between a 'bizarre bathroom' for the women and a work-cluttered 'men's space' (p. 5), it has three female characters, Curtains, fiftysomething Bender and her daughter Binder; and two males, Bone (Binder's lover) and Baxter (Curtains' lover). Orchestrating a battle of the sexes is Curtains, who tells numerous stories about Man and Woman. Typically Beckettian, she is 'any age, as she is covered from head to toe in heavy, brocaded curtains and rail. Not an inch of her face or body is seen' (p. 5). *Low in the Dark* has a feminist agenda. As Catherine Rees says:

The play rejects traditional characterisation and instead uses characters who are largely representative of various gender attitudes. What is interesting is that these categorisations are carried forward to her later plays, where women are largely concerned with the emotional aspects of their existences, while men principally aim to cultivate and maintain the physical and monetary parts of their lives.[5]

Women love the 'artistic' and the 'romantic'; men love 'land' and 'money'.[6] Throughout, there is constant role-reversal – 'one day the woman turned to the man and said, "It's time you had a baby"' (p. 51) – and speeches that suggest folk sayings: 'The woman is born full and dies empty. The man is born empty and dies full. He dies full unless he miscarries' (p. 53).

The Mai (1994)

Christopher Morash rightly says that Carr's 'early, experimental plays gave way to a more naturalistic style in plays with midland settings'.[7] The first was *The Mai*, a story of four generations of women set in 1979–80. The play is 'reminiscent of *Hedda Gabler*'[8] in that The Mai is a strong woman who kills herself because she is unable to compromise. On one level, she is 'a cross between a pagan goddess and the Blessed Virgin', dressed in 'pale blue of summer skies and May altars', 'the epitome of romantic marital purity';[9] on another, she is a down-to-earth woman obsessed with her husband, Robert. Her arguments with him are psychologically convincing, but are never enough to explain her suicide. At the end, which echoes *Wuthering Heights*, The Mai acknowledges that 'no one will ever understand how completely and utterly Robert is mine and I am his': she kills herself because she 'can't think of one reason for going on without him' (p. 185). So although The Mai is an independent woman, all of her activities, from having children to building her new house, are done for her husband.

Ellen, The Mai's mother, is absent and this allows the rest of the family to offer competing versions of who she was. These, and other exchanges, often humorous, between the opium-smoking Grandma Fraochlán, her children and grandchildren crackle with wit and a shared history in which romance is valued more than reality. Grandma Fraochlán tells colourful stories about her father, a Spanish or Moroccan sailor called the Sultan, and of her husband, known as the 'nine-fingered fisherman'. But the banter between the women, however enjoyable, sometimes obscures the fact that this is a picture of a troubled married couple. If The Mai is the commanding female presence, Robert is the absent male. Not only has he abandoned the family, but he also withdraws from them when he is at home, preferring to play his cello. 'The psychological transference was expressed in Brian Brady's production of *The Mai* in a surreal moment when Olwen Fouéré as The Mai was substituted for the cello.'[10] Carr points out that, in symbolic terms, 'the female body it's very like a cello'.[11] Robert plays on The Mai, successfully exploiting her love for him, and, in return, she tries to play him, but ultimately fails.

> Carr's central dramatic device is to use the daughter Millie as the story's narrator. The play breaks with the non-realistic structure of her earlier work by employing a dramatic conceit – also found in Brian Friel's *Dancing at Lughnasa* (1990) – by which the child of the play, in this case Millie, acts as the narrator.[12]

She is not a passive narrator, but actively struggles to establish her version of her mother's story. And her adversary is her father. She says that when she meets Robert, they both fight viciously until the point when both use 'the language of the gutter, where he'll call me a fuckin' cunt and I'll call him an ignorant bollix!' (p. 128). Millie is The Mai's oldest child and, in Carr's words, 'she's telling the story, at a slant'.[13] Furthermore, 'The Mai's story is in fact Millie's story [. . .] the story of a parent or parents is the legacy of their children.'[14] More precisely, the women hand down misery to their daughters: Millie is a wronged or damaged child.

Carr's mature style is evident in the complex interweaving of mythic and folkloric elements into the main dramatic situation, a tale of marital infidelity. Usually, this creates a feeling of deep ambiguity. When Millie tells the legend of Owl Lake at the end of Act One, it dramatically foreshadows the tragedy to come, but it also raises questions:

> I am not quite sure what Millie's interpretation of the story is: that Owl Lake is a dangerous place, that The Mai should learn a lesson in patience from Coillte and not make her mistake, or that The Mai should leave Robert.[15]

In terms of language, this play highlights the contrast between midlands speech (especially Grandma Fraochlán) and more refined modes (exemplified by Millie). The use of folklore also suggests that the characters are shadowed by archetypes, of the kind that appear in fairy tales, and this drains them of volition. This is articulated by Grandma Fraochlán: 'We can't help repeatin', Robert, we repeat and we repeat, the orchestration may be different but the tune is always the same' (p. 123). Similar is the idea, voiced by Millie, that the characters are 'sleepwalkers' (p. 148), who know the legend of the Owl Lake but are powerless to heed its warning. The play also presents us with an image of Millie at sixteen, acting as a hesitant confidante to her mother, a role that makes her prematurely adult. Yet despite the darkness of parental neglect, The Mai is Carr's most humorous and easy-going play. Subsequently, the mood darkened.

Portia Coughlan (1996)

Portia Coughlan is similar to The Mai in its portrait of a dissatisfied woman whose life is out of control. In the names Portia and Belmont, there is an echo of The Merchant of Venice, which influenced Carr at school.[16] This Portia, however, is no Shakespearean lady but, in Carr's words, 'a savage in the woods'.[17] Portia is radically dissatisfied, split between wanting to live and knowing that death is close. Her desperation means she can act as a truth-teller. Her doomed situation also means that she can be many contradictory things at once: brave and afraid, coarse and sensitive, selfish and in pain. Finally, although she is pulled towards death by her love for her dead brother, Gabriel, she is able to admit that, when he was alive, she didn't even like him (p. 241). Her love for him has a sense of the incestuous, although it is not necessary to take her claim that the twins 'made love' (p. 253) since the age of five entirely literally. The pair are twins and one cannot thrive in the absence of the other. In one striking image, she says that they 'Came out of the womb holdin' hands – When God was handin' out souls he must've got mine and Gabriel's mixed up' (p. 211). Typical of the play's ambiguity is the way this image is put into question by Portia's mother, who claims that Gabriel 'Came out of the womb clutchin' your leg' (p. 247). The notion of inseparable twins also relates to Portia's 'melancholic state' following the loss of her twin and 'involves a profound failure, or refusal, to fulfil the gender expectations of her environment'.[18]

In an 'Afterword' published in *The Dazzling Dark*, Carr remarks about 'the rough exoticism' of the play's language, 'for we speak differently [. . .] We talk long and slow and flat' (p. 310). In the first published versions, the dialogue was spelt phonetically, although this was later changed: thus Portia's 'Cem bache ta cheche an me' (1996, p. 1) becomes 'Came back to check on me' (p. 193). In the original,

> her spelling forces the reader (and the actors) to hear the flat open nasality of the midlands, its fluid energy. She creates a medium as flexible as Synge's, one capable of intellectual force, emotional range, and the sheer exhilaration of heart-scorching anger.[19]

On stage, the language is not always easy for audiences: the 1996 play text, which was also a programme, included a glossary.

In *Portia Coughlan*, the landscape is an actor. At one point, Portia says, 'I know the topography of your mind as well as I know every inch and ditch and drain of Belmont Farm' (p. 210). When her father tells her to forget Gabriel, she says that 'the very river tells me that once he was here' (p. 214). Nature, in Carr's work, is invested with human memory. For Portia, the river is a place where 'me and Gabriel made love all the time down be the Belmont River among the swale'

(p. 253). As Carr says, 'the river is her. It's her and Gabriel.'[20] But its flowing water is also connected with her feeling of being in the womb with Gabriel, when 'we don't know which of us is the other' (p. 254). The Belmont River is also a place of myth: a local legend says that the place is named after a river God called Bel, who came and rescued a woman – seen by some as a 'mad hoor of a witch' but whom Portia just calls 'different' – left to die on a stake by locals (p. 219).

Also typical is a brooding sense of biological inheritance. This is clear not only in Portia's ideas about her twin, but also in the revelation that 'Marianne and Sly [Portia's parents] are brother and sister. Same father, different mothers' (p. 244), one explanation of the family tragedy being that 'Young Gabriel Scully was insane from too much inbreedin'' (p. 245). As in *The Mai*, the fierce grandmother sees the family's problems as the result of the mixing of bad blood: 'Fuckin' tinkers, the Joyces' with their 'waxy blood' and 'dirty ignorant blood' (p. 229). Suspicion falls on anyone of unknown ancestry: 'We don't know where ye came from, the histories of yeer blood' (p. 215). Images of blood, especially bad blood ('black blood' [p. 215]), spatter the text: at one point, Marianne even accuses Portia of vampirism (p. 249). The final question, again typical of Carr's work, is Portia's 'Is our lives followin' a minute and careful plan designed on high or are we just flittin' from chance to chance?' (p. 239). The play suggests that life can be read as both predetermined (Portia is doomed because of her twin's death) and chance (Portia might have been saved if Raphael had been less exhausted).

By the Bog of Cats . . . (1998)

Carr's next play, *By the Bog of Cats . . .*, is also set in the midlands and its main theme is loss. Like Carr's other heroines, Hester is a strong-minded outsider. Living in a caravan on the edge of the stable settlements of ordinary folk, she is proud of her 'tinker blood' (p. 289). Abandoned by her mother, she is wilful and anti-social. As is clear from Joseph's ghost, she is also guilty of fratricide – motivated by jealousy of his closeness to their mother. The image of the mother looms large across the play, with Hester appearing to be a bad mother, as well as there being a series of alternative maternal figures, from the darkly symbolic witch-mother, the Catwoman, to the terrestrial clinging mother, Mrs Kilbride, or the weak mother, Monica. Hester is also tied to her location, part of the bog landscape: 'everythin' I'm connected to is here. I'd rather die [than leave]' (p. 273). Hester is linked to nature symbolically in her relationship with Black Wing, the dead black swan she drags ominously on to the stage at the start. At the end, Hester has 'cut her heart out – it's lyin' there on top of her chest like some dark feathered bird' (p. 341).

By the Bog of Cats . . . has classical allusions, such as the name of Hester's lover, Carthage, and the figure of the blind seer, and is a modern version of *Medea*. In terms of form, the three-act play has 'the concentrated unity of time and action' that aligns it with Greek tragedy.[21] Hester fulfils a curse that she would live only as long as the black swan, and believes that she is incomplete without her mother's return: 'For too long now I've imagined her comin' towards me across the Bog of Cats and she would find me here standin' strong' (p. 336). But if Hester refuses the offer of a new house in the town, preferring to live in the wild, the land she occupies is contested territory. Stolen money is used to buy it; the 'blood money' paid to Hester comes from the profits of land. Significantly, land is a place farmed by men. And it obsesses them. As Xavier says about Carthage, 'He loves the land and like me he'd rather die than part with it wance he gets his greedy hands on it' (p. 328). There is also a sense that the bog is a shifting locale whose ability to change suggests the effects of time, and liminality. The midlands are a symbolic mid-place, betwixt and between, neither completely settled nor utterly wild. Here ordinary human rules do not apply. 'In *By the Bog of Cats* . . . we are presented with an almost pre-lapsarian vision of the bonds between the human figure and her landscape.'[22] As Hester says, 'I left Eden, Monica, at the age of seven' (p. 322). Thrown off the land that is part of her psyche, she is driven into self-destruction. But death solves nothing: 'the restored order will not bring happiness to the surviving community which has been irreparably damaged by the events leading to this extremity'.[23]

On Raftery's Hill (2000)

Carr's next play, *On Raftery's Hill*, 'presents a shocking picture of one of the less progressive aspects of modern Ireland'.[24] Set in the midlands, it is about an impoverished rural clan, beset by the evils of incest, abuse and brutality. The main character is the monstrous Red, '*an imposing man in his sixties*', who enters with '*two shot hares around his neck*' (p. 14). The incest theme is central. Dinah and her father, Red, have been having sex ever since she was twelve years old, and, according to Sorrel, this still continues. Dinah's defence is that they do it 'in the pitch dark' without a word, and that it hurts no one, and 'we want ud to stop' but cannot (p. 57). Clearly, Dinah is not only trapped in this relationship, but she is motivated by the desire to protect her daughter/sister, Sorrel. At the same time, she is bitter that no one protected her when she was a child. The result is that Sorrel is a 'double Raftery' (p. 47), since her father and sister are her parents. When Dara says he hates Red, Sorrel points out that since 'hees blood runs through me so what you are sayin is ya can't abide me' (p. 53). The incest theme is also highlighted by the story of Brophy, as told by Dara (p. 19). And Isaac, Red's hunting companion, points out the mythological perspective: 'Zeus and Hera, sure they were brother and sister' (p. 43).

In Ded's cry: 'I want me mother, I miss her fierce so I do' (p. 24), the absent parent of the family is the uncaring mother who shoulders the blame for the abusive father. But, according to Red, she was 'a lunatic wud an antique violin and an eternal case a' migraine' (p. 30). Dinah claims that her mother first 'sent me into bed aside him [her father]' (p. 57). And, once again, the landscape is part of this corrupt family. The Hill (household) contrasts with the Valley (surrounding farmland). As Red says, 'There was alas skul duggery in the Valley' (p. 20). Rural ignorance, genetic collapse and widespread abuse prevail. Just as Red is shown to have polluted his farm, so his family relationships are riddled with lies. Just as Shalome tries every night to return to her long dead father, so Red and Dinah's solution to family problems is to pretend that nothing is happening. It is Sorrel's determination to tell the truth that prevents her from marrying Dara:

she prefers loyalty to her father and mother/sister. As a metaphorical figure, Red symbolises masculinity as a universal pollutant.

> This play, more than her others, can be seen as having an 'in-yer-face' sensibility, with its coarse language, bleak outlook (it has little of the poetry of her earlier work) and its exploration of the brutality of human relationships.[25]

At one point, Dinah says, 'Thah's whah we are, gorillas in clothes pretendin to be human' (p. 28). Monstrosity has a human face.

Ariel (2002)

Carr's next play, *Ariel*, is based on Euripides' *Iphigenia at Aulis* and tells the story of Fermoy Fitzgerald, a father who sacrifices his teenage daughter. Carr dramatises this classical theme in the context of contemporary Irish politics. *Ariel* also draws on other ancient Greek sources, such as 'Aeschylus' Oresteia and Sophocles' and Euripides' Electras'.[26] For example, Elaine and Stephen embody aspects of Electra and Orestes. In addition, there are a number of Shakespearean allusions, most obviously the title. Ariel is 'a figure of light in a dark landscape (Tempest) in addition to being a fallen angel in the Bible'.[27] In the final scene, when Elaine addresses Ariel's skull, there is a clear allusion to *Hamlet*. Intertwined with elements of Greek mythology and the theme of blood vengeance are numerous references to Christian theology – especially in Fermoy's discussions with Boniface – as well as several satirical points about contemporary Irish politics. The watery legends suggested by Cuura Lake are the folk tale strand in the play, and, in the play text, a reproduction of the 'Vision of Hell' from Gustave Doré's illustrations to Dante's *Inferno* (p. 77) emphasises the theme of human suffering. In these ways, the play can be seen as an 'unstable theatrical hybrid of psychotic visions and social realism'.[28] The result is an extremely dense work, packed with numerous allusions that don't always sit easily with the contemporary idiom of the self-made politician, and the whole offers few opportunities for humour.

Ariel focuses on the life of a self-made man who has built up a cement business and gone into politics. Clearly, the portrait of the Agamemnon-like Fermoy is complicated by his attitudes to Christianity. In the interview with the journalist, who points out that 'the Church has spoken out against you on several occasions', Fermoy claims that he 'was talkin abouh the sullen nature a Christ', and uses Piero della Francesca's 1463 painting of the *Resurrection* as an example (p. 43). He argues that Christ was killed by us, not for us, and that he was resurrected for his own sake, not ours. Fermoy's idea that there is 'no forgiveness in them eyes' (p. 44) suggests a vengeful Christ-figure much nearer to the ancient Greek idea of the all-too-human gods than to traditional New Testament teachings. Added to this, Fermoy is also motivated by a love of the Napoleonic legacy in Europe and by a vision of the need for a much larger imagination in nation-building: 'The legacy the Brihish have left us was the till, whereas for Napoleon the world was wan big battlefield. He talked abouh hees battlefields like they were women' (p. 42). In summary,

> Carr's study of the corrupting force of politics is new ground for her, but the melodramatic ghostly visitations and bloody on-stage murders keep this play firmly rooted in her familiar genre of dramatic and emotive family tragedy.[29]

But the play does not follow its tragic templates completely:

> here there is no Eumenides, or Aeschylean law court which attempts to free these characters from their cycle of crime in a civilized way, which is surely the great moralizing force of the original *Oresteia* by Aeschylus. This is also not T. S. Eliot's *Family Reunion*, based on the Eumenides, with its redemptive message.[30]

Woman and Scarecrow (2006)

Finally, Carr's *Woman and Scarecrow* has affinities with her earlier, absurdist style. The set is a bare room with a large double bed. Woman lies dying, and talks to her alter ego, Scarecrow, who treats her to a comic mix of heartfelt truths and spot-on criticism.

> Unseen by any but Woman, Scarecrow assumes the qualities of a ker (female death-spirits in Greek mythology), yet the dialogue between the two bears the wit and casual spite of long acquaintanceship.[31]

Influenced by Samuel Beckett and Tom Murphy, Carr's play is less about death than about the life that death – the 'thing in the wardrobe' (p. 24) – will inevitably terminate. It makes uncomfortable points about the value of our lives, the price we pay for staying with those we love, and the bitterness we feel about not fulfilling ourselves. Claustrophobic, distressing and stomach-twisting, Carr's muscular humour is unsentimental and ranges over the whole of life's bumpy ground: from the messy business of having kids to how poorly most of us are prepared to face the end: 'the whole point of living is preparing to die' (p. 47). In *Woman and Scarecrow*, 'the marital relationship proves too diseased for deathbed reconciliation' and while 'children are traditionally a cipher for immortality, at least in the genetic sense',[32] here they are absent, and the only one that Woman remembers with any vividness is her stillborn child, 'My little half-moon baby with the livid face' (p. 12). The play ends with a mixture of exhausted resignation and fighting spirit: 'Living is almost nothing and we brave little mortals investing so much in it' (p. 76).

Summary

Carr's achievements have been aptly summarised by Cathy Leeney: her place as 'the most visionary Irish playwright of her generation is marked by huge creativity, restless courage and epic ambition'.[33] It is also significant, as Clare Wallace points out, that she is 'the most widely known and successful female dramatist to emerge in Ireland in decades'.[34] As Catherine Rees adds, 'Carr has been nurtured by the Abbey Theatre'.[35] But this nurturing has been problematic. For example, Dominic Dromgoole writes that association with the Abbey has had a negative effect on her writing because this institution values literary Yeatsian plays, which are usually 'sorrowful, washed by water and weeping women'. Her work, he argues, has an 'unbruised preciousness, which can get a trifle wearing. But there is a dark humour, and a suppressed sexuality which enlivens it.'[36]

In the 1990s, Irish theatre had at its disposal what Christopher Morash calls 'a palette of styles' and playwrights could utilise

> realism as one legitimate style among many [. . .] Where *A* [sic] *Low in the Dark* was radical in both its feminist politics and its form, *The Mai* showed an awareness that the theatrical forms of early modernism still retained their oblique power.[37]

Carr's plays typically 'revolve around characters for whom a world of ghosts is more compelling than the reality around them'.[38] In terms of form, Carr's use of the monologue is also significant. Christopher Fitz-Simon says, 'as with many of the younger Irish dramatists, much use is made of the searching monologue through which the desperation in the speaker's soul finds its expression'.[39] And 'Carr is among those who have restored the storyteller's perspective to the drama'.[40] Allied to the use of individual storytellers is 'the deceptive nature of memory'.[41] It should also be noted that the reality in which Carr's stage characters exist is a traditional and instantly recognisable theatrical place. Comparing Synge's *In the Shadow of the Glen* (1903) with Carr's work, Robert Welch writes,

> It is exactly the world Marina Carr, the playwright of the midlands, has brought back in the 1990s, revealing that Irish country life has, in some ways, hardly changed at all in close on a hundred years.[42]

At the same time, her work also reflects the Celtic Tiger economy, those unprecedented boom times which have exploded social mores and created a feeling of cultural confidence. What gives Carr her individual voice is precisely this mix of tradition and innovation, of clear-eyed realism and dreamy fantasy.

Carr is also an example of a playwright who was part of a recent 'rediscovery of the resources of language.'[43] especially its poetry. In her writing, language often appears with an orthography which assaults the conventions of written English, thus creating both a challenge to readers and 'an aural vision for performance'.[44] Despite her use of antique comedy, the general tone of Carr's work is tragic. Indeed, '[a]n intriguing feature of Irish writing towards the end of the millennium was a notable turn to the classics for models and inspiration'.[45] Carr's heroines, especially, face 'an impossible future, and are sometimes defeated', but what strikes you is 'the vehemence of their resistance, their will to freedom and fulfilment'.[46] The influence of the tragic genre also results in a hyperbolic quality about her writing that provokes commentators to strain for adjectives: her relationships are 'recklessly unhappy'[47] and her heroines have a 'furious sense of dissatisfaction'.[48] Moreover, Carr's use of elements of Greek and Shakespearean is complex. Typically, she blends several different notions of tragedy, ancient and modern, in her work:

> In her assemblage of references and influences Carr produces a problematic contemporary tragedy and her heroines are subject to the paradox of a unified narrative or destiny which returns to and is founded upon fragmentation and lack.[49]

Carr's use of folkloric elements has also attracted comment. Her plays are set in a rural landscape drained of modernity – the locale of fairy tales. The outlandish names of her characters 'also reflect those used in fairytales'.[50] Indeed,

> Carr's world is a strange mix of folk tale, memory, raddled affliction and sadness, longing, and a sense that the incredible may become all too real in a world which obeys laws not subject to our will.[51]

Allied to folklore is landscape. In Carr's words, 'I've always thought that landscape was another character in the work.'[52] The typical oppositions are between home as a sanctuary and as a place of fear; between a land that is beautiful and treacherous, in which bogs or rivers represent the opposite of firm ground. Like the midlands themselves, which are symbolically liminal, the landscape of her plays is ever-changeable, unreliable. Her setting 'is depicted as increasingly harsh, isolated, dystopic and removed from modernity'.[53] Places of shifting water become sinks of loss, wells of sadness. For example, 'both women [The Mai and Portia] drown themselves, but The Mai's lake reminds us of the character's inability to leave the site of her fantasy, while Portia's river suggests the possibility of motion', of escape.[54]

Seen through the lens of M. M. Bakhtin's theories, *By the Bog of Cats . . .* is one instance of how 'disorder and turbulence permeate her plays, and lend to them a grotesque and carnivalesque dimension, which can be monstrous or poignant, but is absolutely compelling'.[55] The recurring image of the younger generation being betrayed by the older generation, most bleakly seen in *On Raftery's Hill*, is 'also metonymic of the betrayal by older generations in their failure to husband the resources of the natural world for those coming after'.[56] In this way, Carr's work can be seen as exemplifying a green politics. It is also possible to interpret Carr's troubled families as examples of anthropological practices. For example, '*On Raftery's Hill* reveals a patriarchal family structure that recalls Claude Lévi-Strauss's naturalisation of the exchange of women as objects or gifts.'[57] The incest taboo and the dominance of the menfolk are the objects of the playwright's critique. Some of Carr's plays exemplify the psychoanalytical ideas of Freud, as for instance the melancholia following loss: Christina Wald sees *Portia Coughlan* as

> The play [that] demonstrates the degree to which Portia's unresolved mourning for her twin brother troubles normative femininity. Portraying melancholia as a malady which oscillates between performing and being performed, the play highlights the way Portia on the one hand deliberately rebels against the restrictive rural gender models, but on the other cannot help failing gender ideals.[58]

Similarly, it is worth stressing, as Clare Wallace does, the fact that Carr depends heavily on 'the modalities of repetition', using ghost figures, myth and repeated motifs to create a claustrophobic world.[59]

Carr's work has been interpreted as part of a larger trend in contemporary Irish culture, in which 'the nation's post-coloniality appears to be overlaid, or at least interwoven, with a kind of postmodernism'.[60] Clare Wallace developed this argument in a chapter of her *Suspect Cultures*, showing how the 'tensions between nostalgia and a desire for authenticity'[61] permeate the plays. When 'nostalgia and simulacra interact' the result is 'a kind of neo-primitivist reflex action'.[62] Similarly, Victor Merriman interprets Carr as celebrating a 'spurious post-coloniality' giving reactionary portraits of the nation in a time of social and economic change.[63] And Bruce Stewart sees Hester as 'a proxy for the political violence upon which the Irish state was founded' but which is now being jettisoned in recent decades.[64] On the other hand, Cathy Leeney and Anna McMullan see Carr's postmodernism as exemplified by her hybridity, with mischievous references to Greek and Irish dramatic canons, Shakespeare, Rabelais, Brontë and local legend, with typical characters being 'offspring of mixed origins, half gods, half monsters'.[65]

Carr's work is contemporary in that it shows how traditional institutions, such as marriage, are subject to new strains. Some commentators have seen her themes, especially that of incestuous love, as an implicit criticism of society:

> The ideal of the family was a cohesive force at the very heart of the Irish social contract, and for that reason it sometimes acted as a covering device beneath which tyrannies, abuses, and perversions could take place [. . .] a society that overvalues the family will, inevitably, have certain families that are cauldrons of hell.[66]

Yet Carr never writes plays that denounce specific abuses: more subtly, she shows 'what it is like to be in the midlands of existence' – caught between the desire for love and the reality of love.[67] The result is a sense of futility which drives her characters to the brink. Yet this despair is simultaneously an affirmation: 'Carr's success suggests that her work speaks to the social instability that accompanies cultural growth [. . .] a world confronting its own darkness.'[68] These are Carr's central themes, and her genius has been to give them satisfying theatrical form over a whole body of work.

Primary Sources

Works by Marina Carr

Ariel (Meath: Gallery Press, 2002).

Low in the Dark, in David Grant (ed.), *The Crack in the Emerald: New Irish Plays* (London: Nick Hern, 1990), pp. 63–140.

On Raftery's Hill (London: Faber, 2000).

Plays One: Low in the Dark; The Mai; Portia Coughlan; By the Bog of Cats . . . (London: Faber, 1999).

Portia Coughlan, in Frank McGuinness (ed.), *The Dazzling Dark: New Irish Plays* (London: Faber, 1996), pp. 235–311.

Portia Coughlan (London: Faber, 1996).

Woman and Scarecrow (London: Faber, 2006).

Secondary Sources

Bourke, Bernadette, 'Carr's "Cut-throats and gargiyles": Grotesque and Carnivalesque Elements in *By the Bog of Cats . . .*', in Cathy Leeney and Anna McMullan (eds), *The Theatre of Marina Carr*, pp. 128–44.

Dean, Tanya, 'Review of *Woman and Scarecrow*', *Irish Theatre Magazine*, autumn 2007 <www.irishtheatremagazine.ie/home/ dublintheatrefestivalWomanAndScarecrow.htm>.

Doyle, Maria, 'Dead Center: Tragedy and the Reanimated Body in Marina Carr's *The Mai* and *Portia Coughlan*', *Modern Drama*, Vol. 49, No. 1 (Spring 2006), pp. 41–59.

Dromgoole, Dominic, *The Full Room: An A–Z of Contemporary Playwriting*, 2nd edn (London: Methuen, 2002).

Fitz-Simon, Christopher, 'Carr, Marina', in Colin Chambers (ed.), *The Continuum Companion to Twentieth Century Theatre* (London: Continuum, 2002), p. 139.

—, *The Abbey Theatre: Ireland's National Theatre – The First 100 Years* (London: Thames & Hudson, 2003).

Irish Theatre Institute, 'Marina Carr', *Irish Playography* <www.irishplayography.com/search/person.asp?PersonID=300>.

Leeney, Cathy, 'Ireland's "Exiled" Women Playwrights: Teresa Deevy and Marina Carr', in Shaun Richards (ed.), *The Cambridge Companion to Twentieth-Century Irish Drama* (Cambridge: Cambridge UP, 2004), pp. 150–63.

—, 'Marina Carr: Violence and Destruction: Language, Space and Landscape', in Mary Luckhurst (ed.), *A Companion to Modern British and Irish Drama 1880–2005* (Oxford: Blackwell, 2006), pp. 509–18.

Leeney, Cathy and Anna McMullan (eds), *The Theatre of Marina Carr: 'before rules was made'* (Dublin: Carysfort Press, 2003).

McDonald, Marianne, 'A Light Angel in a Dark Landscape', Review of Marina Carr's *Ariel* (2002) <www.didaskalia.net/reviews/2002_10_02_01.html>.

Merriman, Victor, 'Decolonisation Postponed: The Theatre of Tiger Trash', *Irish University Review*, Vol. 29, No. 2 (1999), pp. 305–17.

Morash, Christopher, *A History of Irish Theatre 1601–2000* (Cambridge: Cambridge UP, 2002).

Murphy, Mike, 'Interview with Marina Carr' [Reading the Future, RTÉ interviews], *University of Glasgow's School of English and Scottish Language and Literature (SESLL)* <www2.arts.gla.ac.uk/SESLL/EngLit/ugrad/hons/IrishLit/Carr/interview.rtf>.

Ni Dhuibhne, Eilis, 'Playing the Story: Narrative Techniques in *The Mai*', in Cathy Leeney and Anna McMullan (eds), *The Theatre of Marina Carr*, pp. 65–73.

Rees, Catherine, 'Marina Carr', *The Literary Encyclopaedia* <www.litencyc.com/php/speople.php?rec=true&UID=5854>.

Roche, Anthony, 'Woman on the Threshold: J. M. Synge's *The Shadow of the Glen* [sic], Teresa Deevy's *Katie Roche*, and Marina Carr's *The Mai*', in Cathy Leeney and Anna McMullan (eds), *The Theatre of Marina Carr*, pp. 17–42.

Scaife, Sarahjane, 'Mutual Beginnings: Marina Carr's *Low in the Dark*', in Cathy Leeney and Anna McMullan (eds), *The Theatre of Marina Carr*, pp. 1–16.

Stephenson, Heidi and Natasha Langridge, 'Marina Carr', in Heidi Stephenson and Natasha Langridge (eds), *Rage and Reason: Women Playwrights on Playwriting* (London: Methuen, 1997).

Wald, Christina, *Hysteria, Trauma and Melancholia: Performative Maladies in Contemporary Anglophone Drama* (Basingstoke: Palgrave Macmillan, 2007).

Wallace, Clare, '"A Crossroads Between Worlds": Marina Carr and the Use of Tragedy', *Litteraria Pragensia*, Vol. 10, No. 20 (2000), pp. 76–89 <http://komparatistika.ff.cuni.cz/litteraria/no20-10/wallace.htm>.

—, 'Authentic Reproductions: Marina Carr and the Inevitable', in Cathy Leeney and Anna McMullan (eds), *The Theatre of Marina Carr*, pp. 43–64.

—, 'Versions and Reversions: The New Old Story and Contemporary Irish Drama', in Michael Böss and Eamon Maher (eds), *Engaging Modernity: Readings of Irish Politics, Culture and Literature at the Turn of the Century* (Dublin: Veritas, 2003), pp. 112–20.

—, *Suspect Cultures: Narrative, Identity and Citation in 1990s New Drama* (Prague: Litteraria Progensia, 2006).

Welch, Robert, *The Abbey Theatre 1899–1999: Form and Pressure* (Oxford: Oxford UP, 1999).

Notes

1. Christopher Fitz-Simon, 'Carr, Marina', p. 139.
2. Cathy Leeney and Anna McMullan, *The Theatre of Marina Carr*, p. xv.
3. Christopher Fitz-Simon, *The Abbey Theatre*, p. 169.
4. Sarahjane Scaife, 'Mutual Beginnings', pp. 4–6.
5. Catherine Rees, 'Marina Carr'.
6. Scaife, op. cit., p. 12.
7. Christopher Morash, *A History of Irish Theatre*, p. 278.
8. Ibid., p. 265.
9. Eilis Ni Dhuibhne, 'Playing the Story', p. 67.
10. Anthony Roche, 'Woman on the Threshold', p. 37.
11. Heidi Stephenson and Natasha Langridge, 'Marina Carr', p. 151.
12. Rees, op. cit.
13. Stephenson and Langridge, op. cit., p. 150.
14. Ni Dhuibhne, op. cit., p. 68
15. Ibid., p. 69.
16. Mike Murphy, 'Interview with Maria Carr'.
17. Stephenson and Langridge, op. cit., p. 152.
18. Christina Wald, *Hysteria, Trauma and Melancholia*, p. 190.
19. Robert Welch, *The Abbey Theatre 1899–1999*, p. 239.
20. Stephenson and Langridge, op. cit., p. 154.
21. Cathy Leeney, 'Ireland's "Exiled" Women Playwrights', p. 160.
22. Cathy Leeney, 'Violence and Destruction', p. 516.
23. Bernadette Bourke, 'Carr's "Cut-throats and gargiyles"', p. 144.
24. Clare Wallace, 'Versions and Reversions', p. 118.
25. Rees, op. cit.
26. Marianne McDonald, 'A Light Angel'.
27. Ibid.
28. Leeney, 'Violence and Destruction', p. 511.
29. Rees, op. cit.
30. McDonald, op. cit.
31. Tanya Dean, 'Review of *Woman and Scarecrow*'.
32. Ibid.
33. Leeney, 'Violence and Destruction', p. 509.
34. Clare Wallace, *Suspect Cultures*, p. 236.

35. Rees, op. cit.

36. Dominic Dromgoole, *The Full Room*, p. 48.

37. Morash, op. cit., p. 265.

38. Ibid., p. 267.

39. Fitz-Simon, *The Abbey Theatre*, p. 178.

40. Roche, op. cit., p. 39.

41. Wallace, *Suspect Cultures*, p. 239.

42. Welch, op. cit., p. 25.

43. Welch, op. cit., pp. 235, 250.

44. Leeney, 'Violence and Destruction', p. 510.

45. Welch, op. cit., p. 240.

46. Leeney, 'Ireland's "Exiled" Women Playwrights', p. 150.

47. Fitz-Simon, *The Abbey Theatre*, p. 178.

48. Leeney, 'Ireland's "Exiled" Women Playwrights', p. 158.

49. Wallace, *Suspect Cultures*, p. 260.

50. Ni Dhuibhne, op. cit., p. 70.

51. Fitz-Simon, *The Abbey Theatre*, p. 239.

52. Murphy, op. cit.

53. Wallace, 'Versions and Reversions', p. 118.

54. Maria Doyle, 'Dead Center', p. 56.

55. Bourke, op. cit., p. 128.

56. Leeney, 'Violence and Destruction', p. 512.

57. Ibid., p. 516.

58. Wald, op. cit., p. 191.

59. Wallace, *Suspect Cultures*, p. 263.

60. Clare Wallace, 'Authentic Reproductions', p. 46.

61. Wallace, *Suspect Cultures*, p. 242.

62. Ibid., p. 247.

63. Victor Merriman, 'Decolonisation Postponed', p. 305.

64. Quoted in Wallace, *Suspect Cultures*, pp. 239–40.

65. Leeney, 'Violence and Destruction', p. 510.

66. Welch, op. cit., pp. 239–40.

67. Ibid., p. 240. Doyle, op. cit., p. 57.

4 ANNE DEVLIN

Enrica Cerquoni

Ourselves Alone; *Heartlanders*; *After Easter*

Introduction

Anne Devlin was born on the Grosvenor Road in Belfast in 1951 to a socialist father and a Catholic mother; she lived there until she was twelve, when her family moved to Andersonstown, off the Falls Road. Raised in Belfast, she went to live in England in 1976. In 2007, Devlin moved back to Belfast. During her prolific career, Devlin was visiting lecturer in playwriting at the University of Birmingham in 1987; and writer-in-residence at the University of Lund, Sweden, in 1990, and at Trinity College, Dublin, in 2004.

The complex dramaturgical texture of her playwriting is informed by her career in different art media – theatre, television, radio and cinema. Some of the nine short stories included in the prose collection *The Way-Paver* have fed into her theatrical works. Devlin's concern with redressing gendered iconographies of womanhood and nationhood marks all of her work. In *Naming the Names*, a television play adapted from the eponymous short story in 1987, Devlin portrayed a female IRA agent who appropriates a traditional male political role. The name of Devlin's female protagonist, Finn, identifies her with a heroic male warrior of the Celtic tradition. When imprisoned, she, like the ancient warriors, pledges to clan loyalty and refuses to betray her 'affiliates' or to 'name the names'.

There is a sense of a disguised biography in her work. Her experience of teaching at a Protestant school provided the raw material for the television drama *The Venus de Milo, Instead* (1987). The constituency of her playwriting, however, is more complex than this.

The plays are written to address my problem with the biography at a particular time. I fiercely say they're not biographical plays, because they are plays of experience, because they are in that gap between experience and biography. A biography is one life; experience is the story of the knowledge of the stories of many who have touched your own. So they are also history plays and of course they are political plays too.[1]

The Plays

I wrote two stage plays between 1985 and 1994: *Ourselves Alone*, from the bipolar axis of my student attachment to Marxism, and *After Easter*, from the diametrically opposed axis of spirituality. My unconscious simply banged like a drum on the doors of my perceptions and demanded to be included. And this fact alone, this invasion of consciousness in the decade of terror – which is what the '70s was – is largely responsible for my approach to writing.[2]

Ourselves Alone (1985)

Ourselves Alone, Devlin's first stage play, developed out of a sense of loss and absence, diasporically and ontologically experienced. *Ourselves Alone* was written after Devlin had left Ireland and moved to England, yet, as she herself admits, 'in my head I was still there, and so I was creating the sounds that I needed to hear, and they were women's voices'.[3]

Ourselves Alone originated from the short story 'Five Notes After a Visit', in which 'the leading characters' relationship becomes the basis for Frieda and John McDermot',[4] two of the protagonists in *Ourselves Alone*, thus indirectly linking the play to George Orwell's *Nineteen Eighty-Four*, to which the short story is a response.

In *Ourselves Alone*, Devlin's complex theatrical form, juxtaposing naturalism and surrealism, sidelines box rooms of confinement with women's poetic rooms of memory and absence. Indeed, the play's spatial dramaturgy alternates actual interior locations such as a club, the house of one of the three women protagonists, Donna, a flat, a Dublin hotel, Belfast's Botanic Gardens with women protagonists' soliloquies in the form of verbal and bodily recounting of flash-like memories, dreams and stream of consciousness. Already in *Ourselves Alone* Devlin starts the process of transforming the role of soliloquy and monologue as it becomes a powerful theatrical strategy within her dramaturgy to map out in an affective way the process of woman's subjectivity and agency. Dreams, the unconscious, what cannot be seen, play a seminal role in Devlin's creative practice, which draws on the raw material of dream states and their cognate worlds of pain or pleasure in order to widen the literal confines and entrapments the three women inhabit.

Ourselves Alone opened at the Liverpool Playhouse on 24 October 1985. The play's title is a literal translation of the Gaelic Sinn Féin into English. Sinn Féin is the title of the nationalist party in Ireland, the political wing of the Irish Republican Army. The play denounces the political hollowness of the phrase, revealing it as gender-coded. Through the title, Devlin reveals the state of outsideness and internal exile to which women in Northern Ireland are subjected.

Influenced by Devlin's work in radio drama, the play is comprised of long and short scenes; it is mostly set in rooms in west Belfast, although it expands outside of it, moving geographically between the North and the South of Ireland, and, indirectly, including England as well within its topography, through the character of Joe Conran, a British agent and Republican recruit.

The play focuses on Belfast sisters Frieda and Josie McCoy and their sister-in-law Donna over a period of eight months of their lives during the mid-1980s shortly after the hunger strikes. As Devlin herself asserts, the three female characters are 'representative' of her own experience in Andersonstown, thus expressing different aspects of herself at different moments in her life.[5]

At the end of the play, in order to escape the stifling contours of patriarchal hegemony and to fully realise herself and her creative potential, Frieda recognises the need to leave Ireland and go to

England. She would rather 'be lonely than suffocate' (*Ourselves Alone*, p. 99). She wants to compose songs, her own songs. The 'collective psychic and personal space established by the three women' in the course of the play[6] cannot replace Frieda's lack of self-expression and freedom. She needs to physically get out of her room, Ireland, which turns out to be a confining and unsatisfactory space to fulfil her yearning for selfhood, for a voice singing to tunes of her own choosing. The room needs emptying in order to be inhabited again.

While Frieda chooses to reject the imposition of her nationalist roots, her sister Josie, the play's 'serious' voice, fully performs the role of the insider within it. Josie's position within the frame of the nationalist ideology, however, is never one of equality. Despite her rejection of the traditional role women are typically given within the nationalist struggle, since the very beginning she is 'waiting on a man' (p. 11), having devoted herself for years to Cathal O'Donnell, an IRA leader.

The play's final line is given to Donna and it frames Frieda's verbal statement on leaving. Donna's poetic vision, 'how quietly the light comes' followed by '*Darkness*' (p. 90), resonates vastly within the suspension of Frieda's imaginative departure. Donna is the listening figure in the play: she is often seen leaning against doors and windows in order to perceive voices and sounds offstage. She is referred to in the play as an individual who has 'spent her life listening' (p. 20). She is the auditor to the other women's voices, stories and inner worlds; to the baby's voice; to the warnings of potential threats and dangers towards them; to the silence of her tragic losses, hinted at in the play. She is the filtering agent between the 'here and now' of the play, the 'real' world, and the 'beyond', the world 'other', brought in through the female protagonists' nightmares, sleepwalking, dreams, visions. In the tripartite exchange of the play she is also the figure who acts as a 'bridge between the two sisters Frieda and Josie'.[7] As Brendan MacGurk has remarked, Donna possesses an uncanny 'perception and understanding of things, even in the face of seeming powerlessness'.[8] Because of her sensorial permeability, she metaphorically remains in the doorway, even at the play's closure. Beside her function as the listening figure, Donna's first stage appearance links her to visibility:

entering the room where Josie is sitting in the dark, she 'turns on the light' (p. 15), she makes the space visible for the characters and for the audience. Significantly, in her final line her acoustic permeability is transformed into a seeing one. Donna's performative statement is about the prophetic, hopeful approaching of light, of visibility as a new ontological and ideological state of possibility, as a doorway of morphed perceptibility where the capability of seeing sounds and hearing images opens a 'thirding' of experiential nuances and modes of being.

Heartlanders (1989)

Before getting to *After Easter*, in 1989, Devlin co-wrote the community play *Heartlanders* with playwrights Stephen Bill and David Edgar. The play was commissioned by the Birmingham Repertory Theatre to commemorate Birmingham's centenary and was directed by Chris Parr. In the play the notion of being an outsider informs the work's collaborative creative process as well as its themes. Each playwright did not write out of his/her experience; instead each of them took on something else: Stephen Bill, for instance, wrote the Irish character in Birmingham and Anne Devlin wrote the character of a Hindu girl. Reflecting on the genesis of the project, Devlin remarked that:

> Since we weren't as representative a group of artists as we would like to be for all the communities in Birmingham, the only thing we could do was not to write to our strengths, so I was not going to write about the Irish community, as there would have been a misrepresentation. It would have meant that only the Irish can be representative for the Irish if you lock the biography in that way in a play.[9]

After Easter (1994)

While *Ourselves Alone* deals with the notion of being an outsider within one's own community, *After Easter* dramatises a very different analysis of the theme of outsideness. The Kristevan notion of being a stranger to oneself is at the core of the play.[10] As a quest play, it is about a human journey and the possibility of finding free expression against the fixity of experience.

The main protagonist, Greta, is a Northern Irish woman living in Oxford who, when the play opens, has been committed to a mental hospital suffering from a nervous breakdown. Her unfaithful husband is seeking to gain custody of their children, one of them a recently born son. Her quest to rediscover her identity involves a return to her Irish hearth and a protracted confrontation with her mother, two sisters, Aoife and Helen, and a brother, Manus. The play is punctuated with dreams and semi-mystical visions and does not follow a linear development. This inner and family drama is played out against the backdrop of her father's heart attack and subsequent death.

The play deploys wide frameworks of time and space: it covers events between 1981 and 1994 (the year of the play's first production) and moves between England and Northern Ireland, between inner and outer rooms, open and closed spaces, metaphysical roller coaster and literalness of experience, surrealism and realism. Greta emigrates to England and 'turns away from everything that once could have been called her identity, including her religion'.[11] The bipolar axes of England and the North of Ireland are deceptive, as constant references to Irishness, to the 'whole of Ireland' (p. 11), and to Catholic nationalism, indirectly include the South of Ireland and sever the topographical binary. Greta's identification with dislocated minority groups living away from their homeland within hostile cultures opens further the geographical and cultural boundaries of her act of self-exile. The national geography of the play is then one of in-betweenness, of rootlessness, of a broad home against the fixity and singularity of essentialist nationalisms, but it is also one of double estrangement within her home culture and within the host country. While *Ourselves Alone* explores the theme of being an outsider within one's own community from the perspectives of women, *After Easter* develops out of that internal isolation and engages with the double invisibility that self-exile inflicts on women.

In Devlin's account of the play's dramaturgical process, *After Easter* was originally born as a series of monologues spread between the characters. This reflected the playwright's willingness to establish equality among the multiplicity of voices and visions within the play. This polyphony of narrative dimensions reflects Richard Kearney's argument that 'every life is in search of narrative [. . .] as a stay against confusion'.[12] Greta's 'verbalisation of the unconscious',[13] her taking over of the main narratorial position reflects Devlin's dramaturgical journey 'to give Greta the authority among the other seven voices (also the nun's silent voice)'.[14] Devlin argues that 'even if you have a central character, a sense of democracy and equality of voices is still maintained'.[15] As a proactive narrator and seer, however, Greta predominates and 'subjects everybody to her storytelling'.[16] This revisiting of the role of the storyteller can present risks: as Devlin notes, 'if you are telling a story, you don't engage with the present'.[17] Storytelling can prevent the dynamics of the present from moving.

As the chief narrator, Greta's role is further complicated. Catriona Clutterbuck states that:

> . . . what the play does is [. . .] to fragment the narrator's traditional detachment by having Greta as a character fully involved with the internal action of the play that she also frames by her various acts of narration.[18]

Devlin's disruptive dramaturgy is a watershed and a point of beginning within the scenario of plays written about the Northern Irish situation. Although the play is strongly embedded in the politics of that context, the different women-based languages through which audiences are invited to access the play open up alternative, broader ways of writing about the Northern Irish situation.

While playing to packed houses, the play generated hostility among some critics for not operating within familiar moulds of theatrical presentation and investigation, within 'known rooms' of expectations.[19] It could be suggested that this critical response betrayed a resistance to being exposed, to being outside frames and paradoxically reiterated the main themes in the play, the inner correspondent worlds of Greta's dreams and visions and the literalness of her experience. The very dispute over the identity of a particular constellation of stars brings to the surface 'the dual poles of certainty'[20] and nationalist consciousness in establishing meanings, and Greta's feelings have 'lots of meanings' (p. 52); while Aoife sees the constellation of stars as the Plough, the symbol of the Irish Citizen Army; and, for Helen, it 'could have been the Pleiades, the seven sisters' (p. 15). In the 'dual poles of certainty'[21] the complexity of woman's being gets reduced. Significantly, the play's position between discourses and counter-discourses is reflected in the politics of the location of its theatrical site, that is in the contentious way in which the play 'was to be seen' within the RSC theatrical frame: as Michael Attenborough remarks, 'Anne Devlin wanted her play [*After Easter*] about nationhood and identity to be seen in Stratford alongside classical work [such as *A Midsummer Nights' Dream*] that was exploring similar timeless themes'.[22]

The opening scene resonates at more than one level with the work of Samuel Beckett. Reminiscent of the three heads in Beckett's *Play*, at once disclosed and questioned by light, the figure of the cross-legged woman sitting on the room's floor is made manifest through light and sound.[23] In addition, the disturbing presence of the man 'standing by a window in the shadow' (p. 1), as well as Greta's sudden flood of words out of the theatrical nowhere, recalls Beckett's *Not I*.[24] Like Mouth, Greta is suspended in, and surrounded by, the space of the stage; she is observed both by the undisclosed figure in the dark and by the spectators. I would argue then that the opening stage image could be viewed as a 'postdramatic'[25] refusal to begin, if beginning is meant not as a process but as a given of established coordinates of space, time and character. It is a refusal to begin a theatrical existence framed by a controlled visibility. This interpretation sheds further light on Greta's line 'Goodbye, room'. It is only when this has been said that the play can really begin (p. 8).

In 'classic realist' and naturalistic theatre,[26] immateriality and its undesirable regions are anxiously hidden offstage as the aim of those movements is the disputably full view of an omniscient onstage of verifiability, explicability and tangibility. In 'classic realism' the complex interplay of this dichotomous opposition – the purged, normative surface of life versus the drama of the invisible – is gender-coded.[27] In Devlin's *After Easter*, however, immateriality and absence are treated differently as they become the filtering agents through which spectators glimpse woman's presence. *After Easter* unfolds a quest on the potentiality of perception within the metaphysical structures of theatre and its physical structures of containment in making room for an empowered, polyvalent female presence.

Yet there is the risk in *After Easter* that the dark room of invisibility is going to be rehearsed again. In scene seven, 'crouched'[28] on the top of Westminster Bridge, Greta's tragedy consumes her as she struggles between life and death. The bridge wall, on which Greta is standing, is the last insubstantial border. Were she to jump, this final liminal place will obstruct her from seeing and being seen and will prevent her from 'entering the mainstream of her larger existence'[29] and from operating the transition 'from the language of the hearth to the language of the heart'.[30] Were Greta to disappear from view and from life, her act would proximate a closure from 'classic realism'[31] and curtail Devlin's 'aesthetics of the disappeared'. The instability and alterity of the space of the emptied room at the play's opening prompt the female protagonist to an early departure in order to re-enter the space and remorph it into a lived space of consciousness.

In relation to the key role of scene seven within the play's dramaturgy, Devlin argues for the need to keep on the side of life, of visibility.[32] This allows for the introduction in the creative process of the image of the birth myth in the last scene: 'this could happen just if Greta stays alive; then the play can finish'.[33] Spatially removed from west Belfast, the bridge functions as a structure of transition. The polarities of meanings and national selfhoods upon which the play's dramaturgy has relied so far, break down. Helen, Greta's 'alter-ego' throughout the play, becomes now contiguous. As Foley observes, 'in a beautiful movement of formal achievement Devlin shifts the emphasis from one sister on to another and, in so doing, shifts the textual emphasis on to another level, formally embracing all characters in a future, whether abstract or lived'.[34]

As the scene draws to a close, Greta's inner voices and visions have turned into the sound of a baby laughing.

In the surreal coda that ends the play, it is after Easter, and Greta is *'at home, rocking a baby, telling it a story. The traditional empty chair is placed near the storyteller'* (p. 75). The story she narrates is a fraught one:

> After Easter we came to the place. It was snowing in the forest and very cold into the fifth month. My mother and I were hunting. But because of the cold we couldn't feel anything or find anything to eat. So we sat down by the stream. I looked up and I saw it suddenly, a stag, antlered and black, profiled against the sky. (p. 75)

From a spatial perspective, the scene breaks down the fourth wall and returns the play to its 'postdramatic' point of non-beginning. The play opens and closes with spatially indeterminate images from monologues that resist conventional notions of theatrical beginning and closure. While the spatial ambiguity of the stage directions in the opening scene re-enters arguably a realist frame with the appearance of the doctor, the surreal monologue of the last scene stays in a state of hybridity. Significantly, this 'unmarked' status of free-floating is marked in the stage directions as *'home'* (p. 75) for Greta. In the plurality of her fractured selves, which have been given expression through emotional, spiritual and psychic images, voices and other characters' experiences, the female protagonist finds the 'inner room she has sought for so long'.[35]

Summary

Devlin is among the playwrights in the North who have changed the way in which the Troubles and nationalism in the theatre are represented, and has opted for a different approach and practice, starting to write plays that interrogated and 'turned a critical eye on the events of the recent past'.[36] As Anna McMullan has argued, 'because of the political sensitivity of the situation, it was some years before dramatists were prepared or allowed to overtly explore "The

Troubles" in the theatre'.[37] Despite the unprecedented wave of sectarian violence in the 1970s in the North, the theatrical landscape of the 1970s responded mainly by reinforcing the status quo and 'absolving the theatre spectator of all political responsibility [. . .]' and representing the conflict 'in terms of an irresolvable social pathology [which] tends to foreclose the possibility of its political resolution'.[38] Devlin's eclectic body of work has mostly expressed preoccupations with the representation and the experience of women surviving in the political crisis of the Troubles. In some of her short stories, as well as in her stage plays, especially *Ourselves Alone* and *After Easter*, Devlin chooses to dramatise 'the nonhistorical violence that is deprioritized by the very historic Troubles'[39] by making the audience aware that politically motivated war was fought inside people's homes. In *Ourselves Alone* homes are camp-like interiors and theatres of war, reflecting how war crimes fought outside were just one aspect of violence: inside homes women were silenced, abused, beaten and made invisible and inaudible. By foregrounding the experiences of women and choosing a feminist lens to analyse the Troubles, Devlin's theatrical practice could posit alternative social formations, disclose the damaging power of nationalism in pushing women into corners of invisibility and pave the way for a reconsideration of the concept of nation. In *Ourselves Alone*, her stage debut about three Irish women's voices whose presences are obscured by their involvement with Irish Republican Army (IRA) men, 'the female community is the play nexus [which] might serve as an alternative social grouping to the nation' in the period immediately after the hunger strike events.[40] In her later play *After Easter* Devlin anticipates and foregrounds the problems of a post-conflict environment and does it through a migrant Northern Irish woman's 'anguished quest, both spiritual and psychological, for roots and identity and meaning'.[41]

In all Devlin's works, the deployment of storytelling in the different forms of dreams, sleepwalking, visions, bodily experiences, art, songs, often expresses 'feelings of terrified powerlessness'.[42] It is also a dramaturgical tool to convey in each of her works the female protagonist's reaction 'to the duties that are imposed upon her as a woman, her own divided loyalties toward her family and country, and the patriarchal hegemony that seeks to control her life'.[43]

Devlin's creative practice, from her radio drama, through her prose and her stage plays offers a whole world that is forgotten by the media: women in Northern Ireland. Devlin's aesthetics of the disappeared interrogates new ways of presenting occluded female energies onstage and attempts to break down framing ideologies and narratives that assert their defeat. Nationhood, and the notion of getting beyond nations also fed into her body of work. As Laura Kane has argued, 'Devlin ha[s] succeeded in identifying stumbling blocks to be cleared on the way to creating post-nations communities and encourage[s] us, through the plays' open endings, to grapple with the issues of lingering, misogyny and entrenched nationalism'.[44]

Rejecting a 'realistic reality' and the parameters of theatrical realism, Devlin's female personae become conjurers of other spaces and times: in some cases they reinvent realities and selves and achieve a plenitude of visibility and audibility beyond the restrictions of fixed identities.

Emblematic of this innovative process of human subjectivity is the last 'room' of the play *After Easter*, Greta's 'own story' (p. 75). Greta's quest for home, voice and her inner room as well as Devlin's attempt to 'unearth the sources of [her] language'[45] have been accomplished.

Primary Sources

Works by Anne Devlin

After Easter (London: Faber and Faber, 1994).
Heartlanders (London: Nick Herne, 1989).
Ourselves Alone (London: Faber and Faber, 1990).
The Way-Paver (London: Faber and Faber, 1986).

Secondary Sources

Arrowsmith, Aidan, 'M/otherlands: Literature, Gender, Diasporic Identity', in Scott Brewster, Virginia Crossman, Fiona Becket and David Alderson (eds), *Ireland in Proximity: History, Gender, Space* (London: Routledge, 1999), pp. 129–44.

Aston, Elaine, *The Cambridge Companion to Modern British Women Playwrights* (Cambridge: Cambridge UP, 2000).

Attenborough, Michael, 'Directing for the RSC: The Classic and the New', in Ronnie Mulryne and Margaret Shewring (eds), *Making Space for Theatre: British Architecture and Theatre Since 1958* (Stratford-upon-Avon: Mulryne and Shewring, 1995), pp. 89–91.

Balme, Christopher, 'Editorial', *Theatre Research International*, Vol. 29 (2004), pp. 1–3.

Belasry, Catherine, *Critical Practice* (London; Methuen, 1980).

Buijs, Marian, 'Suffering Women in Irish Tribal Wars', *Volkskant*, 20 March 1990.

Cerquoni, Enrica, 'Women in Rooms: Landscapes of the Missing in Anne Devlin's *Ourselves Alone*', in Melissa Sihra (ed.), *Women in Irish Drama: A Century of Authorship and Representation* (London: Palgrave Macmillan, 2007), pp. 160–74.

Clutterbuck, Catriona, 'Lughnasa After Easter: Treatments of Narrative Imperialism in Friel and Devlin', *Irish University Review*, Vol. 29 (1999), pp. 101–18.

Cottreau, Deborah, 'Ascending: The Feminist Mytho-Poetics of Anne Devlin's *After Easter*', *Hungarian Journal of English and American Studies*, Vol. 5 (1999), pp. 199–223.

Cousin, Geraldine, *Women in Dramatic Place and Time* (London: Routledge, 1996).

Denman, Peter, 'The Complexities of Being Irish', *Irish Literary Supplement*, Vol. 6 (1987).

Devlin, Anne, 'About That: Irish Plays, Bill Morrison, Anne Devlin, Conor McPherson', in David Edgar (ed.), *State of Play. Issue I: Playwrights on Playwriting* (London: Faber and Faber, 1999), pp. 93–103.

—, 'After Easter', programme note for *After Easter*, Royal Shakespeare Company, May 1994.

—, 'Anne Devlin in Conversation with Enrica Cerquoni', in Lilian Chambers, Ger FitzGibbon, Eamonn Jordan, Dan Farrelly and Cathy Leeney (eds), *Theatre Talk: Voices of Irish Theatre Practitioners* (Dublin: Carysfort Press, 2001), pp. 107–23.

—, *Landmarks of Contemporary Drama* ed. Emilie S. Kilgore (London: Methuen, 1992).

—, 'Letter to Elizabeth Doyle', in Elizabeth Doyle, 'Women and War in Christina Reid's and Anne Devlin's Plays' (unpublished master thesis, University College Dublin, 1993).

—, 'Seminar on *Ourselves Alone*', Drama Studies Centre, University College Dublin, 6 April 2004.

—, 'Writing the Troubles: Talks by Glenn Patterson, Anne Devlin and Colm Tóibín', in Brian Cliff and Éibhear Walshe (eds), *Representing the Troubles: Texts and Image, 1970–2000* (Dublin: Four Courts Press, 2004), pp. 15–26.

Fitzpatrick, Lisa, 'Disrupting Metanarratives: Anne Devlin, Christina Reid, Marina Carr, and the Irish Dramatic Repertory', *Irish University Review*, Vol. 35 (2005), pp. 320–33.

Foley, Imelda, *The Girls in the Big Picture: Gender in Contemporary Ulster Theatre* (Belfast: Blackstaff Press, 2003).

Godiwala, Dimple, *Breaking the Bounds: British Feminist Dramatists Writing in the Mainstream since c.1980* (New York: Peter Lang, 2003), pp. 154–76.

Greene, Alexis (ed.), *Women Writing Plays: Three Decades of the Susan Smith Blackburn Prize* (Austin: University of Texas Press, 2006).

Kane, Laura, 'De/re/construction Work: Female Performances of Northern Irish Nationalism in the Works of Anne Devlin and Christina Reid', in Ruth Connolly and Ann Coughlan (eds), *New Voices in Irish Criticism 5* (Dublin: Four Court Press, 2005).

Kao, Wei H., 'Awakening, Memory and Reconciliation in Anne Devlin's Belfast Trilogy', *Feminist Studies in English Literature*, Vol 2, (2008), pp. 31–61.

Kearney Richard, *On Stories* (London: Routledge, 2002).

Kristeva, Julia, *Strangers to 'Ourselves*, trans. Leon S. Roudieg (London: Harvester Wheatsheaf, 1991).

Kirkpatrick, Kathryn (ed.), *Border Crossings: Irish Women Writers and National Identities* (Tuscaloosa: University of Alabama Press, 2000).

Kurdi, Maria, 'Female Self Cure Through Revisioning and Refashioning Male/Master Narratives in Anne Devlin's *After Easter*', *Hungarian Journal of Irish Studies*, Vol. 2 (1996), pp. 97–100.

Liefhebber, Peter, '*Ourselves Alone* Remains Hard Going/Something to Brood Over', *Telegraaf*, 19 March 1990.

Lojek, Helen, 'Difference without Indifference: The Drama of Frank McGuinness and Anne Devlin', *Éire-Ireland: A Journal of Irish Studies*, Vol. 25 (1990), pp. 56–68.

Macaulay, Alastair, 'An Irish Woman in Crisis', *Financial Times*, 28 May 1994.

MacGurk, Brendan, 'Commitment and Risk in Anne Devlin's *Ourselves Alone* and *After Easter*', in Eberhard Bort (ed.), *The State of Play: Irish Theatre in the Nineties* (Trier: WVT Wissenschaftlicher Verlag Trier, 1996).

McMullan, Anna, 'Irish Womens playrights in Trevor Griffiths and Margaret Llewellyn-Jones (eds), *British and Irish Women Dramatists Since 1958: A Critical Handbook* (Buckingham: Open Up, 1993), p. 112.

—, 'Unhomely Stages: Women Taking (a) Place in Irish Theatre', in Dermot Bolger (ed.), *Druids, Dudes and Beauty Queens: The Changing Face of Irish Theatre* (Dublin: New Island, 2001), pp. 72–90.

Murray, Christopher, *Twentieth-Century Irish Drama: Mirror up to Nation* (Manchester: Manchester UP, 1997).

Nightingale, Benedict, 'Lost on the Road from Ulster', *The Times*, 30 May 1994.

Nowlan, David, 'Theatre Festival Openings: *Ourselves Alone* at John Player Theatre', *Irish Times*, 7 October 1987.

O'Reilly, Anne F., *Sacred Play: Soul-Journeys in Contemporary Irish Plays* (Dublin: Carysfort Press, 2004).

O'Toole, Fintan, 'Ourselves Alone', in Julia Furay and Redmond O'Hanlon (eds), *Critical Moments: Fintan O'Toole on Modern Irish Theatre* (Dublin: Carysfort Press, 2003).

Pilkington, Lionel, *Theatre and State in Twentieth-Century Ireland: Cultivating the People* (London: Routledge, 1993).

Roche, Anthony, *Contemporary Irish Drama: From Beckett to McGuinness* (Dublin: Gill and Macmillan, 2009).

Stratton, Kate, '*After Easter*', *Time Out*, 12 April 1995.

Sullivan, Esther Beth, 'What is "Left to a Woman of the House" When the Irish Situation is Staged', in J. M. Colleran and J. Spencer (eds), *Staging Resistance: Essays on Political Theatre* (Ann Arbor: Michigan Press, 1998), pp. 213–26.

Trotter, Mary, 'Translating Women into Irish Theatre History', in Stephen Watt, Eileen Morgan and Shakir Mustafa (eds), *A Century of Irish Drama: Widening the Stage* (Bloomington: Indiana UP, 2000), pp. 163–78.

Upton, Carole-Anne, 'Anne Devlin', in John Bull (ed.), *British and Irish Dramatists Since World War II* (Detroit, MI: Gale, 2001), pp. 121–28.

Walsh, Catherine, 'Eulogy to a Lost Generation: Caroline Walsh talks to Anne Devlin', *Irish Times*, 25 September 1986.

Woddis, Carole, '*After Easter*', *What's On*, 8 June 1994, in *Theatre Records*, 21 May to 3 June 1994, pp. 697–701.

Wood, Chris, '"My Own Story": Woman's Place, Divided Loyalty, and Patriarchal Hegemony in the Plays of Anne Devlin', *Canadian Journal of Irish Studies*, Vol. 25 (1999), pp. 291–308.

Notes

1. Anne Devlin, *State of Play*, p. 98.
2. Anne Devlin, 'Writing the Troubles', p. 21.
3. Anne Devlin, 'About That', p. 97.
4. Anne Devlin, 'Anne Devlin in Conversation', p. 109. Further references to this edition are given after quotations in the text.
5. Anne Devlin, *Landmarks of Contemporary Drama*, p. 231.
6. Anthony Roche, *Contemporary Irish Drama*, p. 238.
7. Anne Devlin, 'Seminar'.
8. Brendan MacGurk, 'Commitment', p. 60.
9. Anne Devlin, unpublished interview.
10. See Julia Kristeva, *Strangers to Ourselves*.
11. Anne Devlin, 'After Easter'.
12. Richard Kearney, *On Stories*, p. 4.
13. Imelda Foley, 'The Girls in the Big Picture', p. 100.
14. Anne Devlin, unpublished lecture. Further references to this lecture are given after quotations in the text.
15. Devlin, 'Writing the Troubles'.
16. Ibid.
17. Ibid.
18. Catriona Clutterbuck, 'Lughnasa After Easter', p. 108.
19. Benedict Nightingale, 'Lost on the Road from Ulster', p. 20.

20. Aidan Arrowsmith, 'M/otherlands', pp. 129–44, p. 138. Further references to this edition are given after quotations in the text.

21. Ibid., p. 138.

22. Michael Attenborough, 'Directing for the RSC', pp. 89–91, at 91.

23. Samuel Beckett, *Play*, in *Samuel Beckett: The Complete Dramatic Works* (London: Faber, 1990).

24. Not I, in ibid.

25. Hans-Thies Lehmann, quoted in Christopher Balme, 'Editorial', p. 1. The original text in which Lehmann exposes his theories about 'postdramatic theatre' is in German: Hans-Thies Lehmann, *Postdramatisches Theater: Essay* (Frankfurt am Main: Verlag der Autoren, 1999), now published by Routledge. See Hans-Thies Lehmann, *Postdramatic Theatre*, trans. Karen Jürs-Munby (London: Routledge, 2006). This explains my indirect source of bibliographical reference. Further references to this article are given after quotations in the text.

26. Catherine, Belsey, *Critical Practice*, p. 67.

27. Ibid.

28. RSC Promptbook, *After Easter* by Anne Devlin, directed by Michael Attenborough (Stratford-upon-Avon: Royal Shakespeare Theatre Collections, 1994), p. 79.

29. Anne Devlin, in ibid.

30. Ibid.

31. Belsey, op. cit., p. 67.

32. Devlin, 'Seminar'.

33. Ibid.

34. Foley, op. cit., p. 102.

35. Geraldine Cousin, *Women in Dramatic Place and Time*, p. 198.

36. Laura Kane, 'De/re/construction Work', pp. 32–40, p. 33.

37. Anna McMullan, 'Irish Women Playwrights Since 1958', p. 112.

38. Lionel Pilkington, *Theatre and State in Twentieth-Century Ireland*, p. 209.

39. Esther Beth Sullivan, 'What is "Left to a Woman of the House"',p. 221.

40. Kane, op. cit., p. 112.

41. Dimple Godiwala, *Breaking the Bounds*, p. 171.

42. Helen Lojek, 'Difference without Indifference', p. 67.

43. Chris Wood, '"My Own Story"', p. 291.

44. Kane, op. cit., p. 40.

45. Anne Devlin, 'Letter to Elizabeth Doyle', p. 73.

5 EMMA DONOGHUE

Cathy Leeney

I Know My Own Heart; Ladies and Gentlemen

Introduction

Emma Donoghue was born in Dublin in 1969 into a middle-class background. She has lived and worked in Ireland and the United Kingdom and now lives in Canada with her lover and their son and daughter. She has been open about her sexuality in the context of an Ireland highly resistant to lesbian identity, despite significant changes in attitudes to homosexuality, marked by decriminalisation and anti-discrimination legislation in 1993.

She is an accomplished, successful and prolific writer of novels, short stories, biography and history, yet currently Donoghue's name is not as widely recognised in Ireland as it deserves to be. Donoghue's imaginatively wide and scholarly knowledge of and interest in lives in earlier centuries and in a variety of locations reveals how prominence in the contemporary Irish canon continues largely to demand national navel gazing, as well as valuing the male gaze over the female.

With her first novels, *Stir Fry* (1994) and *Hood* (1995), Donoghue explored the love lives of young gay Irish women. Her academic research into women's friendships led to her *Passions Between Women: British Lesbian Culture 1668–1801* (1993), and her novels subsequently foreground the experience of women in different historical contexts and are often based on historical documentation.

Alongside her fiction output, Donoghue has continued to write intermittently for the stage, and for radio. In Ireland, her career as a playwright points towards a hugely vital and influential sphere of theatrical production by independent companies and festivals that is often under-recognised culturally and critically in favour of production in mainstream venues, most especially the dominant Abbey Theatre. Glasshouse Productions, the company responsible for two of Donoghue's successful Dublin productions, is a case in point. Glasshouse was set up in 1990 by four talented women to perform the work of Irish women playwrights. Among an impressive record of innovative and challenging productions, many of new writing, two of the most valuable shows they devised were entitled *There are No Irish Women Playwrights 1* and *2*. Ironically titled, the performances comprised excerpts from both contemporary plays (Part 1) and from the work of neglected and forgotten writers such as Teresa Deevy and Kate O'Brien (Part 2). Glasshouse premiered *I Know My Own Heart*; then, with financial support from the Arts Council of Ireland, Glasshouse commissioned Donoghue to write *Ladies and Gentlemen*, which they initially produced as a rehearsed reading (directed by Katy Hayes), and then as a full production (directed by David Byrne), both at Project Arts Centre.

Emma Donoghue occupies a contested and contesting space in Irish literature and theatre. As a gay woman, working across the genres of fiction, theatre and history, she is a writer challenging categories of gender and national identity interests, history and contemporary experience.

In this essay I will suggest some of the key themes and images arising from Donoghue's plays for theatre, focusing particularly on *I Know My Own Heart* (1993) and *Ladies and Gentlemen* (1996). As an Irish woman playwright Donoghue is one of a marginalised group. Her plays illustrate a feminist concern with women in history, the historicisation of lesbian identity, the recovery of the stories of remarkable women, and with ongoing aspects of patriarchal control across centuries. Women's access to subjectivity has not improved progressively, but is a continuing contest for expression and meaning, as the critic Catherine Belsey would describe it, advancing and receding through a combination of particular political, social and individual circumstances that offer a ground for subjectivity.[1] Donoghue chooses surprising and invigorating stories of women who found space to live as they wished and to fulfil their desires. Her dramas, both fictional and theatrical, relate to Adrienne Rich's concept of a 'lesbian continuum' in their representations of the many aspects of women's bonds, while in the plays examined here, women's sexual bonds are placed centre stage.

Donoghue has a strong sense of the complexity of interrelationship between the personal and the historical/political, and this allows her to explore gender as a key aspect of human identity, dramatising the struggle of individual characters bound by the limits of gender regulation. Basing much of her drama on real people's lives and historical events, Donoghue reveals the feminist investment in truths overlooked or discounted; the recovery of women's experience is a necessary counter to its hegemonic erasure. She also subverts expectations of gender and of lesbian identity, and our understanding of their historical contexts. In writing for theatre she exploits the unique opportunity offered by the stage to explore gender as performance and to destabilise essentialist notions of gender identity as a business of binaries: masculine versus feminine, women versus men.

The Irish context for women playwrights continues to marginalise women's work, with key exceptions. The context for women playwrights in the UK has developed differently, chiefly through the establishment in the 1970s and 1980s of feminist and left-wing theatre companies that prioritised new writing by women and valued the new dramaturgies they brought to performance. When Donoghue foregrounds remarkable women she takes a different approach, showing how women step outside the boundaries placed on heterosexual definitions of womanhood. Thus, it is in their lesbian content that the plays are truly radical.

As a gay playwright Donoghue's work counters the cultural invisibility of lesbian experience. The development of gay theatre, traced by Nicholas de Jongh in his history of stage representations in London and New York in the twentieth century, moves from virtual invisibility into codified representations of gay characters whose queerness remained invisible to straight audiences while being understood by those cognisant of the codes. De Jongh draws the reader's attention to the separate history of lesbian theatre, but many of the same issues of reticence, evasion and avoidance of censorship through coding apply to both homosexual and lesbian representations on stage. The relationship between the stage and the audience is definitive in recognising how discourses of gay identity are regarded. Until the gay liberation movement of the 1960s, audiences were straight-identified, so that gay meanings had to be disguised. In more recent decades, writers may assume gay identity as the premise of the play, and challenge straight audiences to acknowledge same-sex desire.

The requirement of codification in the style of Wilde and Coward lapsed with censorship, and it would seem obvious that Donoghue, writing from the 1990s onwards, should have no need of it. However, her plays are concerned with codification in two ways: first, historically, how gay women found ways of expressing their sexuality by inventing coded expressions in language, gesture and appearance; second, how the theatre both reflects and imposes an expectation of conventional feminine behaviours represented by performance codes that may be linked with genres such as vaudeville, comedy or melodrama. One example of this expectation is how female characters are acceptable as protagonists in comedy, while this is virtually unknown, and would be considered unseemly, in melodrama. Donoghue uses theatrical images of performativity to play with theatrical gender conventions and to reveal the material, historicised limits placed around femininity both onstage and in real life.

The Plays

I Know My Own Heart (1993)

I Know My Own Heart: A Lesbian Regency Romance received its first professional production in April 1993 by Glasshouse Productions at Project Arts Centre in Dublin. For this lunchtime production Donoghue edited the original script so that it ran within the requisite sixty-minute limit of the lunchtime form. In the autumn of that year the full-length script, in two acts, was restored for evening performance in Dublin's Andrew's Lane Theatre. The director, Katy Hayes, has remarked that the subtitle of the play drew in audiences for whom the content was refreshingly novel.[2]

The play is based on the diaries of Anne Lister (1791–1849), who lived near Halifax in Yorkshire. During the period dramatised Lister was heiress-in-waiting of her uncle's estate; at the end of the play she finally comes into her inheritance and packs her bag for Paris. In fact, Lister travelled widely and died in Georgia. Lister, as Donoghue describes in her programme note for the production, 'broke all the rules of Regency ladyhood'. She was not interested in marriage but in geometry and Greek; she travelled alone, had a vigorous sexual appetite, and wrote intimate details of her 'romantic friendships' in her diary. Parts of her diary were, literally, coded. The hieroglyphic script, a combination of arithmetical symbols, numerals and Greek letters, was deciphered by historian Helena Whitbread, who published selections from the years 1817–24 with Virago Press in 1988 under the title *I Know My Own Heart*. Donoghue pointedly remarks that although she has taken liberties in shaping the diaries into dramatic form, the play and Lister's sexuality 'is no invention: it is grounded in the startling details she chose to record for posterity'.

The title *I Know My Own Heart* applies at a variety of levels in the play. It is ironic as it applies to the succession of Lister's lovers and to the confusing attractions to women of conventional wifehood and motherhood. Lister's sexual desires are active and changeable, yet the title also asserts across the action of the play Lister's determination to remain proud of her love for women. As the spotlight of her sexual needs falls on different women, Lister refuses the pressure to censor her actions, and (at least privately) to accept the silence surrounding her sexuality. Her social position is privileged, yet compromised by her lack of independent means while her uncle lives. Marianne and Nancy Brown are the daughters of a respectable local farmer, at a lower level in the social hierarchy, but not entirely out of bounds. Lister falls in love with Marianne, who then accepts a financially advantageous proposal of marriage, despite her reciprocal feelings for Lister. The affair between the two women continues under the pressure of separation, of the sexually transmitted infection originating from Marianne's profligate husband, and of Lister's promiscuity. Another exquisite irony is that Lister and Marianne's liaison is made possible by the latter's marriage, since they can now spend time together without giving rise to social censure.

In the meantime, Lister's friend Tibs shares her confidences and allows the playwright to make explicit the nature of the women's relationships. Dramatic irony comes into play as the audience realises Tibs's unrequited love for Lister, who is entirely careless of her friend's feelings. Tibs assuages her jealousy of Marianne by luring Lister into an affair with the younger sister Nancy, but the strategy is unsuccessful in unseating Marianne in Lister's heart. As Lister guiltily logs the conquest in her diary she remarks, 'Strictly speaking, I know the word "incest" is not appropriate, there being no link of marriage or blood' (p. 145), wryly pointing towards how lesbian identity subverts patriarchal regulation of sexuality and new paradigms are called for where none exists. A further amusing example of this arises when Anne questions whether Marianne considers herself, as a married woman, to be committing adultery when they have sex: 'You are, after all, another man's wife' (p. 131).

It is Marianne's pregnancy and her discovery of Anne's affair with her sister that precipitates the end of their relationship. This coincides in the play with Anne coming into her inheritance, whereupon she departs for Paris, taking with her Rousseau's *Confessions*, from which the title of the play is taken. In their last dialogue, Marianne asks Anne: 'Do you think we're being punished?' (p. 158), recalling the conservative theatrical convention whereby gay characters were penalised for their unorthodox sexuality, ending as exiles or suicides. But Donoghue refuses to punish her characters, and Lister leaves the audience in a mood of optimistic excitement as she sets out alone on a new adventure.

The form of the play is highly unusual; excerpts from Lister's diary, and from selected letters between the characters delivered to the audience, are written fluidly in one continuous sequence with scenes of dialogue between characters. Thus, the script indicates a shared space where the private discourse of diary witness is continuous with the public discourse of conversation at a variety of social levels. As Anne Ubersfeld writes, '[i]t is commonplace to demonstrate how spatial relations among characters [. . .] correspond to a material hierarchicisation'.[3] In this case the borderless playing space works to destabilise social hierarchies. The borders between private and public, between the physical body and the body politic fail, and the pain of loss, silence and uncertainty marks each character's transgression of patriarchal definitions of femininity.

Although the divisiveness of social class challenges essentialist notions of allegiance between women in the play, it does not always win out over sexual desire. The space of the action is criss-crossed with tensions arising from Anne's own social snobbery, Marianne's and Nancy's social ambitions, and all characters' awareness of the expectations of their behaviour in public. Early on, Anne is dismayed by her attraction to Marianne, 'a girl completely outside my social sphere', and in the same conversation displays a hilarious snobbery about her suspicion that Marianne's mother drinks too much: 'Tipsiness is undesirable in any woman [. . .] but quite unacceptable in the mother of the girl I . . .' (p. 110). Donoghue's sensitivity to registers of language is evident in all of her work, and *I Know My Own Heart* achieves a seductive playfulness while it functions to define what is sayable and unsayable. In the first scene, sisters Marianne and Nancy remark the artificiality of expression required in phrasing a letter: 'it's merely a polite code' (p. 105) and prepare the audience for the masks that language affords and enforces in what follows. Elsewhere the codes required for use by women in describing their experience recur: 'a female complaint' [menstruation] (p. 108), 'interesting condition' [pregnancy] (p. 133), and most strikingly where Anne teases Marianne to specify where she wishes to be touched, a playful scene that suddenly turns angry:

Anne   [. . .] What is the word you are looking for?
Marianne There is no word for it. (p. 151)

Women's bodies, their specifically womanly experiences, are betrayed by the silences observed by society, and invention must fill the space. Thus, Nancy observes: 'People like you must make your own rules' (p. 141). Marianne's Lacanian statement reflects how the body requires language to attain subjectivity, and recognition, to express desire.

Codified expressions for sexual activity include the word 'kisses' in both its usual meaning, and in its codified meaning as orgasms, an ambiguity that reflects the play's suggestion of a fluid continuity between stages of physical intimacy, and a challenge to singularly purposive phallic sexuality. Playfully, Donoghue draws the audience into exchanges that are discreet and yet entirely explicit, but also tantalises them with what remains to be revealed, for example when Anne whispers of her exploits into her lover's ear, leaving the audience to read its own meaning into Marianne's astonished reaction (p. 116).

The body is the terrain on which the conflicting forces of desire and social propriety are engaged, so that the performance challenges the audience to confront not only the language of lesbian desire, but its embodiment too. In a series of love scenes the intimacies that fuel the psychological and emotional drama are enacted, the actors' bodies showing what cannot be told in a powerful erotic subtext. The details of codification through gesture, appearance, physicality and costume have the potential to reshape conventional theatrical representations of woman, to confuse divisions between masculinity and femininity, and to interrogate the limits we place around gender identity. Decisions that reflect secure gender binaries, however, may work to reassure an audience's heterosexual expectations and reassert conventional masculine/feminine polarities. In the Glasshouse production of the play, the director Katy Hayes remembers how Donoghue, having seen a dress rehearsal, considered that the dress of the actor playing Anne should not be so pretty. Claire Dowling, however, who played the lead, felt it impossible to perform the role in the alternative, much plainer dress that was suggested. Paradoxically, she required the more 'feminine' costume in order to characterise Anne Lister's extraordinarily proactive desires, energy and hunger for experience.[4]

In the Regency period, the sartorial division between women and men was absolute, a difficult set of prohibitions for a contemporary audience to grasp. Marianne is appalled to think that Anne might actually appear in trousers, for example. When Anne says she may take to wearing frills and bonnets for the sake of more female company, Tibs reacts: 'How very unnatural that would be' (p. 134), and Anne secretly dreams of dressing completely in men's clothes, 'driving my own carriage, being my own master' (p. 133). Her gender identity, if not feminine, is deflected into masculinity as the only alternative. The question of what clothes are 'natural' is effectively historicised. As Marjorie Garber has argued, clothes are an aspect of gendered discourse of power and are no more natural than any aspect of social control.[3]

A Brechtian sense of gesture as gender transgression appears textually in the play when Anne reflects on how taking Marianne's arm in public may lead to social ruin: 'a slight readjustment of the muscles, no more. Such a small gesture to bear so much weight' (p. 107); *I Know My Own Heart* in performance creates a daring and invigorating framework to bear the weight of our gender anxieties, to gaze into the almost lost life of Anne Lister, and through her, to reimagine womanhood.

Ladies and Gentlemen (1996)

In his book entitled *Camp: The Lie That Tells the Truth*, Philip Core explores the connection between camp and 'a secret within the personality which one ironically wishes to conceal and to exploit' (p. 9). *Ladies and Gentlemen* is set against a background of American vaudeville and features characters whose identity is expanded and made complex through the trope of performance. In the play, what is concealed and what is exploited or revealed on late-nineteenth-century US popular stages is analogous to the social boundaries defining gender, and the two worlds of the stage and the real lives of the performers blur, often to liberating effect. The cross-dressing traditions of vaudeville, and centrally, female impersonations of the male made famous by performers such as Vesta Tilley, become in Donoghue's play a mode of communication, a way in which, as Core notes, 'homosexuals and other groups of people with double lives can find a *lingua franca*' (p. 9). Speech and song lyrics operating on several levels of meaning at once reflect this double vision, parallel meanings coexisting, destabilising orthodoxies.

Again Donoghue bases her narrative on real-life events and real persons. Annie Hindle worked as a vaudeville performer and was married twice, to a man and to a woman. The other performers' careers are archived in the New York Public Library, and the songs that run throughout the action are a combination of adaptations from Victorian originals and additional lyrics by Donoghue which in the first production were set to original music composed by Carole Nelson. The playwright introduces an Irish character in Annie Ryan, a poor immigrant woman who finds work as Annie's dresser.

At one level then, *Ladies and Gentlemen* recovers and explores a remarkable life or lives, but it is also a postmodern piece of theatre, deconstructing the fiction of gender binaries, dramatising the performativity of gender roles, playfully staging the linguistic and bodily texts of representation itself so as to interrogate their workings. Several key images of self-reflexivity and meta-theatricality punctuate the play, while the stage space floats between representation of a historical scene and being its Pirandellian self.

Annie Hindle is an English/American male impersonator at the centre of a group of vaudevillians: Gilbert Saroney (an American female impersonator), Ella Wesner (a dresser who launches a career as a performer), and Tony Pastor (an Italian/American vaudeville manager). Into this world of costumed identity and popular songs that veer from sentimentality into vulgar double entendre – 'Dirt's in the eye of the beholder' as Gilbert remarks (p. 90) – comes Annie Ryan, a young Irish orphan who has run away from the convent that paid her fare to the States. Two Annies in the dressing room (and in the cast) are soon distinguished by Annie Hindle when she rechristens her namesake Ryanny. The point of identification between the two is not lost, however, and lies waiting to be fulfilled in the narrative.

The play opens with Annie on the night of her comeback to the stage in 1891 and from this point the action is played in flashback as she remembers events over the past eleven years, including the failure of her abusive marriage, her first meeting with Ryanny, Ella's departure to make a career of her own, Annie's and Ryanny's falling in love and their happiness in marriage, and Ryanny's illness and untimely death. These scenes move year by year from 1880, while between each year we return to the 'end' of the story in 1891, emphasising Annie's memory as the framing device. The looped time structure of the play relates closely to the use of stage space, both aspects transforming on the instant in location and period through Annie's recollection.

The energising relationship in the play is that between Annie and Ryanny, their falling in love, and their marriage. Helen Thompson, referring to aspects of Donoghue's novels, remarks that the writer's 'work is an alternative narrative to the marriage plot',[6] but in *Ladies and Gentlemen*, marriage between women is central to the play. Early on Ryanny states that she is determined to get married, and this creates narrative tension as the action proceeds and the audience speculates whom she will wed. The prolonged scene at the end of Act I leads up to the resolution of this.

Annie's first effort at proposal becomes an absurd performance. Lacking the courage to address Ryanny herself, she addresses instead the dressing room costume dummy, comically named Miss Dimity. To find the words for her feelings is a challenge to Annie; the songs she sings in her performances remind her constantly of normative values: '[h]omes, weddings and partings, that's what they're all about' she observes (p. 47). When Ella recommends persuasion, Annie exclaims. 'How? [. . .] There aren't any songs about things like *this*' (p. 49).

Ryanny finally suggests that they marry 'for real' (p. 56), Annie taking the name Charles Hindle. Once they have agreed and are reeling with elation, Annie's cue is called. She sings 'Home' '*accompanied, with all the romance she can muster*', while '**Ryanny** *watches* [. . .] *as if from the wings*' (p. 58). In this moment, the stage occupies two spaces: the fictional space of the play, the vaudeville stage on which Annie performs, and the actual space of the venue where the performance is taking place. In parallel, the audience occupies two identities: its members are the 1886 audience watching Annie Hindle, with Ryanny peeking from the sidelines, and they are the audience of *Ladies and Gentlemen*. Donoghue places us in a spatial 'not/but', the phrase Brecht used to express the double vision of theatre, its facility in accommodating conflicting images or realities without one eliding the other. The audience is not in 1886, but it is. Annie Hindle is not a man, but in performance she is.

When Gilbert finds a Unitarian minister who will perform the ceremony, the wedding proceeds. Annie asks Gilbert if he will prompt her if she dries during the service, pointing up the porous membrane separating a vow from a line in a theatre script, separating ritual from the ritual performed onstage; Gilbert replies: 'But if I whisper "I do" I'll end up married to Ryanny, and then you'll have to shoot me' (p. 63). The first act ends with an *'imaginary'* tableau of Annie and Ryanny in *'the formal pose of a Victorian husband-and-wife photograph; a flash goes off'* (p. 65). When Ryanny tosses her bouquet over her shoulder at the audience, the theatre space has become their imagined space.

In Act I the rhythm of movement between different times in Annie's life develops at a regular pace, settling with an extended scene at the end of the act. In contrast Act II switches into higher gear in a whirligig of reflection and enactment. The effect of this is to blur the historic moment onstage with the present moment of performance, releasing the audience into a pure space of performance. Annie's closing delivery of the song 'A Real Man' is the apotheosis of this effect.

Throughout Act I and in most of Act II the scene is set in a theatre dressing room, the only exception being the home scenes set in Annie's and Ryanny's New Jersey cottage. The dressing room, equipped with a skip full of costume items, a costume dummy, mirror and make-up box (p. 7), is a reinvented closet. This closet is not a place of hiding but a theatrical laboratory for gender identity. The show-business context of the play invites reflexive images of theatricality and self-consciousness, and objects onstage speak of pretence and transformation. Annie's 'letters box', in which she keeps correspondence from adoring female fans, attests to the effectiveness of her identity as a man on the vaudeville stage, while the company manager's 'show-book', recording his script as master of ceremonies and the order of acts in the show, brings the metatext of performance on stage.

Dressing and re-dressing themselves as women, as men, Annie and Gilbert reveal gender as gesture, rehearsed and perfected, appropriated and discarded. In Act I, Annie, preparing to take to the stage again, *'is remembering how to walk in trousers'* (p. 22). The image of Annie binding her breasts in preparation for her act becomes ironic and moving after Ryanny's death from breast cancer. Perhaps the relationship between clothes and behaviour is best expressed by Gilbert when he says, 'I can't sing in a suit' (p. 94).

Ladies and Gentlemen exploits the entertainment value of vaudeville performance, musical, comic, playful and fluidly structured in time and space. It tracks the growing censorship of performers in American vaudeville as the nineteenth century progressed and standards of respectability were increasingly demanded by bourgeois audiences. However, it also uses Annie Hindle's story to evidence, across history, a precedent for happy marriage between women. When Tony jeers at her relationship with Ryanny, Annie retorts 'We were a family' (p. 98). History for Donoghue is not 'fixed and defined', but is rather, as Steve Pile and Nigel Thrift describe it, like a map, 'detachable, reversible, susceptible to constant modification'.[7] The play recovers Annie Hindle's remarkable life, while it enacts real challenges to the limiting certainties enforced in gender regulation.

Summary

Donoghue's work for theatre meets the feminist purpose of recovering women's experience in history, marking their struggles and their often extraordinary initiative in finding space to express their subjectivity, their sexuality and their love for one another.

In *Ladies and Gentlemen*, Ryanny urges Annie not to forget their happy life together despite the lengthening shadow of her imminent death:

Annie What use is remembering?
Ryanny [. . .] You must. If you don't remember everything, it'll be like it never happened. Like I never got across the ocean, or we never met, or there was never this house at all, just the bare beach. That's what scares me most: being forgotten.

Critical commentary on Donoghue's plays is rare. Her profile as a novelist is more developed. As a lesbian playwright, her work may be doubly marginalised: first as women's work, and second as lesbian work. However, the success of Dublin productions of *I Know My Own Heart* and *Ladies and Gentlemen*, both in well-respected venues, proves that there is an audience for lesbian plays.

Theatre companies aiming to perform representations of gay and lesbian lives such as Muted Cupid (founded in Dublin in 1984) have made important contributions to Irish theatre, and have been largely written out of critical commentaries. A key change has been the development of the Dublin Gay Theatre festival which features an impressive programme of visiting and home-grown work for gay and straight audiences. *I Know My Own Heart* was revived as part of the festival in 2006. *Don't Die Wondering*, broadcast on BBC Radio four in 2000, was adapted for stage and produced by DAYMS at the Teachers' Club in May 2005 as part of the festival. This later play is set in contemporary Celtic Tiger Ireland, and deals with the return home of a young lesbian chef and her attempt to live 'out' in a small Irish community. It presents issues of discrimination against gay women at work and socially, in a convincing and engaging way, and declares its purpose frankly, using conventional form, but with wit and humour.

As a writer whose interests and subject matter reach way beyond Ireland, one might expect that Donoghue's work would be particularly relevant in studies of cultural interchange and trends of globalisation in Irish theatre. Patrick Lonergan's recent study, however, limits discussion of the 'queering' of Irish stages to male homosexuality, and confines detailed discussion to homosexuality on the Abbey Theatre stage.[8]

Emma Donoghue's work as a playwright points towards a growing counter-movement in Irish theatre, in its concern with diasporic Irishness, with life outside Ireland, with the history of lesbian sexuality and gender identity. Her dramaturgies are original in form and radical in content, but they have huge audience appeal through her foregrounding of the appeal of character, and wryly empathic concern for human fates.

Primary Sources

Works by Emma Donoghue

Don't Die Wondering: Radio Play, unpublished manuscript (2000).
I Know My Own Heart, in *Seen and Heard: Six New Plays by Irish Women*, Cathy Leeney (ed.) (Dublin: Carysfort Press, 2001), pp. 99–160.
Ladies and Gentlemen (Dublin: New Island Books, 1998).

Secondary Sources

Belsey, Catherine, *The Subject of Tragedy: Identity and Difference in Renaissance Drama* (London: Routledge, 1985).
Conrad, Kathryn, 'Occupied Country: The Negotiation of Lesbianism in Irish Feminist Narrative', *Eire-Ireland*, Vol. 36, Nos 1–2 (Spring/Summer 1996), pp. 123–36.
Core, Philip, *Camp: The Lie That Tells the Truth* (Louisville, KY: Plexus Publishing, 1984).
de Jongh, Nicholas, *Not in Front of the Audience: Homosexuality on Stage* (London: Routledge, 1992).
Dolan, Jill, 'Gender Impersonation Onstage: Destroying or Maintaining the Mirror of Gender Roles?', *Women and Performance*, Vol. 2, No. 2 (1985), pp. 5–11.
Garber, Marjorie, *Vested Interests: Cross-Dressing and Cultural Anxiety* (London: Routledge, 1992)
Hayes, Katy, telephone interview, Dublin, 3 July 2009.
Lonergan, Patrick, *Theatre and Globalization: Irish Drama in the Celtic Tiger Era* (Basingstoke: Palgrave Macmillan, 2009).
Morales Ladrón, Marisol, 'The Representation of Motherhood in Emma Donoghue's *Slammerkin*', *Irish University Review*, Vol. 39, No. 1 (2009), pp. 107–21.
Peach, Linden, *The Contemporary Irish Novel: Critical Readings* (Basingstoke: Palgrave Macmillan, 2004), quoting Steve Pile and Nigel Thrift, *Mapping the Subject: Geographies of Cultural Transformation* (London: Routledge, 1995).
Rich, Adrienne, 'Compulsory Heterosexuality and Lesbian Existence', in Catharine R. Stimpson and Ethel Spector Person (eds), *Women, Sex, and Sexuality* (New York: William Morrow, 1980), pp. 62–91.
Sedgwick, Eve Kosofsky, *Tendencies* (Durham, NC: Duke UP, 1993).
Thompson, Helen, 'Emma Donoghue: Interview', in Caitriona Moloney and Helen Thompson (eds), *Irish Women Writers Speak Out: Voices from the Field* (Syracuse, NY: Syracuse UP, 2003), pp. 169–80.
Ubersfeld, Anne, *Reading Theatre*, trans. Frank Collins (Toronto, ON: University of Toronto Press, 1999).
Wandor, Michelene, *Carry On, Understudies: Theatre and Sexual Politics* (London: Routledge & Kegan Paul, 1986).

Notes

1. Catherine Belsey, *The Subject of Tragedy*, pp. 1–10.
2. Katy Hayes, telephone interview, 2009.
3. Anne Ubersfeld, *Reading Theatre*, p. 104.
4. Hayes, op. cit.
5. Marjorie Garber, *Vested Interests*, pp. 1–20.
6. Helen Thompson, 'Emma Donoghue: Interview', p. 169.
7. Quoted in Linden Peach, *The Contemporary Irish Novel*, pp. 76–7.
8. Patrick Lonergan, *Theatre and Globalization*, pp. 145–52.

6 BRIAN FRIEL

Nicholas Grene

The Enemy Within; Philadelphia Here I Come!; The Loves of Cass McGuire; Crystal and Fox; The Mundy Scheme; The Gentle Island; The Freedom of the City; Volunteers; Aristocrats; Faith Healer; Translations; The Communication Cord; Making History; Dancing at Lughnasa; Wonderful Tennessee; Molly Sweeney; Performances; The Home Place

Introduction

Brian Friel is widely regarded as Ireland's greatest living playwright, with a career spanning almost fifty years, a range of plays that have won international success, much translated and often revived, attracting a considerable body of academic criticism. Born in Omagh, Co. Tyrone, in the North of Ireland in 1929, at the age of ten he moved with his family to the city of Derry, where his father taught at a school, and where he himself was educated at St Columb's College, later the school of his friend and colleague Seamus Heaney. He went to St Patrick's College, Maynooth initially as a seminarian but, deciding against the priesthood, transferred to teacher's training at St Joseph's College, Belfast, working as a school teacher in the Derry area from 1950 to 1960. At that point his short stories (some of which had been published in the *New Yorker*) and his radio plays broadcast by BBC Northern Ireland enabled him to give up teaching to become a full-time writer.

His accomplished short stories, published in two collections, *A Saucer of Larks* (1962) and *The Gold in the Sea* (1966), and his radio plays provided an apprenticeship for the theatre; his first staged play, *The Enemy Within*, was produced by the Abbey at the Queen's Theatre in 1962. By his own account, a crucial experience in his formation as a playwright, initiating him into theatrical practice, was a period of two months in 1963 spent as a theatre observer in Minneapolis at the invitation of the Irish director Tyrone Guthrie. His breakthrough play, *Philadelphia Here I Come!*, was produced the following year at the Dublin Theatre Festival by the veteran Gate Theatre director Hilton Edwards. Its remarkable success when it transferred to New York in 1966 made Friel a bankable name on Broadway.

Married with five children, Friel moved in 1967 across the border to Co. Donegal, where he located the signature setting of so many of his plays, Ballybeg, literally 'small town'. Most of his earlier plays were concerned with such a small-town environment and the personal and social issues of the characters who lived there. However, the increasingly violent situation in Northern Ireland in the wake of the Civil Rights movement of the 1960s (in which Friel took part), brought a new political concern to his drama in the 1970s plays *The Freedom of the City* and *Volunteers*. These, along with other major plays of the period such as *Aristocrats* and *Faith Healer*, were staged by the Abbey. But in 1980, Friel, with the actor Stephen Rea, founded Field Day as an independent touring theatre company designed to respond constructively to the Northern violence and the entrenched political positions that generated it. *Translations*, which like subsequent Field Day productions opened in the symbolically significant Guildhall in Derry, was an enormous success in Ireland and abroad.

Much of Friel's energy in the 1980s was devoted to Field Day, which expanded its directorate to include Seamus Heaney and the academic Seamus Deane among others and widened its activities to publishing pamphlets and an anthology of Irish writing. In this period Field Day staged two more of Friel's own plays, *The Communication Cord* and *Making History*, as well as a version of Chekhov's *Three Sisters*, the first of a number of later adaptations including Turgenev's *Fathers and Sons*, commissioned by the National Theatre in London (1987), and *Uncle Vanya* (1998). Though reluctant to play an active public role in politics, Friel served a term in the Senate, the upper house of the Irish parliament (1987–89).

Dancing at Lughnasa, staged by the Abbey Theatre in 1990, proved to be Friel's most popular play to date. The 1990s continued to be a prolific period for Friel, in which he took on a new role as the director of two of his plays, *Molly Sweeney* and *Give Me Your Answer Do!*, both produced at the Abbey. Since then most of his new work, including original plays such as *The Home Place* (2005) and adaptations such as *Hedda Gabler* (2008), have been staged at the Gate Theatre.

Friel has been given many honours and awards for his writing, including several honorary degrees; he is a member of Aosdána and the American Academy of Arts and Letters, and a Fellow of the Royal Society of Literature. For his seventieth birthday in 1999 there was a nation-wide festival of productions of his work, and his eightieth in 2009 has been celebrated in academic journals and conferences as well as the naming of a Brian Friel Theatre in Queen's University, Belfast. While Friel's plays are valued for their vivid representation of a specifically Irish society and culture, the themes with which he engages give them a much wider currency across the world.

The Plays

The Enemy Within (1962)

The Enemy Within is a dramatisation of the life of the sixth-century Saint Columba, known in Irish as Columcille, Colum of the Churches, because of his outstanding missionary achievements in establishing monasteries, most famously that of Iona where the play is set. As in his later history plays, Friel makes no effort to imagine his characters in their historical difference, but familiarises them for a modern audience by giving them an easily colloquial regional speech; St Columba is the playwright's own contemporary. We see him at the start of the play in vigorous middle age, managing the Iona community as an efficient and humane administrator, dealing with reports as they are brought in to him from around the region: converted Picts who are rumoured to be reverting to paganism, continuing feuds back in Ulster. It is these feuds that provide the occasion for the play's central drama. For Columba is imagined not only as the ascetic saint who has renounced the world, apostle of the Christian way of peace, but still the tribesman whose clan loyalty is roused when the appeal comes to him to join his kindred in battle. This is the 'enemy within' of the title, the continuing attachment to family and locality, a passionate longing for his home territory and familiar associations. He succumbs to this temptation in Act I, but after a series of traumatic consequences when he returns to Iona in Act II, he is able to resist a second call to join another Ulster feud. This is not a definitive success – Columba will still need to battle to combat the enemy within – but it is one significant victory along the way. With its crafted three-act structure, skilful characterisation and lively dialogue, *The Enemy Within* is a well-made play of a fairly conventional, old-fashioned sort.

Philadelphia Here I Come! (1964)

It was the change of dramaturgy in *Philadelphia Here I Come!* that was so striking and contributed to the play's huge success and continuing popularity. On the face of it, this seemed a wholly traditional subject for the sort of Irish play the Abbey Theatre had made formulaic: the young man about to emigrate from the stagnant small town, with the elderly uncommunicative father, the comic housekeeper, the priest, the schoolmaster and the local 'lads'. But this stock subject was transformed by the decision to split the central part into two, with Public Gar and Private Gar, played by two different actors. Public was the tongue-tied, emotionally handicapped young man incapable of articulating his complex and conflicted feelings about his home town, his relationship with his father, the reasons that are driving him to leave. But Private, the alter ego, the unseen man, is there to speak the thoughts that Public cannot utter. While there have been suggestions Eugene O'Neill's play *Days without End* was a source for this device, the stage convention as Friel employs it in *Philadelphia* is wholly original and wholly effective.[1]

It works so well theatrically in part because it allows for a play of fantastic possibility around the humdrum ordinariness of Gar's life in Ballybeg. At a very simple level, an audience is allowed to appreciate the sheer boredom of Ballybeg without being bored themselves. For

Friel does not observe rigidly the division of roles by which Private is merely Public's silent unspoken self. When alone together the two indulge in a comic cross-talk act, which adds to the theatrical vitality and brio of the play. The depressed economy of 1950s Ireland led many young people to emigrate as Gar is doing, and the play dramatises the reasons why. Gar is treated as ill-paid hey-you to his ageing widower father with no prospects of increased income or authority. His one romance is thwarted by the social snobbery of Senator Doogan, father of his girlfriend Katie. The banal Canon and the drunken Master are all Ballybeg has to offer by way of spiritual leadership or education, and the loutish, boastful, sex-starved 'lads' are Gar's only available companions. But Friel maintained that the play was not about the social issue of emigration as such; its theme, he said, was love.[2] Certainly the failure of the relationship between S.B. and Gar, which is a failure to be able to speak their feelings for one another, is central. The exaggerated generation gap of late-married father and young son, housekeeper replacing the absent mother, leaves Gar especially hungry for the nurturing of feminine love. His mantra for warding off unwelcome thoughts is the recitation of Edmund Burke's speech idealising the young Marie Antoinette, he is constantly trying to imagine his dead mother, and it is the emotional need of his childless Aunt Lizzie that has tempted him to join her in Philadelphia. It is because of this sense of unfulfilled attachment that the play ends in uncertainty:

> **Private** . . . God, Boy, why do you have to leave? Why? Why?
> **Public** I don't know. I – I – I don't know. (p. 99)

The Loves of Cass McGuire (1966)

The Loves of Cass McGuire can be seen as a companion play to *Philadelphia*, the earlier study of the young man about to leave for the US matched by the old woman returning to Ballybeg after a life spent in New York. Cass's rowdiness, her drinking and memories of life as a bar attendant in the Bowery make her a scandal to her respectable Irish family, who consign her to the geriatric home that is the play's setting.

Her one source of pride is shattered when it transpires that the emigrant's remittance which she has sent back regularly was not needed, but has been banked for her old age. The play combines a satire on the middle-class proprieties of the family, eager to distance themselves from the disreputable Cass, with an exploration of her life of memory and fantasy. A meta-theatrical opening, with Cass commenting on the drama, insisting the story should be told her way, disrupts any conventional theatrical representation. But the most striking non-naturalistic feature of the play is the series of 'rhapsodies' in which two other inmates of the home at first, and then Cass herself, indulge in fantastically romanticised versions of their past lives. Friel makes clear in an introductory note that the term 'rhapsody' is chosen for its musical associations and the speeches were designed to be underscored with the music of Wagner. While typically Frielian in its preoccupation with exile and return, memory and loss, it is also the first of many of his plays in which music, and musical structures, are integral to theatrical effect.

Crystal and Fox (1968)

Though he has his own characteristic themes, Friel has never settled into a single mode or style in his playwriting. So, for example, *Crystal and Fox* and *The Mundy Scheme* could not be less like one another. *Crystal and Fox* is a study in the self-destructive character of Fox Melarkey, the manager of a fit-up variety show touring Ireland with his adored wife Crystal. He systematically alienates other members of the company, deliberately courts failure, until he and Crystal are left alone together. It might appear that this is what he has sought, a return to the pristine purity of their first love, but then he drives Crystal herself away by falsely telling her that he betrayed their delinquent son to the police. He is left finally alone with nothing but the roulette wheel with which he began his show-business career. In spite of a fine performance by Cyril Cusack in the title role, the unaccountable motivation of Fox remained a puzzle for audiences in the theatre.

The Mundy Scheme (1969)

The Mundy Scheme, by contrast, was a broad-brush satire on the corruption of contemporary Irish politics: '*The place is Dublin. The time is at hand*', the opening direction tells us (p. 154). The caricatures of the politicians and the situation, however, are generic – the mother-fixated, ex-auctioneer Taoiseach F. X. Ryan, the drunken Minister of External Affairs, the anxious Jesuit-educated Minister of Finance contrasted with the boorish ministers up from the country. The state is all but bankrupt, the unions are threatening revolution. Financial salvation comes in the form of the Mundy scheme by which an American realtor will lease large tracts of west of Ireland bog for an industrial-scale cemetery to inter the dead of all nations. In the scramble for a slice of the action that follows, we see the wholly self interested politicians jockey for position, double-crossing one another to the point where Ryan is left alone at the top of the greasy pole, with the Mundy scheme a huge success. A sardonic commentary at once on the state of the nation, as well as Ireland's historical death-consciousness, it might appear prophetic of the much later scandal-ridden period of the globalised 'Celtic tiger'.

The Gentle Island (1971)

The target of Friel's scrutiny in *The Gentle Island* is the primitivist myth of island life which was one of the main icons of the Irish literary revival from Synge's *The Aran Islands* to the Blasket Island autobiographies of the 1930s. To the romantic tourist Peter from Dublin, the play's Iniskeen looks exactly like the 'gentle island' that its name signifies in Irish, a pastoral idyll of peace and tranquillity. But the audience sees how little the one-armed king of the island, Manus, who stubbornly insists on remaining with his family when all the other islanders have left, resembles the benign patriarch Peter imagines him to be. There is a terrible history of how he lost his arm, maimed by the uncles of the woman he had seduced and abandoned, Rosie Dubh (the name ironically close to Roisin Dubh, allegorical female personification of Ireland) who subsequently committed suicide by walking into the sea.

And that background story is matched by the play's action when Shane, Peter's younger partner, is left paralysed by a violent attack on him by Sarah, frustrated wife of Philly, Manus's gay son, whom she has seen making love to Shane. Friel was ahead of his time in Irish theatre in dealing explicitly with homosexuality. The play powerfully reveals the homophobia that overshadows the ideals of patriarchy and the atavistic violence lying beneath the surface of the Irish island idyll.

The Freedom of the City (1973)

The terrible events of 30 January 1972, which became known as Bloody Sunday, when thirteen unarmed civilians on a Civil Rights march in Derry were killed by British paratroopers, provoked a new level of political engagement in Friel, who had himself been on that march. The outrage that he, like many people in Ireland, felt at the findings of the Widgery Tribunal, which effectively exculpated the soldiers responsible, was expressed in *The Freedom of the City*. Though Friel fictionalises the actual event, setting it back in time to 1970 and making the victims three marchers who have found themselves by accident in the Derry Guildhall and are taken to be occupying terrorists, the framing enquiry into the circumstances of their killing obviously satirises the Widgery Tribunal, with literal quotations from the tribunal report included in the text. Yet the evident prejudice of the presiding judge is only one of many forms of misrepresentation to which the three central characters are subjected. The play works as a collage, showing the onstage reality of Lily, garrulous mother of eleven, Michael the earnest Civil Rights protester with aspirations, and Skinner the anarchist cynic and clown, intercut with distorted versions of their story from the Republican Balladeer, alternative politically skewed sermons by a priest, the vapid commentary of an RTE journalist at their funeral. An unrelated sociologist's lecture on 'the culture of poverty', which the Derry characters' action ironically illustrates, further complicates the interplay between truth and representation. Although the play was criticised for its political bias, and it was no doubt fuelled by Friel's anger, it can be related to his general continuing concern with the misconstructions of narrative.

Volunteers (1975)

Volunteers related more obliquely to the Northern political crisis, drawing also upon topical events in the Republic of Ireland at the time. In the course of developing the Dublin riverside site at Wood Quay for a new corporation headquarters in the early 1970s, important Viking archaeological remains had been discovered. A very strong, but ultimately unsuccessful, public campaign was mounted to stop the building work going forward. Friel's play, which shows a group of political prisoners who have volunteered to work on a Wood Quay-like archaeological site, represents simultaneously a satiric protest against the Philistinism of the political establishment indifferent to cultural heritage, and an exploration of the mentality of Republican dissidents. We see the range of different temperaments of the 'volunteers' at once IRA Volunteers and volunteers for this work – and the group dynamics of them, their guards and overseers. These men stand in isolation and opposition at once to the established state apparatus and their fellow-paramilitary prisoners, who have sentenced them to death for collaborating with the state. The play is dedicated to Seamus Heaney and uses a very similar technique to that in his collection of poems *North*, published in the year the play was produced, with excavated vestiges of violent past history in imaginative relation to the politics of the present.

Aristocrats (1979)

Not all his plays from this productive period were explicitly political; *Living Quarters* (1977) focused instead on the dysfunctional family. Subtitled 'after Hippolytus', it represents a deliberate modern-day reconception of Euripides' tragedy.

The family remains at the centre of *Aristocrats*, though the theatrical precursor here is neither Euripides nor Pirandello but Chekhov. The crumbling house of the O'Donnells in *Aristocrats* is an Irish equivalent to the Chekhovian *Cherry Orchard*, and it is likely that the imaginary croquet game of the eccentric son Casimir owes something to the mental billiards that Gayev plays with his umbrella in Chekhov's play.

But these are 'aristocrats' with a difference; unlike most of the much-mythologised inhabitants of the Irish Big House, they are Catholics not Protestants. Friel emphasises this special sociological dimension by the presence of Tom Hoffnung, an American historian writing a thesis specifically on this class of Catholic gentry, and who listens with increasing bewilderment to the impossible family legends of the historical figures who visited the house. This fantasia serves to underline the stranded alienation of such a family, cut off from real power by their religion, but isolated from the wider community by their class. The dislocation of social role is matched by the defor-mations of the family itself: an authoritarian father who is a retired judge (as so often in Friel), now only a senile voice transmitted from an offstage bedroom, a dead mother who suffered from chronic mental illness, their son and daughters variously afflicted emotionally and psychologically. Friel's vision is at once sterner and more obviously diagnostic than Chekhov's, though with the death of the father he allows the family something of an upbeat ending.

Faith Healer (1979)

Many critics now consider *Faith Healer* to be Friel's greatest play. It is certainly one of his most challenging theatrically, consisting as it does of four monologues by three characters who never occupy the stage together. An audience is left to try to sift the truth from the incompatible narratives of Frank Hardy, the eponymous faith healer, his wife Grace, and their business manager Teddy, who spent years touring Scotland and Wales with them. The power of the play derives from its openness to interpretation. Each of the characters in turn holds the audience completely with what seems like a compelling narrative, yet the inconsistencies between their stories mean that they must be misrepresenting the facts, whether deliberately (as appears to be the case with Frank) or inadvertently (with Grace and Teddy). The status of the stories and the nature of the unbreakable co-dependence between the three figures are made more mysterious by the fact that two of them are already dead: Frank having been murdered in Ballybeg by a group of drunken young men whose paralysed friend he failed to cure, and Grace, unable to bear his loss, having killed herself. Faith healing itself is an ambiguous profession; the alcoholic, obsessive Frank cannot decide whether he is a histrionic charlatan or has a genuine gift – he can on occasions heal the sick. As such it adumbrates the uncertain mentality of the creative artist. The faith healer's tours of the peripheral regions of Scotland and Wales, his reluctance to return to Ireland and the disastrous consequences of his final homecoming are suggestive of the prophet without honour in his own country, his death that of a sacrificial scapegoat. No other play of Friel's has ever quite matched *Faith Healer* for the intensity of its emotional feeling and the depth of its symbolic resonance.

Translations (1980)

The year 1980 was an extraordinary one for Friel, with the successful revival of *Faith Healer* at the Abbey coming within weeks of the opening of *Translations* as the inaugural production of the Field Day Theatre Company. The setting of the play in a Donegal hedge school in 1833 allowed Friel to dramatise an imagined moment in the historical process of modernising colonisation. The introduction at this time of the national school system, in which the language of instruction was to be English, the simultaneous Ordnance Survey mapping operation of the British Army and premonitions of the Famine of twelve years later, are brought together to represent the approaching extinction of traditional Gaelic culture. As a potent theatrical symbol for the failure of communication between coloniser and colonised, the Irish speakers of Baile Beag are assumed not to be able to understand the British soldiers and vice versa, even though all the dialogue is actually in English. Both sides are dependent on the equivocal interpreting of Owen, the English-speaking son of Hugh, the drunken hedge schoolmaster. While the Anglicisation of the place names by the map-makers represents the colonial process of occupation, the play explores more fundamental questions of how far language ever can be truly translated, drawing on George Steiner's *After Babel*, from which several of Hugh's lines are derived. The play ends with the tragic disappearance (presumed murder) of the well-intentioned English officer who has fallen in love with the local girl Maire, with devastating consequences for Baile Beag.

The play, with an outstanding cast led by Ray McAnally and Stephen Rea, and including a young Liam Neeson, was a huge success with audiences of every political persuasion, both at its opening in Derry, on its tour through other parts of Ireland and in Britain. Although there was some criticism of the play's historical accuracy and what was felt to be its nationalist bias in the representation of the Ordnance Survey as a brutal instrument of colonisation, it gave Field Day great impetus in their mission of creating a new sort of theatre for Ireland. Friel himself, however, was wary of some of the more emotional responses to the work and wrote his next original play to be staged by Field Day as a sort of antidote to *Translations*.

The Communication Cord (1982)

The Communication Cord is a contemporary farce that satirises the sentimental romanticisation of rural origins typified in the reproduction peasant cottage in modern Ballybeg where the play is set. The central character Tim, a lecturer in linguistics, is researching 'response cries' as a form of communication, allowing Friel to pursue the interest in language theory initiated in *Translations*. The disguises, cross-purposes and mistaken identities typical of farce, enhanced by characters who are assumed only to be able to speak French or German, creates an anarchic theatrical Babel. While farce is not Friel's strongest theatrical genre, the final scene of the characters trapped in the cowhouse chains of the converted cottage about to collapse on their heads is a satiric revenge on the pretentious Irish idolaters of the past, including some admirers of Friel's own work.

Making History (1988)

In staging *Translations*, Friel and Field Day were accused of a nationalist distortion of historical fact. Such distortion was made the central subject of Friel's final play for the company, *Making History*. The central character is Hugh O'Neill, the leader of the last major

Gaelic rebellion against British power at the end of the sixteenth century. Drawing on Sean O'Faolain's revisionist biography *The Great O'Neill* (1942), Friel emphasises O'Neill's mixed cultural identity: his upbringing in England represented theatrically by an upper-class English accent, his marriage to Mabel Bagenal, sister to one of his most implacable adversaries in the Irish colonial wars. The drama of his fraught relationship with Mabel, her death and the disaster of the Battle of Kinsale, O'Neill's last desperate years in exile in Rome, are counterpointed by the hagiographical version of the story planned by Archbishop Lombard, in which the inconvenient facts will be airbrushed out. The play dramatises the way in which any history creates narrative out of the facts of the past, shaped by the conditions of the present. It could be said itself to illustrate that very proposition in producing a revised story of O'Neill suitable for the needs of Field Day in the 1980s bent on questioning orthodox Irish historiography.

Dancing at Lughnasa (1990)

Dancing at Lughnasa, staged by the Abbey, in its move away from the more explicitly political Field Day plays of the 1980s, can be seen as another change of direction for Friel. Explicitly autobiographical in content, dedicated as it is to 'those five brave Glenties women', sisters of the playwright's own mother, it is a memory play set in 1936; the middle-aged narrator Michael is remembering the summer when he, like Friel himself, would have been aged seven. The boy Michael is invisible on stage, his lines spoken by his adult counterpart, on the principle that the recollecting mind can see everyone but himself. The Celtic harvest festival of Lughnasa, of which vestiges remain in the remote Ballybeg back hills, is evoked as the emblem of the pagan culture underlying the ascetic Irish Catholicism that represses the lives of the five unmarried sisters – Michael is his mother's illegitimate son. The spectacular onstage dance by the five women in Act I represents an instinctual protest against that repression. The image of dancing, whether the ballroom dancing of Gerry, Michael's sporadically appearing Welsh father, or the festive African dancing remembered by

Uncle Jack, the missionary priest who has been converted to animism by those he set out to convert, provides the play's central leitmotif down to Michael's concluding lyrical monologue where memory itself becomes 'Dancing as if language no longer existed because words were no longer necessary . . .' (p. 71).

Though admired when it first opened in Dublin, the legendary success of *Dancing at Lughnasa* really grew on the basis of its international reception first in London and then in New York. Although the play emphasised the harshness of the lives of the Mundy sisters, two of whom die homeless in London, as Friel's own aunts had done, an element of nostalgia no doubt conditioned audience responses. For first- and second-generation Irish emigrants, this was an Ireland they need not regret having left but which could be recalled fondly in retrospect. The real power of the play, however, derives from its celebration of female energy – apart from anything else it has continued to provide showcase parts for Irish women actors in its frequent revivals – and its subtle and theatrically compelling rendering of a moment in remembered time. Its 1930s period is stressed with references to the Italian invasion of Abyssinia, the Spanish Civil War, and particularly the coming of the radio to Ballybeg, representing the modernisation of rural Ireland. The personal memory of childhood in the play stands in for the recollection of the historical past going back to mythic rituals enacted here in a latter-day secular theatrical form.

Wonderful Tennessee (1993)

This concern with the rediscovery of ritual in a contemporary setting was pushed further in *Wonderful Tennessee*. A group of six friends from Dublin arrive at remote Ballybeg pier for a birthday celebration on an island off the coast. They never reach the island, but spend the night in a frenzied effort at festivity that by degrees exposes the failings, neuroses and despair of the three interrelated couples. The 'Oileán Draíochta', 'Island of Otherness; Island of Mystery' (p. 28), becomes a mirage which each of them imagines differently, representing all that is lacking in their own secular urban lives. In that sense, it is a satire that relates back to *The Gentle Island* and *The Communication Cord*. But with the story of an actual human sacrifice supposed to have taken place on Oileán Draíochta in the wake of the 1932 Eucharistic Congress (an early historic high point in independent Ireland's celebration of its Catholicism), and a disquisition on the Eleusinian mysteries of ancient Greek religion by one of the characters who is a classicist, Friel, as in *Dancing at Lughnasa*, emphasises continuities between pagan and Christian ritual. By the end of the play, the characters find themselves inventing their own versions of such rituals. The most interesting feature of *Wonderful Tennessee* theatrically was the use of the accordion playing of George, the character dying of throat cancer, as a non-verbal orchestration of the moods and meanings of the play through popular and classical music. In spite of this, however, the necessarily static nature of the action and the over-explicitness of the symbolism damagingly weakened the play in production

Molly Sweeney (1994)

With *Molly Sweeney* Friel returned to the three-character monologue format of *Faith Healer*, though here the monologues are intercut and the three characters, Molly Sweeney, the blind woman cured of her sight, Frank her husband, and the eye surgeon Mr Rice, are all onstage throughout. Based on a real-life case popularised by neurologist Oliver Sacks, Friel significantly changed the gender of the middle-aged man who was restored to sight in middle age but failed to adapt to the sighted world. Molly Sweeney, who has been tutored by her father – again a judge – in the names of the things she cannot see, becomes a victim of the enthusiastic zeal of her quixotic husband and the self-interest of the surgeon who wants to regain his damaged reputation by a spectacular miracle cure. Clearly related to Synge's *The Well of the Saints* about the blind couple who are so disillusioned by their restored sight that they choose to stay blind rather than submit to a second cure, Friel's play differs from Synge in its emphasis on issues of gender. The distinctiveness of Molly's blind world, in which she is happy and fulfilled, reflects her feminine interiority, subjected to arbitrary, patriarchal control with its destructive insistence on her joining and conforming to an outward sphere of vision.

Performances (2003)

Music has always played an important part in Friel's theatre, most obviously in *Wonderful Tennessee*. *Performances* was his most radical musical experiment, with the onstage performance of Janáček's Second String Quartet integrated into the action. Taking off from a collection of passionate love letters Janáček wrote in the last year of his life when writing the string quartet, the composer, imagined back from the dead, flatly denies the biographical interpretation put upon them by the earnest researcher who comes to visit him, asserting the primacy of the work of art and the supremacy of music over language: 'The people who huckster in words merely report on feeling. We *speak* feeling' (p. 31). That belief is put to the test for an audience in the theatre by having actual musicians rehearsing and finally playing the last two movements of the string quartet. The play must be taken as the tribute to the superiority of music by a playwright especially gifted in language who regards the script of a play as equivalent to a musical score.

The Home Place (2005)

Friel's last original play to date is *The Home Place*. The historical setting in 1878 at the start of the Irish land war, which was to result ultimately in the mass transfer of property from Anglo-Irish estate owners to small tenant farmers, was an opportunity for Friel to revisit the colonial situation of *Translations* fifty years on. The Ordnance Survey map-making has its imperialist equivalent in a late-nine-teenth-century phrenology project of racist classification. But, where in the 1830s it was the old Gaelic culture of the hedge school that was on the point of extinction, here it is the life of the Ascendancy landlords represented by the Gores, the widowed father Christopher and his son David, both in love with the housekeeper Margaret. That love, in the end (it is to be assumed) unfulfilled for both suitors, may be taken to be representative of the attachment of the landowning class to their Irish surroundings. They are imagined as colonists incapable of real acculturation because of a continuing allegiance to 'the home place', the English estate from which their ancestors came to Ireland. While this hardly reflects the mentality of most Anglo-Irish Protestants of the period who (often insistently) regarded themselves as Irish rather than English, Friel uses it to represent the displaced alienation of the class and the tragic inevitability of their dispossession by the native Irish they originally dispossessed.

Summary

Brian Friel began his career as a writer of short stories, and storytelling has remained central to his work as a playwright. His characters typically make themselves up in often illusory or fantastic self-narrations. So, for instance, Friel made use of a childhood memory of his own in the lyrical evocation of the outing in the blue boat given to Private Gar in *Philadelphia*, and even though the memory could not be authenticated, it remains an emotional or imaginative truth. In many of his later plays, also, Friel shows a tender respect for this sort of romantic personal myth-making. It is there in the 'rhapsodies' of Cass McGuire, and in the legendary family anecdotes of Casimir in *Aristocrats*. As Eamonn says protectively to Casimir, when the historian Tom Hoffnung has exposed the impossibility of one of these stories, 'There are certain things, certain truths [. . .] that are beyond Tom's kind of scrutiny' (pp. 309–10).

However, Friel also creates theatrical forms that embody truer, or at least more factual, narratives challenging these alternative realities. The narrating Man and Woman in 'Winners', the first part of *Lovers* (1967), provide the bare forensic report on the events leading up to the couple's death. In *Living Quarters*, the ledger overseen by Sir represents the unalterable course of action that the characters retrospectively try in vain to rewrite. In one sense, such narratives in their very neutral objectivity must be seen as inadequate to the spontaneity of the lived experience with all its play of possibility. Yet, particularly in *Living Quarters*, the factual narrative constitutes a fated inevitability of tragic truth against which the self-deceiving illusions of the individual characters are weighed and found wanting.

Friel has thus shown himself exceptionally fond of narrators and narration in his drama, but often with a tension between narrative and performance. This is most obvious in *Faith Healer*, where the performance of each monologue by the characters given the stage alone in turn compels audience belief while it is being performed. And yet the incompatibility of the different accounts of their shared story makes us aware of their unreliability. The contrast between narrative and performance works differently in *The Freedom of the City*, where the staged actions of the three figures in the Guildhall are understood to be the authentic reality as against the distorting discourses that purport to tell their story. This tension is especially striking in the case of a memory play such as *Dancing at Lughnasa*. There the live drama is mediated through the recollecting mind of Michael; his speeches introduce, comment on and conclude the play with the authority of considered reflection. Yet the lives of the women onstage exceed his powers of narrative control. He is not present when they perform their Act I dance and, even after he has told the story of the deaths of two of them in Act II, they remain stubbornly alive in the theatre. The embodied life of women, here and in *Molly Sweeney*, challenges the male narrative of the word.

That there is a clear interrelationship of personal stories and memories with the collective national narratives of history is an obvious transition, caught well in the subtitle to Martine Pelletier's French study of Friel, '*histoire et histoires*'.[3] In an early play such as *The Enemy Within* the historical situation is merely a backdrop for Columba's drama of inner struggle. But from the 1970s on, with the urgencies of political violence in the North pressing upon him, Friel became concerned with how far the life of the past could be recovered and how it might be shaped into narrative. *Volunteers* presents a theatrical image of literal digging below the surface of a modern present as a metaphor for trying to create meaning out of past history. This was the impetus also behind the historical plays written for Field Day. Although Friel was to be accused of political tendentiousness in *Translations*, his objective in that play was to dramatise a moment in the colonial process that shaped the condition of modern Ireland. In *Making History* it was precisely the political imperatives that drove the production of historical narratives that he sought to show.

Below history again there is myth; below Christian culture, in Friel's view, lie the archetypes of paganism. Already in *Faith Healer* there are traces of this mythic pattern in Frank's murder in Ballybeg at the end of a 'Dionysian night. A Bacchanalian night [. . .] when ritual was consciously and relentlessly debauched' (p. 340). It is more obvious in *Dancing at Lughnasa*, where the dance of the women, inspired by thoughts of the harvest festival, is linked to the descriptions by Father Jack of dancing at East African fertility rites. And it is fully explicit in the discursive *Wonderful Tennessee*, where the group improvise on stage a mimic form of dismemberment of their rich leader Terry, the Fisher King for a night. For Friel, 'Ritual is part of all drama. [. . .] Drama is a RITE, and always religious in the purest sense.'[4] Much of his work in the theatre has been a search for modern theatrical counterparts to this deep structure of myth and ritual.

In terms of his dramaturgy, Friel has not been a radically innovative playwright. From early in his career he absorbed the influence of American and European contemporaries and predecessors. So, for example, Thornton Wilder's *Our Town* (1938) may have provided an exemplar for Friel, both for the representation of Ballybeg, generic 'little town', and for the figure of the controlling, reflecting Stage Manager, forerunner of so many of Friel's own narrators. It is clear that Tennessee Williams's *The Glass Menagerie* (1944) was the memory-play model for *Dancing at Lughnasa*, the childhood family scene mediated through the remembering consciousness of the autobiographical retrospective. Pirandello is a presence in Friel's experiments with metatheatre in *The Loves of Cass McGuire* and *Living Quarters*. Friel's great master, however, reflected in the number of works he has 'translated' or adapted, is Chekhov. His affinities with Chekhov have often been pointed out: their common liking for extended, disjunctive, family groups; a preference for indirect rather than direct action; the unstable combination of absurd comedy with a plangent pessimism.

Friel may be classified as a playwright of ideas in so far as he has frequently drawn upon one or more discursive or theoretical sources and made them central to the substance of individual plays. So, the idea of the 'culture of poverty' which features in the lecture by the sociologist Dodds in *The Freedom of the City* was derived from the anthropologist Oscar Lewis's *La Vida*.[5] *Translations* drew heavily not only on Steiner's *After Babel* but on *A Paper Landscape*, the geographer J. H. Andrews's book on the nineteenth-century Ordnance Survey of Ireland. Sociologist Erving Goffman was used in *The Communication Cord*, Sean O'Faolain in *Making History* and Oliver Sacks in *Molly Sweeney*.[6] Friel's skill has been to make use of such materials in dramatic and accessible theatrical forms, to make of them literally a play of ideas. Playful comedy has been an essential part of his dramatic idiom throughout from the cross-talk of the doubled Private and Public Gar on. A quick-talking, cynical clown is a commonly recurring figure – Shane in *The Gentle Island*, Skinner in *The Freedom of the City*, Keeney in *Volunteers* – animating what are essentially tragic situations with joking parodies and mocking improvisations. While never a self-consciously avant-garde playwright, Friel has been continually inventive in finding new theatrical conventions for engaging his audiences: the split persona of *Philadelphia*, the mutually incomprehensible Irish and English speakers in *Translations*, the juxtaposition of dead and living characters in many of his plays. While not all of these experiments have worked equally well, they have made for a theatre that is fresher, livelier and more interesting than more conventionally naturalistic or representational work.

Friel's early successes in the 1960s and continuing importance in international theatre have attracted a considerable body of criticism. Beginning with the study by D. E. S. Maxwell in 1973, there have been a number of introductory overviews of his work by Ulf Dantanus, George O'Brien and Tony Corbett.[7] He has been made the subject of several collections of essays or special issues of academic journals.[8] The most ambitious works on Friel to date, taking in the full range of his writing, have been those of Elmer Andrews, Martine Pelletier and Richard Pine.[9] Given the significance of Friel's commitment to Field Day, there has been an increased concentration of the political dimensions to his work. F. C. McGrath, for instance, taking a cue from the influential introduction by Seamus Deane to

Friel's 1984 *Selected Plays*, has relegated the early work to an apprenticeship period, arguing that Friel's long-standing interest in truth and illusion only became fully significant when theorised and politicised from the 1970s on.[10] The most recent monograph on Friel, by Scott Boltwood, interrogates the problematic nature of Friel's politics and his relationship to nationalist ideologies.[11]

Friel belongs, with Hugh Leonard, Tom Murphy and Thomas Kilroy, to an older generation of Irish playwrights who began working in the 1960s. Their plays together served to create a dramaturgical revolution, modernising, introducing new techniques and challenging themes to an Irish theatre that had become stultified in the period since the early achievements of Synge, Yeats and O'Casey. Of this group, Friel has had the most sustained success, not only in Ireland (where Murphy's work would be almost as widely respected) but internationally in Britain, the United States and in Europe. Although in many plays distrustful of language, making crucial use of music in much of his drama, he still has to be seen as an inheritor of the language-based theatre so endemic in the Irish tradition; his dialogue is crisp, witty and colloquial, his long speeches and monologues lyrically eloquent. He has always been insistent on the paramount position of the playwright in the theatre and the integrity of the dramatic script, having little time for the interpretative pretensions of ambitious directors. As such he can be related to younger Irish playwrights such as Frank McGuinness and Marina Carr, who are equally reliant on the power of dramatic language. He could, however, be considered conservative in practice compared with the movement-based or ensemble-generated work which is becoming more popular recently, or with the rougher and more demotic style of Martin McDonagh, Conor McPherson, Enda Walsh and Mark O'Rowe. He remains, none the less, the towering presence of contemporary Irish theatre in the first decade of the twenty-first century.

Primary Sources

Works by Brian Friel

Aristocrats (Dublin: Gallery Press, 1980).

The Communication Cord (London: Faber and Faber, 1983).

Crystal and Fox and *The Mundy Scheme* (New York: Farrar, Strauss and Giroux, 1970).

Dancing at Lughnasa (London: Faber and Faber, 1990).

The Enemy Within (Oldcastle: Gallery Press, 1979).

Faith Healer (London: Faber and Faber, 1980).

The Freedom of the City (London: Faber and Faber, 1974).

The Gentle Island (London: Davis-Poynter, 1973).

Give Me Your Answer Do! (Oldcastle: Gallery Press, 1997).

The Home Place (Oldcastle: Gallery Press, 2005).

Living Quarters (London: Faber and Faber, 1978).

Lovers (Oldcastle: Gallery Press, 1984).

The Loves of Cass McGuire (London: Faber and Faber, 1966).

Making History (London: Faber and Faber, 1989).

Molly Sweeney (Oldcastle: Gallery Press, 1994).

Performances (Oldcastle: Gallery Press, 2003).

Philadelphia Here I Come! (London: Faber and Faber, 1965).

Translations (London: Faber and Faber, 1981).

Volunteers (London: Faber and Faber, 1979).

Wonderful Tennessee (Oldcastle: Gallery Press, 1993).

Secondary Sources

Andrews, Elmer (ed.), *The Art of Brian Friel* (Basingstoke: Macmillan, 1995).

Boltwood, Scott, *Brian Friel, Ireland and the North* (Cambridge: Cambridge UP, 2007).

Corbett, Tony, *Brian Friel: Decoding the Language of the Tribe* (Dublin: Liffey Press, 2002).

Dantanus, Ulf, *Brian Friel: A Study* (London: Faber and Faber, 1988).

Friel, Brian, *Essays, Diaries Interviews: 1964–1999*, ed. Christopher Murray (London: Faber and Faber, 2000).

Maxwell, D. E. S., *Brian Friel* (Lewisburg, PA: Bucknell UP).

McGrath, F. C., *Brian Friel's (Post) Colonial Drama* (Syracuse, NY: Syracuse UP, 1999).

Morse, Donald E., Csilla Bertha and Mária Kurdi (eds), *Brian Friel's Dramatic Artistry* (Dublin: Carysfort Press, 2006).

O'Brien, George, *Brian Friel* (Dublin: Gill and Macmillan, 1989).

Peacock, Alan, *The Achievement of Brian Friel* (Gerrards Cross: Colin Smythe, 1993).

Pelletier, Martine, *Le Théâtre de Brian Friel: Histoire et Histoires* (Villeneuve d'Ascq: PU de Septentrion, 1997).

Pine, Richard, *The Diviner: The Art of Brian Friel* (Dublin: University College Dublin Press, 1999).

Roche, Anthony (ed.), *Irish University Review*, Special Issue on Brian Friel, Vol. 29, No. 1 (1999).

Notes

1. For a discussion of the issue see Ulf Dantanus, *Brian Friel: A Study*, pp. 89–93.
2. Brian Friel, *Essays, Diaries, Interviews, 1964–1999*, p. 47.
3. Martine Pelletier, *Le Théâtre de Brian Friel: Histoire et Histoires.*
4. Quoted in Dantanus, op. cit., p. 87.
5. For a full discussion of the significance of the borrowings here, see F. C. McGrath, *Brian Friel's (Post) Colonial Drama*, pp. 112–18.
6. See Richard Pine, *The Diviner: The Art of Brian Friel*, p. 9.
7. D. E. S. Maxwell, *Brian Friel*; Dantanus, op. cit.; George O'Brien, *Brian Friel*; Tony Corbett, *Brian Friel: Decoding the Language of the Tribe.*
8. See, for example, Alan Peacock, *The Achievement of Brian Friel*; Donald E. Morse *et al.* (eds), *Brian Friel's Dramatic Artistry.*
9. Elmer Andrews (ed.) *The Art of Brian Friel*; Pelletier, op. cit.; Pine, op. cit.
10. See McGrath, op. cit., passim.
11. Scott Boltwood, *Brian Friel, Ireland and the North.*

7 MARIE JONES

Catrin Siedenbiedel

Somewhere Over the Balcony; The Hamster Wheel; A Night in November; Stones in His Pockets; Women on the Verge of HRT; The Blind Fiddler

Introduction

Born in 1955, Marie Jones grew up in Protestant working-class surroundings in east Belfast.[1] She left school at fifteen, without any 'formal preparation'[2] she started her theatre career as an actress in Belfast in 1968 and in 1976 she joined the Young Lyric Players at Belfast's Lyric Theatre, but she complained that the main Belfast theatres at that time neither produced many local plays nor employed any local actresses.[3] A group comprising Jones and four other unemployed Northern Irish Catholic and Protestant actresses (Carol Scanlon, Eleanor Methven, Maureen Macauley and Brenda Winter) therefore started to write their own plays with many female parts and in language and dealing with topics related to their Northern Irish background. They were supported by playwright Martin Lynch.[4]

At this point, the young women worked together on their first play, *Lay Up Your Ends*, about the 1911 strike of woman mill workers, an action called to protest against a law that forbade the workers to talk or sing at work and which led to the formation of the first Textile Workers Union in 1913. It had a specifically Northern Irish impact because both Protestants and Catholics were involved in the play. In order to produce this play in 1983, the five women had to found their own feminist theatre company: the Charabanc.[5] Marie Jones was the company's writer-in-residence until 1990.

During these years she also wrote several plays for Replay Productions, a professional Theatre-in-Education Company founded by Brenda Winter in 1988. These plays included, *Under Napoleon's Nose* (1988), on the history of Belfast, and *The Cow, the Ship and the Indian* (1991), a children's play about a boy and his family living in nineteenth-century Ireland in which the child compares his own colonial situation to that of the Native Americans.

In 1991 Marie Jones, together with Pam Brighton and Mark Lambert, set up another company in Belfast, the DubbelJoint Theatre, for which she wrote plays that dealt with the Troubles. In 2002 she was awarded the Order of the British Empire (OBE) for her services to drama.

Marie Jones also works as an actress, most prominently for film productions such as Jim Sheridan's *In the Name of the Father* (UK/Ireland) in 1993 and Brian Kirk's *Middletown* (UK/Ireland) in 2006.

The Plays

Somewhere Over the Balcony (1987)

Somewhere Over the Balcony is a two-act play written together with Eleanor Methven, Carol Moore and Peter Sheridan for the Charabanc Theatre Company.[6] Situated in between 'political drama' and 'black farce',[7] it also contains some musical elements. Set in the Catholic Divis Flats, in a west Belfast neighbourhood severely affected by the Troubles, on 9 August 1987, 'Internment Day',[8] it focuses on three local women, Kate Tidy, Ceely Cash and Rose Marie Noble.

Like spectators in a theatre Kate, Ceely and Rose watch the everyday war-like action and comment on it, in a kind of modern teichoscopy (the technique of reporting offstage action rather than showing it). But they are not the only ones who observe others: there is a group of British Army soldiers who have, some time before, moved into the tower block opposite the flats to watch the supposed enemies' actions or – as Kate Tidy puts it in her local working-class vernacular – 'Them bastards are watching us' (p. 447).

That day, there are two groups of foreigners in this Catholic neighbourhood: the supporters of Internment Day, who celebrate the British power over the IRA, and the members of the 'Troops Out' movement. Acting as war profiteers, like Brecht's Mother Courage, the women offer those war tourists: 'Rubber bullets? [. . .] Gas masks, riot gear, souvenirs. / Collected with care over many years' (p. 451).

Even though obviously the battlefield of the Troubles seems to be right in front of their doors, they are more concerned with their everyday life problems than with what is going on around them politically. Since they are used to what others might call an emergency state, their lives take their 'normal' courses: 'the parameters of sanity shift and the idea arises that violence has reached an acceptable level'.[9] The most striking of the surreal events in the play is a wedding that takes place in a church nearby – surrounded by the British Army because they suspect the best man to be a fugitive from justice.

In the second act the situation in the besieged church seems to worsen since the bride is about to give birth to a child. Again the three Catholic women – connected to the events in that church by a ridiculous 'can-telephone' – are more worried that the child might be born before its parents are lawfully married than concerned with what the British Army soldiers do (p. 464).

At the end of the play the solution comes in the form of a modern-day *deus ex machina*: together with some of their children and a tortoise, Grandfather Tucker, who has neither spoken nor moved in twelve years, has hijacked a British helicopter and makes sure that the baby is born in matrimony. Here, the stereotypical 'victims' of a war become the heroes of the day. Again the women relax and the play ends with their song 'The Sun is Shining'.

A play showing the 'long-term effect of perpetual violence on the streets',[10] *Somewhere Over the Balcony*'s inside, ironic perspective on the Troubles could be seen as a particular accomplishment of the joint authorship of both Protestant and Catholic playwrights.

The Hamster Wheel (1990)

The Hamster Wheel, a two-act play subsequently adapted for both radio and television, focuses on the changes a family has to undergo after the father has suffered a stroke. It is the last play that Marie Jones wrote for the Charabanc company.[11]

At the beginning of the first act middle-aged Kenny, who has been a lorry driver, comes home from hospital in a wheelchair unable to communicate properly with Jeanette, his wife, and Cathy, his daughter. Initially his role is a silent one and even as time goes on he still has difficulty talking. Even though he is in the centre of the action, the play does not primarily focus on his perspective but rather on that of his wife and his daughter, who from the beginning have very different means of coping with the new situation.

Whereas Jeanette tries to ignore the gravity and permanence of his stroke's effects (p. 195), his adult daughter Cathy quickly focuses on its practical consequences. While her mother is afraid of facing reality, Cathy feels torn between her feeling of responsibility towards her parents and her plan to go to Germany on a scholarship to continue her political science studies abroad (p. 200f.). Other characters in the play are Jeanette's sister, Patsy, and her husband, Norman, who mirror the typical reactions of third parties towards the new situation of a family after a tragic event.

The different attitudes of the characters are shown synchronously in a scene including two dialogues set at different places but which overlap like the four voices in a quartet.[12] The characters in the play 'can't hear each other' (p. 197), whereas the audience is aware of the simultaneity. The spectator feels rather like Kenny: '. . . all he ever hears is muffled voices in the background discussin' him' (p. 225). This dramatic arrangement gives the audience an omniscient point of view in order to make them reflect the different positions in a slightly disillusioning manner. Additionally, it adds a comical twist to the serious topic of the conversations – and grants the audience some comic (or rather grotesque) relief.

This leads to the last scene of the first act, in which wife and husband have a serious conversation for the first time after the stroke. Both have learned to express their fears and hopes. As a result, Kenny decides to overcome his prejudice and go to a day care centre to get some help.

Just at the moment when everything seems to have settled, Kenny has yet another stroke. Jeanette feels as if they are 'back at square one' (p. 258). Hence at the end of the play the images of the wheelchair and the hamster wheel melt into one with the ancient image of the relentlessly spinning wheel of fortune. The final freeze frame, recalling the initial one, indeed suggests such a never-ending story. But since modern scientists would describe time as moving in a spiral-like structure rather than in circles,[13] this, too, is a repetition with a difference: there are some changes visible, as Jeanette has learned to realise the gravity of the situation and that neither she nor Cathy can go through such a situation again without help from the outside.

A Night in November (1994)

A Night in November is a multi-character one-man show dealing with the outburst of sectarian hatred during a football match. The historical background is the match on 17 November 1993, 'that awful night in November' (p. 76), when the Republic of Ireland beat Northern Ireland 3–0 in Belfast. The manager of the Northern Ireland team, Billy Bingham, was criticised afterwards for sparking sectarian hatred, because he conducted the crowd in singing loyalist songs such as 'Billy Boys' in order to boost support for the team.

Shortly before that match, on the evening of 30 October 1993, three masked members of the Ulster Freedom Fighters shot into the crowd in a pub in Greysteel, County Londonderry, killing eight people, one of whom was a Protestant. This situation is presented from the perspective of a fictional character, Kenneth McCallister, a mildly prejudiced Protestant dole clerk, who lives in a Protestant middle-class neighbourhood in Belfast together with his wife Debrah and two children. The actor playing Kenneth takes over the roles of all the other characters as well, which sometimes has a deeply comical effect.

Right at the beginning of the play, Kenneth's fear of the IRA's violence is shown as severely affecting his daily life. He is introduced lying under his car to look for 'explosive devices' (p. 63) and being ridiculed by his wife, who tells him that he is not important enough to be the target of an IRA attack. One could see his initial position, literally lying on the ground before her, as an iconographic reflection of his voluntary subordination to her and the Protestant petit bourgeois social rules she represents. Of course, the arrangement of one actor taking over both roles gives a comical twist to this hierarchical situation. At the end of the play this image is turned upside down: Kenneth leaves their house in Belfast when Debrah lies in bed asleep (p. 96). And his newly developed open-minded superiority to her stubborn narrow-mindedness is taken even further – it takes him off the ground: 'As I walked across the tarmac, my feet were not even touching the ground . . .' (p. 100).

The reason for his inner change on the question of nationality is to be seen in his experience of the football match, which is the leitmotif of the text.[14] Right from the beginning of the match Kenneth realises that the hatred of the Northern Irish fans against their opponents is disproportionate. As the tension rises, the abuse gets worse and begins alluding to terrorist attacks: the opposing football players and their fans are likened to the IRA, by being called 'the men that blow up our peelers or kill our soldiers' (p. 71), whereas the deeds of the Ulster Freedom Fighters are idealised, their killings during the Greysteel attack celebrated like goals scored by sportsmen: 'Greysteel seven, Ireland nil . . .' (p. 71).

This is the initial moment of Kenneth's change, 'his epiphany'.[15] But it takes some time to be completed. Coming back from the match emotionally enraged, he fails to communicate his experience to his wife. In order to keep up his old life, he internally emigrates to 'some insignificant little town in the middle of England' (p. 81). What makes him change this position is his experience of 'crossing borders'. When he goes to a Catholic neighbourhood in Belfast for the first time, he makes friends with his Catholic boss Jerry whose idea of supporting the Irish football team in New York initiates Kenneth's wish to go to the USA as well, together with the fans from Dublin. This makes him – literally and figuratively – overcome the Irish border.

Watching the match together with other Irishmen in an Irish-American pub, he experiences a new feeling of national community beyond political borders, one based on their common support of the

Irish team. He seems to have come of age in finding his national identity: 'even me, even me who never considered himself an Irishman [. . .] I am an Irishman from Belfast' (pp. 103, 107). He even adds the precarious religious aspect into his new self-definition: 'I am a Protestant Man, I'm an Irish Man' (p. 108). What consequences this new insight has on his everyday life are, however, left open at the end of the play.

Stones in His Pockets (1999)

Stones in His Pockets is a multi-character two-man-show divided into two acts. The background action of this 'meta-cinematic drama'[16] concerns an Irish-American film crew occupied with the production of a fictional Hollywood movie called *The Quiet Valley*,[17] set in County Kerry. The plot of the play deals with the backstage story of that movie, which uses American film stars, Irish landscape and Irish 'natives' (p. 42) as extras for creating 'a nice romantic rural Irish scene' (p. 27).

The story is told from the most marginal perspective imaginable at the set: that of two local extras, Jake Quinn and Charlie Conlon,[18] who become, in a reversal of the traditional role hierarchy, not only the two central but in a way all eleven characters of the play: the actors of Jake and Charlie take over all the other roles as well, using only different pairs of shoes to mark the change. Thus in at least two meanings of the phrase this is a 'piece for actors'.[19]

The extras of *The Quiet Valley* dream of getting their share in the film industry. Jake wants to become a film star (p. 22) and Charlie has written his own script (p. 14). But as the story unfolds they have to realise that none of the crew is really interested in them, but only in furthering their own careers. The extras' job is reduced to populating the scenery and – behind the scenes – to coaching the American actors in their Irish accents. Ironically, these accents are not meant to become too realistic in the end because 'you won't get away with it in Hollywood, they won't understand' (p. 15).

The climax of the film crew's ignorance of the protagonists' concerns occurs at the end of Act I in the suicide of Sean Harkin, a young extra eager to find his identity: 'Yis all think yis are movie stars, yis are nothing, I'm Sean Harkin and I am a somebody' (p. 20). Unfortunately, his identity seems to be based on drug abuse. Sean is removed from his local pub because the American actress, Caroline, is afraid of him (p. 47). This makes him feel denuded of all his dreams (p. 43) and causes him to drown himself, 'his pockets [. . .] full of stones . . .' (p. 35). Ignoring their share in the responsibility for the young man's death, the art directors of the movie only reluctantly allow the extras to attend the funeral.

Their ignorance results in the turning point, so that in the second act Charlie and Jake decide to produce their own film, the plot of which – another metadramatical twist in the play – seems to resemble that of which they are the protagonists. The main topic of it is the reversal of traditional film role hierarchies: 'a story about a film being made and a young lad commits suicide . . . in other words the stars become the extras and the extras become the stars . . .' (p. 54).

Thus the play becomes one that breaks on different levels with traditional role hierarchies, but that is not the only topic of *Stones in His Pockets*. The question of Irish identity is discussed here on different levels. To begin with, the Northern Ireland conflict is touched upon in the first scene. Set in the Republic of Ireland, it introduces Charlie as a 'Ballycastle man' (p. 9) from Northern Ireland with 'the RUC' and its 'Special Branch' (p. 9) on his mind. But Charlie has not left the North to escape from the Troubles but because his video shop went broke due to the competition of a multinational franchise company. Hence the Northern Ireland question does not really serve as a modifier of Irish identity in this play. It is rather an ironic twist in the question of Irish identity since Charlie is regarded as 'local' by the film crew but as an 'outsider' by the locals (p. 12f.).

Caroline, the American actress, seems to identify with the Irish culture or what she considers it to be: 'I'm not just here to exploit the beauty of the land, I love it . . . I know the history and the poets' (p. 26). But this is an out-of-date romanticised image of Ireland in which the 'real' cows are 'not Irish enough' (p. 28) and the colonial structures have not evaporated, since the film crew treat the local people as inferiors, partly because they are not considered to be their main consumers: 'Don't worry . . . Caroline . . . Ireland is only one per cent of the market' (p. 13). And even those crew members who are themselves Irish speak about 'the natives' or 'the Irish' (pp. 42, 48) as if they saw their countrymen from the outside. Charlie and Jake reflect on Simon's attempt to escape from his national identity:

> **Charlie** You would think he wasn't Irish.
> **Jake** He just wishes he wasn't. (p. 49)

At the end of *Stones in His Pockets* Jake and Charlie dream about making their own movie, telling their own story and that of Sean Harkin – to escape the reality of the commercial film industry. In Jake's and Charlie's cinematic iconography cows would represent 'real Ireland' as a kind of naturalistic leitmotif or even a kind of 'in-yer-face' cinema: 'So all you see is cows, every inch of screen, cows [. . .] big slabbery dribblin' cows. [. . .] Udders, tails, arses, in your face' (p. 58).

Women on the Verge of HRT (1999)

Women on the Verge of HRT is a two-act play that contains seven songs by Neil Martin. The background to the play is the phenomenon of middle-aged women travelling to a concert of the schmaltzy Irish country singer Daniel O'Donnell. A room of his hotel in Donegal is the setting of the first act, the 'naturalistic first half'[20] of the play. Vera McClure and her friend Anna Morrison, both middle-aged, i.e. 'on the verge of hormone replacement therapy (HRT)', have come there from Belfast to flee their frustrating everyday lives for a weekend. The relationship of Anna and her husband Marty has considerably cooled down and Vera has been abandoned by Dessie, her husband and father of her three daughters. He has left her for a woman twenty-five years his junior with whom he has just had the long-desired baby boy.

In the hotel room the two women discuss their situation. Vera feels that searching for a partner at her age is as desperate as 'going for the groceries at a quarter past five and you hear this voice, "This store will be closing in fifteen minutes"' (p. 5). Rebelling against this situation, she wants the men 'all lined up so I could tell them exactly what they are doing to us' (p. 19). Anna, on the other hand, suggests she 'put up' quietly with everything and look for surrogates such as putting 'all the love into the cat' (p. 7f.), reading 'a good love story' (p. 7) – or talking to Daniel O'Donnell (p. 4).

The second act, 'the expressionistic second half',[21] is set outdoors on '*a plateau overlooking the sea in Donegal. Just before dawn*' (p. 21). This is where Fergal, the waiter, and the two women meet. The howling of the wind in the background is taken by him to be the wailing of the Banshee, who according to the old belief foretells somebody's death (p. 22). This very Irish setting is the scenery for a play-within-the-play: Fergal as an actor or 'shape-shifter' evokes different characters from the women's lives, as if they were in a kind of psychodramatic session. Vera's ex-husband 'Dessie' and his young wife 'Susie' talk to Vera as if they were real characters and 'Marty' appears to Anna. On these grounds they have the chance to do what they wished for: talk to them. Fergal's dramatic aim within the fictional plot is similar to that which Maguire attributes to Marie Jones's (or Charabanc's) plays as such: 'the goal is to empower ordinary people by presenting them with visions of their own lives and heritage, heightened and made significant in theatrical performances'.[22]

In order to distract the women from their self-pity Fergal offers literary relief of a different genre: he tells them the fairy tale of the 'true' reason for the Banshee's wailing – 'she would not accept she was no longer beautiful' (p. 34) – in order to make Vera accept 'the change' instead of 'wailing' about it like the Banshee.

This story-within-the-play helps neither Vera nor Anna and in the end Fergal offers the last remaining literary genre to cure them: he dedicates a love poem to Vera. This, along with his promise that he could love her, seems to cause a mental change in her. But when she wants to give their love a physical dimension by touching him, '*There is a puff of smoke and* **Fergal** *disappears*' (p. 39). At the end of the play the Banshee is still wailing and Anna and Vera join in singing the 'Finale Song', expressing their wish to be heard: 'All we're asking is the right to reply / When we're told our passion must lie down and die' (pp. 39–40). They, too, have found no other solution but 'wailing' – but they put it into a more productive form: a song with a clear message.

Criticising traditional gender roles, the play is placed in the tradition of suffrage drama.[23] Only 'the cause' of the women's fight is not a political message but rather a revolt against their own ageing process.

Accordingly, the ending is neither happy nor tragical but open: the two women sing their finale song, recalling the first song's chorus, which gives the play an apparently circular structure, which means that no kind of catharsis has taken place. But whereas the echoing of the play's opening suggests that everything remains unchanged, there are new stanzas to the song which turn it – as in the *Hamster Wheel* – into a repetition with a difference: the women show some kind of Freudian life instinct (compared to their depressed mood in the first act) as they revolt against death by resisting viewing themselves as being in a 'sex hospice' (p. 39).

The Blind Fiddler (2004)

The Blind Fiddler is a two-act memory play[24] based on an earlier one-act play by Marie Jones called *The Blind Fiddler of Glenadauch* (1990), which was produced by Charabanc Theatre Company. The story of a Catholic Belfast family, which is slowly revealed throughout the play, shows how the social backwater of the Troubles can estrange even an ordinary family. The structure of this drama resembles a Chinese box with a frame story, an inner story and a story within that story. In the frame story, Kathleen, the daughter of the family, then at adult age, is on a pilgrim's journey to Lough Derg (Republic of Ireland) in an attempt to understand why her late father in the last thirty years of his life escaped his family every year for a week in order to embark on a pilgrimage there – even though he was not even religious. In a flashback, the audience gets to know the earlier story of the family. Pat, the father, runs a pub for both Catholic and Protestant customers which is always in danger of losing its better-off Protestant customers for sticking to Catholic habits such as traditional live music. His wife Mary is very ambitious and wants their children Kathleen and Joe to have a better life than this. She forbids her husband not only to play his beloved fiddle in the pub – 'You have bin told – no music in this pub' (p. 4) – but also to speak in the Irish language: 'and none of that oul talk either – it's dangerous' (p. 5). She makes the family move to a supposedly better neighbourhood in Cave Hill Road and pushes the children's school careers and Joe's piano lessons rigorously. Everyone in the house has to follow her rules. Her strategy is partly successful: Kathleen works as a civil servant and Joe indeed becomes a famous concert pianist – but his success estranges him from his family. As an adult, Kathleen learns – only after her father's death – that Pat had never been on a pilgrimage at all but instead fulfilled his own dream of a musical career: he used to go to a music festival to play his fiddle there.

The title of the play thus attains dual meanings: on the one hand, it refers to a story-within-the-story: 'The Blind Fiddler of Glenadauch' (p. 22ff.). This is enacted in Pat's pub as keeping alive Irish oral tradition. This story mirrors the plot of the play by contrasting the same basic principles of either devoting your life to art for art's sake or to the idea of improving your social conditions – but with reversed messages. The blind fiddler comes to a poor family and plays for them. They know that according to popular belief '[y]ou haft to feed and water' him (p. 23). Indeed, the family manages to share their last food and forget their hunger for a while with the blind fiddler playing for them. But in the end, they have to face reality and the son leaves to get work in Belfast.

The 'blind fiddler' is also Pat, with his hidden musical career, who thus becomes a modern version of the 'blind seer' from Greek mythology. The play has been criticised for being sentimental and 'slow-moving'[25] but praised for being a 'reminder that in the rush to do the best for our children we may do them harm by forgetting that education and money are no substitute for love . . .'[26]

Summary

Overall, Marie Jones's plays have a strong socio-political impact, discussing different issues such as gender roles, the ageing process, social justice, responsibility towards other people and national identity. Taking the topics directly from interviewing and observing the people of her community, Jones attains a high degree of authenticity in her plays, a likely reason for their popularity.

The form of her plays is basically realistic with some Brechtian alienation techniques:[27] in the course of them, the characters 'only' learn to express themselves in words a little better and realise the importance of doing so, like Jake and Charlie in *Stones in His Pockets*, who in the end resolve to tell their own story in their own movie.

Marie Jones's plays focus more on telling than on showing, their characters presented by their way of storytelling rather than by their appearance. This can be observed in the development towards plays with one or two characters who are simultaneously actors of all the other characters (*A Night in November* and *Stones in His Pockets*). An earlier stage of this development can be seen in the second act of *Women on the Verge of HRT*, where Fergal acts out the absent characters. The 'possibility of transformation'[28] is therefore the theme of Jones's plays in more than one sense; the protagonists in a way 'dissolve' into their story, tranforming into minor characters. At the same time, the identities of the protagonists within the story are also unstable and in need of transformation.

Jones thus includes challenges for actors. For that reason and because she falls back on other forms of popular culture as well, Lonergan praises Jones's plays as 'amongst the most theatrical currently being written in Ireland'.[29] This is not to deny that her plays are in a very basic sense epic. After all, her characters are storytellers, very good, very Irish storytellers, who make the world a stage. This always seems to have been Jones's idea – from the moment she observed her mother and aunt exchanging gossip in ever new and more dramatic ways:[30] that theatre brings stories to life. And that is what her most recent characters do: essentially they are the onstage fictional narrators of their own stories, bringing vividly to life all the other characters involved. Simultaneously, this dramatic strategy calls upon the audience actively to take part in the process of creating a fictional reality.

Primary Sources

Works by Marie Jones

The Blind Fiddler (London: Samuel French, 2008).

'Court No. 2', in Ophelia Byrne (ed.), *Convictions* (Belfast: Tinderbox Theatre Company, 2000), pp. 9–12.

The Hamster Wheel, in David Grant (ed.), *The Crack in the Emerald:*

A Night in November, in: Marie Jones, *Stones in His Pockets. Two Plays* (London: Nick Hern Books, 2000), pp. 61–108.

Somewhere Over the Balcony, in Helen Gilbert (ed.), *Postcolonial Plays: An Anthology* (London: Routledge, 2001), pp. 443–69.

Stones in His Pockets, in Marie Jones, *Stones in His Pockets: Two Plays* (London: Nick Hern Books, 2000), pp. 5–59.

New Irish Plays (London: Nick Hern Books, 1990), pp. 189–258.

Women on the Verge of HRT (London: Samuel French, 1999).

Secondary Sources

Anon., 'Best receives honorary degree', *BBC News*, 13 December 2001 <http://news.bbc.co.uk/1/hi/northern_ireland/1709558.stm>.

——, 'New honour for Sir Ronnie', *BBC News*, 15 June 2002 <http://news.bbc.co.uk/1/hi/northern_ireland/2045970.stm>.

Aston, Elaine and Janelle Reinelt, 'A Century in View: From Suffrage to the 1990s', *The Cambridge Companion to Modern British Women Playwrights* (Cambridge: Cambridge UP, 2000), pp. 1–19.

Bassett, Kate, 'Killing Paul McCartney/Bombshells/The Blind Fiddler, Assembly Rooms Thom Pain/New Spaces for Role Models/Nine Days Crazy/The Elephant Woman, Pleasance, Harry and Me, Gilded Balloon Birma & Bramati, Traverse – What's So Funny About Pain, Murder and Mania?', *Independent*, 15 August 2004.

Byrne, Ophelia, 'Marie Jones – One of Northern Ireland's Most Successful Playwrights' <http://www.culturenorthernireland.org/ article.aspx?art_id=821>.

Carlson, Marvin, 'The Mother Tongue and the Other Tongue: The American Challenge in Recent Drama', in Jochen Achilles, Ina Bergmann and Birgit Däwes (eds), *Global Challenges and Regional Responses in Contemporary Drama in English. Contemporary Drama in English 10* (Trier: Wissenschaftlicher Verlag Trier, 2002), pp. 151–69.

Gardner, Lyn, 'The Bard of Belfast', *Guardian Unlimited*, 11 August 2004 <http://www.guardian.co.uk/stage/2004/aug/11/theatre. edinburghfestival20048>.

——, 'The Blind Fiddler – Assembly Rooms, Edinburgh', guardian.co.uk, 9 August 2004 <http://www.guardian.co.uk/ stage/2004/aug/09/theatre.edinburghfestival20046>.

Gelder, Lawrence von, 'In Many Guises, a Plea for Peace: Theater Review', *New York Times*, 13 October 1998.

Gilbert, Helen, 'Charabanc Theatre Company: *Somewhere Over the Balcony*. Northern Ireland: Introduction', *Postcolonial Plays. An Anthology* (London: Routledge, 2001), pp. 443–5.

Goodman, Lizbeth, 'Charabanc Theatre Company on Irish Women's Theatres', in Lizbeth Goodman *et al.* (eds), *Feminist Stages. Interviews with Women on Contemporary British Theatre* (Amsterdam: Overseas Publishers Association, 1996), pp. 278–82.

Gussow, Mel, 'Introduction', in Marie Jones, *Stones in His Pockets* (New York, London: Applause, 2001).

Habermas, Jürgen, *Theorie des kommunikativen Handelns* (Frankfurt am Main: Suhrkamp, 1981).

Harvie, Jen, 'Tinderbox's Convictions', *Staging the UK* (Manchester: Manchester UP, 2005), pp. 53–73.

Huber, Werner, 'Contemporary Drama as Meta-Cinema: Martin McDonagh and Marie Jones', in Margarete Rubik and Elke Mettinger-Schartmann (eds), *(Dis)Continuities – Trends and Traditions in Contemporary Theatre and Drama in English. Contemporary Drama in English 9* (Trier: Wissenschaftlicher Verlag Trier, 2002), pp. 13–23.

Irish Theatre Institute (eds), 'Marie Jones (1)', *Irish Playography. Biography* <http://www.irishplayography.com/search/person.asp? PersonID=279>.

Leonard, Garry M., 'Women on the Market: Commodity Culture, "Femininity", and "Those Lovely Seaside Girls" in Joyce's *Ulysses*', *Joyce Studies Annual*, Vol. 2 (1991), pp. 27–68.

Lonergan, Patrick, 'Marie Jones', in Alexander G. Gonzales (ed.), *Irish Women Writers: An A-to-Z Guide* (Westport, CT: Greenwood Press, 2006), pp. 164–8.

Maguire, Tom, 'Marie Jones', in John Bull, *British and Irish Dramatists Since WWII* (Detroit, MI: Gale Group, 2001), pp. 182–7.

Malkin, Jeanette R., *Memory-Theater and Postmodern Drama* (Ann Arbor University of Michigan Press, 1999).

Martin, Carol, 'Charabanc Theatre Company: "Quare" Women "Sleggin" and "Geggin" the Standards of Northern Ireland by "Tappin" the People', *Drama Review*, Vol. 31, No. 2 (1987), pp. 88–99.

McKittrick, David, 'Courthouse Takes Centre Stage as Actors Revisit Horrors of Belfast', *Independent*, 15 November 2000.

McMullan, Anna, 'Gender, Authorship and Performance in Selected Plays by Contemporary Women Playwrights: Mary Elizabeth Burke-Kennedy, Marie Jones, Marina Carr, Emma Donoghue', in Eamonn Jordan (ed.), *Theatre Stuff: Critical Essays on Contemporary Irish Theatre* (Dublin: Carysfort Press, 2000), pp. 34–46.

Middeke, Martin, *Die Kunst der gelebten Zeit: Zur Phänomenologie literarischer Subjektivität im englischen Roman des ausgehenden 19. Jahrhunderts* (Würzburg: Königshausen und Neumann, 2004).

Moylan, Pat, 'Marie Jones in Conversation with Pat Moylan', in Lilian Chambers, Ger

FitzGibbon and Eamonn Jordan (eds), *Theatre Talk. Voices of Irish Theatre Practitioners* (Dublin: Carysfort Press, 2001), pp. 213–19.

Trotter, Mary, 'Women Playwrights in Northern Ireland', in Elaine Aston and Janelle Reinelt (eds), *The Cambridge Companion to Modern British Women Playwrights* (Cambridge: Cambridge UP, 2000), pp. 119–33.

Wilmer, Steve, 'Women's Theatre in Ireland', *New Theatre Quarterly*, Vol. 7, No. 28 (1991), pp. 353–60.

Notes

1. I follow the information given by Patrick Lonergan in 'Marie Jones', p. 164. Other sources claim 1951 to be her year of birth. See Ophelia Byrne, 'Marie Jones – One of Northern Ireland's Most Successful Playwrights'.

2. Tom Maguire, 'Marie Jones', p. 183.

3. Pat Moylan, 'Marie Jones in Conversation with Pat Moylan', p. 213.

4. Marie Jones quoted in Gardner, 'The Bard of Belfast'.

5. The name is taken 'from a benched open-air wagon used in Ireland early in the twentieth century for day trips'. Helen Gilbert, 'Charabanc Theatre Company: *Somewhere Over the Balcony*. Northern Ireland: Introduction', p. 443. About Charabanc's feminist impact see Lizbeth Goodman, 'Charabanc Theatre Company on Irish Women's Theatres', pp. 278–82.

6. It was later published in Helen Gilbert's anthology of *Postcolonial Plays* (2001).

7. See Gilbert, op. cit., p. 444.

8. 'On 9 August 1971, the British government introduced internment to Northern Ireland, allowing the arrest and imprisonment without trial of many Catholics who were suspected members of the IRA. [. . .] Internment Day is now marked, on the anniversary of introduction, every year in Nationalist areas with bonfires' (Helen Gilbert, Notes on *Somewhere Over the Balcony*, in op. cit., p. 469).

9. From the programme to *Somewhere Over the Balcony*, Charabanc Theatre Company (ed.) (1987), p. 3. Quoted in: Mary Trotter, 'Women Playwrights in Northern Ireland', p. 128.

10. Trotter, op. cit., p. 128.

11. See Maguire, op. cit., p. 184.

12. The musicality of this scene is underlined by its ending which, according to the stage directions, requires a '*Musical link to the next scene*' (p. 198).

13. See Martin Middeke, *Die Kunst der gelebten Zeit*, p. 95.

14. The two-act structure of the play relates to the two halves of a football match, and the scenery creates the idea of a football stadium: the backdrop shows a 'football crowd' and the 'terrace' of a stadium. In a German-language production by Arved Birnbaum in April 2006 the play was even set in front of a panoramic window giving a view on the north stand of the RheinEnergie Stadium in Cologne.

15. Lawrence von Gelder, 'In Many Guises, a Plea for Peace: Theater Review'.

16. See Werner Huber, 'Contemporary Drama as Meta-Cinema: Martin McDonagh and Marie Jones', pp. 13–23.

17. The title alludes to Ford's *The Quiet Man* (1952).

18. See Marie Jones's role name in *In the Name of the Father*: Sarah Conlon, a minor character of the movie.

19. Mel Gussow, 'Introduction', p. 6.

20. Lonergan, op. cit., p. 166.

21. Ibid. p. 166.

22. Maguire, op. cit., p. 184.

23. Aston and Reinelt define it as follows: 'The message needed to be clear and immediately accessible, politically instructive, and entertaining, which promoted a style of agitprop comic-realism.' (Elaine Aston and Janelle Reinelt, 'A Century in View: From Suffrage to the 1990s', p. 4f).

24. Kate Bassett calls it a 'memory play' in her review. See Kate Bassett, 'Killing Paul McCartney' (2004).

25. Ibid.

26. Lyn Gardner, 'The Blind Fiddler – Assembly Rooms, Edinburgh'.

27. See Lonergan, op. cit., p. 167.

28. Ibid., p. 165.

29. Ibid., p. 166.

30. Marie Jones, quoted in Gardner, 'The Bard of Belfast'.

8 JOHN B. KEANE

Jürgen Kamm

Sive; Sharon's Grave; Many Young Men of Twenty; The Field; The Rain at the End of the Summer; Big Maggie; Moll; The Change in Mame Fadden; The Crazy Wall; Values; The Chastitute

Introduction

John Brendan Keane was born in Listowel, County Kerry, on 21 July 1928. After his training as a chemist's assistant he took on several jobs as a labourer in England – an experience reflected in some of his later plays – and returned in 1955 to his native Listowel, where he opened up a public house which he ran until his death on 30 May 2002. Much of the raw material for his writing was delivered by his customers, and Keane listened carefully to the stories exchanged in his bar over pints of porter, usually taking notes and making sketches after closing time. In his early autobiography, *Self-Portrait* (1964), Keane writes about his way of working:

> After two years in the pub I started to write again. I would begin at twelve o'clock at night when all the customers had departed. I'd fill a pint and draw the table near to the fire. I started with short stories and poems and I would write till three or four o'clock in the morning, writing a thousand words an hour and drinking a pint every hour, maybe boiling three or four hardboiled eggs if the hunger was prodding me. (pp. 83–4).

This immediacy of writing lends his entire work an astounding degree of authenticity, especially since it is paired with a shrewd sense of observation and the courage to address even unpalatable subjects.

Keane himself firmly believed that all a writer needs is 'heart, guts, courage, and never to be ashamed of himself or of his own people' (p. 95). Keane demonstrated his audacity in different literary genres, notably in poems, satiric essays and in his much-acclaimed novels *The Bodhrán Makers* (1986) and *Durango* (1992), but he is certainly best remembered for his dramatic writings in which he openly addressed a number of pressing social problems such as rural poverty, emigration, gender issues and the concerns of women, the attachment to land, human relationships and the loss of love. Such topics were stimulated by the comprehensive changes that have put their stamp on Ireland and its society since the late 1950s. Keane addressed these various concerns in 'plays set in rural Ireland, but an Ireland torn apart by new psychological growing pains'.[1]

Keane's talents as a writer were widely recognised during his lifetime. He received a Doctorate of Honours from Trinity College, Dublin, in 1977 and a Doctorate of Fine Arts from Marymount College, Manhattan, in 1984. In addition, Keane served as president of Irish PEN and was awarded the title of Honorary Life Member of the Royal Dublin Society in 1991. He was a founding member of the Society of Irish Playwrights, a member of Aosdána, the affiliation of creative artists in Ireland, and an outspoken member of the Fine Gael Party.

The Plays

Sive (1959)

Most of Keane's plays, and arguably his best ones, are informed by the conflict between the characters' desires, ambitions and dreams on the one hand, and their eventual frustration on the other, frequently resulting in agony and torture. These thematic preoccupations can be discerned in his debut play *Sive*, a domestic tragedy set in an isolated farmhouse in the Irish countryside in the late 1950s. The play centres on the eponymous Sive, a young girl aged eighteen, whose mother died when she was an infant and whose father was, so the story goes, killed in a mining accident in England. Having been born out of wedlock and being uncertain of her parentage and identity, Sive is at the mercy of her uncle Mike and her aunt Mena who have raised their niece. However, the domestic atmosphere is far from harmonious since Mena, in her early forties and as yet childless, would like to have the house to herself and would gladly be rid of Sive and her grandmother Nanna. A solution seems to suggest itself when Thomasheen, the local matchmaker, brings news that the old, but rich farmer Sean Dóta has fallen in love with Sive and offers a reward of £200 once the match is concluded. Mena is not willing to forgo this singular chance of marrying off the illegitimate girl and of finally refurbishing her own household comfortably with Sean's money. Despite the protests of her husband and the fierce opposition of her mother-in-law, Mena pursues her stratagem with single-minded determination, and the second act opens with the preparations for the wedding. If Mike has sympathy with Sive, his mother Nanna is even more determined to protect her granddaughter, and with the help of the minstrel-tinkers Pats and Carthalawn she concocts a plan for Sive to elope with her youthful boyfriend Liam Scub, but the design is thwarted by the watchful Thomasheen who does not wish to lose his reward. As Sean appears to pay his respects to his bride, Sive's room is found empty, and soon afterwards Liam carries the girl's dead body on to the stage: she has drowned herself in desperation. The play closes with Nanna silently weeping over the dead body of her grandchild and the tinkers mourning the death of Sive.

The tinkers are interesting characters, representing mythical lore as minstrels, poets and travellers, but also serving as chorus figures. Towards the end of the play, Pats acts as both a character from mythology and a shrewd sociologist who comments on the social changes in the country, which has come increasingly into the grasp of a ruthless materialism and where 'Money will be a-plenty' (p. 84). These social changes affect the characters in different ways. Sive is the tragic heroine who, much like Shakespeare's Ophelia, drowns herself because she cannot solve the conflict between her own desire for emotional fulfilment and the materialistic demands of those sur-rounding her. The suicide of the orphaned girl, however, also destroys the hope of constructing an individual identity for the representatives of the younger generation. Moreover, the tragic conflict is partly fuelled by the characters' resistance to honesty. 'Thou shalt not lie' is a commandment which is disobeyed by the representatives of both the old and the new generation. In this way, Sive may be seen as the tragic victim of two generations of Catholic liars who pursue their individual interests.

Sharon's Grave (1960)

Materialism, gender conflicts, the quest for love and its frequent loss are topics to which Keane returns in the following plays. *Sharon's Grave* is set 'in a small farmhouse on an isolated headland on the south-western seaboard of Ireland' (p. 9). In its reliance on Irish mythology the play is rather indebted to the tradition of Irish stagecraft as advocated by W. B. Yeats and as exemplified in plays such as *Cathleen ni Houlihan* (1902).

Sharon's Grave opens with old Donal Conlee on his deathbed, mourned by his daughter Trassie and his mentally retarded son Neelus. Donal's impending death opens up three interwoven plot lines. The first of these deals with the love affair between Trassie and the itinerant thatcher Peadar Minogue. The second plot line concerns the fate of Neelus, who has the reputation of being popular with the ladies and who has always been fascinated by the mythical tale of the young and beautiful princess Sharon who, as the legend has it, travelled south to meet her future husband, a handsome chieftain, for their marriage. At the centre of the third plot line are the dying Donal's nephews, the deformed and depraved Dinzie Conlee and his submissive brother Jack. Immediately after Donal's death Dinzie attempts to evict his cousins by threatening them with physical and psychological violence. However, his destructive force returns on Dinzie with a vengeance as Neelus, towards the end of the play, carries him off on his shoulders, drowning himself and Dinzie in a deep hole near the coast, the eponymous Sharon's Grave – a ritual death which restores liberty to the legendary characters and, at the same time, sets Trassie and Peadar free to marry and to enjoy both property and sexuality in their own home.

Many Young Men of Twenty (1961)

The topics of emigration and exile touched upon in *The Highest House on the Mountain* (1961) are more thoroughly explored in the following play. *Many Young Men of Twenty* offers a serious criticism of Irish politics, especially with a view to the slackening economy and growing emigration, but it does so, curiously, in the format of the musical, the action being interspersed with numerous songs and recitals. The play is set in the backroom of a public house in the small town of Keelty in southern Ireland run by Seelie Hannigan and her brother Tom. Their maid Peg Finnerty struggles to earn a meagre income for herself and her child since her lover has abandoned her. At the beginning of the play the woeful sons Kevin and Dinny are shipped off by their parents to England. Before Kevin takes his leave he talks to Peg, to whom he is attracted, and he promises to write to her from England. The action in the second act takes place exactly one year later as the boys are expected to return from England for a short holiday. The young Dinny brings his newly married English wife with him, and his brother Kevin continues to court Peg, although she never answered his letters. Meanwhile Peg also receives the advances of Maurice Browne, the new teacher at the local school who is thoroughly disgusted with the way the country is run. He talks himself into a fearful rage which culminates in a sweeping criticism of Irish politics and of political corruption in the 1960s:

> We're sick to death of hypocrisy and the glories of the past.
> Keep the Irish Language and find jobs for the lads that have
> to go to England. Forget about the Six Counties and
> straighten out the twenty-six first. (p. 38)

Towards the end of the play, the majority of the characters decide to leave Ireland for England since there is simply no decent future for them in their own country. In the end, Maurice also offers Peg a future across the Irish Sea, but Peg implores him to stay in Ireland with her and work for a brighter future there. As the last curtain falls '*Maurice Brown and Peg Finnerty embrace*' (p. 46) and their union radiates a faint glimmer of hope in an otherwise dark and depressing scene of emigration and exile.

The Field (1965)

If *The Year of the Hiker* (1963) is concerned with parental irres-ponsibility and the neglect of land, *The Field*, beyond doubt one of Keane's most distinguished plays, offers an impressive analysis of the hunger for land and the desire for survival in a rapidly changing and industrialised Ireland. Keane's international reputation increased sig-nificantly when the play was turned into a highly acclaimed movie in 1990, directed by Jim Sheridan and starring Richard Harris as Bull McCabe and Sean Bean as his son Tadgh. The eponymous field belongs to a local widow who would like to sell it to top up her meagre pension. Mick Flanagan, local publican and auctioneer, promises that he will strike a good bargain, but there is bound to be trouble because 'The Bull' McCabe has used the field for the past five years and is desperate to buy it now. Problems arise with the appearance of William Dee. Born in Ireland, he moved with his Irish wife to England, where he made a successful business career; he has arrived to make a bid for the field himself. While the Bull wants to use the field for pasture, William is keen to invest his capital in order to expand his business by building a factory producing blocks of concrete. Bull and William stand for two diametrically opposed concepts of land use, and the auction develops into a fierce struggle between the representatives of agriculture and of industry, with William eventually offering the higher bid. The Bull is not prepared to accept his defeat. With his son Tadgh he concocts the plan to give William a sound beating in order to frighten him away, while the villagers are intimidated by physical threats into providing an alibi for father and son. However, what was intended as a mild pounding ends up in murder as William dies from the injuries received at the hands of father and son McCabe. From this point on, the play develops into a whodunit with a well-informed audience watching the Bull and Tadgh cleverly shifting the blame on to others.

Unlike in the classic whodunit, the culprits escape scot-free in this case so that, from the point of view of the audience, 'the law is law no more' (p. 74). The Bull's idea of the law is the law of the land and the law of the individual fighting for survival in a rapidly changing world where the likes of William Dee buy land for industrial, rather than for agricultural purposes. The Bull's idea of law and land dates back to an earlier, pre-industrial age when man and land formed a closely knit unit and when landowners took the law into their own hands. However, social and economic conditions in the country were changing in the 1960s. William's death can hardly be read in symbolic terms, since industrialisation began to sweep over Ireland during the decade and not even murder could prevent the growth of industries which would eventually spell out the downfall of the likes of the Bull McCabe, hanging on ruthlessly, if tragically, to an older order.

The Rain at the End of the Summer (1967)

These changes are also reflected in the development of Keane's thematic interests. *The Field* is the last play which deals with issues of land and which is firmly set in a rural farming community, and it concludes the first phase of his dramatic writings. In the five plays which follow, the lonely cottage is frequently replaced by the suburban villa, and instead of farmers struggling for survival, Keane presents the psychological pains of middle-class characters struggling to adapt to a new set of norms and values. This new direction in his dramatic writing is immediately evident in *The Rain at the End of the Summer*. Joss O'Brien had to face the most serious crisis in his life when his wife died nine years ago and he started to drink heavily. However, he managed to overcome his difficulties, largely with the help of his housekeeper Kate, with whom he conducts a clandestine love affair. At the beginning of the play, Joss has arranged his life as a widower and is rather pleased by his smug, bourgeois lifestyle. His eldest son Toddy is a respected solicitor while his younger son Jamesy has taken over the father's prospering business, and his daughter Ellie, the youngest of the family, works as a secretary in the most successful company in the city. This façade of middle-class complacency and respectability is soon demolished as Ellie announces her decision to become a nun and to join the Salutation Order, thus destroying Joss's aspirations to grandfatherhood. While the father still believes that his youthful daughter will change her mind once the right man crosses her path, he is even more shocked by Jamesy's confession of having fathered a child on a young woman who is not even his girlfriend. Joss tries to convince his son that he must show responsibility, marry the pregnant girl and give a name to his yet unborn child, but Jamesy plans to send her to England and to have the baby reared by adoptive parents.

The clash between generations representing different sets of values in the rapidly changing Ireland of the 1960s becomes evident in the diverging attitudes towards the problem assumed by father and son. While Joss, despite Kate's fervent pleas not to ruin the boy's future, firmly insists on Jamesy marrying the pregnant girl, the representatives of the younger generation display a significantly more tolerant approach to sexuality and parenthood. If these representatives are characterised by a more lenient attitude to morals, their response to Joss's announcement of his impending marriage with Kate indicates that such tolerance does not necessarily encompass the parental generation. The conflicts between the characters come to a head in the final act as Joss hits the whiskey bottle again, much to the dismay of Kate, who eventually leaves the house and puts a stop to their previous wedding plans. Instead, Joss, in a state of serious intoxication, reveals to his children his grand proposal to solve all their problems: he is prepared to sacrifice himself by marrying the pregnant girl so that the child will have a home in its own family. However, he is then informed that the girl has been happily shipped off – a notion of happiness which collides with the father's more traditional idea of moral responsibility. In a furious state of excitement he orders his sons out of his house and, indeed, out of his life. The play closes with the stage direction, '(*His right hand stiffens as if he were about to suffer a stroke*)' (p. 72), indicating that the traditional set of moral standards as embodied in the character of Joss is no longer fit to survive in the tolerant climate of the 1960s.

Big Maggie (1969)

The titular hero of *Big Maggie* is the female opposite to the father-figure in *The Rain at the End of the Summer*. At the age of sixty-one Walter Poplin died, leaving behind his wife Maggie, his sons Maurice and Mick and his daughters Katie and Gert. The late Walter, once handsome and rich, had the reputation of being a boozer and a womaniser, much to the chagrin of his wife Maggie, who is quite happy to see him buried. Walter left his family financially well settled, and his widowed wife is determined to run the shop and the farm as a proper businesswoman with an iron fist.

Mick, who had hoped that the farm would be divided between himself and his brother Maurice, bids his family farewell and leaves for England. Katie, her late father's favourite child, is punished for her pampered upbringing and her lax morals in the past. Since Maggie fears that her daughter might be pregnant, Katie is forced into an unhappy marriage with an older man to shield her from public shame. Katie's younger sister Gert is treated in a similar fashion and decides to join her brother in England. With two of her children in enforced exile and Katie tamed into a loveless marriage, Maurice, her elder son, is the last of her children to learn his lesson. His wish to marry the penniless Mary Madden meets with ill-disguised hostility on the part of his mother, who expects a significant dowry from a daughter-in-law. When Maurice tells his mother that for him it is either marriage or exile in England with his brother and sister, Maggie remains unmoved. Finally, the humbled and pregnant Mary pays a visit to Maggie, who takes no pity on the girl because she believes that Mary took the risk of pregnancy deliberately in order to coax Maurice into marriage and to turn her out of her house. Maggie is her own mistress for the first time in her life and she does not intend to lose her independence. She can afford neither pity nor compassion for her children, who will survive only if they are hardened to cope with the cruel, money-grubbing world outside. If Joss in *The Rain at the End of the Summer* despairs at the thought of his unborn grandchild being reared by adoptive parents in England, Big Maggie feels no compunction about pushing her children into exile. In her own way

Maggie does care about her children and grandchildren, but this care is alloyed with a cruelty and heartlessness that her embittered life and changing social circumstances have forced on her.

Moll (1971)

Moll again features a strong-minded female character but otherwise has little in common with *Big Maggie*. *Moll* is a comedy set in the presbytery of Ballast, County Cork, where Cannon Pratt and his two curates are desperate to find a new housekeeper. Eventually they settle on Miss Maureen (Mollie) Kettle, who has previous experience of housekeeping for priests. The play spans four years, during which Moll gradually takes charge of the place until she is eventually in full command. Getting rid of Moll becomes impossible after the bishop is full of praise for the exemplary state of the parish and the progress which his priests seem to have achieved. The play's overall comic note cannot entirely disguise the mild satire on the Church, whose representatives are criticised for being too complacent and too far removed from ordinary life to tackle the problems of a changing society with resolution and modern strategies.

The Change in Mame Fadden (1971)

A distinctly more serious note is struck in *The Change in Mame Fadden*, yet another play set in a middle-class milieu and which again centres on a heroine. It is a domestic tragedy which contrasts questions of social class and public reputation with the human longing for love, tenderness and understanding. Mame Fadden, an attractive woman in her mid-forties, feels that her life is disintegrating around her. Not only does she feel neglected and humiliated by her husband; to make matters worse, she has lost contact with her two sons, Jack and Jim, because 'their precious wives are ashamed of me' (p. 4). In order to find a bit of silence and repose, she regularly visits the quayside along the river at night. Mame's husband Edward and his sons are deeply worried because Mame has been acting in very strange ways lately and insulting the neighbours. Father and sons are afraid that Mame's condition might ruin their reputation in the community, affecting their professional standing and, more importantly, destroying Edward's lifelong wish to be accepted as a member of the Royal Atlantic Golf Club. Mame admits that she feels lonely and that she has no one to talk to. Also she complains that Edward has always kept her short and that she has never been able to enjoy any luxuries. To escape from her mid-life crisis she suggests that they do something crazy, spend money and enjoy themselves. But it is not just the money Mame has missed in her life, and she speaks very openly about her emotional and, indeed, sexual neglect. If she has experienced anything in her life, it is loneliness, and she is afraid of being lonely in old age. She now yearns for a change of atmosphere, but all her suggestions to spice up their lives are sternly refused by her ill-humoured husband, who also forbids her nightly ramblings. To solve his marital problems Edward seeks advice from Canon Doodle, who married the couple twenty-five years ago. When Mame returns home the Canon proves to be knowledge-able in the ways of married couples, gives them a mild lecture, proposes a second honeymoon and finally makes both of them promise that they will be kind to one another from now on. Despite a moment of brief tenderness, the tensions between them soon flare up again as Edward continues to criticise his wife for her irresponsible behaviour. Now bereft of any hope for an emotionally gratifying future, Mame goes for a final walk at night and, like Sive before her, drowns herself in frustration.

The Crazy Wall (1973)

Conflicts between generations and frustrated aspirations also dominate *The Crazy Wall*, another domestic drama set in a middle-class milieu, but with fewer tragic dimensions. The play is set in the small town of Lolinn in the South of Ireland and it opens with a scene in 1963 when the members of the Barnett family have come together for the funeral of their father, Michael Barnett. In the style of epic drama the four brothers Tony, Tom, Lelum and Paddy Barnett, introduce the audience to the setting and the plot and they explain that the last time they were together in their parents' back garden was in 1943 when their father was trying to build a crazy wall. In the second scene of the first act the clock is turned back by twenty years. At this time, Tony serves in the Irish Army, Tom and Paddy attend school, and Lelum whiles away his time doing nothing. In order to keep his family usefully employed Michael has decided to build a wall around his garden, which is regularly used by trespassers and neighbours. What he wants is a bit of privacy for himself and his family, but his friend Jack warns him that other people will want to build walls themselves and that soon the entire street will be walled in. Moreover, building a wall does not only mean keeping people out but also walling oneself in. Not heeding such warnings, Michael is ready to start with the construction of his wall on the following day when bad news arrives: his son Tom has been caught with girls in a neighbouring shed and the school's headmaster has complained about his misconduct.

Michael's wife Mary is furious, but Michael insists on his tolerance in matters of education: he wants his sons to be different from the other boys of their generation, to become observant and sensitive to life. Mary, however, believes that her husband's pretended tolerance is nothing less than an escape from reality: 'When things get difficult you go and build a wall' (p. 45). Consequently, she forces Michael to face the fact that their servant maid Lilly is pregnant and that their son Tom is the most likely candidate as father of the child. Michael must learn the bitter lesson that his sons might all be failures by his own standards: Tony has preferred to remain a private soldier rather than being promoted to officer, Lelum wants to become an actor, Tom is a fornicator, and Paddy a failed poet. With his family life crumbling away, Michael, in a gesture of final fury, grasps a sledgehammer and desperately attacks the wall. Twenty years later, on the occasion of Michael's funeral, the wall is in ruins. However, in 1963, Tony wears the uniform of an army officer and his brothers also seem to have done well for themselves. If the ruined wall appears to symbolise Michael's futile attempt at mastering life, his sons' fond memories of their father and their successful careers indicate that Michael's tolerant education was not entirely fruitless in the end.

9 THOMAS KILROY

Anthony Roche

The Death and Resurrection of Mr. Roche; *The O'Neill*; *Tea and Sex and Shakespeare*; *Talbot's Box*; *Double Cross*; *The Madame MacAdam Travelling Theatre*; *The Secret Fall of Constance Wilde*; *The Shape of Metal*

Introduction

Thomas Kilroy was born in Callan, County Kilkenny, on 23 September 1934. The son of a policeman, Kilroy received his education from the Christian Brothers in Callan before going on to a boarding school on a County Council Scholarship. In 1953, on a University Scholarship from the same source, he went to University College Dublin to take a degree in English. During his summer vacations, Kilroy worked in England and regularly attended theatre in Stratford and London, notably the work of George Devine at the Royal Court and Joan Littlewood at Stratford East. This led him to bemoan the current state of Irish theatre and argue for a more dynamic and radical approach in such influential articles as 'Groundwork for an Irish Theatre', published in 1959 in the Jesuit journal, *Studies*. Having trained as a teacher, he earned the Higher Diploma in Education and from 1959 to 1964 was headmaster at Stratford College in Dublin. In 1965 Kilroy was appointed Assistant Lecturer in the Department of English at his *alma mater* and was soon promoted to College Lecturer. The original plays he had been writing finally came to fruition with two important premieres in the late 1960s: *The Death and Resurrection of Mr. Roche* at the 1968 Dublin Theatre Festival and *The O'Neill* at the Peacock Theatre the following year.

In 1973 he resigned from university teaching to devote more time to his writing. The troubled period which followed is reflected in the portrayal of writer's block and a troubled marriage in his 1976 play, the dark comedy *Tea and Sex and Shakespeare*. In 1977, Kilroy began an important collaboration with the director Patrick Mason in *Talbot's Box* at the Peacock Theatre; the play, based on the life of the Dublin mystic Matt Talbot, was his most formally adventurous to date. Between 1973 and 1979 Kilroy took a number of short-term teaching positions both in Ireland and abroad. One of these was at University College Galway (now National University of Ireland – Galway) where in 1979 he was appointed Professor of Modern English, a position he held until 1989. In the 1980s his playwriting became closely involved with some of the most innovative theatrical companies in Ireland and England: London's Royal Court Theatre, where his version of Chekhov's *The Seagull* was produced in 1981; and Dublin's Rough Magic Theatre Company, for whom he produced a reworked version of *Tea and Sex and Shakespeare*. His most important and sustained involvement was with Derry's Field Day Theatre Company, co-founded by playwright Brian Friel and actor Stephen Rea in 1980. Kilroy provided Field Day with his greatest play to date in 1986, *Double Cross*, interweaving the lives of two Irishmen who reinvented themselves and occupied opposing sides in the Second World War: in a tour-de-force performance, Stephen Rea played both roles, including a London run at the Royal Court. During the 1980s Field Day widened its intervention in the politics of the island through debates, pamphlets and ultimately a multi-volume anthology of Irish literature and in 1988 Kilroy accepted an invitation to join the board. In 1991 Field Day produced a second play by him, *The Madame MacAdam Travelling Theatre*, again set during the Second World War but this time along the Irish border; this had a more mixed reception. In 1992 he resigned from the Field Day board. During Patrick Mason's tenure as artistic director at the Abbey Theatre in the 1990s Kilroy produced, first, a version of Pirandello's *Six Characters in Search of an Author* (1996) and then a play which began as a stage version of Oscar Wilde's novel *The Picture of Dorian Gray* before metamorphosing into an original work, *The Secret Fall of Constance Wilde* (1997). In the 2000s Kilroy has had a new work staged at the Abbey, *The Shape of Metal* (2003) and his version of Frank

Wedekind's *Spring Awakening, Christ, Deliver Us!* is to be staged there in February 2010.

The Plays

The Death and Resurrection of Mr. Roche (1968)

The Death and Resurrection of Mr. Roche was the first Irish play to feature a homosexual on stage, and as such can be seen as exemplary of the greater sexual freedom which the stage enjoyed worldwide in the late 1960s. Although he is the title character, the gay Mr. Roche is not the central one. Rather, the dramatic emphasis is on Kelly, a civil servant engaged in the pursuit of alcohol and amusement after a numbing week at work. The play is also focused on the group dynamic as it surveys the ensemble of after-hours revellers gathered in Kelly's flat. What starts out as horseplay at the expense of Mr. Roche, their belated and unexpected party guest, on the score of his homosexuality escalates when he in turn calls their masculinity into question. The high jinks turn homicidal when Mr. Roche succumbs to an apparent heart attack. While the others are out in the fields trying to dispose of the corpse, Kelly confesses to his best friend that he has had a brief homosexual incident with Mr. Roche and this in turn leads him to reflect on what he has made of his life, the intellectual ambitions he once nurtured. The play lives up to its title with the return of the revived corpse to the flat, miraculously restored after a thunderstorm, and the play ends with Mr. Roche firmly ensconced in Kelly's armchair, answering his phone. Kilroy's play took a resolutely contemporary look at the Ireland of the 1960s, not only through tackling the then-taboo subject of homosexuality but through its forensic examination of the other (heterosexual) males, who rely for a sense of self on a boisterous camaraderie and the Saturday-night ritual of drinking themselves blind to their condition. To this extent the play is naturalistic, with a keen ear for the sharp wit and casual obscenity of male conversation. Increasingly, the play chafes at those naturalistic boundaries as it seeks to offer a spiritual diagnosis of the characters and society it is representing, never more so than when the resurrected Mr. Roche speaks of the experience of transformation and new birth he has undergone out there in the fields: 'And – it [the sun] came! Like the beginning of life again. A great white egg at the foot of the sky. Breaking up into light. Breaking up into life. Consider the mystery of it' (p. 72). A clear precedent here is the drama of T. S. Eliot and the staging of the rituals of Greek tragedies in the drawing rooms of the contemporary English upper middle classes. Even though a struggle to accommodate the mystical in the mundane is evident in both plays, Kilroy's grasp of his lower-middle-class demotic is assured and his comedic instinct stronger. *The Death and Resurrection of Mr. Roche* made for a stunning debut and was staged the following year at London's Hampstead Theatre. The Abbey Theatre mounted a mainstage production in 1973, a revival in 1989, and in 2004 chose it to represent the decade of the 1960s in a series of ten staged readings for the theatre's centenary. And on the occasion of Brian Friel's eightieth birthday in 2009, he nominated *The Death and Resurrection of Mr. Roche* as one of the plays which had most inspired him.

The O'Neill (1969)

One of Kilroy's declared aims as a writer is to examine what he perceives as 'a failure to achieve a wholeness of community in the Irish experience'. This motive helps to explain why he should have started out as a dramatist by writing a history play in *The O'Neill*. (The play, though staged after *The Death and Resurrection of Mr. Roche*, was written first.) Kilroy goes back to Ireland in the sixteenth century and examines the conditions which contribute to a lack of community through the emblematic figure of the Earl of Tyrone, Hugh O'Neill, 'called The O'Neill by the Irish in their ancient fashion' (p. 12). The question that animates Kilroy's play is how this figure could have led a rebellious Irish army to victory against the English at the Battle of the Yellow Ford in 1598 when he had been expatriated and bred up to a civilised ideal at the court of Queen Elizabeth I. *The O'Neill* instigates a retrospective inquiry into what caused the change of loyalties by focusing on the complex nature of Hugh O'Neill as an

Anglicised native and hence the locus of two conflicting ideologies of Irishness and of Englishness. As in so much of Kilroy's work, the vision is double, shifting from the more obvious external conflict between the individual and the demands of his society to the conflicts within that individual. One strong aspect of the conflict between the old Gaelic order into which Hugh O'Neill was born and the new world of the English Renaissance in which he was raised hinges on issues of gender and sexuality. For Hugh desires and is determined to take as his wife Mabel Bagenal, much younger than he is and not Irish but English, a member of the English planter stock who have seized Irish land. The strength of desire that Hugh articulates not only breaks with propriety but is the spur to drive him beyond all inherited political and family loyalties. The attraction is reciprocal: O'Neill is longing for the 'good order and civil security' of English society, Mabel for the 'romance' of Ireland. But his decision to make Mabel Bagenal his third wife and to impose her on his people has the opposite effect from integrating and reconciling the conflicting halves of his personality; rather, it drives them apart. In the play's second act, the conflict shifts to the political and the military as a dramatic interplay is developed between O'Neill and Lord Mountjoy, the man sent over by the English to deal with the situation. The dramatic seeds of the *doppelgänger* or double motif Kilroy would so brilliantly orchestrate in *Double Cross* (1986) are present here between the Irish chieftain and the English lord and emerge through the play's carefully wrought symmetries of scene and speech. The concepts of victory and defeat have no real meaning for O'Neill or Mountjoy as each is increasingly isolated on the stage, mutually trapped in tragic recognition of the atavistic forces released by the conflict between the Irish and the English.

Tea and Sex and Shakespeare (1976)

Kilroy wanted to treat of the conflict between individual and society, and the essentially artificial nature of the self. To do so required a much greater degree of theatrical freedom from the naturalism to which his first two plays had largely adhered. In *Tea and Sex and Shakespeare* the explicit subject of writer's block paradoxically generated the greatest range of theatrical effects in Kilroy's work so far. From its opening image of a mock-hanging, the play declares open season on the norms of naturalism and proceeds instead to pull rabbits out of hats – or surrealistically dressed characters out of a cupboard or wall. A base of reality is provided through the character of Brien and the play's central situation of a man alone in a room, writing. Brien attempts to preserve his isolation against a pressing world but repeatedly fails to do so, as a wide range of characters force their way onstage: his wife Elmina and her parents, the landlady Mrs O and her nubile daughter, Deirdre. Brien only slams one door to open another: the Pandora's (theatrical) box of a large onstage cupboard out of which emerge surrealistic versions of all the forces against which the beleaguered writer is trying to secure himself. As Brien and the play ask: 'Am I inside or outside or what?' (p. 21). The play he is seeking to write, like *Tea and Sex and Shakespeare* itself, requires a whole range of theatrical representation: mime, costume, music and stylised imagery. As always in Kilroy, the crucial issue of identity is bound up with the struggle to devise an appropriate theatrical form. Brien in comic desperation tries to deal with his married life to Elmina and the various guilts it has engendered while the play explores the intimate connection between his literary and sexual impotence. Part of his neurosis, and a reason for Shakespeare's presence in the title, is the attempt to keep rewriting his own life as a version of *Othello*. He casts himself in the role of the jealous, insecure husband, Elmina as his Desdemona, and the Anglo-Irish neighbour Sylvester as a psychologically and culturally intimidating Iago. But if Brien convinces himself he is inhabiting *Othello*, the play itself pushes in the direction of a late 'dark' Shakespearean comedy such as *The Winter's Tale*, where the self-generated tragedy of a Leontes is reworked by confessedly artificial means into a comic resolution. *Tea and Sex and Shakespeare* climaxes when the other characters force from Brien the secret hurt at the heart of his imaginings, one which can be exorcised only by a final gust of purgative laughter. The ending draws audaciously on Wilde's *The Importance of Being Earnest* and its missing handbag to disclose a baby over which Brien weeps real tears. The baby is transparently an artificial one, a dummy.

Talbot's Box (1976)

If the figure of the blocked writer was rather too close for comfort, Kilroy's choice of Matt Talbot in *Talbot's Box* provided a figure with whom it was difficult for him to identify: a Dublin working-class mystic who burdened himself with the trappings of devout Catholicism – chains, scapulars, fasting, daily Mass – to the point of eccentric extremism. In dramatising such a life, Kilroy challenged his own sympathies while choosing a public figure who held a recognised place in the affections of his Irish audience. *Talbot's Box* begins in a morgue with the title character's body already laid out for burial, the other four members of the cast assembled to perform the last rites. But the stage form adopted is not narrowly mimetic. Rather, the action is framed with '*a huge box occupying virtually the whole stage*' (p. 9) and Kilroy develops this as a resonant theatrical metaphor. The box suggests in turn a coffin, a confession box, a witness stand, a wooden bulwark constructed by Talbot the carpenter against the encroaching chaos and Tom Kilroy's own box of theatrical tricks, with the props and stratagems of the playwright's trade openly on display. A statue of the Virgin Mary speaks up to enquire: 'How long do I have to stand like this?' (p. 9). The answer is 'not long' since each actor apart from Talbot is called on to play many parts in the course of the drama. The play from the start is Talbot's dream in his long sleep of death and as in the act of dreaming, one identity readily blurs into another and the figures who gather about his reanimated body are in part the fevered, accusatory fragments of his past. In a series of retrospective scenes, Talbot struggles first with the potentially lethal legacy of his father's drunkenness, then with the more equivocal family claims of brother and sister, finally with a young chambermaid whose offer of a shared life is rejected. Talbot is subject not just to familial pressures but to social ones. In the trial-like situation which emerges and places him in the witness-box, the charge most frequently levelled against him is that of strike-breaking. For one of the several specific time-periods with which the play aligns itself is 1913, the time of the Dublin Lock-Out from which the Irish Labour Movement dates its origins. Matt Talbot's private mysticism cannot readily be assimilated to the social protests of his fellow-workers. The forces ranged against him bring Talbot to his knees and culminate in a series of physical assaults: first, the littering of the dazed figure with a pile of religious texts, then a full-scale assault on the box itself, as we sense but do not see the collective force of a large crowd pressing on its (and Talbot's) outer limits. None of the nets of explanation or inquisition flung at Matt Talbot succeeds finally in capturing or defining him, a suitably Pyrrhic outcome for a play which relentlessly examines its own processes and the effort to render a singular vision public as drama. Talbot recognises the violence in himself and others and sees it as proceeding from a 'terrible hunger' for what others might have. In turning to look for what is missing inside himself, he learns to embrace that darkness: "'Tis because I wanta meet the darkness as meself. [. . .] I think meself the darkness is Gawd' (p. 47).

Double Cross (1986)

Kilroy's earlier plays ultimately endorse the singular vision of a Roche or Talbot by setting it against the claims of a conformist society. Such radical individuality is a good deal more suspect, and its social implications gauged in a more political way, in *Double Cross*, the first of Kilroy's two works for Field Day. Of the play's two roughly contemporary Irish protagonists, Brendan Bracken and William Joyce, the first became Churchill's Minister for Information in the Second World War while Joyce adopted the persona of Lord Haw Haw in his notorious radio broadcasts from Nazi Germany. In Kilroy's theatrical representation, both rely uniquely on the power and projection of their voices as a means of self-realisation. This lends an ironic appropriateness to their fates, one killed by cancer of the throat, the other hanged as a traitor. Brendan Bracken's story occupies the first half. English – specifically London – society has always proved, in Kilroy's words, 'susceptible to the charm of a master Thespian' (p. 12); and so Bracken is presented as in the line of Anglo-Irishmen from Farquhar to Wilde and Shaw who made their way by means of on- and offstage theatricalisation to a position of influence in English society. The transfer involves the shedding of Irish identity and a complete reinvention of the self. As a result, the role is an actor's delight, since Bracken responds with a different face or rather voice to each encounter. The question dramatised by the scenes with his lover Popsie is whether there is a stable, enduring identity behind all the protean impersonations. While Bracken plays the time-honoured Anglo-Irish role of court jester to English society, William Joyce in Act Two (the same actor is to play both roles) seizes on his more absolute displacement and the medium of radio to delight in the possibilities of subversion at every level. As Lord Haw Haw, he takes pleasure in detonating verbal bombs in the primed imaginations of the British public. He finally scripts his own end by handing himself over. Preferring to submit to trial and execution, he perversely confirms his fabricated identity as a subject of the British crown. Through Bracken and Joyce, Kilroy demonstrates the inevitability of self-betrayal in the course of any movement outwards towards a world of possibilities. Bracken speaks eloquently at one point about distance and space as freedom; but the play notes that the results may be either criminal or artistic. Even as art, the aestheticisation of that choice is a denial of history. Each character becomes not a free individual who has shed his Irish past, but someone who has traded in the role of historical victim for the mirror-image of oppressor and placed all his faith in the symbols of the culturally dominant race. Both Bracken and Joyce have mastered those symbols, as signified in the fluency of their language, and become their perfect embodiment for demonstration through the media. *Double Cross* began life as a radio play, *That Man Bracken* (1986). But staging it gives Kilroy the opportunity to subject the histrionic appeal of voice as presence to a full battery of deconstructive and demystifying effects. Theatrical embodiment offers the possibility of a true doubleness which admits the other, the presence which both Bracken and Joyce's endless subjective monologues seek to crowd out and deny.

The Madame MacAdam Travelling Theatre (1991)

Five years later, Kilroy offered in his second Field Day play, *The Madame MacAdam Travelling Theatre*, not so much a sequel to *Double*

Cross as its parallel or counterpart. Also set during the Second World War, this play returned the scene to Ireland and more explicitly used theatrics and costuming as a means of interrogating questions of identity. It centres on a theatrical troupe which has just crossed the border from a Northern Ireland directly involved in the conflict into an independent Ireland committed to neutrality. But the play will not allow for that kind of absolute separation; it opens in unlocalised space and the sound of a bomber flying overhead. Madame MacAdam and her consort Lyle Jones are English. Lyle gets to play all the lead parts in the Shakespearean or melodramatic scenarios they perform, while Madame MacAdam accompanies on the piano or fills the lesser roles. But offstage it is Madame MacAdam who gives Lyle his directions, whose name fronts the troupe and who maintains its equilibrium. The gender dynamic which began to emerge in *Double Cross* is coming to the fore in terms of artistic partnerships. The English troupe has crossed the Irish Sea to Belfast, where they have acquired Sally, whose Northern Irish accent and perspective are used to disturb any absolute distinction between the English players and the Irish locals. The other key member of the troupe is Rabe, from England, but Jewish, whose abiding memory is the burning of his father's shop by Blackshirts. The apocalyptic imagination which drives Rabe allows him no respite or hiding place in Ireland, and he has found only temporary refuge with the players. For, as the play vividly demonstrates, Ireland for all of its proclaimed neutrality is not immune from fascism. The visit of the theatricals has had a disturbing effect upon the local community, as is demonstrated through the blurring of gender and identity boundaries as much as the political. The most serious example of this crossover between theatre and life is the manoeuvrings throughout of the uniformed Local Defence Force and of Bun Bourke, local baker and squad leader. At the end of Part One, in a chillingly effective theatrical coup, we see projected '*in silhouette, the figures of Bun Bourke and his LDF men but now in Nazi uniforms*' (p. 49). The shadows of war, of Fascism and of Nazism, which the florid onstage theatrics and the Irish setting keep in the background, here dominate the foreground. The shadows fall on Ireland, which is not immune, and on the naked, terrified figure of Rabe, who is in bed with the young local girl Jo in their travelling caravan. The 'real' Bun, who has consistently denounced the amorality and reality-shifting of the theatricals, lurks outside, ready to expose them. Jo is the most overlooked character in the play and, despite the fact that she wears heavy glasses, the most clear-sighted. This quirky, determined, comically serious young woman, teetering over from adolescence into adulthood, has an ability to intuit the future which links her with Rabe sexually and with Madame MacAdam psychically. After the players have departed and the town returned to normal, the pregnant Jo is the one who is most fully attuned to that future. She stands out in the play's crowded ensemble and might have had the direction of the play more fully entrusted to her.

The Secret Fall of Constance Wilde (1997)

Constance Wilde (née Lloyd) has been consistently sidelined and erased in almost every account of Oscar Wilde. Kilroy has undertaken in this play consciously to redress that balance, to place the passionate and probing intelligence of Constance at the dramatic centre while Oscar for once is sidelined. Kilroy has drawn throughout on mime, choreography, abstract and symbolic design to do so. But most daringly of all to the three human figures of the tragedy, Constance, Oscar and his lover, Lord Alfred Douglas ('Bosie'), he adds puppets – small white puppets to represent the two boys and *'a gigantic puppet [of] a Victorian gentleman, red cheeks, black moustache, bowler hat, umbrella [and] frock coat'* to represent the play's oppressive patriarchs. These puppets are manipulated onstage by six attendant figures wearing *'white, faceless masks'* who remain present throughout and (it is suggested) are also 'Figures of Fate' manipulating the lives of the three human protagonists. The play is framed by Constance and Oscar both seriously ill and near the end of their comparatively short lives. He is broken by the years in prison, she by the mysterious 'fall' down the stairs in their beautiful white house in Tite Street. Husband and wife confront one another over an abyss, of the graves which they are about to enter, of the past which they must seek to enter once again. Kilroy views the three characters at its centre as all fleeing from

Victorian patriarchs: Constance's respectable father, had up on a charge of sexual abuse; Sir William Wilde, only briefly referred to by his son ('I despise my father'); and Bosie's father, the Marquess of Queensberry, whose pursuit of Oscar provokes the libel suit the latter brought against him, disastrously as it turned out. In seeking to escape their pasts, the three characters are doomed to repeat them and carry them forward into their subsequent relationships. Constance is offered a role as sister by Oscar but insists on that of wife. As she acknowledges, she has been cast – by her husband and society – in the role of the 'good' woman 'who ran away with her children, away from the horror, the filth; the good wife who kept him in money throughout even while he betrayed her'. As she increasingly comes to realise, it is a process in which she herself has colluded and which she now seeks to redress. Constance has been mute witness to the embraces Oscar has shared with Bosie before the play brings wife and lover together in a series of charged encounters. Each wants to be all-in-all to Oscar but has to concede that each has access only to separated areas of his multiple personality. Constance and Bosie are the two sexual and psychic opposites between which Oscar Wilde oscillates. For Oscar, the perfection of the home life they have built together offers him a refuge from the fleshly reality he pursues in the streets of London. It is a perfection Constance must finally refuse. Her 'fall' is as much sexual as actual: into knowledge of the sexual variations her husband practises with other men and into an admission of the sexual abuse she has suffered in her own family household. *The Secret Fall of Constance Wilde* offers a brilliant meditation on the contrasts between role-playing in life and in the theatre. It also allows for an ethical probing of guilt and of the conflict between body and soul.

The Shape of Metal (2003)

In Kilroy's most recent plays – *The Madame MacAdam Travelling Theatre*, *The Secret Fall of Constance Wilde* and an unproduced play on William Blake – women have come to the fore, but all of them have remained helpmeets to the male artists at their core. The plays, however, have increasingly dramatised a process of the female usurping on the male, protesting at the absolute identification of the artist with the masculine principle. In *The Shape of Metal* the central character Nell Jeffrey claims the autonomy so long accorded male artists. Nell is an eighty-two-year-old sculptor and the setting throughout is her studio, cleared now of all but a single piece, which is shrouded. In the play's extended flashback to 1972, we see the sculptor actively at work as a dynamic fifty-two-year-old. But even in her decrepitude, with her hands too weak to work, Nell is still trying to shape some meaning, not only out of metal but out of the mess which is her life. Like Tom Murphy's *Bailegangaire* (1985) and Brian Friel's *Dancing at Lughnasa* (1990), *The Shape of Metal* is centred on female energies and three women, Nell and her two daughters. The youngest, Judith, now in her forties, is alive and present throughout, an active force driving and goading her wayward mother to confront and tackle issues she has shirked. One is the issue of her paternity. Nell Jeffrey has never married, has had multiple sexual relations throughout her life and more than one father for her two children. At one level, she has claimed for herself the same freedom from traditional sexual mores as the male modernist artist; at another, she has left tangled emotional wreckage in her wake for her children to deal with. This is also a play about artistic fathers, with Nell reminiscing about her meeting with Swiss sculptor Alberto Giacometti in Paris of the 1930s. The meeting was facilitated by a family friend called Sam 'who was childishly pleased to show his two Dublin gels . . . the artistic sights. All the Becketts are like that.' In this way, Kilroy ingeniously creates life tissue for Nell Jeffrey, a great artistic figure who never existed (unlike Wilde or Blake). But Samuel Beckett is a singularly important figure for Thomas Kilroy: their theatre is constructed out of empty space which is filled with human sounds and man-made objects. Beckett once defined his artistic imperative as finding a form to accommodate the mess. Nell Jeffreys speaks in *The Shape of Metal* of 'a lifetime trying to create perfect form'. Thomas Kilroy has always striven with form but there has always been a central human conflict at the core of his drama. Here, form and feeling converge in the tragic figure of Nell's other daughter, Grace. She never appears directly in the present of the play, only as a twenty-five-year-old in the flashback, where her chronic depression is already all too evident. The play opens with Nell calling out Grace's name in her sleep while she dreams of her daughter pleading with her 'to sculpt my head, Mummy, as promised'. The Grace who speaks onstage does so not in the flesh but as an illuminated speaking head, a live sculpture, as it were. Nell is confronted with the perfection of art as that which she has always sought: something finished, complete, dead. Grace's words confirm this even as they mock Nell for her failure to address her daughter's suffering in life rather than remove it through art.

Summary

The premieres of two successive plays in the late 1960s, *The Death and Resurrection of Mr. Roche* and *The O'Neill*, announced the arrival of a singular new talent on the Irish dramatic scene. Thomas Kilroy has always stood out as a playwright committed to the urban and the modern rather than the rural and the nostalgic, a playwright of ideas in the European tradition and a radical experimenter in form and language, but one who has also trained his satiric eye on Irish society and the pressures it exerted on the individual vision. His plays were influential on fellow-playwrights: Brian Friel followed Kilroy's *The Death and Resurrection of Mr. Roche* with a gay couple in his 1971 play, *The Gentle Island*; and was later to write his own stage play about Hugh O'Neill, *Making History* (1988). Kilroy won an initial following with these two plays. Their radical implications were somewhat concealed by the efforts of both protagonists to identify with the group. Their ultimate failure to do so, and the existential crisis they undergo as a result, points the way to the development of the later works. In *Tea and Sex and Shakespeare* and *Talbot's Box* the central figure is already an outsider, an eccentric, and the dramatic emphasis falls on those isolated figures and their interrogative impact on society. To treat of the conflict between the individual and his society and of the essentially artificial nature of the self required a much greater range of theatrical freedom than the conventions of naturalism would allow. In Kilroy's plays of the 1970s, there is a sense of both the central characters and of the playwright breaking free of the bonds of naturalism into an overtly theatrical realm – where dead characters stand up, where apart from the central character all of the actors rapidly trade roles and costumes, where realistic dialogue can give way to monologue and chant, and where the bodily movements of the actors are halfway to mime. All of his plays thus far have engaged with the notion of personal freedom, of resisting the pressures of social conformity and marking out a space of existential possibility. These issues have been dramatised through such socially displaced figures as the homosexual, the writer and the Catholic mystic. In *Double Cross*, such radical individuality is a good deal more suspect and its social implications gauged in a more political way, with its two Anglo-Irish outsiders taking on roles in British and German society. As Kilroy makes clear in his notes on the play, he perceives Bracken as an actor, Joyce as a writer, 'a creator of fictions'. Role-playing on stage and in society is further linked in *The Madame MacAdam Travelling Theatre* through its emphasis on costuming; if the actors disturb the other characters through the ease with which they trade roles, it is the donning of military costume by some of the townspeople that instead asserts dominance and control. After his two Field Day plays, Kilroy returned to Ireland's national theatre with *The Secret Fall of Constance Wilde* and *The Shape of Metal*. His lifelong concern with the man of vision has increasingly developed into an explicit engagement with the figure of the artist; Kilroy's fertile theatrical experimentation is deeply linked to the challenge of representing those visions on stage. The plays of the 1990s and 2000s dramatise an ever greater emphasis on the human cost of such a pursuit. As the title of Kilroy's Wilde play indicates, Oscar is not the centre of this particular drama, however much he would like to be; instead, Constance's tragedy takes centre stage. Most of *Blake* is set in an asylum, where the incarcerated artist is being scrutinised by the authorities; but the most sustained scrutiny is being directed at him by his wife, Catherine. In both of these plays, the women perform a traditional role in relation to the male artist, a combination of helpmate, mother and muse. But in *The Shape of Metal* Kilroy crosses the gender divide in attributing artistic agency to a woman, the fictitious sculptor Nell Jeffrey. Her fraught relations with her two daughters are brought into fruitful interchange with the artistic process she enacts on stage. Nowhere has Kilroy's view of the stage as a place where form and feeling meet been rendered with more clarity.

Primary Sources

Works by Thomas Kilroy

The Death and Resurrection of Mr. Roche: A Comedy in Three Acts (London; Faber and Faber, 1969).
Double Cross (London: Faber and Faber, 1986).
Ghosts (after Ibsen) (Oldcastle: The Gallery Press, 2002).
Henry (after Pirandello, *Henry IV*), in Thomas Kilroy, *Pirandellos: Two Plays* (Oldcastle: The Gallery Press, 2007).
The Madame MacAdam Travelling Theatre (London: Methuen, 1991).
My Scandalous Life (Oldcastle: The Gallery Press, 2004).
The O'Neill (Oldcastle: The Gallery Press, 1995).
The Seagull: A New Version (after Chekhov) (London: Eyre Methuen, 1981).
The Secret Fall of Constance Wilde (Oldcastle: The Gallery Press, 1997).
The Shape of Metal (Oldcastle: The Gallery Press, 2003).
Six Characters in Search of an Author (after Pirandello), in Thomas Kilroy, *Pirandellos: Two Plays* (Oldcastle: The Gallery Press, 2007).
Talbot's Box, with Author's Note (Dublin: The Gallery Press, 1979).
Tea and Sex and Shakespeare (Oldcastle: The Gallery Press, 1998).

Secondary Sources

Bertha, Csilla, 'Thomas Kilroy's *The Shape of Metal*: "Metal . . . Transformed into Grace"', *Brazilian Journal of Irish Studies/ABEI Journal*, Vol. 9 (2007), pp. 85–97.
Cosgrove, Brian, 'Ego Contra Mundum: Thomas Kilroy's *The Big Chapel*', in Patrick Rafroidi and Maurice Harmon (eds), *The Irish Novel in Our Time* (Lille: Publications de l'Université de Lille III, 1975–76), pp. 297–309.
Dubost, Thierry, *The Plays of Thomas Kilroy: A Critical Study* (Jefferson, NC: McFarland and Company, 2007).
Etherton, Michael, *Contemporary Irish Dramatists* (Houndmills: Macmillan, 1989).
Hayley, Barbara, 'Self-Denial and Self-Assertion in Some Plays by Thomas Kilroy: *The Madame MacAdam Travelling Theatre*', in Jacqueline Genet and Elisabeth

Hellegouarc'h (eds), *Studies on the Contemporary Irish Theatre* (Caen: Centre de Publications de l'Université de Caen, 1991), pp. 47–56.

Hunt Mahony, Christina, *Contemporary Irish Literature: Transforming Tradition* (Houndmills: Macmillan, 1998).

Kilroy, Thomas, 'Groundwork for an Irish Theatre', *Studies: An Irish Quarterly*, Vol. 48 (1959), pp. 192–8.

—, '*The Seagull*: an Adaptation', in Vera Gottlieb and Paul Allain (eds), *The Cambridge Companion to Anton Chekhov* (Cambridge: Cambridge UP, 2000), pp. 80–90.

Long, Joseph, 'An Irish *Seagull*: Chekhov and the New Irish Theatre', *Revue de Litterature Comparée*, Vol. 64, No. 4 (1995), pp. 419–26.

Maxwell, D. E. S., *A Critical History of Modern Irish Drama 1891–1980* (Cambridge: Cambridge UP, 1984).

McGuinness, Frank, 'A Voice from the Trees: Thomas Kilroy's Version of Chekhov's *The Seagull*', *Irish University Review*, Vol. 21, No. 1 (1991), pp. 3–14.

Murray, Christopher, 'Thomas Kilroy's Worlds Elsewhere', in Jacqueline Genet and Wynne Hellegouarc'h (eds), *Irish Writers and Their Creative Process* (Gerrards Cross: Colin Smythe, 1996), pp. 63–77.

—, *Twentieth Century Irish Drama: Mirror up to Nation* (Manchester: Manchester UP, 1997).

—, 'Thomas Kilroy', in Anthony Roche (ed.), *The UCD Aesthetic* (Dublin: New Island Books, 2005), pp. 173–8.

Roche, Anthony, 'The Fortunate Fall: Two Plays by Thomas Kilroy', in Maurice Harmon (ed.), *The Irish Writer and the City* (Gerrards Cross: Colin Smythe, 1984), pp. 159–68.

—, *Contemporary Irish Drama: Second Edition* (Houndmills: Palgrave Macmillan, 2009).

— (ed.), Special Issue on Thomas Kilroy, *Irish University Review*, Vol. 32, No. 1 (2002).

Sampson, Denis, 'The Theatre of Thomas Kilroy: Boxes of Words', in Jacqueline Genet and Richard Allen Cave (eds), *Perspectives of Irish Drama and Theatre* (Gerrards Cross: Colin Smythe, 1991), pp. 130–9.

Trotter, Mary, '"Double Crossing" Irish Borders: The Field Day Production of Tom Kilroy's *Double Cross*', *New Hibernia Review*, Vol. 1, No. 1 (1997), pp. 31–43.

Welch, Robert, *The Abbey Theatre 1899–1999: Form and Pressure* (Oxford: Oxford UP, 1999).

10 HUGH LEONARD

Emilie Pine

The Au Pair Man; *The Patrick Pearse Motel*; *Da*; *Summer*; *Time Was*; *A Life*; *Kill*; *Moving*

Introduction

Hugh Leonard is the pen-name of John (Jack) Keyes Byrne, who was born in Dublin, 9 November 1926. Leonard began writing plays for amateur productions, until 1956 when he submitted *The Big Birthday* to the Abbey Theatre, Dublin. By then Leonard had made a name for himself as a dramatist, particularly with the production at the Dublin Theatre Festival of *Stephen D* (1962), a version of Joyce's autobiographical works *Stephen Hero* and *A Portrait of the Artist as a Young Man*. In *Stephen D*, Leonard played with stage conventions and impressionistic techniques in an accessible style, a format that would inform much of his own original drama in later years. In 1968 *The Au Pair Man* was produced at the Dublin Theatre Festival with success and in 1970 the Leonard family returned to Ireland. Leonard's association with the Dublin Theatre Festival was strong, having contributed a total of eighteen plays to the festival, and this link was further established when he served as Programme Director in 1978. In the 1970s, Leonard had considerable dramatic success, the highlight of which was *Da* (1973), which won the Tony award for best play in New York in 1978 (two other plays, *The Au Pair Man* and *A Life*, were also nominated, in 1974 and 1981), and was later made into a film, starring Martin Sheen, in 1988, for which Leonard wrote the screenplay. In later years, many of Leonard's plays have been revived, in particular *Da* and *A Life*. Leonard's most recent play is *Love in the Title* (1999). In addition to his dramatic works, Leonard wrote a weekly column for the *Irish Independent*, entitled 'Leonard's Log'.

Leonard's prose output included the publication of his columns in book form and several novels, as well as several books of auto-biographical writings, including *Home Before Night* (1979) and *Out After Dark* (1989). He died at home in Dalkey on 12 February 2009.

The Plays

The Au Pair Man (1968)

Set in London, *The Au Pair Man* dramatises the relationship between Mrs Elizabeth Rogers and Eugene Hartigan. Hartigan, an Irishman, comes to Rogers's home to repossess an item of furniture that she has not paid for. Rogers feigns innocence and invites Hartigan to apply for the position of au pair man, to fill the position of her often absent husband. In lieu of payment, Rogers offers to tutor Hartigan in the art of being a gentleman, while he reciprocates with sexual favours. Hartigan believes that Rogers is grooming him so that he can be a gentleman in public society, and in particular dreams of returning to Ireland to impress his family, yet he is disturbed to learn that Rogers intends to keep him as her au pair man 'indefinitely'. Hartigan leaves the house and embarks upon his own career and becomes involved with an upper-class girl named Rose. However, he is brought back to Mrs Rogers's home when she faces eviction and he encourages her to sign the rights to her home away, so that she can be moved unproblematically to the suburbs. Mrs Rogers retaliates by revealing that she has used her niece Rose to deceive Hartigan so that she might manoeuvre him back into her own life, and the play ends with his acceptance of his enslavement to her, as he puts the signed lease into the bin and takes up his position as the au pair man once more.

The Au Pair Man is Hugh Leonard's first major play, and its mix of clever wordplay, sexual farce and focus on class sets the tone for much of his later work. The play picks up on the *Pygmalion* myth, using the Irish–English divide to replace the class division of Shaw's play, as at one point Mrs Rogers comments on Hartigan's unfortunate 'colonial accent' and refers to her education of him in colonising terms reminiscent of Shakespeare's *The Tempest*, as she says that '[y]our mind was a blank page and I wrote my name on it' (p. 58). Hartigan's rationale for wanting to improve himself is his impoverished background and his sense of social inferiority. Mrs Rogers is well aware of this and uses it to her advantage, playing on his insecurity when she makes comments such as 'You possess [. . .] [t]he rich, good taste to despise yourself' (pp. 65–6). It seems in Act III when Hartigan returns as a polished businessman that he has not only escaped her control, but has outstripped his teacher by achieving respect and status. Mrs Rogers's home, a symbol of her allegiance to the British Empire, is crumbling, the walls are buckling from the 'increasing pressure' on both it and the Empire. Humorous touches include the doorbell, which chimes the British National Anthem, displaying simultaneously the all-encompassing nature of Empire and its reduction to a jingle. Mrs Rogers faces being 'put out' of her home, a symbolic demolishing of the Empire at the hands of one of its former subjects, and she fears that her kind is becoming 'extinct' (p. 83). Yet, her final triumph and her ability to control not only Hartigan, but also her niece Rose, reveals the residual power of the Empire. Mrs Rogers's enslavement of Hartigan also displays a favourite Leonard trope of farcical sexual relations in the upper middle classes, a trope that he later transferred to an Irish setting.

The Patrick Pearse Motel (1971)

The Patrick Pearse Motel opens in the Gibbons' living room as the Gibbons and the Kinnores listen to the sound of a ping-pong game being played in stereo on a new and very impressive sound system that the Gibbons have recently bought. Dermod Gibbon and Fintan Kinnore are business partners who are about to open a motel, named after the Irish patriot, Patrick Pearse. The partners hope to exploit the connection to Pearse and plan to name the other rooms after other Irish martyrs, such as Robert Emmet. The motel is also graced with a restaurant called the Famine Dining Room. Dermod and Fintan are planning to travel to Cork to purchase another motel, leaving their wives at home to keep each other company. However, Grainne

Gibbon, though she seems an affectionate and devoted wife, has plans to have an affair with television celebrity James Usheen and spend the night with him in the Patrick Pearse Motel. This is foiled when Fintan intercepts a letter written between Grainne and Usheen and jumps to the conclusion that it's about his own wife, Niamh. He sidetracks Dermod so that they all end up in the Patrick Pearse Motel, and a farcical chase ensues in which Grainne attempts to seduce Usheen, Niamh tries to hide, Dermod tries to find Grainne and Fintan tries to find Niamh. Into this mix are added Miss Manning, the English manager of the motel, who tries to seduce Dermod, and Hoolihan, the night-watchman. Eventually, it turns out that Miss Manning is James Usheen's former fiancée whom he left because he couldn't face marrying a divorced woman and the threat of excommunication from the Catholic Church. Through Manning's machinations, however, they are reunited, and both married couples are reconciled as well. Usheen promises that he will launch the motel on his television show and the venture seems personally and professionally successful.

The Patrick Pearse Motel is a Feydeau-esque bedroom farce, mocking the new Catholic middle-class aspirations to wealth and taste. The play makes very real W. B. Yeats's accusation that the middle class 'fumble in a greasy till', by displaying the avarice of money-driven businessmen Dermod and Fintan. At the end of the play, Miss Manning is able to convince the men to forgive their wives, whom they assume have been adulterous, on the basis that the scandal will negatively affect the launch and financial prospects of the motel. The men's need to put commercial concerns first and their marriages second is a mockery of their supposed Catholic and Republican morals. For, though it is primarily a farce on the sexual mores of the Irish bourgeoisie, the play also satirises the mythologisation of Irish history and the empty rhetoric of Irish republicanism. Fintan is disgusted when the night-watchman Hoolihan, himself a veteran of the 1916 Rising, is not as reverential as he should be towards Pearse and the heroes of the Rising, saying 'wasn't Mr Pearse full of ou' codology [. . .]?' (p. 140). Yet Hoolihan is quite clearly correct in his observation that the new generation of Republicans, claiming that the motel is 'the fulfilment of the dreams of the men who died for this green island' (p. 158), are really only in it for the money. Hoolihan declares that 'Yous lot has more sense. I do like to see the big motor cars and the women with all the rings [. . .]. If I hadda had brains, I'd be rich too, because it's the best nationality' (p. 140). Leonard offers a satirical view of the Irish bourgeoisie and the values they espouse. Moreover, he suggests that the Irish are willing to use their national heritage for economic, rather than moral or spiritual, gain.

Da (1973)

The play dramatises the homecoming of the middle-aged Charlie for his father's funeral. The play opens as Charlie sorts through the detritus of his father's life: old bills and letters. Charlie's father, however, refuses to let death banish him and his ghost returns to haunt his son. He can be seen and heard only by Charlie in the present and Charlie is aghast at his continued presence. The ghost of Da moves between the present and other fragments of Charlie's memories that we see played out on the stage, so that the play exists in two time frames. Leonard manipulates the stage so that these two time frames coexist in the kitchen of the family home, and other parts of the action occur to the side of and above the kitchen, a 'neutral area, defined by lighting' (p. 12) that can represent multiple locales, and a bench which denotes the sea front. In one key scene, the adult Charlie and Da re-enact one of Charlie's memories in which he confides in his father that he's afraid his biological mother will return and claim him. Other memories are of the day his father retired and was given a paltry pension by the Protestant family he had worked for for fifty-four years. Young Charlie grows up, gets married and is offered a job by Drumm, a civil servant. He moves abroad to London and becomes a successful playwright, returning only for the day of his father's funeral. At the end of the play, having tidied his father's affairs and remembered his childhood in the house, Charlie leaves, locking the door behind him. However, his father's ghost follows him and though Charlie is returning to England, there is no absolute resolution as Leonard suggests that the ghost of Da will always be with him.

Da is Leonard's most autobiographical play. When *Da* was staged in Ireland in 1973 at the Dublin Theatre Festival it gained him not only commercial success, which he was used to, but critical plaudits also, for its exploration of growing up and coming to terms with your past. Leonard himself was an adopted child, something he had kept secret all his life. The play also matches his career as he moved from the civil service to being a writer in London. The autobiographical nature of the play gives it a meaning and seriousness beyond the farce of earlier plays, and the fears of Young Charlie are very real ones, that his identity is somehow insecure. This compares with the exploration of Ireland's post-colonial past and the insecurity of national identity, as represented in the plays of, for example, Brian Friel and Tom Murphy. For Charlie, there is both shame and strength in being adopted – he remembers his mother's 'party-piece' in which she describes how she 'took him out of Holles Street' maternity hospital against the advice of her mother and raised him so that he was a 'credit to us' (p. 29). The autobiographical content of the play meant that Leonard was under public scrutiny now as a character as well as writer, and Charlie's situation may have been one way of Leonard working through his own recent return to Ireland from London. There is thus a personal bravery to *Da* that underscores the black humour of the play and makes it, perhaps, Leonard's most lasting.

The device of father, son and younger self in dialogue brings into focus the contrast between the dreams of youth and the realities of old age, as well as the inevitable generational misunderstandings and lost opportunities to express love and find connections. Young Charlie and Charlie in the present talk to each other, across the chasm of youth and age, and Young Charlie is predictably disappointed in what he became, all 'dried up. Dead.' Leonard manipulates stage conventions, yet maintains the unity of place, keeping the play's experiment with chronology and flashback within a safe framework of a recognisable family and home. This is a device that he would later use in *A Life*, in which the character of Drumm reappears. Though *Da* is a departure in terms of its serious tone, certain themes are consistent with Leonard's comedies, such as the debilitating power of social status and class.

Summer (1974)

The play is set in two time frames; the first act takes place in 1968, while the second act occurs in 1974. Both acts take place on a hillside overlooking Dublin, as three families share a picnic on a summer's day. In Act I the couples reminisce about their younger days, discuss their children and health. Myra and Jess White have three young children who have stayed at home, though Myra is missing them, while the Halveys and the Loftuses have brought their teenage son and daughter, Michael and Lou. The group goes for a post-prandial walk, while Michael and Lou stay behind and discuss philosophy and deem themselves far superior to their parents. Jan Loftus and Richard Halvey are the first to return from the walk and they argue about whether or not they should start an affair. When the others join them, Stormy Loftus comments on the boom in the building industry, while it becomes clear that Jess is the least financially secure of the group. Stormy tries to give Jess money, but is rebuffed.

As Act II opens, six years have passed and the hillside has changed – a Celtic Cross has been removed, and there are fewer trees, suggesting that the area is zoned for development, another sign of the building industry expanding. The group are initially put off by the changes and aren't sure if it is even the same place. Lou has also changed, losing so much weight that she is at first not recognised by the others. As the act progresses, it is revealed that she has been discarded by her husband, is pregnant and determined to get her husband back. In the intervening six years, Jess's health has not been good and he is still struggling financially, especially as his daughter is about to get married. He asks Stormy for a loan but is disgusted when Stormy refuses to lend him the money and proposes instead to give it to him. Richard has recently ended the affair with Jan, against her wishes, and when she gets angry with him, Myra overhears and realises about the affair. Myra is a devout Catholic and is scandalised. When she tries to tell Stormy and Trina Halvey, however, they refuse to believe her, telling her that she made a mistake, at which she becomes extremely upset. The play ends with the couples dancing, Jan and Richard with each other, Trina with Stormy, and Jess with Myra.

Summer is Leonard's favourite among his own plays, and was written so that it would be as if the audience were merely eavesdropping on a group of people. As a result, the action is minimal, with the emphasis on the exchanges between characters. The gap of six years allows Leonard to darken the tone, so that Jess's financial insecurity in the first act becomes a real issue in the second, and in each act he has an altercation with Stormy over money. Jess's health has also suffered in the intervening time, leading him to worry about death, again heightening the sense of decay. This is also brought out in the relationship between Jan and Richard, which was in Act I a source of promise and potential, but is in Act II bitter and exhausted. Myra is held up in the play as the only character with religious faith, and Leonard illustrates the distance between the image of Ireland as a Catholic nation and the attitude of most Irish towards religion. When Myra is shocked by what she overhears between Jan and Richard, the others assume that it is her naïveté, though Jess simply tells her that it's none of her business, implying that he realises the truth. Stormy and Trina are the most successful in business, as Stormy's building business has expanded, while Trina runs a prosperous boutique. As a result, their refusal to believe Myra's revelation is perhaps due to their own concerns outside their families. The play's tone is gentle, but there are signs of changing Ireland – Lou faces a future as a single mother, while the expansion of Dublin city has literally changed the landscape, and not necessarily for the better. *Summer* uses the double time frame to map these changes and to diagnose the mood of contemporary Ireland in the mid-1970s.

Time Was (1976)

Set on a summer evening in the wealthy south Dublin suburb of Killiney, *Time Was* satirises the fascination with nostalgia and all things past. Two couples, P.J. and Ellie, and John and Bea, return to the former's house for an after-dinner drink. John works with the government and hints that recent scandals of disappearing people in North America, Britain and Ireland are linked to each other, and somehow connected with the current vogue for nostalgia. The four characters get their own taste of this when P.J.'s reminiscences about his childhood cause the appearance of Tish, a woman he remembers all too powerfully. Tish has been whisked from 1949 to the present day and her appearance creates much confusion, until John reveals that so many people from the past have been appearing spontaneously in the present, caused by people longing for the past, that the government has had to create a refugee camp for them in a remote part of the country. P.J. then adds to the confusion when he summons up Harry, a Foreign Legion soldier from *Beau Geste*, an old film set in the desert. Unfortunately for the foursome, Harry is accompanied by a band of Arabs who attack the house and shoot John, whose ear is badly injured. The humour in this episode has dated in regard to its racial politics, though the Arab characters never appear onstage. The comic resolution to the play is assured, however, when P.J. accidentally conjures up the United States Cavalry from the film *She Wore a Yellow Ribbon* and the 'Yanks' rescue them from the siege situation. By the end of the play, Harry and Tish team up and head off into their own modern sunset, but the ending is bittersweet for Ellie, as her husband's nostalgia becomes so strong that P.J. gets his wish and returns to his own past, disappearing out of the present and leaving Ellie alone. Two decorators appear at the end, looking like Laurel and Hardy, and signalling that P.J. has gone permanently.

In *Time Was* Leonard picks up on the central themes of *The Patrick Pearse Motel* and *Summer*, combining the farce and the superficial desire for a heroic version of the past of the former, with the sense of lost youth and love in the later play. *Time Was* effectively satirises the infatuation with the past and the notion that life used to be better: homes were secure, values were intact, and the future was full of hope. Indeed, it is this last issue that emerges through P.J.'s reminiscing about his youth and, in particular, when he and Ellie first met and fell in love. Their current situation is clearly at a deadlock as they rehearse the same lines and events day after day and weekend after weekend. What P.J. wants to recapture, in his return to the past, is the sense of a future. Though the character of John decries the willingness of people to believe in the past as a better, simpler or freer place, there is something seductive about P.J.'s personal nostalgia. The results of this nostalgia, however, though at times hilarious, are more often disastrous, including the loss of John's ear-lobe and the ending of P.J. and Ellie's marriage. It is clear in the play that the deleterious effects of nostalgia are not limited to Ireland, but prevalent elsewhere also, but at the same time, by targeting nostalgia, Leonard displays his concern that Irish culture in particular is overly backward-looking. The device of the two decorators reflects Leonard's enjoyment of playful structural devices, and looks forward to the two movers who provide the chorus in *Moving*.

A Life (1979)

In *A Life* Leonard revisits the same landscape as *Da*, and one of the earlier play's marginal characters, Desmond Drumm, now becomes the centre of the drama. Drumm has a terminal illness, but cannot confide in his wife Dolly about it. Instead, he chooses to confide in his old friend Mary. In recent years Drumm has fallen out with Mary over his dislike of her husband Lar Kearns. Drumm is determined, however, to make good the friendship again instead of wasting his last days quarrelling with her. In tandem with these scenes, Drumm also reminisces about his youth, before he was married, and his love for Mary. The remembered scenes reveal that Mary had feelings for Drumm, but his overly serious manner and inability to express himself led to her marriage to the easy-going but prospectless Lar instead, while the young Desmond had to settle for the naïve and adoring Dorothy. Yet at the end of the play Mary reveals how Drumm had his subtle and unconscious revenge, as he fostered their son Sean's reading and education, paying for his schooling and slowly turning Sean against his father, as the young boy copied Drumm's distaste for Lar.

Like *Da*, *A Life* strikes a more serious tone than Leonard's farces. Drumm was a serious and slightly resented figure in the earlier play, but here we see the other side of him and realise that he is vulnerable. As in *Da*, too, there is the double time frame, in which the old man Drumm can see his own past being enacted, while he is also an actor himself in the present world. Drumm was too serious as a boy, and is now a bitter man. He is depicted as unable to soften himself, except occasionally with Mary, and he suffers for this both in terms of an uneasy relationship with others and with himself. Yet despite his stand-offishness, Leonard is making a point about the way in which those who want to be different by being intelligent and serious can isolate themselves. While Lar Kearns in contrast is open and easy-going, it is also clear that Mary has not had an easy life with him. Their son Sean's emigration to England is, at the end of the play, revealed to have taken place because he suspected that he might have been Drumm's biological son, and it is clear that Drumm felt much more affinity with him than with his own two daughters. *A Life* is low on action, but functions instead as a character study, charting the disappointments of four different characters, in particular Drumm and Mary, neither of whom has ended up with the life anticipated in youth. Drumm, at the end, asks Dolly what his life has amounted to, sure that he has achieved nothing, but perhaps at the end the audience is allowed a glimpse of the small joys of their relationship, which is a small achievement in itself.

Kill (1982)

Kill is Leonard's most political play, dramatising a dinner party at the house of the Taoiseach (Prime Minister), who is revealed to be both corrupt and linked to a paramilitary terrorist organisation. The Taoiseach, Wade, hosts the dinner party, with the help of his assistant, Therese, in order to consolidate his stewardship of the estate he currently lives on. However, he has let the land and house run down and, as a result, faces being evicted. Judge Lawless is on the trustee board that decides on Wade's tenancy, but his wife Madge is determined that Wade should lose the estate. Wade is also determined and enlists Tony Sleehaun to help him manipulate Madge into a situation where she has to support his continued tenancy. Wade's other concern is that the estate become unified, by repossessing the alms house which stands at the entrance to the estate and which has been taken over by others – currently it is occupied by Mort Mongan, a terrorist intent on destruction. Mongan makes a couple of appearances during the party, and intimidates the guests, who also include a bishop masquerading as a parish priest, and Iseult, a musician who plays the saw. Mrs Wade also makes an appearance, but she is barely aware of what is going on. The dinner party descends into chaos, and Madge withstands Wade's many attempts to persuade her, until he finally finds a way of blackmailing her, by implicating her in an explosion that Mongan has set off.

The play is a thinly disguised comment on the tenure of Charles Haughey as Irish Taoiseach, while the relationship between the estate and the gate lodge is an allegory for the cause of the reunification of the Republic of Ireland with the six counties of Northern Ireland. The house – a deconsecrated church – represents a laicised Ireland. The Taoiseach is depicted as pandering to both the Catholic Church and the arts, and through this pandering, ensuring their support for his machinations. Each time Wade contradicts the logical explanation for events, giving instead his own corrupt version of the facts, Father Bishop acquiesces, while Iseult Mullarkey is concerned only with her own pseudo-spiritual and mythological music. Though the play is a black comedy or farce, Leonard spells out the allegory on the opening page, arguing that it is a 'lampooning – more accurately a harpooning of Irish attitudes towards the North' (p. 380). Leonard was vocal in his opposition to the IRA and what he saw as an accepting and casual attitude towards it by the majority of the people in the Republic. The final triumph of Wade is an apt illustration of his opinion that it is the figures of political power in Ireland who have fostered this attitude and who will continue to harbour the terrorists in order to move closer to the promise of reunification, which is here reduced to the ridiculous image of a run-down estate and its alms house.

Moving (1992)

Moving depicts one family's physical and social movements, first into a house on Martello Road in 1957 and secondly into a grander house on Martello Lawn in 1987. Both moves represent an achievement in terms of economic and social status. Although there is a thirty . . . year gap between the two parts of the play, the characters do not age, and they act out the same values and issues, though the details are different in 1957 and 1987: the family remains essentially the same, but some roles are altered, in particular John Turvey and Colleen/Ingrid Quirke. The Removals Man and his Assistant function in the play as the Chorus, watching and commenting on the family's changing status, and beginning and ending the play.

In 1957 Ellie Noone has to be cajoled into the new house by her upwardly mobile husband Tom; she is made slightly nervous by the increase in space and living standards. By 1987 Ellie has grown into her role and inhabits the grander house of Martello Lawn with ease. Tom and Ellie's children Karl/Carlos and Madeleine are confident and clear about their own roles in the future and they give the play a lightness and optimism. There is also conflict within the family, as Ellie's mother Mary Quirke turns up drunk in Part One, bemoaning the loss of her 'favourite' daughter Colleen, and claiming Madeleine's bedroom as her own, while in Part Two Mary is much more dynamic and does not live with them but comes to call with her daughter, 'poor' Ingrid. In Part Two the spectre of the dead Colleen is entirely absent, and instead Ingrid plays the role of the once attractive sister now past her best. Tom's attitude to Ellie's sister in Part One is wistful; it's implied that he was secretly in love with Colleen and married Ellie as a consolation prize when Colleen died; Colleen appears only briefly before the curtain falls on Act One, still eighteen years old and radiant, in Tom's imagination. In Part Two, however, there are signs of friction between Tom and Ingrid, as Tom resents her attempts to flirt with him and her belief that she could have married him had she wished.

In Part One, John Turvey is a family friend and local teacher, who is also an avid Irish speaker, keen to remind people of the value of the past, as well as the future. In Part Two, John is cast as a controversial figure as, since revealing his homosexuality, he has lost his job as a teacher. When he is supported by the children and Tom, Ellie reacts angrily, revealing that despite her modern appearance, she still holds outdated and bigoted views.

Moving confirms again Leonard's focus on the family, highlighting through character study and dialogue their subtle interactions and viewpoints. The gap of thirty years enables Leonard to depict changing social outlooks, though Ellie's anger towards John, and her determination to bar him from her house, reveal an ugly and illiberal outlook. In both parts, Tom is a businessman who pushes forward his family's upward mobility, while Ellie is more anxious about the potential for financial disaster. The gap in years also displays, as the Removals Man points out, that families are always the same, despite changes in outward appearances.

Summary

The central topics of Hugh Leonard's dramatic work are: class, hypocrisy, family and sexual politics. Leonard's plays, after *The Au Pair Man*, are set in and around Dublin and represent the Catholic middle class, particularly concentrating on the domestic lives of the urban middle class of south County Dublin. Leonard's comedies satirise this class, which he ironically referred to as 'the new Quality'. His comedies point out the amorality of this new class and their naked pursuit of wealth. Plays like *The Patrick Pearse Motel, Summer* and *Moving* give a portrait of this class against the background of a rapidly changing Irish culture, which Leonard diagnoses as the simultaneous growth of property development and extra-marital affairs. In *Kill* Leonard is at his most severe, highlighting the empty rhetoric and moral corruption of the dominant political and social classes. His writing in these plays is cutting and sharp, making witty and acid lines its *modus operandi*.

Leonard's work also has more serious notes to it, particularly in *Da* and *A Life*, which are both set in a wealthy Dublin suburb, but instead focus on those who are not part of the monied landowning class. These two plays bring to the fore issues of family and emotional vulnerability, not always evident in some of Leonard's farces. However, aspects of *Summer* and *Moving* do combine Leonard's satirical eye with a degree of sympathy and seriousness, as when Lou Loftus is facing the future as a single parent, or John Turvey loses his teaching job because of his sexuality.

Another key element of Leonard's work is the use of the double time frame, as in *Da*, *A Life*, *Summer* and *Moving*. This technique clearly shows the changes that characters have undergone, from the distortions of their early hopes and ambitions, to the evolution of a family and their relationships. This bi-temporality also allows Leonard to catalogue the pace of Irish social change. A play such as *Moving* clearly shows that the expansion of the Irish economy has not necessarily led to a more liberalised social outlook.

Despite Leonard's popular success, driven by his desire to entertain audiences, he occupies a marginal position in the Irish theatrical canon. On the one hand, Leonard's body of work has been consistently well received by audiences, his plays have won awards, and he has been described as a 'major playwright of international importance', yet on the other hand, despite these accolades, Leonard's work has given rise to minimal critical scholarship. One explanation for this is that Leonard's plays simply do not fit into the dominantly realist or naturalist context of plays that represent the experiences of colonialism, post-colonialism and emigration. Moreover, their modern, urban focus stands apart from the predominantly historical and rural dramas of other notable Irish playwrights. However, in recent years Leonard's achievement has perhaps come into clearer focus, and this may be due to a greater interest in farce, as evident in the popular and critical success of Martin McDonagh. Leonard's enormous body of work certainly makes him one of Ireland's most popular and prolific playwrights, if not its most critically lauded.

Primary Sources

Works by Hugh Leonard

The Au Pair Man, in *Selected Plays Hugh Leonard* (Gerrards Cross: Colin Smythe, 1992).
Da; A Life; and Time Was (Harmondsworth: Penguin, 1981).
Kill, in *Selected Plays: Hugh Leonard* (Gerrards Cross: Colin Smythe, 1982).
Moving (London: Samuel French, 1992).
The Patrick Pearse Motel, in *Selected Plays Hugh Leonard* (Gerrards Cross: Colin Smythe, 1992).
Summer (London: Samuel French, 1979).

Secondary Sources

Chaillet, Ned, 'Hugh Leonard', in D. L. Kirkpatrick (ed.), *Contemporary Dramatists*, 4th edn (Chicago, IL: St James, 1988).

Pine, Emilie, 'Leonard's Progress: Hugh Leonard at the Dublin Theatre Festival', in Nicholas Grene and Patrick Lonergan (eds), *Interactions: Dublin Theatre Festival 1957–2007* (Dublin: Carysfort Press, 2008), pp. 47–60.

11 MARTIN LYNCH

Tom Maguire

The Interrogation of Ambrose Fogarty; Castles in the Air; Welcome to Bladonmore Road; Rinty; Pictures of Tomorrow; The History of the Troubles (accordin' to my Da)

Introduction

Since his earliest work in the late 1970s, Martin Lynch has created a body of work rooted in the working-class culture of his native Belfast in both its content and its formal properties. His life and concerns as a dramatist echo those of his predecessors, Thomas Carnduff and Sam Thompson. He comes from a working-class background; he learnt his craft as a playwright without a substantial formal education or any training as a dramatist; and his work is marked by a socialist perspective. Born in the city in 1950, he was brought up initially in the York Road area, until his family was relocated to Turf Lodge, one of Belfast's peripheral housing schemes.[1] The seventh of twelve children, when he left school at fifteen, he was apprenticed as a cloth-cutter, worked as a casual labourer in the docks and in a variety of temporary jobs, interspersed with periods of unemployment. His working life as a dramatist began despite a very limited experience of theatre, and yet he has sustained a career over thirty years through a body of work which has included some of the most popular plays produced over the period.

It was through his activism with the socialist Republican Clubs movement that Lynch first engaged with the theatre. He helped organise a community tour around Belfast of Arden and D'Arcy's *The Non-Stop Connolly Show* in 1975. Then, a year later, he was persuaded by friends to see Patrick Galvin's *We Do It for Love* at the Lyric Players' Theatre. The epic form of each excited him. As he deepened his own reading of Marx and James Connolly, he began to see drama as an instrument through which working-class political consciousness might be developed. With a small group of fellow-activists, he formed the Turf Lodge Fellowship Community Theatre, initially writing and performing skits and sketches around local clubs. Their first play, penned by Lynch in 1976, was the short epic piece *We Want Work, We Want Bread*, a title taken from the slogan of the hunger marchers during Belfast's Outdoor Relief Riots in 1932. It was followed by *Is There Life Before Death?* which depicted the barren prospects of six teenagers from Turf Lodge on the cusp of leaving school. The Fellowship went on to produce three further plays by Lynch: *What About Your Ma is Your Da Still Workin'?*, *They're Taking the Barricades Down* and *A Roof Under Our Heads*. Through this engagement with the process of writing, Lynch achieved a double shift in his development as a playwright: away from political abstraction and into his own lived experience as the source of his inspiration. It is this avoidance of programmatic politics and his celebration of the working-class culture around him that mark his subsequent career as a professional writer.

Lynch's professional debut came with *Dockers* (1981), following his appointment as writer-in-residence at Belfast's Lyric Players' Theatre in 1980. Both it and its successor, *The Interrogation of Ambrose Fogarty* (1982), demonstrate Lynch's developing craft, particularly under the influence of Sam McCready at the Lyric. This was recognised, too, in the approach by the founding members of Charabanc Theatre Company to write a play for them in 1982, which eventually was jointly authored by Lynch and the company as *Lay Up Your Ends* (1983). At the time, Lynch was being fêted as a Northern O'Casey[2] and he took up a further writer-in-residence post at the University of Ulster between 1985 and 1988. Since then, his output has included work for film (*A Prayer for the Dying*, 1986), radio, and significant community theatre projects, such as *The Stone Chair* (1989) and *The Wedding Community Play*.

Lynch's work as a writer has been accompanied by a continued commitment to providing a platform for the development of theatre accessible to a popular audience. Thus, alongside a sustained engagement as a writer with community arts projects, such as the 1994

Bonjour Mucker, a play written in close association with delinquent boys from St Patrick's Boys' Home, west Belfast, he was founding chairman of Northern Ireland's Community Arts Forum.

The Plays

The Interrogation of Ambrose Fogarty (1982)

In *The Interrogation of Ambrose Fogarty*, Lynch engaged directly with the violence of Northern Ireland's political conflict. The play shows the brutal treatment of a terrorist suspect, Ambrose Fogarty, while he is being held without charge by the police under Northern Ireland's anti-terrorism legislation. Alongside Fogarty, the police are holding Willie Lagan, a country and western singer who had been inadvertently caught up in a riot and arrested by the British Army. The play exposes the methods by which the police's Special Branch forced confessions out of people being interrogated or implicated them by pressuring others into testifying against them. While Fogarty has had a record as a Republican activist, the play ends with Lagan being charged and held. Lagan's innocence indicts the system which allows his incarceration. The play was controversial, however, not just because it exposed police interrogation methods, but also because it sought to humanise the ordinary policemen and -women. This is achieved through the rivalry between Constable Davy McFadden and the British Army officer, Captain Levington, for the affections of policewoman Yvonne Lundy; and through the avuncular Sergeant Knox, who dreams of walking down the street to police the community.

Castles in the Air (1983)

In *Castles in the Air*, Lynch reworked *A Roof Under Our Heads* for professional production. A lack of quality public housing had arguably been the spur to the political violence in the North, and Lynch clearly delineates the personal cost to the Fullerton family of living in crowded and damp conditions in Turf Lodge. Mary Fullerton is struggling to raise her adult daughter Pauline, teenage son Eddie, and their two younger siblings. Separated from her brutal husband Frank, she is recovering from the violence he meted out to her and her own abuse of drink and pills. Despite constantly pestering the Housing Office, there seems little prospect of her being rehoused and when Eddie is caught joyriding, her problems are only multiplied. Lynch is careful, however, not to present a uniform picture of the working class as innocent or long-suffering victims. Pauline is proactive in pursuing the possibility of a new house, in dealing with the police and in developing a possible life that will take her away from Turf Lodge through marriage to boyfriend Kieran. Through the chicanery of Tommy 'Razor Blade' and his sidekick, Bap O'Hare, Lynch demonstrates also how the same system which maltreats some is manipulated by others.

Welcome to Bladonmore Road (1988)

Welcome to Bladonmore Road centres on the McFadden family who have moved from Belfast's docks area to Bladonmore Road, 'the snobbiest district in Belfast'.[3] A comedy of manners, the play satirises the materialistic pretensions of the matriarch Bernadette McFadden, who through marriage to Alex, a take-away owner, is able to instal her family among Belfast's middle classes. However, the family has not embraced bourgeois values and between her drunken sister Julia, and tearaway son Camillus, it soon becomes clear that Bernadette's aspirations for her family will come to nothing. At the same time, Lynch excoriates the hypocrisy of the well-to-do neighbours with whom Bernadette wants to fit in. They are corrupt in their business dealings and their personal lives, with the married Roisin Blakely conducting an affair with Eamon Connery, secretary to the local residents' group. Lynch demonstrates how class solidarity operates between the respectable professionals of Bladonmore Road and how they are able to mobilise the law when faced with the uncouth McFaddens. Eventually Bernadette decides to return to her old home, where the values of community are more important than a big house.

Irrespective of this social commentary, as drama, it is as notable for its set-piece jokes and stories.

Rinty (1990)

Rinty tells the story of John (Rinty) Monaghan, the Belfast boxer who became Flyweight Champion of the World in 1947, but was forced to retire on health grounds in 1950. While boxing, Monaghan was also noted for his talents as a singer, which he maintained as a sideline, before beginning a second career when he retired as a fighter. Monaghan's spendthrift ways and the failure of his business investments mean, however, that the benefit of his income as a boxer was short-lived and he ended up in the only low-level jobs for which he was qualified. When his career as a singer is revived some years later, it is cut short by the cancer which ended his life. This is both a celebration of Monaghan's achievement and an indictment of the social conditions which meant that, for men of his generation and class, there were few opportunities for material betterment or cultural enrichment. A key scene is where Monaghan fights against an old school friend, Bunty Doran, where instead of trading punches they exchange a dialogue about why it is that they have had to turn to fighting to earn a living. The play is notable not only for its celebration of an iconic working-class figure, but for the use of multiple narrative strands, linked together by the narration of old Rinty who addresses his younger self. In production, the use of multiple role-playing enhanced the epic dramaturgy.

Pictures of Tomorrow (1994)

Pictures of Tomorrow sits apart from the rest of Lynch's oeuvre. The action is split between the contemporary London flat of Ray Oliver and Spain during the Civil War. Ray is hosting a reunion with Len and Hugo alongside whom he fought in the International Brigade. At the same time, his granddaughter, Kate, is trying to get him to move to an old folks' home since he is suffering from Alzheimer's disease. The plot juxtaposes the personal loyalty and vitality of their younger selves, with the difficulties they have with their families and ageing bodies. Ray was a respected leader during the war, becoming a celebrated member of the Communist Party, but has lost his faith in the Party, something which Hugo, who has always idolised him, cannot accept. Len has been a successful union leader and remains a member of the Labour Party, but is estranged from his own daughter. Each then is alienated from the world in which he finds himself, struggling to come to terms with the man he has become.

The History of the Troubles (accordin' to my Da) (2002)

Lynch's most commercially successful play, *The History of the Troubles (accordin' to my Da)*, was co-written with local actors Conor Grimes and Alan McKee. It is principally the story of Gerry Courteney, a fifty-six-year-old man from west Belfast, who has lived for most of his adult life through Northern Ireland's violent conflict. Courteney is, like Hasek's Schweik, an innocent little man caught up in the sweep of history. He is interned without trial, but he is more interested in drinking, the Rolling Stones and raising his family than he is in politics. He manages to negotiate the worst of the violence unscathed, and there is a tragic irony when his son is kicked to death by a local gang in an unmotivated attack. Nevertheless, Courteney's achievement is to endure, and the play ends joyfully with the declaration of the Good Friday Agreement and Courteney serenading his baby granddaughter.

Summary

The late John McGrath's formulation of the characteristics of 'popular theatre' captures much of what is distinctive about Martin Lynch's work. Derived from McGrath's own experience of touring theatre to popular audiences in Britain, these characteristics are listed as: directness; variety, comedy, effect, music, immediacy, emotion and localism.[4] Here the idea of a play is expanded beyond the bounds of any universalist literary genre and is viewed as a situated act of human interaction between performers and spectators. It is based on an understanding of a fundamental Gramscian distinction between popular and bourgeois culture. Lynch himself has articulated such a distinction:

> I've tried to build up working-class values and to make working-class people conscious and proud of them. Middle-class humour and life-style – and thus sense of theatre – is much different from working-class behaviour.[5]

He treated this distinction directly in *Welcome to Bladonmore Road*, but it underpins all of his work. It is articulated through two particular aspects of his work: its relationship to Belfast's working-class communities, and the performance forms it takes.

As can be seen from the short summaries of his published work, Lynch has consistently drawn his material from the lived culture of Belfast's working class, what McGrath termed localism. His plays are situated in recognisable communities, and the dramatic worlds he creates are informed by the values and behaviours of those communities. Thus, his plays can be seen as charting the daily struggle of ordinary people trying to survive the poverty of their conditions. He celebrates the neighbourliness that co-dependency brings. In *Welcome to Bladonmore Road*, Bernie realises that she will never be at home in her new surroundings:

> A really do miss the oul' district, the neighbours. There's wee Mrs Ferran – I used t'collect her pension for her every Tuesday and run her messages cause she wasn't able t'get out. A haven't seen nor heard of her since we left. A haven't seen any of m'oul neighbours since w'left.[6]

In some instances, such class solidarity is evidenced in the camaraderie of drinking culture, where alcohol becomes a great social leveller. In *Welcome to Bladonmore Road* a party to celebrate Bernadette's passing of her driving test turns into an open house for old friends from the local pub, in sharp contrast to the polite drinks hosted by the Blakelys earlier in the play. In *The History of the Troubles (accordin' to my Da)* Gerry celebrates his daughter's wedding by attempting to buy everyone a drink. There is a distinctive rhythm to the way he lists off the drinks: 'Four vodkas, two white lemonade, two pints of Guinness, half a cider. A big bottle of Harp, a wee bottle of Harp and a pint of Harp. And a fizzy orange poured.'[7] Gerry's joyful exuberance is expressed by ordering the round for as many of the guests as he can.

Lynch's writing articulates and celebrates the demotic speech of Belfast in ways that stretch the bounds of standard orthography and, occasionally, are incomprehensible to outsiders. Lynch commented about the opening night of *Dockers* that 'Apparently quite a lot of people didn't know what was being said. Belfast middle-class people didn't know what Belfast working-class people were saying to each other.'[8] His writing not only follows the syntax and rhythm of Belfast speech, but abounds with local dialect and phrases. When young Rinty is flirting with the woman who would become his wife, they banter,

> **Young Rinty** Hiya. [*Declaring*] Did anybody ever tell you your face resembles a meadow full of roses in the full bloom of summer?
> **Frances** Did anybody ever tell you yours resembles a basinful of willickes?[9]

In *The History of the Troubles (accordin' to my Da)* Fireball declares that he is so hungry, 'I could eat a child's arse through a gap in the hedge.'[10] A further characteristic of Lynch's dialogue which this points to is the prolific use of swearing and swear words. Bernadette cautions her son Ignatius when they move to Bladonmore Road: 'Bad language is one of the things that will have to stop,'[11] recognising that while swearing is an unremarkable trait of working-class culture, it is unacceptable in bourgeois culture. Indeed while swearing is marked as an act of aggression and violence among the middle classes, in Lynch's dialogue and working-class speech more generally, swear words are used to punctuate speech, and qualify expressions as a marker of verbal dexterity. Willie Lagan reacts to being imprisoned by declaring, 'This is out of order. Cat! Rough McFucking Duff, what?'[12] He later describes the chairman of the local darts club as, 'a no-good, wasting, bastarding parasite'.[13] 'Sleggin', the joking abuse of one character by another, is a further constant feature of Lynch's dialogue. Young Rinty tells fellow-boxer-musician, Eddie McCullough, 'I thought Maxie was away in the head, Eddie, but you're a complete buffalo's arse.'[14]

In his early works, Lynch's drama was predominantly issue-based, such as those works dealing with youth unemployment or poor public housing. In some instances this was derived from Lynch's personal experience, such as in *The Interrogation of Ambrose Fogarty*, which was based on incidents where Lynch was held in various detention centres by the police or British Army. Indeed, the outlandish character of Willie Lagan was based on a well-known local man, Hughie Dargan. *Minstrel Boys* (1985) focused on the divided loyalties of young men living in west Belfast during the hunger strikes of the early 1980s, reflecting Lynch's own sense of contradiction. In *The History of the Troubles (accordin' to my Da)*, there is a match between many of the characteristics of the central figure of Gerry Courteney and Lynch himself that was accentuated in production by the casting of an actor with a close physical resemblance to Lynch.

More than this, however, Lynch's attempt to build up working-class culture has led him to mine the lore of that culture for his work. While the fate of John Graham in *Dockers* was based on an actual incident involving Kipper Lynch, the playwright's cousin, much of the success of that play was in capturing the sense of the culture around the docks, including widely shared stories and jokes. Choosing Rinty Monaghan as a subject also allowed Lynch to explore the history of a local working-class hero well known to his audience. Even in *Pictures of Tomorrow* he was able to represent the heroism of the working-class volunteers to the International Brigade while at the same time expressing his own disillusionment with Soviet-style socialism. In his unpublished *Holding Hands at Paschendale* (2006), Lynch was inspired to write an account of a soldier being taken to a firing squad for cowardice during the Great War after hearing an account from his own grandfather, Patrick, of his experiences as one of many working-class men from Ireland who served in the British Army.

Lynch's engagement with working-class culture is perhaps most obvious in his community plays. For *The Stone Chair*, for example, he worked directly with the community of Belfast's Short Strand to gather stories about the experience of the Belfast Blitz which became the basis of his final script;[15] while *The Wedding Community Play* also involved local people in the devising process and performance. Lynch's most recent work, *The Chronicles of Long Kesh* (2009), as yet unpublished, has further combined this direct engagement with the community with Lynch's own craft as a writer. The play provides a history of Her Majesty's Maze Prison where all of Northern Ireland's political prisoners were held during the conflict, through the perspectives of both prisoners and prison officers. The research process for that play involved interviews with over forty former prisoners and prison officers, which was combined with Lynch's own personal knowledge and experience. This last aspect is important. Lynch is resolutely working-class in his perspective and lifestyle, so that his engagement with popular culture is as an insider.

The form of his work, therefore, has much more in common with forms of popular entertainment which Lynch himself enjoys, than with well-made literary drama; as he says, 'Working-class culture today isn't particularly literary. It's all based on light entertainment – TV, discos, pubs. Give us a laugh. Entertain us because we've been working all day.'[16] Structurally, many of the plays are organised episodically, and shift between locales, storylines, or in tone from one scene to the next. This is true even of work which might otherwise have the deceptive appearance of a classic realist representation. This produces the effect of a variety performance where, for example, a set-piece comic routine might be juxtaposed with a scene of heightened tragedy, or give way to a song. This does not mean that the plays do not have a central action; rather, it means that such action is always placed within a broader and more complex perspective than Aristotelian unities allow. His is a drama of social processes, rather than the problems of individuals.[17]

In this respect, Lynch's deployment of comedy is particularly noteworthy. While his dialogue is consistently peppered with the witticisms of the street and one-liners, humour has a more sophisticated function than merely to provide comic relief. In a number of the plays, it is used to contrast the heroic with the anti-heroic. In *Dockers*, Lynch contrasts the idealism of Graham with Buckets McGuinness who has the insight but lacks the personal will and energy to lead the change which he sees is needed. In *The Interrogation of Ambrose Fogarty*, Lynch's creation of the comic foil of Willie Lagan is juxtaposed with the idealistic Fogarty. Lagan ironically characterises himself as a Republican hero through song when he is taken to be interviewed, and even threatening to go on hunger strike. When Lagan is charged and Fogarty is released, two aspects are contrasted: Lagan's ill-fit as a Republican hero and the capacity of the justice system to render the innocent as guilty. In *Rinty* Lynch presents Choke-the-Dog who repeatedly borrows money from Monaghan to bet against him each time he has a major fight. In *Pictures of Tomorrow*, the young Hugo's appetite for alcohol and women are set against the intransigence of his older self in holding on to his allegiance to the Communist Party. The lisping mortuary attendant, Fireball, accompanies Courteney's life in *The History of the Troubles* and his insensitivity to the tribulations which Courteney endures undercuts the pathos of both Courteney's experiences and the wider political situations. When Courteney asks him about the death of Republican hunger striker, Bobby Sands, he replies, 'Ah, poor Bobby. [*Pause*] And y'see Pat Ederry?[18] He's another one. Thon fucker couldn't ride the Turf Lodge bus.'[19] Lynch's plays return continually to this anti-heroic comic figure, often presented as a sage drunk or wise fool. Rather like Shaw's Mr Doolittle, such work-shy characters also expose the internal contradictions of capitalism by their refusal to obey bourgeois norms of behaviour. Buckets McGuinness comments, 'If work was any good, the wealthy would be doing it.'[20] Likewise, Tommy 'Razor Blade' in *Castles in the Air* is a ne'er-do-well whose primary goal is to exploit his role as a painter for the Housing Executive to do as little work as possible while earning money to spend on drink.

Each of these stage figures is given a limited characterisation, depicted through a defining mannerism or catchphrase. A number of reviewers have regarded such characterisation as a weakness, identifying these as one-dimensional stereotypes deployed for easy laughs. This is a fundamental misunderstanding of the relationship between such characters and the audiences for which they are written. As Cashman has pointed out in relation to communal anecdotes, apparently flat characters, that is those that seem to be most typical in the way in which they are treated textually by the storyteller or writer, can none the less be received with a greater degree of complexity by the audience.[21] Thus, Lynch can rely on an economy of expression when delineating character in the knowledge that his audience can read the complexity of these types who can be regarded as 'representing the range of human responses to shared conditions and providing ready-made rhetorical resources for narrative'.[22] Moreover, Lynch is careful also to create such characters as sites of contradiction, often providing them with insight that illuminates the situation, in addition to the defining weaknesses which are the source of their humour. Buckets McGuinness, for example, acts as a conscience to John Graham in *Dockers*, despite his self-confessed commitment to drink:

> Stick it out, kid, stick it out. The future depends on you. You wouldn't like to think that in twenty years' time, things were just as bad for the dockers, just because you got fed up and made a pig's arse of things.[23]

In *Castles in the Air*, it is Razor who reads Brecht's poems, encouraging Dap to recite one at a local concert.

Alongside comedy, music is a consistent characteristic of Lynch's work. While in some instances music is specified as an extra-diegetic soundtrack, more consistently characters are called on or volunteer to sing within the narrative. The dockers' committee enjoys a sing-song to celebrate May Day in the pub, before Graham's rendition of 'The Red Flag' results in his beating. Willie Lagan is a country and western singer in *The Interrogation of Ambrose Fogarty* and regales both his captors and the audience with snatches of music. Razor thinks of himself as a singer, and drops into song at any opportunity in *Castles in the Air*. The party in *Welcome to Bladonmore Road* is marked by a sing-song to which Bernie and Jan Blakely each contribute. *Rinty* contains songs from the character of Monaghan – he ends the first act with 'The Gypsy' – as well as snatches of street ballads from other characters. In Act Two, there is a physical action sequence to a speeded-up version of 'Bye, Bye Blues', acting as a form of gestus for Monaghan's life:

> **Billy Burns** *lays down his Double-Bass, takes his glasses off and approaches* **Young Rinty**, *as though he were a boxing opponent. The two men square up to each other.* **Billy** *stretches out his arm and places the palm of his hand on* **Young Rinty**'s *head.* **Young Rinty** *then swings punches furiously at* **Billy**, *all coming short, in the pretence that he can't reach* **Billy**. **Billy** *laughs at the audience. Then* **Billy** *brings his other hand up in a closed fist and slams it against his hand placed on* **Young Rinty**'s *head.* **Young Rinty** *staggers backwards. The music slows in tempo, in time with his staggered movements.*[24]

In *The History of the Troubles (accordin' to my Da)*, Gerry Courteney is a fan of the Rolling Stones and this music provides a soundtrack to the performance. It is important narratively, too, when Courteney encounters a former Protestant workmate, Benny Elder, from whom he has been kept apart as a consequence of the Troubles. When they bump into each other, they mark the moment with a version of 'Baby Please Don't Go'. Music provides for them the common culture which endures through the divided society and which contradicts the monolithic identities of nationalist and unionist. In *Chronicles*, Lynch takes this further, with the Republican prisoners giving concerts with Tamla Motown songs as a way of maintaining morale.

Lynch's commitment to the values he shares with his audience does not mean that his engagement with working-class culture is uncritical, what McGrath termed 'tailism', 'trailing along behind the tastes of the working class, debased as they are by capitalism, and merely translating an otherwise bourgeois message into this inferior language'.[25] While he celebrates many aspects of working-class culture, he also demonstrates the limitations of that culture. Drinking may bring people together, but it also is demonstrated to be a debilitating curse on individuals and their families. The ways in which class loyalty can also inhibit individual development are shown in John Graham's reluctance to consider educating his son in *Dockers*; while in *The History of the Troubles (accordin' to my Da)*, Courteney is proud that his son, Colm, is managing to escape the confines of the housing estate by getting to university. Lynch also includes characters who reflect on and analyse the class system, sometimes a little heavy-handedly, but always from the position that poor people are not poor by accident or as a result of their own failures.

Like a number of other Irish playwrights whose objective has been to reach out to a popular audience, Lynch has been paid scant critical attention. While the early plays, *Dockers* and *The Interrogation of Ambrose Fogarty*, earned him praise, the rest of his oeuvre has been largely ignored by critics. Indeed, while some of his work has toured outside of Northern Ireland, it has not been widely regarded nor, until the publication of a series of his works by Belfast's Lagan Press since 2002, has it been widely available. Even within Northern Ireland, middle-class newspaper reviewers have complained that his work panders to sentiment or that it deploys simplistic stereotypes, substituting humour for depth of characterisation or complexity of dramaturgy. In many respects, however, there has been a significant failure to understand the form of Lynch's plays and to engage with the culture which informs them. They view his work from the outside. He does not engage with the rural Ireland of Brian Friel, nor the hard edged urban dramas of Dublin and Cork. His Belfast does not repeat the clichés of much of the cinematic representation of the violence there. Instead, he expands the idea of Ireland to include a class much vilified and rarely celebrated. Lynch's popular success is due to his ability to engage with his audience. Yet his is always a contrary position. Despite his socialist activism, his work is marked by a distrust of political orthodoxy and social conformity from whatever source. Ultimately, then, he is a socialist playwright because of this commitment to a dialectical engagement with an audience which he knows and respects too much to preach to.

Primary Sources

Works by Martin Lynch

Dockers and *Welcome to Bladonmore Road* (Belfast: Lagan Press, 2003), pp. 9–72.

The History of the Troubles (accordin' to my Da) [with Connor Grimes and Alan McKee] (Belfast: Lagan Press, 2005).

The Interrogation of Ambrose Fogarty and *Castles in the Air* (Belfast: Lagan Press, 2003), pp. 83–141.

Lay Up Your Ends. A Twenty-Fifth Anniversary Edition, Richard Palmer (ed.) and Brenda Winter (introd.) (Belfast: Lagan Press, 2008).

Pictures of Tomorrow, Rinty and *What Did I Know When I was Nineteen?* (Belfast: Lagan Press, 2003), pp. 9–62.

Secondary Sources

Cashman, Ray, *Storytelling on the Northern Irish Border. Characters and Community* (Bloomington, IN: Indiana UP, 2008).

Connolly, Roy, 'Martin Lynch', in John Bull (ed. and introd.), *British and Irish Dramatists Since World War II* (Detroit, MI: Thomson Gale, 2005), pp. 143–50.

Klein, Michael, 'Life and Theatre in Northern Ireland: An Interview with Martin Lynch', *Red Letters: A Journal of Cultural Politics*, Vol. 16 (1984), pp. 26–31.

Maguire, Tom, *Making Theatre in Northern Ireland: Through and Beyond the Troubles* (Exeter: University of Exeter Press, 2006).

McAughtry, Sam, 'Workers' Writer', *Irish Times*, 5 March 1981, p. 8.

McGrath, John, *A Good Night Out. Popular Theatre: Audience, Class and Form* (London: Methuen, 1981).

McGuinness, Frank, 'Beyond O'Casey: Working-Class Dramatists', *Irish Literary Supplement*, Vol. 3, No. 1 (1984), p. 35.

Mengel, Hagal, '"What is the Point of Livin"': On Some Early Plays of Martin Lynch', *Etudes Irlandaises: Revue Française d'Histoire, Civilisation et Littérature de l'Irelande*, Vol. 8 (1983), pp. 145–63.

Triesman, susan and Martin Lynch, 'Caught by the Goolies', Platform, Val. S (1983), pp. 2–6.

Notes

1. These biographical details are based on an unpublished interview with the author, and a range of sources including Michael Klein, 'Life and Theatre in Northern Ireland', Hagal Mengel, '"What is the Point of Livin"', Sam McAughtry, 'Workers' Writer', and Susan Triesman and Martin Lynch, 'Caught by the Goolies'.

2. Frank McGuiness, 'Beyond O'Casey', p. 35.
3. Martin Lynch, *Dockers* and *Welcome*, p. 78.
4. John McGrath, *A Good Night Out*, pp. 53–8.
5. Klein, op. cit., p. 29.
6. Lynch, *Dockers* and *Welcome*, p. 142.
7. Martin Lynch, Connor Grimes and Alan McKee, *The History of the Troubles*, p. 57.
8. Triesman and Lynch, op. cit., p. 3.
9. Martin Lynch, *Pictures, Rinty* and *What Did I Know*, p. 75 – 'willickes' are local shellfish (whelks) which are boiled and pickled and sold by local fishmongers.
10. Lynch, Grimes and McKee, op. cit., p. 43.
11. Lynch, *Dockers* and *Welcome*, p. 78.
12. Martin Lynch, *The Interrogation* and *Castles in the Air*, p. 21.
13. Ibid., p. 57.
14. Lynch, *Pictures, Rinty* and *What Did I Know*, p. 83.
15. See Tom Maguire, *Making Theatre in Northern Ireland*.
16. Klein, op. cit., p. 28.
17. Mengel, op. cit., p. 146.
18. Ederry is a national hunt jockey, on whom Fireball has staked a lot of bets unsuccessfully.
19. Lynch, Grimes and McKee, op. cit., p. 51.
20. Lynch, *Dockers* and *Welcome*, p. 16.
21. Ray Cashman, *Storytelling on the Northern Irish Border*, p. 166.
22. Ibid., p. 162.
23. Lynch, *Dockers* and *Welcome*, p. 41.
24. Lynch, *Pictures, Rinty* and *What Did I Know*, p. 105.
25. McGrath, op. cit., p. 59.

12 OWEN McCAFFERTY

Mark Phelan

I Won't Dance Don't Ask Me; Damage Done; The Waiting List;
Freefalling; Shoot the Crow; Mojo Mickybo; 'Courtroom No. 1'; *No*
Place Like Home; Closing Time; Scenes from the Big Picture; Cold
Comfort; Antigone

Introduction

One of the most important and original playwrights working in
Ireland today, Owen McCafferty's impressive body of work has been
produced by every major theatre company in his native Belfast (the
Lyric, Tinderbox, Kabosh, Prime Cut) as well as Galway's Druid
Theatre Company and the National Theatre London, where he served
as writer-on-attachment in 1999. Although all his work is characterised by his unique adaptation of Belfast speech, the universalism of
his subjects and lyricism of his language transcend its local roots as the
global routes of new productions of his work can testify, with his work
being translated and performed in Japan, Germany, Chile, France,
America and Australia in recent years.

McCafferty was born in Belfast in 1961; his father was the manager
of a bookmaker's office and his mother worked as a civil servant. Soon
after his birth, the family relocated to London before returning to
Belfast in 1971, 'which was quite a culture shock, everything was
starting up, politically. It wasn't a good time to have an English
accent. So I immediately lost it.'[1] The family settled into the Ormeau
Road, now segregated on sectarian terms: the Lower Ormeau mainly
Catholic and nationalist; the upper Ormeau mainly Protestant and
loyalist, with the bridge over the river Lagan forming the border
between both communities (the landscape mapped in *Mojo Mickybo*).
Educated locally, McCafferty later left school to work in the civil

service before travelling to the US for several months. Upon returning to Belfast, he worked in an abattoir before going back to college to study for A-levels, which later enabled him to enrol at the University of Ulster, where he studied philosophy. After graduating, he subsequently worked as an office manager, an accountant, a civil servant and a tiler before he started to write short stories in the late 1980s. His wife Peggy pointed out to him that his stories relied heavily on dialogue and suggested he try writing for theatre instead. Since then, he has been prolific and has produced a substantial body of work comprising sixteen stage plays and adaptations, as well as two radio plays (*The Elasticity of Supply and Demand* [2000]; *The Law of Diminishing Returns* [2002]). His latest play, *The Absence of Women*, will be produced by the Lyric Theatre in 2010.

The Plays

I Won't Dance Don't Ask Me (1993)

This poignant monologue beautifully captures many of the insecurities and anxieties of an older generation of Irish men as Gus McMahon suffers an emotional breakdown after being made redundant. Deprived of the rhythm and routine of his working life and reduced to the role of house husband, Gus reflects on the mundane details of daily life and his profound sense of emptiness, which is only emphasised by the busy lives led by his wife and son:

> What the fuck's happening to me? The boy thinks I drink too much . . . He doesn't know what he's talking about, he doesn't know the story. It's about who I am, what I did. He thinks it's enough to call me Gus – I know who you are because we're on first name terms – no, there's more to it than that. (p. 138)

He recalls the confidence and competence he had when he managed a successful bookmaker's office: 'I was an artist . . . It wasn't much but I was the best' before ruefully reflecting 'that's been taken away from me' (p. 141). Feeling increasingly useless and utterly crushed by the petty humiliations of daily life, Gus's ensuing depression destroys his self-esteem and identity. His psychological problems are further compounded by his failing health and physical strength, for he is no longer able to do push-ups and his prostate problems now cause him to wet the bed: 'After fifty-four years I'm starting to piss the bed': an ominous augury that leaves him very 'frightened . . . that frightens me' (p. 148).

Though Gus can cope with these fears and frustrations, his failure to communicate meaningfully with his family, to express his love or to ask for their support, proves his most difficult problem. Towards the end of the play though, he realises:

> when you've too much time on your hands you start thinking about these things and everything gets jumbled up. You start examining yourself and then you look at your family and think 'Who am I? Who are they? Do they know me? Do I know them?' (p. 156)

The play closes with his defiant declaration:

> tomorrow can't be like today, something has to turn up you see or I'll keep asking questions and it'll destroy me . . . Tomorrow will be different. I'll take up ballroom dancing . . . (pp. 156–7)

and as the lights fade, his frail figure starts to waltz across the stage; an evocative image eloquent with possibilities and yet freighted by the suspicion that tomorrow may well be the same. At the same time, Gus has generated the will to struggle on, to continue, to dance. These closing lines can be played as a redemptive release from the past or as a poignantly empty gesture and are reminiscent of the famous final lines of another old man reflecting on his life in Beckett's *Krapp's Last Tape*.

Damage Done (1994)

This short two-hander features Him and Her: 'an ancient couple [who] sit in armchairs . . . in silence' (p. 80) before they begin bickering with each other. The rhythm of their ritualised exchanges suggests their conversation is cyclical; a repetitive routine that goes 'up and down and round and round' like Him's hazy memory of his ride at a fun fair (p. 80). This short piece is Beckettian in both its form and themes: its ritualised language; the vagaries of memory; and the failure of communication between an elderly couple whose relationship brinks on breakdown and yet who remain together 'motionless' as they 'sit in silence' (p. 81) as the lights fade at the end of the play.

The Waiting List (1994)

Performed a few months before the IRA ceasefire, this auto-biographically informed monologue relays the thoughts of a young Catholic father locking up his home in an interface area of Belfast. In a sombre mood he reminisces on his childhood, though this is not some clichéd invocation of innocence but a disturbing evocation of the damaging effects sectarian violence has had on children. His experiences are emblematic in many ways of an entire generation who have been deprived of the innocence of childhood; their lives circumscribed by territorial boundaries and parental admonitions: 'Don't go here, don't go there, watch who you play with, be in before dark' (p. 87).

One memory of cycling freely around the city with his friends in the hot summer of 1971 vividly captures how children encounter (and enforce) the sectarian geography of the city. When he and his friends accidentally stray into a playground in 'enemy territory' they are immediately interrogated by other children:

'Where you from?'
'What school do you go to?'
'What football team do you support?'
'Say the alphabet?'

'Sing "The Sash".'
. . . Smack. (p. 88)

Such incidents reveal not only how 'children can be cruel bastards
they're like adults that way', but how such experiences shape their
collective identity: 'I'm starting to get the hang of this now. I'm a Taig
and they're Orangemen – what could be simpler?' (p. 88). Another
significant memory is the murder of his 'hip' history teacher, a
'community worker, hands across the divide type' who 'took a shine
to me' and gets him involved in local youth club where one night:

> Bang, bang, bang, bang . . . A hole in the head, thick purple
> blood on a cord jacket, a smart man with brains hanging out
> of him. The ante had just been upped. Men steal lives while
> boys play games. (p. 90).

This last line hauntingly captures the essence of *Mojo Mickybo*, while
the incident itself is based on McCafferty's memory of the murder of
his history teacher (to whom he later dedicated the play when it was
republished in 2002). As a precursor to *Mojo Mickybo*, the *Waiting
List* reveals the invidious ways in which children are acculturated to
violence and conditioned to sectarianism and segregation, and both
plays examine 'the loss of innocence that was a reality for so many
Belfast children of his generation'.[2] *The Waiting List* is also autobiographical in that the central character temporarily exiles himself in
America before returning home with 'eyes opened, mind broadened';
goes 'back to school . . . University, philosophy, a higher plane . . .'
(p. 92); and briefly mixes with a group of Guinesss-drinking
Guardianistas whose communist ideals belie the practicalities and
politics of everyday life, especially after he meets 'a girl, by chance at a
dance' and the arrival of children signals it's 'time to settle down.
Philosophers don't earn much readies' (p. 93). And so, one day he
ends up working as a tiler to support his family.

The closing section of the monologue concisely expresses the
accommodation he has made with life in this city, 'I'm thinking this
place isn't so bad so long as you stick to a routine' (p. 94). If

earlier sections of the monologue chronicle how children become acculturated to sectarianism, the closing sequence expresses how adults adjust to accept life in the city as 'normal' as they learn to

> ignore everything around you . . . it's like you can be here and not really live here – you look but don't see, you hear but don't listen and you think but seldom question, it's great. (p. 94)

Freefalling (1996)

Aptly described by Grant as a 'kind of staged "road movie"'[3] and by another critic as 'a play that wishes it were a movie',[4] this short two-hander is similar to Enda Walsh's *Disco Pigs* in its form and content. Performed by two actors playing multiple roles, its central characters, Him and Her, are disaffected urban teenagers utterly alienated from their dead-end lives. Their brief romance and risqué adventure when they steal a car offers some release from the monotony of their lives; however, this is both brief and brutal as the discovery of a gun in the vehicle has violent consequences.

Shoot the Crow (1997)

Nominated for the Best New Play category in the Irish Times/ESB Irish Theatre awards, *Shoot the Crow* was first performed by Druid Theatre Company and tells the story of four tilers working on a building site, where it is sixty-five-year-old Ding-Ding's last day of work. Worried about life after retirement, Ding-Ding intends to keep working as a window cleaner, 'It's not gonna make me Rockafella but it'll get me a few shillins everyweek an' give me somethin' t'do'; though he needs some 'readies . . . t'buy somebody else's roun' off them' (p. 25). Ding-Ding's plans appear daft to nineteen-year-old Randolph, who dreams of buying a motorbike and travelling abroad though he hasn't got the necessary 'readies' either. The last two tilers, Socrates and Petesy, are also financially pressured; the former is tormented by his failure as a father to pay the maintenance for his separated wife and son, while Petesy cannot subsidise his daughter's school trip to France.

Consequently, the four men concoct separate schemes to steal a pallet of tiles, all of which comically unravel. McCafferty's socialist politics and personal experiences of working as a tiler obviously inform the play and its theme of unfulfilled aspirations and ambitions ('tilers that have nothing, are going nowhere and lead empty fucking lives', p. 64) is a recurrent one in McCafferty's work.

Mojo Mickybo (1998)

First performed by Kabosh, a company originally committed to producing an innovative, visual and physical style of performance, *Mojo Mickybo* marked a major milestone in McCafferty's career. Set in the summer of 1970, Mojo from 'up the road' meets Mickybo, from 'over the bridge', and they become the best of friends. Acting out their fantasies of being Butch Cassidy and the Sundance Kid and fending off the Rubber Bullet Gang, both friends are innocently oblivious to the dangers of the real world disintegrating around them until Mickybo returns home to find his father has been shot dead: a discovery that destroys their friendship.

The play demands dynamic physical performances from two actors who play all the roles in the play and inspired award-winning performances from the original cast, who played seventeen different characters, alternating between them at great speed. Their human etch-a-sketch performances generated an extraordinary energy that brilliantly captured the effervescence of children's imagination. The play was subsequently revived several times and toured extensively before being adapted for film (*Mickybo and Me*) by Terry Loane in 2005.

'Courtroom No. 1'; in Convictions (2000)

Arguably, McCafferty's 'Courtroom No. 1' is the most haunting piece of this landmark production comprising seven playlets by different authors which were performed in the derelict Crumlin Road Courthouse. McCafferty's play used the courtroom as a purgatorial setting for a dialogue between a nameless victim of the Troubles and the disembodied voice of his unseen interrogator. The victim seeks answers in the vain hope of finding some form of closure or resolution to his plight; however, his hope for release or redemption is continually denied. This short scene metaphorically embodied the fates of all the victims of the Troubles and the suffering of their families, whose experiences had been cynically sidelined during the peace process in the name of political expediency.

No Place Like Home (2001)

In collaboration with a choreographer, a composer, a visual artist and actors, *No Place Like Home* was commissioned by Tinderbox to explore themes of displacement and dispossession. Obviously such issues and images were especially resonant in Belfast given its benighted history; however, although the play features a Belfast plumber called Archimedes (an aqueous allusion to the Greek who first understood the principle of displacement), the play seeks to open up wider politics and parallels with references to Rwanda, Bosnia and the Holocaust in its investigation of eviction, asylum and refugees. The play is non-naturalistic in form and avoids direct social commentary in favour of a poetic, physical and impressionistic presentation of 'a reality that goes beyond any one community or any particular period'.[5] In its formal experimentation the play was far more successful than *The Private Picture Show* (1994) and for McCafferty the project was an important 'opportunity for a group of artists to see if there was a theatrical way of telling a uniquely Belfast story'.[6] The play also made an important intervention in generating debate about political issues arising from the profound changes affecting the whole of Ireland, as a nation of emigrant emissaries rapidly morphed into the host society of myriad immigrant nationalities.

Closing Time (2002)

Set in the run-down hotel bar that once used to be the 'best run' boozer on the street but is now on the brink of collapse, McCafferty's play eponymously suggests the material and metaphorical condition of both the pub and its punters. Described by Nicholas de Jongh as 'a long day's drinking into the night' he, and other critics, gently criticised the play's darkness as 'too sombre'[7] though McCafferty insists it is 'a play about redemption'.[8]

The play opens the morning after the night before to reveal two men asleep in a Belfast bar: Robbie, the owner; and Joe, a regular. As they both sleep off the booze, Robbie's wife Vera and another regular, Iggy, emerge from upstairs where they spent the night together, and as the drinking session starts all over again the paralysed lives of the paralytic inhabitants are played out in increasingly slurred terms. The hotel itself had been bombed thirteen years earlier, a catastrophic incident that has profoundly affected the lives of Joe, Vera and Robbie. Robbie has drunk away the compensation money for the hotel and destroyed his marriage in the process; while Joe's wife, who had been caught up in the bombing, never recovered and ran away leaving her grief-struck, guilt-ridden husband unable to return home, and so he has slept in the hotel ever since although his home is only across the street. Iggy is also homeless, evicted by his estranged wife and family whom he repeatedly promises to call; he never does. The fifth and final character, a brain-damaged handyman employed by Robbie to help out at the hotel, is the most haunting figure of all:

Iggy	he always like that?
Robbie	what ya mean from birth or what?
Iggy	aye
Robbie	no/postman was he?/milkman?
Joe	somethin like that/delivery or something /don't know
Robbie	doing his roun's/this is away at the start like – twenty years an more
Joe	would be that
Robbie	jumped out a car they did – shot 'im in the head an away/not right since/slowed 'im up y'know/ couldn't repair whatever damage was done / said it wasn't him they were lookin for to alec had taken somebody elses shift or something / no good t'him that. (pp. 16–17)

McCafferty never clarifies whether the gunmen are Republican or loyalist; or if his characters are Catholic or Protestant, for these details are of no real importance:

> what I am trying to do when I write is to say that politics are an aspect of our lives, but it's not the complete picture . . . There are things that are more important to us – the debris and consequences of political acts that have failed and that we carry around with us.[9]

The characters refer to radical changes taking place in their city, although its regeneration cruelly contrasts with the reality of their own lives. Equally, news on the television relaying the ongoing peace process and 'progress' is also of little consequence. This is characteristic of McCafferty's drama in that he is more interested in the personal than the political, as Belfast-born director Mick Gordon notes: 'The Troubles are very far in the background. They don't impinge on the narrative engine of the play. Or the thematic investigation.'[10]

Scenes from the Big Picture (2003)

McCafferty's most accomplished work and perhaps the greatest play written by an Irish playwright in well over a decade, *Scenes from the Big Picture* premiered at the National Theatre in London and was subsequently awarded the John Whiting Award, the Evening Standard's Charles Wintour Award for New Playwriting and the Meyer-Whitworth Award: the first time all three awards had been bestowed on the same playwright in the same year. *Scenes* is Joycean in its prismatic perspective: presenting twenty-one characters in a twenty-four-hour period to generate the eponymous 'big picture' of modern life in a kaleidoscopic series of snapshots of intensely personal stories. The setting is Belfast, but not as it had ever been staged before: this could almost be any other major city in the world as McCafferty deliberately decontextualises the city to decouple it from the clichéd images and caricatures that characterise its usual (re)presentation:

'The point was that it could have as easily been Leeds as Belfast, and people got that.'[11]

This strategy is embodied in a beautifully understated gesture in one of the shortest scenes in the play. Elderly widower Frank Coin is tying his shoes and listening to a radio playing in the background when the disembodied voice of a newsreader announces, 'the political talks continue although all parties involved have agreed they have reached an impasse . . .' (p. 22), but the rest of the report is truncated as Frank turns off the radio and resolves once more to face the real world without his beloved wife to whom he still converses: 'another day ahead of us Elsie – go out here and stretch my legs' (p. 22). For McCafferty, this is the 'big picture': the personal stories of ordinary people who live their lives against the backdrop of the Troubles (which is usually foregrounded to all other (re)presentations of Northern Ireland). These individual stories are eventually woven into an epic narrative, as in an Altman-like fashion the play unspools the stories of more than a score of characters whose lives intricately coincide and converge; creating a communal image of Belfast utterly unlike any other representation of this city in what one critic hails as 'a more or less perfect play'.[12]

And yet the Troubles do cast their shadows of gunmen on the play: a cache of weapons buried in an allotment serves as a muddy metaphor for the legacies of the past; a drug dealer is kneecapped; while at the very heart of the play is the devastating portrayal of an elderly couple whose son was 'disappeared'. No details are provided as to why this happened or who was responsible, or its relation to the unfolding peace process – all of which effectively concentuates the audience's attention on the anguish experienced by the family and their desperate need for closure: 'we need to bury him so that the fuckers that shot him don't have the last say' (p. 21). As the excavations eventually yield the body of their missing boy, the expiation of their grief is devastating; and a potent condemnation of the peace process's abject failure to represent or redress the victims of violence for fear of endangering its 'progress'.

Cold Comfort (2005)

Cold Comfort is another collaboration with close friend Patrick O'Kane, who played leading roles in *Shoot the Crow*, *Scenes from the Big Picture* and *Closing Time*. This new monologue featured O'Kane as Kevin Toner, an exiled labourer who returns to Belfast from London for his father's funeral and who is forced to confront his own personal grief and guilt. The damaged father–son relationship at the heart of the play reworks a long-established trope in Irish theatre and in the author's words the play 'is about a lack of communication:'[13] a leitmotif in McCafferty's work, as is the alcoholism that has destroyed both Kevin and his father's lives and marriages:

> I live in kilburn / drinker / an a live in a flat on ma tod / right you go / you live in belfast / yer a drinker / an you live in a house on yer tod / I was married an now I'm not / you were married now you're not / we're like fucking twins. (p. 36)

Antigone (2008)

This superb version of Sophocles' tragedy is perhaps the finest of a slew of Irish adaptations and is significant for shifting the emphasis away from its eponymous heroine to focus on the flawed figure of Creon (McCafferty even contemplated retitling the play 'Creon'). Set in the aftermath of a civil war, the political connotations of Sophocles' tragedy for post-conflict Northern Ireland are rather obvious, but McCafferty (commendably) avoids labouring any allegorical connection.

In addition to sympathetically reworking Creon's character to portray a man whose martial mindset is poorly suited to the requirements of peace-time governance, McCafferty's adaptation is also distinctive for his treatment of the Chorus, which appears as a single 'Old Man'. As the play opens, we see the Old Man stacking body bags belonging to both sides of the fratricidal war and throughout the play his world-weary observations undercut the rhetorical hubris of the play's tragic protagonists. Furthermore, we learn that he spends every day sewing and stacking body bags in the forlorn search for his own son, who has been killed in the same battle as Antigone's brothers. The Old Man's rough vernacular speech signals his social position as altogether lower than the aristocratic class and caste of Creon and Antigone: a distinction designed to inject some class politics into Greek tragedy. (Presumably McCafferty's philosophical background meant he was familiar with the precepts of Aristotle's *Poetics* whereby only high-born figures could be classified as tragic heroes.) This crucial element of McCafferty's adaptation leads to an extraordinary confrontation towards the end of the play when the ordinarily servile Old Man suddenly confronts Antigone when she wallows in her grief with the fact that he too has lost a loved one, his beloved son, and he bellows in her face: 'Yours is not the only grief!'

Summary

Several themes consistently recur in McCafferty's work: alcoholism, loneliness, the loss of innocence, the lack of meaningful communication between people. Issues around masculinity also marble his work: men's identities, anxieties and inability to express themselves to friends and families which ultimately damage their own lives and relationships – a theme eponymously emphasised in his forthcoming play *The Absence of Women*. His plays, however, are not as unremittingly bleak and dark as has been claimed; redemption, change and hope are often present, albeit elegiacally.

McCafferty's work often places centre stage those marginalised from mainstream society; indeed the author admits: 'all I've ever wanted to do is tell stories about people who go unnoticed through life'. An explanation for this can be gleaned from his description of the 'artistic partnership' he shares with close friend Patrick O'Kane, with whom he 'shares a socialist view of the world'.[14] However, this perspective is philosophical rather than rigidly ideological (indeed, those espousing the latter are lampooned in *The Waiting List*), for there is little didacticism or dogma in his drama: 'It's not social commentary. I stay away from that.' Indeed, the author regards political and documentary realism as something which detracts from his real job of storytelling: 'I can't see the point of this docudrama reality type of thing where you do loads of research and amass lots of facts . . . all I'm trying to do . . . is get a story across.'[15]

In expressing these stories McCafferty has consistently experimented with Belfast speech; drawing on the rhythms of its idiom, its street slang, sounds and scatology to shape what Tom Paulin calls the city's 'scutching vernacular' into something more lyrical and poetic. In a number of interviews the author has outlined his aesthetic commitment to write 'in a heightened Belfast dialect . . . one of the things that I'm interested in is trying to create a new Belfast theatrical speak'.[16] Nevertheless, as Louis Muinzer correctly observes, his plays 'are not tied to locale and dialect, but simply grounded in them'.[17]

In contradistinction to his peers, McCafferty's drama (written over a period roughly coterminous with the continuing peace process) does not place the Troubles centre stage, nor are they his main theme or focus. (*The Waiting List* is one exception, however; McCafferty had been commissioned to represent the experience of nationalists by Point Fields Theatre Company.) Instead, McCafferty's topics and themes are almost always inflected by his interest in the personal rather than the political, the local rather than the national, but this is precisely what enables his work to transcend these oppositions and to touch upon universal themes: birth, death, love, loss, suffering, salvation, hope, despair. O'Kane incisively highlights how McCafferty's use of local settings offers few limitations on their global appeal: 'It starts here, then reaches all humanity. It's an irony that in touching the specific, you move into the panoramic.'[18] As O'Kane intimates, McCafferty is a playwright whose work is local without ever being parochial; a Belfast artist whose idea of the 'big picture' is radically different from those audiences and critics outside the city for whom it is always defined (and delimited) by the Troubles. McCafferty's 'big picture' focuses on the local, lived experiences of ordinary people who continue their lives as well as they can, in circumstances often beyond their control.

And yet, at the same time, the Troubles are never ignored or erased from his stage world; their destructive effects are often, if obliquely, registered and recorded in the damaged lives of his characters. The victims (and perpetrators) of paramilitary violence, though, are never identified in terms of their political or religious provenance, as apart from the perforce revelation of *Mojo Mickybo*, we never know if someone is Catholic or Protestant, nationalist or unionist:

> I steer away from doing that . . . The point I want to make is that the emotional impact of everyday life and our relationships are more important to us than continually bickering over politics.

In eschewing a more direct engagement (or exploitation) of the Troubles, McCafferty shows how ordinary people carry on with their lives and reveals the invidious process through which they become inured to violence:

> It seems odd to say that you can have explosions and killings and bombings and not take any notice of them. But when something like that happens day in day out, it becomes part of the fabric of life. That's how it is. You stop seeing it as abnormal.[19]

McCafferty's work is refreshingly free from the clichés, cant and comedy that characterise so much of 'Troubles drama'. There are no political speeches or solutions on offer; nor are there sentimental appeals for some spurious reconciliation, all of which distinguishes his work from that of many contemporaries; however, it also contributes to his canonical and critical neglect.

Theatre critics throughout Ireland and the UK have consistently acclaimed the poeticism and musicality of McCafferty's speech: a quality that regularly prompts favourable (if facile) comparisons with J. M. Synge, David Mamet and others; one critic even hails him as 'a Belfast Eugene O'Neill'.[20] One figure to whom he has not been compared, although there are interesting parallels, is Conor McPherson. Both philosophy graduates have garnered considerable critical acclaim for their gift for storytelling and the lyricism of their language, although the way in which McCafferty works with the earthy vernacular of Belfast speech, crafting sometimes crude language into a more poetic register, is reminiscent of another Dubliner, Mark O'Rowe.

McCafferty, however, is unconvinced by the comparisons critics make to other playwrights, but is even less impressed when their analysis is over-determined by autobiographical interpretations. Although several critics do focus on the connections between McCafferty's own life and the characters of his plays, the vast majority frame him as an important 'post-conflict' author (almost *avant la lettre*) who: 'deals with the emotional fallout of sectarian violence'.[21] Although McCafferty admits his interest in these matters, he insists his work is much more than this, and resents the imposition of such a reductive critical frame:

> The trouble with any play associated with Ireland is that audiences immediately expect it to be about the sectarian divide, but really those problems are superficial and I go out of my way not to tackle them.[22]

In spite of McCafferty's claims to the contrary, critics continue to read his plays as material and metaphysical metaphors for the Troubles. Of *Closing Time*, the *Guardian*'s Michael Billington declared: 'it is impossible not to see the play as a metaphor for Northern Ireland's own political stasis',[23] while the *Irish Times*'s Fintan O'Toole makes the same connection during its Irish run:

> There was a grim appropriateness to . . . *Closing Time*. On a day when the peace process was being spoken of in terms of collapse, lack of momentum and absence of vision, McCafferty's image of things falling apart in Belfast had a more than theatrical resonance.[24]

In an interview McCafferty expresses frustration with such reductivist readings and rejects any assumptions that he is some kind of 'spokesman for the North': 'I don't see that I write about Belfast. I see that I set things in Belfast and that's different. I don't think I'm ever writing a state of the nation thing, ever.'[25] Elsewhere he argues that both authors and audiences 'need to accept the fact that there is more to us than a thirty-year fight over a piece of land';[26] an argument that inspired *Scenes from the Big Picture.*

Although McCafferty is one of the most prolific and original playwrights working in Ireland today, his work, paradoxically, has been grievously neglected by scholars of Irish theatre (Grant's entry in *British and Irish Dramatists Since World War II* remains the single academic overview of his work). The fact that McCafferty is the only name checked twice in Tom Maguire's landmark study of Northern Irish theatre[27] eponymously indicates the reason for this: namely, that the 'Troubles' remains the dominant metanarrative (mis)shaping discourse about theatre in the North of Ireland.

Scholars who have written about plays and playwrights from the North almost exclusively concentrate on those whose work deals explicitly with the causes and/or consequences of political violence; hence the canonical prominence of Martin Lynch, Gary Mitchell, Christina Reid, Anne Devlin, Graham Reid *et al.* It is to be hoped, as the North emerges into a new post-conflict period, that this critical neglect will be redressed.

Primary Sources

Works by Owen McCafferty

Antigone (London: Nick Hern, 2008).
The Chairs (Belfast: Tinderbox Theatre Company, 2003).
Closing Time (London: Nick Hern, 2002).
Cold Comfort (London: Nick Hern, 2002).
'Courtroom No. 1', in *Convictions* (Belfast: Tinderbox Theatre Company, 2000).
Days of Wine and Roses (London: Nick Hern, 2002).
Mojo-Mickybo (London: Nick Hern, 2002).
No Place Like Home (Belfast: Tinderbox Theatre Company, 2001).
Plays and Monologues [*Shoot the Crow; Damage Done; The Waiting List; Freefalling; I Won't Dance Don't Ask Me; The Private Picture Show*] (Belfast: Lagan Press, 1998).
Scenes from the Big Picture (London: Nick Hern, 2003).

Secondary Sources

Allfree, Claire, 'It's the Drink Talking', *London Evening Standard*, 15 February 2005.

Billington, Michael, 'Closing Time', *Guardian*, 11 September 2002.

Byrne, Ophelia, 'Owen McCafferty', <http//:www.culturenorthernireland.org/article.aspx? art_id=744>.

Coyle, Jane, 'Freefalling', *Irish Times*, 6 February 1996.

—, 'Two Men in Search of Resolution', *Irish Times*, 3 May 2005.

de Jongh, Nicholas, 'Pints of Bitterness', *London Evening Standard*, 19 September 2002.

Fricker, Karen, 'Observe the Ulster Playwright', *Irish Times*, 3 April 2004.

—, 'Seeking the Writer Within', *Irish Times*, 24 September 2002.

Grant, David, 'Owen McCafferty', in John Bull (ed.), *British and Irish Dramatists Since World War II* (London: Thompson and Gale, 2005), pp. 151–7.

Macauley, Alastair, 'Scenes from the Big Picture', *Financial Times*, 14 April 2003.

Maddocks, Fiona, 'It's the way he tells them', *London Evening Standard*, 4 February 2005.

Maguire, Tom, *Making Theatre in Northern Ireland: Through and Beyond the Troubles* (Exeter: Exeter UP, 2006).

Muinzer, Louis, 'A Voice on the Stage: The Plays of Owen McCafferty', in Owen McCafferty, *Plays and Monologues* (Belfast: Lagan Press, 1998), pp. 11–16.

O'Toole, Fintan, 'Closing Time', *Irish Times*, 10 October 2002.

Spencer, Charles, 'All Human life is Here', *Daily Telegraph*, 12 April 2003.

Notes

1. Fiona Maddocks, 'It's the way he tells them'.
2. David Grant, 'Owen McCafferty', p. 153.
3. Grant, op. cit., p. 154.
4. Jane Coyle, 'Freefalling'.
5. Fintan O'Toole, 'Closing Time'.
6. Ibid., p. 156.
7. Nicholas de Jongh, 'Pints of Bitterness'.
8. Claire Allfree, 'It's the Drink Talking'.
9. Karen Fricker, 'Observe the Ulster Playwright'.
10. Karen Fricker, 'Seeking the Writer Within'.
11. Fricker, 'Observe the Ulster Playwright'.
12. Alastair Macauley, 'Scenes from the Big Picture'.
13. This and four subsequent statements were privately communicated.
14. Jane Coyle, 'Two Men in Search of Resolution'.
15. Maddocks, op. cit.
16. Ophelia Byrne, 'Owen McCafferty'.

17. Louis Muinzer, 'A Voice on the Stage', p. 13.
18. Coyle, 'Two Men in Search of Resolution'.
19. Maddocks, op. cit.
20. Cited in Fricker, 'Observe the Ulster Playwright'.
21. Allfree, op. cit.
22. Maddocks, op. cit.
23. Michael Billington, 'Closing Time'.
24. O'Toole, op. cit.
25. Fricker, 'Observe the Ulster Playwright'.
26. Allfree, op. cit.
27. Tom Maguire, *Making Theatre in Northern Ireland*.

13 MARTIN McDONAGH

Martin Middeke

The Beauty Queen of Leenane; A Skull in Connemara; The Lonesome West; The Cripple of Inishmaan; The Lieutenant of Inishmore; The Pillowman

Introduction

Martin McDonagh is one of the most celebrated, yet at the same time one of the most controversial playwrights of contemporary Irish drama. His plays have been translated into many languages and have been performed widely all over the world. When he appeared on the scene in the mid-1990s one iconoclastic play was quickly followed by another, and McDonagh was instantly hailed a playwright prodigy.[1] Being still in his twenties at that time, it seems venial that McDonagh was too inexperienced not to occasionally scandalise both the public and the press on his way to quick and early fame. Accordingly, his incredible talent was diagnosed as often as his alleged arrogance. Epithets such as 'shooting star', 'genius', 'loud mouth', 'punk artist'[2] or even 'the Quentin Tarantino of the Emerald Isle',[3] with which the 'McDonagh enigma'[4] has been labelled, are well-established yet often misleading.

Martin McDonagh's biography appears multi-faceted and, in his own words, defies easy categorisation:

> I always felt somewhere kind of in-between . . . I felt half-and-half and neither, which is good [. . .]. I'm not into any kind of definition, any kind of -ism, politically, socially, religiously [. . .]. It's not that I don't think about those things, but I've come to a place where the ambiguities are more interesting than choosing a strict path and following it.[5]

Martin McDonagh was born in London on 26 March 1970 to Irish parents as their second son. In the 1960s his parents had emigrated from rural Ireland to London. McDonagh recalls that he spent almost every summer with his parents on the west coast of Ireland in Connemara.[6] These visits and the London-Irish neighbourhoods in south London he grew up in have been conducive to an anything-but-methodical, rather 'distanced'[7] and highly 'anti-traditional'[8] experience and image of Ireland that has facilitated a more global, cultural rather than national, revisionist way of looking at contemporary (Irish) society.[9]

McDonagh went to Catholic schools and, for the most part, was educated by Irish priests. He left school at the age of sixteen, lived on unemployment benefits, listened to the Clash, the Sex Pistols and the Pogues, watched TV and films (somewhat eclectically including anything from soap operas to Scorsese's *Taxi Driver* and a BBC version of Pinter's *The Birthday Party*), and read everything he could lay his hands on, most notably perhaps short stories by Jorge Luis Borges. By 1992, McDonagh had written around 150 Borges-inspired 'grotesque tales'[10] himself. He also wrote radio plays, film scripts and stage plays. His breakthrough occurred when Garry Hynes, the artistic director of the Druid Theatre Company in Galway, came to read the script of *A Skull in Connemara* in 1995. She instantly recognised the ingenuity of the writing, asked for more, and McDonagh conse-quently sent her the entire rest of the 'Leenane Trilogy', *The Beauty Queen of Leenane* and *The Lonesome West*. By then he had also completed two plays of an 'Aran Islands Trilogy', *The Cripple of Inishmaan* and *The Lieutenant of Inishmore*, and an early version of his 2003 stage play *The Pillowman*, which was set on stage by the Druid Theatre in a reading in Galway as far back as 1997.[11] To the present day he has written and directed two extremely successful screenplays, the short film *Six Shooter* (2005) and the major film *In Bruges* (2008). A new stage play, *A Behanding in Spokane*, his first to be set in the United States, will be premiered on Broadway in New York City in 2010.

McDonagh's plays and films have received prestigious awards; for a full overview see the McDonagh fansite.[12]

The Plays

The Beauty Queen of Leenane (1996)

The Beauty Queen of Leenane was first performed at the Town Hall Theatre in Galway on 1 February 1996. The major target of *The Beauty Queen* is the institution of the family.[13] The play is set in a lonely farmhouse, a deplorable persiflage of the myth of the idyllic country cottage of the olden days in the west of Ireland. The plot centres on the middle-aged protagonist Maureen Folan and her mother Mag, '*a stoutish woman in her early seventies*' (p. 1). Reminiscent of Nagg's wish for 'Me pap!' in Samuel Beckett's *Endgame*, Mag's and Maureen's conversations are mainly concerned with petty household hostilities. From the start their interaction is a destructive one which escalates into a nightmarish albeit compelling vision of emotional and physical violence. In order to chain her daughter to herself, Mag withholds letters from Pato Dooley, who asks Maureen to come to America with him. In an almost Joycean configuration, Mag becomes a distorted Mother Ireland image 'of the old sow that eats her farrow'. Vengeful Maureen, in turn, refuses to be such an obedient 'Eveline' as in Joyce's short story of the same title when she pours boiling oil on her mother's hand and tortures the contents of the letter out of her. Ultimately she kills her mother to finally stop her from interfering with her life.

> *The rocking-chair has stopped its motions.* **Mag** *starts to slowly lean forward at the waist until she finally topples over and falls heavily to the floor, dead. A red chunk of skull hangs from a string of skin at the side of her head.* (p. 51)

In a circular and Beckettian[14] fashion the play ends on a repetition with a difference as Maureen assumes the position of her mother in the rocking-chair. This leaves her behind as a mocking inversion of the protagonist of the sentimental Delia Murphy song 'The Spinning Wheel' played in the background (p. 60). She becomes a veritable death-in-life image of utter paralysis.

The Beauty Queen constitutes an emotional roller coaster ride into the abysses of the human psyche. No matter how macabre, how cruel, how grotesquely absurd the violence might seem, McDonagh succeeds in creating genuinely moving passages amid all the farce. Pato's diagnosis of the unbearable amount of social control in Leenane – 'You can't kick a cow in Leenane without some bastard holding a grudge twenty year' (p. 22) – is, of course, as funny as it is revealing a deep compassion with a situation of social as well as mental inertia. The same holds true for Pato's account of his working conditions in England (p. 34) or Maureen's report of her temporary stay in an English mental institution. Kate Stratton remarked in *Time Out* that the play was 'suspended somewhere between the heartgrip of melodrama and the hysteria of farce',[15] highlighting a psychic vulnerability and a sense of loss emanating from under the surface of both genres.

A Skull in Connemara (1997)

In *A Skull in Connemara*, which opened at the Town Hall Theatre in Galway on 3 June 1997 and subsequently premiered at the Royal Court Theatre in London on 17 July 1997, McDonagh sustains the disrespectful iconoclasms and the unpredictable twists of plot. Mick O'Dowd is the main character of the play, whose gruesome task it is to clear graves that are more than seven years old and to dispose of the mortal remains by smashing the skulls and bones of the dead. After he sees himself confronted with the clearing of his wife Oona's grave events come thick and fast. Pursuing the long-standing rumour in Leenane that Mick had had a hand in Oona's death, zealous and frustrated local policeman Thomas Hanlon boosts his gathering of evidence by stealing Oona's corpse and manipulating her skull. Accidentally, a slip of the tongue of Thomas's brother Mairtin reveals that the pair of them stole Oona's corpse. Mick is furious and hits Mairtin with a mallet. When Thomas urges Mick to write down a confession, he willingly consents, but, as it turns out, he confesses to the killing of Mairtin which the blood-soaked shirt he is wearing seems to testify to. Thomas jumps at Mick to strangle him when – just like Christy Mahon's father in Synge's *The Playboy of the Western World* – the declared-dead Mairtin returns to the scene affirming that he has been merely the victim of drunk driving. Exposing Thomas as the thief of Oona's remains, Mairtin is instantly attacked with a mallet by his brother, who is only by a hair's breadth prevented from fratricide by Mick, who has destroyed his confession before. The play closes on Mick's caressing Oona's skull, leaving the central mystery of the play unresolved.

A Skull is a turbulent farce in which central motifs such as drunk driving, mallets and cracks in foreheads function as absurdly comic repetitions with a difference. They are attributed to different persons alike in different situations representing different stances towards law or morals. Thomas Hanlon, the gung-ho Garda, desecrates a grave and fakes evidence in order to prove a (true?) murder, almost commits a murder himself; Mick confesses to a murder he has not committed and gets away with the murder he (very probably) has. Far from representing realistic characters and realistic situations, McDonagh's hyperbolic farce reflects upon a world of paradox which buries the clear-cut borderline between the lawful and the outlaw.

The Lonesome West (1997)

The main targets of McDonagh's biting satire in the last part of the Leenane Trilogy are the *grand récit* of religion and the institution of the Church.[16] The plot is largely determined by the squabbles of the two middle-aged brothers Coleman and Valene Connor. Their relationship is a complementary one, which seems not a little of an echo of Beckett's Vladimir/Estragon and Pozzo/Lucky in *Waiting for Godot*. Beckett's characters have cogently been read as complementary pairs of body and mind, master and slave. In a similar yet more realistic vein, Valene and Coleman embody two variants of the psychopathological: Coleman is the sadist (his outrageous deeds include patricide and the cutting off of Valene's dog's ears), while Valene's orderliness, parsimony and his manic collection of figurines give abounding evidence of the anankastic.

The unhappy priest – Father Welsh – appears powerless in the face of such madness, resorts to drinking, and then, in a terrifically shocking parody of Jesus Christ (*qui tollit peccata mundi*), he scalds his hands in the burning hot liquid of the plastic figurines, which Coleman has venomously brought to melt in Valene's cherished stove. Finally he kills himself in order to take Valene and Coleman's sins on his shoulders:

> **Father Welsh** I would take that pain and pain a thousand times worse, and bear it with a smile, if only I could restore to ye the love for each other as brothers ye do so woefully lack, that must have been there someday. (p. 169)

Patrick Lonergan is perfectly right in stating that 'like the plastic figures of saints in that play, the Church was experiencing a form of meltdown'[17] in globalised Celtic Tiger Ireland. The outright obsolescence of the Church becomes visible in the plastic figurines which are, in quite a Baudrillardian sense, mere *simulations* or *simulacra* of faith. McDonagh's deconstruction unmasks these simulacra as a proliferation of kitsch. Significantly, each figurine bears the capitalist mark of 'V', indicating that faith in Valene's point of view has become a commodity unthinkable beyond private ownership. In a Marxist sense, this entails exploitation and self-alienation. The title of the play, as has been pointed out by many critics, refers to a line in Synge's *Playboy*, and it also recalls Sam Shepard's *True West*. As in Shepard the myth of the American Dream of freedom and prosperity is shattered, McDonagh's *The Lonesome West* destroys anew both the idyllic pastoral of the West and the hope of (transcendental) redemption.

The Cripple of Inishmaan (1996)

The Cripple, which was first performed at the Cottesloe in London on 12 December 1996, is the first part of a hitherto incomplete 'Aran Islands Trilogy'. The play functions as an intricate Chinese box which deconstructs the myth of the Aran Islands by making myth-making self-reflexive, by turning fiction and fictionalising into its central subject matter. Set in 1934, the play portrays the Aran Islands as a place of unimaginable boredom. One day, chief-gossipmonger and self-fashioned news editor Johnnypateenmike has a piece of truly spectacular news to tell: the Hollywood crew of Robert J. Flaherty has been heralded as coming to the island of Inishmore in order to produce a (fictional) documentary called 'Man of Aran'. We know today, of course, that the strength of Flaherty's film lies in its cinematography and that much else is fabricated. 'Oh thank Christ the fecker's over. A pile of fecking shite' (p. 85) is Slippy Helen's debunking comment after watching the film.[18] Young and handicapped Billy Claven – politically incorrectly but not altogether unaffectionately called 'Cripple Billy' by everyone – is invited to Hollywood for screen tests. Months later he returns to Inishmaan, contemplates suicide, but has second thoughts when Helen agrees to date him. His future, though, seems doomed when the lethal disease he faked before catches up on him:

After the coughing stops he takes his hand away and looks down at it for a moment. It's covered in blood. **Billy** *loses his smile, turns the oil lamp down and exits to the back room. Fade to black.* (p 113).

Three moments of the play stand out: scene seven reveals Billy sick and alone in '*a squalid Hollywood hotel room*' (p. 74). Later we learn that Billy was only rehearsing the part he was given in the Hollywood melodrama he was screen tested for. Here, the melodramatic mode becomes self-reflexive. Accordingly, the sentimentality is suspended by McDonagh's deconstructive *meta-melodrama* and is turned into a bomb which detonates not only to destroy audience expectations but also to blow the myths of Aran, Ireland and the myth-producing machinery of Hollywood to pieces.

As the pre-text of Flaherty's *Man of Aran* amply shows, documentary historiography and objective (historical) truth do necessarily imply fictionality. This meta-historiographic issue is highlighted in an unforgettable scene when Slippy Helen plays 'England versus Ireland' with Bartley and smacks three eggs against her brother's stupefied head, thus giving him 'a lesson about Irish history' (p. 71). Drawing on Declan Kiberd's *Inventing Ireland*, Clare Wallace has excellently shown that this scene very skilfully explores the 'performative space of national identity'[19] which self-reflexively comments on the way Ireland has both been 'invented' by the English and functioned as England's cultural Other.

McDonagh's metafictional aesthetics in *The Cripple* also accentuates the performativity and theatricality inherent in the construction of a social role or a social self. Indeed, Billy's 'biography' turns out to be as crippled as his body since it remains a kaleidoscope of varying projections and umpteen stories (within stories). Such diverging versions illustrate the necessarily 'crippled' nature of (national) identity and historical as well as biographical truth.

The Lieutenant of Inishmore (2001)

The Lieutenant is McDonagh's most controversial play to this day. Set in 1993 just before the Northern Ireland peace process gained momentum, the play centres on psychopathic INLA gunman Padraic Osbourne's returning to Inishmore from Northern Ireland to look after his sick beloved cat Wee Thomas. Padraic finds the cat dead and is determined to satisfy his thirst for revenge by killing his father Donny and young Davey, whom he deems responsible for Wee Thomas's demise. What Padraic does not know is that his cat was killed by fellow-INLA men in order to trick him back to the island and kill him. With the help of young and vicious Mairead, who blinds the three INLA killers with well-directed shots from her air rifle, Padraic escapes his assassination and brutally murders and tortures the INLA men and has their corpses disposed of in a '*blood-soaked living room* [. . .] *strewn with body parts* [. . .] *which* **Donny** *and* **Davey***, blood-soaked also, hack away at to sizeable chunks*' (p. 55). At last Padraic himself is shot in the head by Mairead because he had killed her cat Sir Roger in a rage before. As the absurd (anti-)climax of the play, Wee Thomas happily returns to the scene rendering the entire teleology of the plot line as grotesquely absurd, ultimately pointless and as aleatory as the alternative endings of the play:

Davey Home sweet home.

Donny Home sweet home is right.

Fade to black as the cat eats the Frosties.

Donny Didn't I tell you he likes Frosties, Davey?

[*If, however, the cat doesn't eat the Frosties, the above line should be substituted for:*

Davey He doesn't like Frosties at all, Donny.]

Blackout. (p. 69)

First performed at the RSC in Stratford-upon-Avon on 11 April 2001, the play had been turned down before by both the Royal Court and the National Theatre. Trevor Nunn allegedly went as far as thinking the play might even threaten the peace process.[20] Some critics have remarked that such a topic should have been treated in a more reverent way in order to instigate a 'serious debate'.[21] For an Irish audience especially, the play might run the risk of trivialising terrorism or of being disrespectful to 'actual victims of real terrorist atrocities'.[22]

Indeed, the ethical potential that shines through McDonagh's relentless iconoclasms in *The Lieutenant* crops up *ex negativo* only. There is no ethical let alone moral authority in the play. McDonagh's aesthetics of grotesque violence, however, exposes, deconstructs and thereby castigates the inhumane corruption of the terrorist agenda, its mindless fanaticism, its brutality, and its ignorance of history. Quite tellingly, Padraic recalls that he 'used to have a list of valid targets' but that he 'lost it on a bus' (p. 60). McDonagh unmistakably lays bare how far ends and means have grown apart in the terrorist mind, as the pseudo-intellectual blathering and half-knowledge among the INLA henchmen sufficiently corroborates:

Christy We none of us enjoyed today's business, Joey-o, but hasn't the plan worked? And like the fella said, 'Don't the ends justify the means?' Wasn't it Marx said that, now? I think it was.

Brendan It wasn't Marx, no.

Christy Who was it then?

Brendan I don't know, now. It wasn't Marx is all I'm saying.

(p. 28)

The nihilism inherent in such blatant ignorance and the formal nihilism which, at first sight, characterises McDonagh's farcical yet self-conscious metadrama – 'worse and worse this story gets' (p. 64)[23] – coincide with each other, cancel each other out and, then, turn into a seriously humane, ethical statement. In an interview with Sean O'Hagan, Martin McDonagh emphasised that the play was written in a 'pacifist rage', that it was affected by a feeling of 'wholehearted anti-violence'[24] and that its concern was neither with the English nor with the Irish exclusively. McDonagh's grotesque use of violence in the play does not, as Mary Luckhurst misleadingly assumes, feed prejudices of the Irish as 'backward and inferior',[25] nor does the audience 'become party to the milking of unspeakable wickedness for mirth and entertainment'.[26] Rather, the scenes of grotesque violence portray what Julia Kristeva called the 'abject' – anything that provokes revulsion and repudiation in us (be it corpses, severed body parts, streams of blood or the laughter about them). For Kristeva (and likewise for McDonagh), the abject has but the one function: to confront us with our limitations and our anxieties.[27] McDonagh's thoroughly ethical appeal against terrorism of any kind inherent in this confrontation is unequivocal: base means can *never* serve noble ends.

The Pillowman (2003)

The Pillowman was first staged in the Cottesloe Theatre of the National Theatre London on 13 November 2003. Here McDonagh takes the topic of (anti-)totalitarianism to a more abstract and, hence, more universal level as both the exact time and place of the play remain obscure. The opening tableau of the play introduces the writer Katurian being interrogated by the two secret police agents, Tupolski and Ariel. Initially blindfolded, Katurian does not know what he is detained for, yet in the course of the play he has to learn that some of the violent short stories he has written have been put into terrible practice. All of these short stories are written in a revisionist fairy-tale mode, and their contents strongly oppose the sense of security which the formula of 'Once upon a time' suggests. Important leitmotifs of most of the stories are cruel parent–child relationships which entail torture, mutilation, suicide, matricide and patricide. Eventually Katurian's retarded brother Michal confesses to the murders, and Katurian kills him because he wants to save Michal from being executed. Reasoning that he wants his stories to survive, he confesses to the murders himself and is shot in the head by Tupolski, only to rise again and, in a final twist of plot, to narrate his own version of the ending in which the stories indeed survive their author.

The structure of the play, once more, is a complicated *mise-en-abîme* of stories within a story. The metafictional function of the interlacing of fictions on different logical levels of the plot line is the rigorous questioning of the epistemological as well as the ontological status of the real. Juxtaposing fiction and reality Katurian, on the one hand, insists on the self-sufficiency of all art: 'A great man once said, "The first duty of a storyteller is to tell a story," and I believe in that wholeheartedly' (p. 7). This position, however, does not imply a mere aestheticist or *l'art pour l'art* position. Katurian's terribly frightening story 'The Writer and the Writer's Brother' turns out to be auto-biographical; and the eponymous Pillowman in Katurian's story serves as a role model for both Michal and Katurian himself when the latter chokes Michal with a pillow. Structurally reminiscent of Irish metafiction such as Flann O'Briens *At-Swim-Two-Birds*, McDonagh establishes various interlaced plot levels:

Katurian as Narrator [Katurian as Protagonist (Stories written by Katurian)]

Leitmotifs (child abuse, patricide, the writing of fiction) re-surface on each of these levels and in different characters. At the end, when the dead Katurian self-reflexively narrates his own ending, the entire play is laid open as a metafictional artifice.

Throughout the play the writing of fiction itself becomes an auto-reflexive topic. Much of the discussion between Tupolski and Katurian reflects and comments upon proper titles, cunning twists of plot, narrative tension, (downbeat) endings. The storytelling in *The Pillowman*, of course, echoes the Irish tradition of storytelling, the ancient art of the Seanchaí. Also at issue is the (moral) responsibility of both writer and reader of literature who should know, to borrow from Synge's *The Playboy of the Western World*, the 'gap between a gallous story and a dirty deed'. The metafiction in *The Pillowman* questions the epistemological as well as ontological status of reality and the real. 'This is just like storytelling' (p. 39) says Katurian and, thus, characterises the totalitarian manipulation of 'facts' during the interrogation. Yet at the same time, the blurring of facts is a sign of artistic freedom and personal liberty. In an aesthetic sense, this juxtaposition and the question of whether or not art can corrupt and cause moral damage recalls the ancient conflict between Plato and Aristotle. McDonagh's position is clearly that the theatre is *not* a moral and instructive institution providing messages. Artistic mimesis is regarded as being *not* assertoric. Rather, the dramatic 'world' shows us fictional possibilities. Most of all, it does not make any claims to truth beyond the far more sublime concept of poetic truth. In this, McDonagh's poetics reject *normative* ideas of what literature in particular and art in general are supposed to fulfil. McDonagh thwarts normative 'guidelines' (p. 7) and demands of a play by rigorously twisting the plot line again and again and by constantly turning the Pinteresque or Kafkaesque atmosphere of menace into hilarious and truly baffling comedy, and vice versa – 'We like executing writers. Dimwits we can execute any day' (p. 30). At the same time, the intertextual play (with echoes ranging from Kafka, Pinter, Borges, Brothers Grimm, Roald Dahl to Edward Gorey) in accordance with the blackest comedy still retains 'heartening glimmers of humanity' and 'emotional depth'.[28] Katurian's story of the Pillowman, which is evocative of William Butler Yeats's 'The Stolen Child',[29] convincingly (and movingly at that) presents stories and art as a means of compensation for an otherwise unbearable situation of human suffering.

Katurian [. . .] when the Pillowman was successful in his work, a little child would die horrifically. And when the Pillowman was unsuccessful, a little child would have a horrific life, grow into an adult who'd also have a horrific life, and then die horrifically. (p. 45)

In much the same way as Katurian's stories survive, the associative richness of McDonagh's play ultimately denotes the triumph of art and imagination over the restrictions and limitations of reality (and death). The often precarious yet felicitous balance between laughter and fear, between postmodernist experimental play and existential depth turns the *The Pillowman* into a complex play about the incommensurability of life and art, about reality and illusion, about 'politics, society, cruelty and creativity'[30] and certainly into one of the masterpieces of contemporary metadrama worldwide.

Summary

McDonagh's oeuvre is a complex postmodern hybrid fuelled by a plethora of traditions and genres, transforming facets of drama, TV, film and fiction into a richly imaginative and perfectly unique kaleidoscope of cultural imagination. The major aesthetic concern of Martin McDonagh's plays is a clearly deconstructive one. This deconstructive drive must be the starting point of any thematic and stylistic analysis of the plays. In this context, it is pivotal to recall the fact that deconstruction is a movement which operates, as Jacques Derrida pointed out, 'necessarily from the inside, borrowing all the strategy and economic resources of subversion from the old structure'.[31] Martin McDonagh's plays have a significant predilection for aesthetic modes such as irony, parody, pastiche and travesty and their practices of intertextuality and self-reflexivity. All these modes and practices – by definition – operate from the inside of an old(er) structure. In effect, then, the iconoclastically explosive devices McDonagh plants in the old structures and their detonation emphasise a juxtaposition of the old and the new, the fragments of which, like an intricate palimpsest, are reassembled in a new, complex and highly original aesthetic formation – albeit constituting, as all meta-art, a drama or a literature 'in the second degree', as Gérard Genette phrased it.[32]

Numerous critics have laid open the multi-layered intertextual and intermedial network that shines through McDonagh's drama ranging from literary sources such as Boucicault, Wilde, Orton, Beckett, Joyce, Kafka, Borges, Pinter, Mamet and, especially, John Millington Synge, to film (Tarantino, Scorsese, Hitchcock), (punk-) music, and TV soap operas.[33] The eclectic playfulness with which McDonagh incorporates these sources adds to the distancing effect, which is visible, for instance, in McDonagh's heightened Hiberno-English and the black humour of 'skull-hammering', 'wife-into-wall-driving', 'cat-braining', 'head-stoning', 'shark-clobbering' or 'mam-trampling'. Many critics have also noted the extremely funny parody of Synge-song in McDonagh's use of the Irish diminutive suffix -een in, for instance, a 'bag of skulleens', a 'plankeen of wood' (to kill a cat with), or 'a nice sliceen' with a razor to be given to nipples. Here, the familiar is unmistakably turned into the unexpected or even abject in order to destabilise, or to demythologise its traditional semantic context.[34] To banally characterise McDonagh's work as a 'pastiche soup',[35] however, as if pastiche functioned like a normative cooking recipe, or to assume that 'pastiche involves a denial, or rather an effacement of history'[36] is both a misunderstanding of McDonagh's art and, more crucially even, a gross understatement of the aesthetic potential that lies in parody or, as its variant, in pastiche. In a postmodern fashion, parody and pastiche self-reflexively challenge notions of authenticity, originality, tradition, origin, and – in a post-structuralist sense – even conventional processes of signification in order to revise or to question their absoluteness or totality. Creative expression is combined with often fierce critical commentary and, in this, the difference between past and present, old and new (Ireland) becomes visible at the heart of the similarity.[37]

Although Martin McDonagh has received thorough critical attention, such aesthetic questions have often been either neglected or eclipsed by the more political questions of authenticity and Irishness, a fact which is all the more surprising as it pertains to a playwright whose main concern so ostensibly is an aesthetic one. Lonergan aptly summarises the extremes in McDonagh-criticism: 'the belief that he is cleverly subverting stereotypes of the Irish, and the conviction that, on the contrary, he is exploiting those stereotypes, earning a great deal of money by making the Irish look like a nation of morons'.[38] The latter opinion has led critics to such misleading statements as that McDonagh's plays 'stage a sustained dystopic vision of a land of gratuitous violence, craven, money-grubbing and crass amorality'[39] or 'offer a kind of voyeuristic aperture on the antics of white trash' in an aesthetics which has split from 'the continuities of an indigenous tradition of dramatic writing'.[40] Mary Luckhurst even felt McDonagh's plays were fouling his own Irish nest and betraying the ideals of the Irish Revival when she concluded her argument by recommending him to reread the Manifesto for the Irish Literary Theatre.[41] In this, she must have forgotten about the fact that in their manifesto Yeats and Lady Gregory hoped

> to find in Ireland an uncorrupted & imaginative audience [. . .], [. . .] *a tolerant welcome* & that *freedom to experiment* which is *not found in the theatres of England*, & *without which no new movement in art or literature can succeed.*[42] [my emphasis]

Luckhurst's severe criticism is preceded by the very normative understanding that (dramatic) art (in Ireland), for some, has got to hold a mirror up to the nation and that drama has got to be characterised by an ultimately realistic moral responsibility. As shown above, this is the very aesthetic stance which is metafictionally deconstructed in *The Pillowman*. Not only does the idea that McDonagh might deprecate Ireland and the Irish ignore that 'gap between a gallous story and a dirty deed' itself, it also falls into the very trap of meta-art which lays bare, to borrow from René Magritte, 'the treachery of images' and the fact that an image of a pipe is *not* a pipe. Merriman, for instance, misinterprets McDonagh's farcical and, hence, rather sublime confrontations of the audience with the abject as morally abject forms of bourgeois reassurance.[43] Rather than that, McDonagh urges us to reflect upon what can be considered as 'real' or as 'reality' at all.[44]

By deconstructing stereotypical ideas of what (an Irish) reality or identity could be, let alone *are*, McDonagh's plays lay bare that authenticity (authentic Ireland or any authentic national identity) is a fiction or a myth, and a veritable straitjacket of a myth at that. The myth of de Valera's 1943 project of a 'home of a people living the life that God desires men should live' is as ruthlessly deconstructed as the globalised marketing of this myth. Hence all the at first sight familiar and idyllic country cottages, fireplaces, mantelpieces and tokens of 'Home Sweet Home' in McDonagh's West are foiled and, accordingly, disillusioned and displaced by disturbing instances of grotesque verbal, emotional, psychological, physical, structural violence – reason enough for Aleks Sierz to consider McDonagh one of his chief witnesses for In-Yer-Face Theatre.[45] The plays are characterised by a sense of cruel and painful personal as well as cultural entrapment and, particularly, of psychic paralysis. Small-town Ireland turns out to be a suffocating death-in-life image. The distancing effect inherent in McDonagh's farce, however, its oversimplification of characters, its relishing of unexpected plot-mechanics combined with the grotesquely heightened instances of violence transpose the particular into the realm of the universal. Nicholas Grene has aptly noted that the time frame of the Leenane Trilogy, for instance, remains unclear as '1990s Leenane is underwritten by a palimpsest of earlier periods'.[46] Leenane (and Aran as well as Éire) are fictional models, synecdoches of the modernised, globalised and disenchanted Western world: traces of the violent, petty small town (be it Leenane, or Spokane, or any other), McDonagh seems to say, are everywhere and in each of us.

On the one hand, McDonagh's presentation of this is a genuinely comic one. There is roaring laughter at the heart of even the most nerve-racking atrocities on stage, and the laughter is put to a liberating and almost cathartic use.[47] Such defusing notwithstanding, the laughter questions authorities and – in a postmodern fashion similar to Eco's *The Name of the Rose*[48] – denies respect towards tradition and institutions alike. In quite a Bakhtinian way, the laughter engenders a radically anti-authoritative, *dialogic* text of different voices, an epitome of the Bakhtinian heteroglossia: 'a special type of double-voiced discourse' and 'another's language, serving to express authorial intentions but in a refracted way'.[49] The everted world in McDonagh's plays challenges traditional authorities and expectations and, ultimately, strives to set reader and audience free from ensuing forms of fear, veneration, piety or etiquette in a carnivalesque counter-world in which the boundaries between the real and the surreal are constantly blurred.

As suggested above, this blurring, on the other hand, does not lack in existential depth. At the heart of *A Skull in Connemara*, to name but one final example, is a sense of deep disorientation in which, to paraphrase Yeats, the traditional centres of law or morals can no longer hold.[50] The title of the play, which is taken from Lucky's speech in Beckett's *Waiting for Godot* – 'abandoned unfinished the skull the skull in Connemara'[51] – is, thus, aptly chosen. As is well known, the chaos in Lucky's monologue derives from the fact that he is, syntactically speaking, interweaving one subordinate clause into another *ad infinitum* with the main c(l)ause absent, the subject (matter) missing, and the sentence, thus, left 'unfinished'. The result is a self-reflexive spiral structure which all of Martin McDonagh's plays share with Beckett. Neither in Beckett nor in McDonagh does a Second Coming seem to be at hand. What we are left with in McDonagh's world replete with murder, violence, spite, hatred, laughter and a tiny rest of affection is the epistemological void of unrelieved tensions and oppositions, mere assumptions in the face of a (transitory) skull. What is at stake in McDonaghland is, thus, less 'contemporary Ireland, but the human condition'.[52]

Primary Sources

Plays: 1: The Beauty Queen of Leenane, A Skull in Connemara, The Lonesome West, ed. Fintan O'Toole (London: Methuen Drama, 1999).
The Cripple of Inishmaan (New York: Vintage, 1998).
The Lieutenant of Inishmore (London: Methuen Drama, 2001).
The Pillowman (London: Faber and Faber, 2003).

Secondary Sources

Achilles, Jochen, ' "Homesick for Abroad": The Transition from National to Cultural Identity in Contemporary Irish Drama', *Modern Drama*, Vol. 38, No. 4 (1995), pp. 435–49.

Bakhtin, Mikhail M., *The Dialogic Imagination: Four Essays*, ed. Michael Holquist, trans. Caryl Emerson and Michael Holquist (Austin: University of Texas Press, 1981).

Beckett, Samuel, *Waiting for Godot* (London: Faber and Faber, 1981).

Chambers, Lilian and Eamonn Jordan (eds), *Martin McDonagh: A World of Savage Stories* (Dublin: Carysfort Press, 2006).

Derrida, Jacques, *Of Grammatology*, trans. Gayatri Chakravorty Spivak (Baltimore, MD: Johns Hopkins UP, 1976), p. 24.

Dromgoole, Dominic, *The Full Room: An A–Z of Contemporary Playwriting* (London: Methuen Drama, 2000).

Feeney, Joseph, 'Martin McDonagh: Dramatist of the West', *Studies*, Vol. 87, No. 345 (1998); pp. 24–32.

Fitzpatrick, Lisa, 'Language Games: *The Pillowman*, *A Skull in Connemara*: Martin McDonagh's Hiberno-English', in Lilian Chambers and Eamonn Jordan (eds), *Martin McDonagh: A World of Savage Stories* (Dublin: Carysfort Press, 2006), pp. 141–54.

Foster, Roy F., *W. B. Yeats: A Life*. Vol. I: *The Apprentice Mage* (Oxford: Oxford UP, 1997).

Genette, Gérard, *Palimpsests: Literature in the Second Degree* (Lincoln: University of Nebraska Press, 1997).

Grene, Nicholas, 'Ireland in Two Minds: Martin McDonagh and Conor McPherson', in Lilian Chambers and Eamonn Jordan (eds), *Martin McDonagh: A World of Savage Stories* (Dublin: Carysfort Press, 2006), pp. 42–59.

Huber, Werner, 'The Early Plays: Shooting Star and Hard Man from South London,' in Lilian Chambers and Eamonn Jordan (eds), *Martin McDonagh: A World of Savage Stories* (Dublin: Carysfort Press, 2006), pp. 13–26.

Hutcheon, Linda, *A Theory of Parody: The Teachings of Twentieth-Century Art Forms* (Champaign: University of Illinois Press, 2000).

Kristeva, Julia, *Powers of Horror. An Essay on Abjection,* trans. Leon S. Roudiez (New York: Columbia UP, 1982).

Lady Gregory, 'Our Irish Theatre', in John P. Harrington (ed.), *Modern Irish Drama* (New York/London: Norton, 1991), pp. 377–84.

Lanters, José, 'The Identity Politics of Martin McDonagh', in Richard Rankin Russell (ed.), *Martin McDonagh. A Casebook* (London: Routledge, 2007), pp. 9–24.

Lonergan, Patrick, 'Martin McDonagh, Globalization, and Irish Theatre Criticism', in Lilian Chambers and Eamonn Jordan (eds), *Martin McDonagh: A World of Savage Stories* (Dublin: Carysfort Press, 2006), pp. 295–323.

—, '"Never mind the shamrocks" – Globalizing Martin McDonagh', in Richard Rankin Russell (ed.), *Martin McDonagh. A Casebook* (London: Routledge, 2007), pp. 149–75.

—, *Theatre and Globalization: Irish Drama in the Celtic Tiger Era* (Basingstoke: Palgrave Macmillan, 2009).

Luckhurst, Mary, 'Martin McDonagh's *The Lieutenant of Inishmore*: Selling (-Out) to the English', in Lilian Chambers and Eamonn Jordan (eds), *Martin McDonagh: A World of Savage Stories* (Dublin: Carysfort Press, 2006), pp. 116–29.

Merriman, Vic, 'Decolonization Postponed: The Theatre of Tiger Trash', in Lilian

Chambers and Eamonn Jordan (eds), *Martin McDonagh: A World of Savage Stories* (Dublin: Carysfort Press, 2006), pp. 264–80.

—, 'Staging Contemporary Ireland: Heartsickness and Hopes Deferred', in Shaun Richards (ed.), *The Cambridge Companion to Twentieth-Century Irish Drama* (Cambridge: Cambridge UP, 2004), pp. 244–57.

Murphy, Paul, 'The Stage Irish are Dead, Long Live the Stage Irish: *The Lonesome West* and *A Skull in Connemara*', in Lilian Chambers and Eamonn Jordan (eds) *Martin McDonagh: A World of Savage Stories* (Dublin: Carysfort Press, 2006), pp. 60–78.

Murray, Christopher, 'The Cripple of Inishmaan Meets Lady Gregory', in Lilian Chambers and Eamonn Jordan (eds), *Martin McDonagh: A World of Savage Stories* (Dublin: Carysfort Press, 2006), pp. 79–95.

O'Hagan, Sean, 'The Wild West', *Guardian*, 24 March 2001 <http://www.guardian.co.uk /lifeandstyle/2001/mar/24/weekend.seanohagan>.

O'Toole, Fintan, 'Nowhere Man', *Irish Times*, 26 April 1997.

—, '"A Mind in Connemara": The Savage World of Martin McDonagh', *The New Yorker*, 6 March 2006 <http://www.newyorker.com/archive/2006/03/06/060306fa_fact_ otoole?printable=true>

Richards, Shaun, 'Plays of (Ever) Changing Ireland', in Shaun Richards (ed.), *The Cambridge Companion to Twentieth Century Irish Drama* (Cambridge: Cambridge UP, 2004), pp. 1–15.

Roche, Anthony, '"Close to Home but Distant": Irish Drama in the 1990s', *Colby Quarterly*, Vol. 34, No. 4 (1998), pp. 265–89.

—, 'Reworking *The Workhouse Ward*: McDonagh, Beckett, and Gregory', *Irish University Review*, Vol. 34, Nos. 1–2 (2002), pp. 171–784.

Russell, Richard Rankin (ed.), *Martin McDonagh. A Casebook* (London: Routledge, 2007).

Sierz, Aleks, *In-Yer-Face-Theatre. British Drama Today* (London: Faber and Faber, 2001).

Theatre Record, Vol. XVI, No. 5 (1996), pp. 288–91.

Theatre Record, Vol. XVI, No. 25 (1996), pp. 1549–52

Theatre Record , Vol. XVII, No. 1 (1997), pp. 17–25.

Theatre Record, Vol. XXI, No. 1 (2001), pp. 6–13.

Theatre Record , Vol. XXI, No. 10 (2001), pp. 631–5.

Theatre Record, Vol. XXIII, No. 23 (2003), pp. 1550–5.

Wallace, Clare, '"Pastiche Soup", Bad Taste, Biting Irony and Martin McDonagh', *Litteraria Pragensia*, Vol. 29, No. 15 (2005), pp. 3–38.

Watt, Stephen, *Beckett and Contemporary Irish Writing* (Cambridge: Cambridge UP, 2009).

Notes

1. Joseph Feeney, 'Martin McDonagh'.
2. Werner Huber, 'The Early Plays', p. 14.

3. Alastair Macaulay, *Financial Times*, 29 July 1997.

4. The phrasing is Charles Spencer's, *Daily Telegraph*, 9 January 1997.

5. Fintan O'Toole, 'Nowhere Man'.

6. Fintan O'Toole, '"A Mind in Connemara"'.

7. Antony Roche, '"Close to Home but Distant"', p. 287.

8. Huber, op. cit., p. 15.

9. The move from the national to the cultural has been analysed by Jochen Achilles, '"Homesick for Abroad"'. See also Patrick Lonergan's excellent *Theatre and Globalization: Irish Drama in the Celtic Tiger Era* (Basingstoke: Palgrave Macmillan, 2009), especially Chapter 5.

10. O'Toole, '"A Mind in Connemara"'.

11. Patrick Lonergan, *Theatre and Globalization*, p. 102.

12. <http://www.martinmcdonagh.net>.

13. Patrick Lonergan, 'Martin McDonagh, Globalization, and Irish Theatre Criticism', p. 296.

14. Huber, op. cit., and Nicholas Grene, 'Ireland in Two Minds', p. 47.

15. Kate Stratton, *Time Out*, 11 December 1996.

16. Lonergan, 'Martin McDonagh, Globalization, and Irish Theatre Criticism', p. 296.

17. See ibid., p. 297, and Paul Murphy, 'The Stage Irish are Dead'.

18. Shaun Richards, 'Plays of (Ever) Changing Ireland', p. 9.

19. Clare Wallace, '"Pastiche Soup"', p. 16.

20. Sean O'Hagan, 'The Wild West'.

21. Mary Luckhurst, 'Martin McDonagh's *The Lieutenant*', p. 119.

22. Lonergan, 'Martin McDonagh, Globalization, and Irish Theatre Criticism', p. 300.

23. Samuel Beckett, *Waiting for Godot*, Act II: 'VLADIMIR: This is becoming really insignificant. / ESTRAGON: Not enough.'

24. O'Hagan, op. cit.

25. Luckhurst, op. cit., p. 121.

26. Patrick Carnegie, *Spectator*, 19 May 2001.

27. Julia Kristeva, *Powers of Horror*.

28. Aleks Sierz, *What's On*, 19 November 2003.

29. 'Come away, O human child! / To the waters and the wild / With a faery, hand in hand, / For the world's more full of weeping than you can understand.' William Butler Yeats, 'The Stolen Child', *The Poems*, ed. and introd. David Albright (London: Everyman's Library, 1992), pp. 44–5.

30. Alastair Macaulay, *Financial Times*, 15 March 2003.

31. Jacques Derrida, *Of Grammatology*, p. 24.

32. Gérard Genette, *Pallinpaesto*.

33. Anthony Roche places McDonagh's black humour in the context of the Irish tradition in 'Reworking *The Workhouse Ward*: McDonagh, Beckett, and Gregory', *Irish University Review*, Vol. 34, Nos. 1–2 (2002), pp. 171–784). For an intensive analysis of intertextuality and intermediality in McDonagh see also: Patrick Lonergan, '"Never

mind the shamrocks" – Globalizing Martin McDonagh', in Richard Rankin Russell (ed.), *Martin McDonagh*, pp. 149–75. For the Beckett-Intertext see also Stephen Watt, *Beckett*, pp. 67–8, 166–7.

34. Undoubtedly the best studies of McDonagh's language are: Christopher Murray's 'The Cripple of Inishmaan Meets Lady Gregory', and Lisa Fitzpatrick's 'Language Games: *The Pillowman, A Skull in Connemara*: Martin McDonagh's Hiberno-English', both of which are anthologised in Lilian Chambers and Eamonn Jordan (eds), *Martin McDonagh*, pp. 79–95, 141–54.

35. Dominic Dromgoole, *The Full Room*, pp. 198–9.

36. Wallace, op. cit., p. 29.

37. Linda Hutcheon, *A Theory of Parody*, and also the excellent article by José Lanters, 'The Identity Politics of Martin McDonagh' in Rankin Russell, op. cit., pp. 9–24.

38. Lonergan, 'Martin McDonagh, Globalization, and Irish Theatre Criticism', p. 295.

39. Vic Merriman, 'Decolonization Postponed' in Chambers and Jordan (eds), op. cit., p. 273.

40. Vic Merriman, 'Staging Contemporary Ireland' in Richards (ed.), op. cit., p. 254.

41. Luckhurst, op. cit.

42. Lady Gregory, 'Our irish Theatre', pp . 378–9.

43. See Vic Merriman, 'Heartsickness and Hopes Deferred', pp. 255–6.

44. See, for instance, Michel Foucault, *Ceci n'est pas une pipe: Sur Margritte* (Saint Clément: Scholies/Edition Fata Morgana, 1973).

45. Aleks Sierz, *In-Yer-Face Theatre*, pp. 219–25.

46. Nicholas Grene, 'Ireland in Two Minds', p. 51.

47. Ibid., p. 57.

48. Ironically, much of the debate between critics about the inappropriateness or the irreverence involved in the laughter in McDonagh's plays recalls the poignant dialogues about the nature of laughter between William of Baskerville and Jorge of Burgos in Eco's novel.

49. Mikhail Bakhtin, *The Dialogic Imagination*, p. 40.

50. See Yeats, 'The Second Coming', in Albright (ed.), op. cit., p. 235.

51. Samuel Beckett, *Waiting for Godot*, p. 45.

52. Lisa Fitzpatrick, 'Language Games', p. 153.

14 FRANK McGUINNESS

Eamonn Jordan

Observe the Sons of Ulster Marching Towards the Somme; Carthaginians; Mary and Lizzie; Mutabilitie; Someone Who'll Watch Over Me

Introduction

Born on 29 July 1953 in Buncrana, which is located on the Inishowen peninsula in County Donegal, Republic of Ireland, Frank McGuinness grew up living close to the border that divides the island of Ireland. In his youth, he spent a good deal of time going back and forth from his home place to Derry. This city is part of the six counties that constitute Northern Ireland; going there required him to cross regularly the border that divided North and South, and to reflect on the causes, impact and issues of partition.[1] In McGuinness's writing, the counties of Donegal and Derry, while both are in the province of Ulster, yet not of the same nation, interplay in a curious, anomalous way to suggest a liminal, divided, doubled and displaced sense of focus and place. McGuinness left his home town in 1971 to study literature at University College Dublin, and while there, the hugely traumatic events of Bloody Sunday (30 January 1972) impacted greatly on him. McGuinness acknowledges that it was on that particular day he lost his 'innocence'. When he had finished his undergraduate degree, he undertook graduate studies in medieval literature, eventually gaining full-time employment at St Patrick's, Maynooth University. Currently, he is Professor of Creative Writing in the School of English, Drama and Film at University College Dublin.

McGuinness regards himself as both a Northern Irish and a Catholic writer in the very broadest senses of both words. But the reach of his dramatic work takes in many different situations and circumstances, well beyond the concerns of the local and the national. His plays have been translated into many different languages and produced successfully internationally for almost thirty years. Further, his adaptations of Greek and modern European plays have been very well received across the globe. For this range of work, McGuinness has won numerous awards. He is also noted for three collections of poetry, short stories, some screenplays, and articles on playwrights, in particular, written for academic journals and books.[2]

More than most writers, McGuinness is someone who regularly experiments with form and content. He is not happy to revisit the same types of scenarios with the same dramaturgical imperatives. Genre-wise, he is equally proficient with tragedy and with comedy, and further, he has the capacity to integrate classical and popular cultural awarenesses with great ease. Indeed, the sensibilities of the plays are normally some amalgam of the tragic and the comic, the real and the surreal, the continuous and the discontinuous. By so doing, McGuinness manages to shift register with considerable frequency and deftness. In terms of form, his work varies from a general heightened or expressive realism in *The Factory Girls* (1982) or *The Breadman* (1990), to a type of perverted, nightmare scenario found in *Innocence* (1986) where Act One captures a grim, deprived and depraved social reality and Act Two, in the main, the inner mechanisms of the haunted mind of the painter Caravaggio; it is as if the second act is layered upon the first. *Carthaginians* (1988) has the episodic/journey structure of ritual, sacrament and pilgrimage, and *Mary and Lizzie* (1989) is a wild, mobile fantasia inspired by Ibsen's *Peer Gynt*. *Mutabilitie* (1996) mimics the Shakespearean five-act form, whereas *Observe the Sons of Ulster Marching Towards the Somme* (1985) is an episodic, almost Brechtian history/memory play that sets out to deny empathy and to alienate, by blending monologue, a basic naturalism, simultaneous scenes and a carnivalesque play-within-a-play format derived from the Battle of the Boyne.

McGuinness's plays are set in a whole host of eras and in very different socio-economic and political circumstances. *The Factory Girls* is set in a Donegal shirt factory, *Innocence* in post-Renaissance Italy, and *Mutabilitie* in Cork in 1598, during the Munster Wars.

Someone Who'll Watch Over Me (1992) is set in a cell in Beirut in the late 1980s to early 1990s, and *The Bird Sanctuary* (1994) in Booterstown, south County Dublin in the early 1990s. More recently, *Speaking Like Magpies* (2005) is set in numerous locations in Britain, around the time of the Gunpowder Plot of 1605, and his latest play *There Came a Gypsy Riding* (2007) is set in present-day Connemara. His stage environments are frequently fluid spaces that have the capacity to be instantly and substantially altered or transformed. The stage space at the end of *The Bird Sanctuary* adapts to reveal a miraculous painting, and in *Mary and Lizzie* scenes shift from a grave scene to a Victorian seaside location, from a dinner party with Karl and Jenny Marx to the camps of Russia, under communist rule. Time and space are fluid. Likewise, stage spaces can be multiple as in *The Sons of Ulster*, where at one point there are four distinctive and simultaneous locations on a divided, segmented and clearly demarcated stage.

Some concepts confidently recur again and again, and others are less frequent or reappear in subtle ways, but ultimately, as with all great writing, it is the interplay between what is similar, familiar and repetitive, and what is diverse, diffuse and different that has the potential to generate quality work. In his writing, the dramatic focus has been on the Troubles in Northern Ireland, the sectarian conflict between Catholics and Protestants, nationalists and loyalists, and on the impact and legacy of imperialism. There is an obsessive compulsion to interrogate the Irish–British relationship, from multiple points of view. An additional layer is added by the introduction of American characters to the clash between the British and Irish ones; sometimes there is a reliance or over-reliance on an American character, usually male, who is deployed as a way of opening up entrenched binaries that had traditionally induced biases, stereotypes, objectifications and persecutions.

There are also the issues of class identities, communities, genders and sexual orientations, which are best evaluated through his fascination with artistry, with the obligations of the artist or visionary to filter, contest or manipulate the circumstances of their existences. McGuinness locates his plays in situations where despite restraint, confinement or imprisonment, the characters reinscribe the space through language, prayers, songs, poems, melded images, gestures, and through the re-enactment or reconfiguration of social norms, rites and customs. He contests culturally embedded rituals by using parody, perversion or sinister takes on such conventions, habits, mindsets and reflexes.

The Plays

Observe the Sons of Ulster Marching Towards the Somme (1985)

After the success of *The Factory Girls* (1982), the next two plays *Borderlands* (1984) and *Gatherers* (1985), which McGuinness scripted for Team Theatre, a Theatre-in-Education company, show evidence of the broader aspirations of the writer. The substance of that ambition struck resolutely home with the extraordinarily elaborate and brilliant *Observe the Sons of Ulster Marching Towards the Somme*. This play deals with a group of eight loyalists, who have signed up to fight for the British Army during the First World War in Ulster's 36th Division. Initially, their almost unanimous, unswerving impetuses to fight are deemed to be an expression of loyalist Ulster's commitment to Britain, which also serves as an inducement to Britain to maintain its rule over the whole island of Ireland. As the action progresses this loyalty is put under increasing pressure, first by the homosexual, upper-class character, Kenneth Pyper, secondly by the horrors of war, and, thirdly, by an emerging sense of personal individuation and maturity that each of the soldiers adopts. This allows the mask of the tribe to slip.

The horrors of war ensure that the soldiers make a whole series of recognitions that complicate and contradict their initial motivations and certainties. McIlwaine notes: 'We're not making a sacrifice. Jesus, you've seen this war. We are the sacrifice' (p. 156). The play opens with the Elder Pyper, the only survivor of the eight, reflecting back on the carnage that was the Battle of the Somme. He is haunted by those who have died, for they refuse to leave him in peace because he misrepresents their actions and betrays their values. The tension between tribal acts of remembrance and false testimony is vital. Part Two is set in an army barracks when the recruits first get to know each other, and Part Four is set just before the soldiers go into battle. Part Three marks the temporary homecomings of the soldiers in pairs, and four locations are discernible onstage with mini-scenes, cinema-like, with cross-cutting and fading from one to the other, until eventually, all four spaces are visible and simultaneously active, and a cacophony of distinct voices and sensations coalesce.

As someone who would have strong nationalist beliefs, and as someone who would be perceived to be Catholic, however lapsed, for McGuinness to write about the rival tradition with such decisiveness and integrity has been praised by many. Of course, McGuinness is reflecting on and dramatising otherness, but he does not romanticise or simplify unionist values and impulses. Instead, he establishes complex motivations for his characters, but he also identifies different strands of loyalism that move away from a stereotyping or homogenisation, something most opponents tend to do when it comes to those they challenge. Further, the soldiers are robust and aggressive individuals, prompted by a self-destructive blood lust. The central character, Pyper, is the source of a trickster consciousness, but his shifting of perspective is brilliantly tracked through the drama. At the initial stages, Pyper is someone out to self-destruct, and is nihilistic and antagonistic in his undermining of others. By the end of the play, he so much wants to belong that he is accused by the others of trying too hard to participate in the rituals of the tribe, before they go into battle. Perversely, he is the only one who survives.

As war plays go, there is considerable tension on stage throughout. As the play is set in 1916 it chimes with nationalist commemorations of the Easter Rising in the same year, which was for many the beginning of the end to British rule. Further, the play is equally about paramilitaries in the 1980s, both loyalist and Republican, who were perversely and delusionally re-enacting the same sacrificial imperatives of the Somme and of the Easter Rising. More crucial still is the fact that the victory of King William over King James at the Boyne is regarded as the mythic moment that consolidated a loyalist sense of destiny. That McGuinness has his soldiers re-enact the Battle of the Boyne, filtered through the loyalist Scarva tradition and permits a novel ending to such a battle, where the traditional outcome is reversed, says as much about the imperiousness of history, as it does about the imperatives of McGuinness's dramaturgy to destabilise and to unsettle expectations.

Innocence (1986)

Pyper is matched by the figure of Italian post-Renaissance painter Caravaggio in *Innocence*. The play is set on the day the artist murders Ranuccio Tomassoni. McGuinness takes not only inspiration from the events in the life of the artist but also from his paintings, and McGuinness utilises and recontextualises images, props and symbols that recur in Caravaggio's works. The play is about creativity and patronage, about sexual orientation and Catholic damnation, and about the historic as well as the contemporary. When first produced in 1986, homosexuality was illegal in Ireland [3] Yet here on the stage of the Gate Theatre was not only a gay artist, but also Cardinal Francesco del Monte paying for sex with rent-boys, Lucio and Antonio, while at the same time using his religious position to justify, damn and deny. By him, homosexuality is equated with vice and damnation. The principally external social reality of the first act is displaced by the act that follows it. The second act takes an audience inside the mind of Caravaggio, in such a way that the acts are not about continuity, but a layering process, the superimposition of one on top of the other. Thus audiences experience a very different type of play.

This is not a history play, more a compression of Caravaggio's life into a tight time span, and is a fictionalised version of the life, of which there are many other narrative accounts. Of course, there is a distinction to be made between the character of Caravaggio and the artist. There is an obvious danger in bleeding one into the other. So authenticity and verisimilitude are not foremost either to the dramaturgy or to the scenography of the play's first production. Joe Vaněk, in his design, utilised objects from across different time-periods in order to establish anachronisms.[4] This is a play not only about perceptions of damnation, but also is about redemption. The vision of the artist is to see salvation in all things. Caravaggio used those trapped in poverty and/or prostitution to pose for him as saints and sinners alike. Famously, Caravaggio used the bloated corpse of a dead prostitute, who had been pulled from a river, as a model for the Virgin Mary. At the core of Caravaggio's artistry is the ability to marry creativity and destructiveness, to balance compositionally light and dark, and to refigure key moments of Christian iconography within a homoerotic template. The intensity of the paintings springs from the corruption and poverty of his society, the impetuous rages of the artist, the unsettled nature of the unconscious, as much as from a transgressive brilliance and stylistic innovation that he brings to his work. Caravaggio is a mass of contradictions, equally creative, aloof, detached, calculating, reflective and caring, as well as being spontaneous, intuitive, violent and murderous. Through patronage and the procedures of commissioning, art is often commodified and its ideological imperatives and expectations implicitly normalised, while the artist functions as a mere possession. Caravaggio is both a confirmation and challenge to that perspective.

The play opens with a nightmare scenario, as Caravaggio sleeps in Lena's hovel. He is haunted by people in his life and by objects and images that recur and dominate his work, such as a skull, the red cloak and a horse. The co-mingling of people and objects, trauma and creativity are clearly established and such an overlap continues on right through the play. As the play progresses, the spectator meets a range of characters including the Cardinal, the young male prostitutes, the artist's brother, and their dead sister as well as Lena, his companion of sorts. By the end of the play, she takes on the mantle of an artist, in a world turned upside-down. It is a carnivalesque reversal: '**Lena** . . . I knew then somehow we'd won, we turned the world upside-down, the goat and the whore, the queer and his woman' (p. 284).

Carthaginians (1988)

The companion piece to *The Sons of Ulster* (the Protestant/loyalist play) is *Carthaginians* (the Catholic/nationalist play). It deals with the trauma and tribulations induced by Bloody Sunday, an occasion on which British paratroopers shot dead fourteen people on the streets of Derry, claiming that they were responding to an attack by Republican paramilitaries. While the time between the play's first production and the actual incident itself is brief, unlike *The Sons of Ulster* where the time span is substantial, *Carthaginians* still should be characterised as a history/memory play. The play's women characters gather in a graveyard, hoping to witness the dead rise. The male characters have different attachments to the same space. The dead do not rise, but the characters who have existed in a liminal space of suffering take the chance to purge their consciousnesses, to rest and move on. Each has to face individual horrors, and each has to connect back into the world of the living.

The playlet, *The Burning Balaclava*, written by the gay character, Dido, who writes under the pseudonym of Fionnuala McGonigle (F. McG . . .) is a key turning point in the drama, as the characters enact a cross-gender cast masquerade that travesties the rhetoric and sensibilities of all religious and political allegiances. As with the mock battle in *The Sons of Ulster*, which of course has a cross-tribal cast and a half-Catholic, Crawford, masquerading as King William of Orange, play or metatheatricality, in both instances, is the liberating, revitalising energy, which facilitates a shift of consciousness. After participating in *The Burning Balaclava*, the characters begin to imagine anew, and the stranglehold of the trauma begins to weaken. By the play's end, each character finds a way of letting go of guilt, denial, the deep hurts, and severe injustices that the events of Bloody Sunday brought about and have come to symbolise.[5] Both directly and indirectly, *The Sons of Ulster* and *Carthaginians* reflect the clash between Protestantism and Catholicism, loyalism and Republicanism. In the work there is this constant binary distinction between Catholic and Protestant; it continues to be expressed in plays such as *Speaking Like Magpies*, which was performed as part of the Royal Shakespeare Company's Gunpowder season and which reflects on the plot by Catholics to murder the Protestant King James I. The play ends with Queen Anne, admitting to her secret Catholicism; thus the cycle of inter-religious conflict has another impetus and another source.

Mary and Lizzie (1989)

Mary and Lizzie is a fantasy piece, inspired loosely by Henrik Ibsen's *Peer Gynt*, which McGuinness was adapting around the time. The two Burns sisters, Mary and Lizzie, flee Ireland having been warned about an impending famine. They head to Manchester, where they live with Frederick Engels, successful businessman, writer, and friend and financial supporter of Karl Marx. These two sisters had been almost written out of history, and McGuinness's work is both an act of retrieval and an assault on Victorian sensibilities, exemplified by Marx particularly, who for all his insight had written disparagingly about the Irish in his book *The Conditions of the Working Class*,[6] despite having lived with these two women for a long time, and despite their role in escorting him through the underworld of poverty and the inhumane living conditions found in industrial Manchester. Scenes range from the women of the camps in Ireland in the middle of the nineteenth century, awaiting the return of British soldiers, to the work camps of Russia under communist rule, from the underworld where the sisters meet their dead mother to an encounter by the seaside with Queen Victoria (performed by a male). Space and time are meshed in most unsettling and brilliant ways, so that poverty and dispossession are registered, and intellectual reflection is shown to be incapable of distilling the essences of inhumanity. The two sisters also challenge the founders of Marxism on the grounds of gender and nationality. These men, despite their brilliance, are confined by many of the prejudices of their own times, classes and cultures. Engels and Marx can clearly reflect on class, power and inequality, but are far less successful on imperialism, race and gender. European class biases as much as British ones are contested by the play.

Mutabilitie (1997)

Moreover, this play's breadth and fluidity contrast sharply with the five-act Shakespearean form of *Mutabilitie* which plots the tensions between the indigenous Irish and the ruling British classes, represented by the poet Edmund Spenser[7] and his partner, Elizabeth.

While ruled by the mythic Queen Maeve and her partner King Sweeney, the Irish revolt is led by the File, or Poetess and her partner Hugh, who work for the Spenser family inside the fortress.[8] File imagines redemption taking the form a of man coming from a river and when a member of an acting troupe, called William Shakespeare, is saved from the water, File believes that she has discovered a redeemer. Neither William nor an uprising bring lasting change. Elizabeth regards the Irish as 'vermin', 'animals' and 'savages' (p. 8). Spenser shares her perceptions:

> We must win this people to England's laws, to England's custom, to her religion. If we fail, then we abandon this people to the devil. (p. 10)

His concept of colonialism is thus substantiated by the civilising imperative of imperialism, which denies the material benefits of conquest or that imperialism itself might be ever construed as evil. While *Mutabilitie* initially imagines redemption through the rescued body from the river, it is later reconstituted, by the Irish finding the lost Spenser child and agreeing to foster rather than take him as a hostage.

Someone Who'll Watch Over Me (1992)

If both previous plays challenge the dominant hegemony of British rule through a dialogical opposition between two hostile, but clearly unequal, groupings, the third part of the trilogy, *Someone Who'll Watch Over Me*, endeavours to diffuse clear binary distinctions between the English/British[9] and Irish characters, Michael and Edward, respectively, through the manipulation of stereotype and through a constant breach of an audience's expectation, grounded as it is in cultural norms and expectations. McGuinness attempts to move away from the imperatives of history and the injustices and misrepresentations that these bring. In this play, Edward and Michael are held hostage with an American, Adam, in a cell in Beirut. The play was inspired by McGuinness's response to the actual cycle of hostage taking that occurred in Lebanon in the late 1980s and early 1990s. Adam is the honest broker, and in many respects, he is the agent of change. Further, in Lebanon, there is little or nothing to distinguish between bearing a British or Irish passport. To the hostage takers, these men are simply citizens of a Western world, enemies to their own values, and representative of Western democracies hostile to their own core beliefs. Edward tells of flashing his Irish passport during his abduction in the hope that his Irishness will bring him some sort of dispensation, but to no avail. By the play's end, the spectator is to assume that Adam is dead, Edward is to be set free, after suffering a nervous breakdown, and Michael, the initially prissy Englishman, is still being held. Michael's strength and his traditions have seen him through thus far. The play is about negotiation and the letting go of national imperatives and prejudice, but is never simplistic. It is through the use of storytelling and the creative imagination that the chained hostages move towards some sort of liberation. There is no happy ending in the traditional sense. Michael's future, in terms of the drama, is notionally precarious.

Summary

McGuinness's work invites careful scrutiny, given that many of his plays are written almost as parallel, even parasitical texts to those he has adapted. Anton Chekhov, Henrik Ibsen and August Strindberg, as well as the major classical Greek figures, all have faced serious challenges to their dramaturgical representations of women. The above cluster of writers are accused at worst of isolating from the dramatic action and immobilising within the theatrical spaces their female characters, thereby unleashing a rampant, deviant misogyny that pandered to the prerequisites of the individual ruling classes of their own times, or at best, of careless objectification and stereotyping, especially in terms of ending plays with the suicide of female characters. In addition, feminist critics have argued that most Irish male playwrights offer their female characters a very limited range of functions within the drama and that a narrow range of behaviours are part of audience expectations. In the traditional Irish play women were almost always obliged to substantiate patriarchal rule and were associated with home, otherness and the land.

Obviously, one can test the dramatic action of a play to see if the women characters have access to similar types of behaviour, thoughts and feelings as those of their male counterparts of the same class, or if not, analogous access to a wide array of simple, complex and comparable emotions, whether there are isolations, immobility, exclusions or the absence or restraints on agency. In *Mutabilitie*, for example, File is willing to commit all kinds of crimes in order to see her country freed, yet when the young son of the Spensers, who has gone missing, wanders into the Irish camp, he is looked after with great care, thanks to her intervention. A gendered identity, culturally and historically shaped, can be almost free floating, and is grounded in artifice, metatheatricality and the sensibility of play, yet alert to its own transitional reality. Artistry is one specific expression of this. McGuinness populates his plays with male and female artists. The advice to most playwrights would be to stay away from writers, painters, actors, theatre directors, especially poets, as these characters tend to be too knowing, overly expressive and perceived as self-indulgently performative. The tendency is to get artists onstage to be the voice of the playwright, all-knowing and self consciously alert to their existences, and more importantly, willing to enunciate at length their predicaments. McGuinness seems to have wholeheartedly ignored that sort of advice. While artistry foregrounds gender, it must be offset by the actions of the characters that cannot be withdrawn as pretence, or shielded from their actions. For instance, murder cannot be retracted.

So, it is not so much that the artist is a visionary, but a troubled artist whose ability is to see others or their own society with a greater clarity than they see themselves. Instead the artists are often uncomfortable and uncertain with their own compulsions. Helen Lojek points out that:

> McGuinness's male artists are typically geographic exiles . . .
> Women artists like Eleanor Henryson in *The Bird Sanctuary*

and File in *Mutabilitie* remain geographically as well as imaginatively in their homes. The male artists launch their quests horizontally across the surface of the earth; the female artists quest vertically, exploring the depths of place and self.[10]

Pyper in *The Sons of Ulster* is a sculptor. Once Pyper survives the war, he sings the piper's tune, that limited mythology of war to which his tribe subscribes, but it is also a narrative which betrays the fundamental memory of his dead comrades. Therefore he is haunted by them to remember the story in all its complexity and not to distil it down to the coherence offered by a blood sacrifice narrative imperative. In *The Sons of Ulster*, Pyper's creativity is stunted by the obligations and conventions of tribe and by an inability to break free of a cycle of control and intervention. The playful and imaginative performativity of Pyper from the play's off is grounded more in his self-destructiveness and pain than in any liberating consciousness. Loyalist destiny is located in repetition, as it is for those who uncritically rehash and recycle mythic patterns of self-sacrifice, in the name of a worldview that is passed down almost unmediated from the Battle of the Boyne. Dido in *Carthaginians* is the budding playwright who writes under a pseudonym, as if such a name will give distance from the trauma of post-Bloody Sunday Derry.

By interrogating the figure of the artist, whether it is a theatre director, playwright, sculptor or poet, issues of gender and sexuality are most clearly explored and revealed. Eleanor is bisexual, Caravaggio is homosexual, as are Dido, Pyper, Gabriel and Conrad in *Gates of Gold* (2002), and Rebecca in *The Factory Girls*. Of this list, Rebecca is the only one not an artist. Her creativity is of a different order. McGuinness is not only opening up a debate about homosexuality, as homosexuality was illegal in Ireland until 1993, but equally he is not just attempting representations that are simply about gender or sexual orientation or discrimination. Instead sexuality is part of his characters' constructions, not the single focus of consideration.

His gay characters can be relatively innocent like Dido or destructive, even murderous: Caravaggio kills, and Eleanor brings death, even if it is through magic. In *Mutabilitie*, File is learned in law, languages, maths, astronomy, poetry, medicine and magic. She is also very violent. Yet, the play concludes with File's invitation to the Spenser child to drink milk and eat (p. 101). She has the power to create and to destroy, as do almost all of McGuinness's artists. Moreover, the plays insist on the responsibility of such awarenesses. So, when it comes to gender and sexual orientation, McGuinness seems to avoid the traditional pitfalls of writing that is accused of a constraining gender bias or prejudicing same-sex passion. If you look across the range of the work it is possible to argue that the female characters, whether heterosexual or homosexual, seem to have the same access as to behaviours, choices, emotions and responses, both positive and negative, as their male counterparts. Further, with some exceptions, women characters have a similar access to ritual and to the contestation of reality through the frameworks of play. Yet, in the early plays, when it comes to mixed-gender casts, I have recently argued that the male characters seem to have greater access to performativity than the females.[11] *Carthaginians* and *Innocence* are obvious evidence of it, but as the work progresses that tendency is countered in plays such as *Mary and Lizzie* and in *The Bird Sanctuary*. It is only in terms of sexual promiscuity that the two genders significantly differ.

McGuinness's work is rich, complex, vigorous, and a huge challenge to academics, audiences, and to those who perform the work. His reputation is advanced by good performances, but more importantly, it will be enhanced by a distance from the immediacy of the work. Already the merits of his early and mid-career work are being revised upwards, and in the future, the questions raised initially by some commentators, about what has been seen as the overwritten or the unwieldy weave of the work, will be seen in far more positive ways. To conclude, in the work the deep sectarian divisions of Northern Ireland are overlaid with the historical imperatives of British imperialism and its control of Ireland. An additional layer is added when artistry, gender and sexualities are deployed to explore and expose entrenchment.

McGuinness's plays are set in borderlands, within a liminal consciousness, in spaces where there is the inarticulateness and the urgency of the language, where there is no intimacy and great warmth, where deviance brings clarity and perversity assertiveness, where the

ritualised imagination breaches conventions, and where the impossible can happen. McGuinness is the Irish playwright who has written
most frequently about the past, about carnage of history, but indeed
he is equally a playwright of and for the future.

Primary Sources

Works by Frank McGuinness

Gates of Gold (London: Faber and Faber, 2002).

Mutabilitie (London: Faber and Faber, 1997).

Plays 1 [*The Factory Girls, Observe the Sons of Ulster Marching Towards the Somme,
Innocence, Carthaginians, Baglady*] (London: Faber and Faber, 1996).

Plays 2 [*Mary and Lizzie, Someone Who'll Watch Over Me, Dolly West's Kitchen, The Bird
Sanctuary*] (London: Faber and Faber, 2002).

Secondary Sources

Cregan, David, '"There's something queer here": Modern Ireland and the Plays of Frank
McGuinness', in Brian Singleton and Anna McMullan (eds), Special Issue: *Performing
Ireland, Australasian Drama Studies*, Vol. 43 (2003), pp. 66–75.

Hiroko Mikami, *Frank McGuinness and His Theatre of Paradox* (Gerrards Cross: Colin
Smythe, 2002).

Jackson, Joe, 'The Healing Touch', *Irish Sunday Independent*, 21 April 2002.

Jordan, Eamonn, *The Feast of Famine: The Plays of Frank McGuinness* (Bern: Peter Lang,
1997).

—, 'Meta-physicality: Women Characters in the Plays of Frank McGuinness', *Women in
Irish Drama: A Century of Authorship and Representation* (London: Palgrave, 2007), p.
142.

Kiberd, Declan, 'Frank McGuinness and the Sons of Ulster', *Yearbook of English Studies*,
Vol. 35 (2005), pp. 279–97.

Kurdi, Maria, 'An Interview with Frank McGuinness', *Nua: Studies in Contemporary Irish
Writing*, Vol. 4, Nos 1–2 (2003), pp. 113–32.

Lojek, Helen (ed.), *The Theatre of Frank McGuinness: Stages of Mutability* (Dublin:
Carysfort Press, 2002).

—, *Contexts for Frank McGuinness's Drama* (Washington, DC: The Catholic University of
America Press, 2004).

Long, Joseph, 'Frank McGuinness in Conversation with Joseph Long', in Lilian Chambers *et al.* (eds), *Theatre Talk: Voices of Irish Theatre Practitioners* (Dublin: Carysfort, 2001), pp. 298–307.

West, Derek, 'Joe Vaněk in Conversation with Derek West', *Theatre Ireland,* Vol. 29 (1992), p. 26.

Notes

1. As Hiroko Mikami establishes, 'For people of the Inishowen peninsula, Derry/Londonderry is a natural capital, to which they still commute for work or shopping, crossing the border on a daily basis.' See Hiroko Mikami, *Frank McGuinness and His Theatre of Paradox,* p. 3.

2. See details of the holdings in the Philip Tilling archive in ibid., pp. 165–232.

3. Joe Jackson notes: 'Because once upon a time – specifically 1990 when I last interviewed McGuinness – we had to rely on subtextual hints when it came to the subject of his homosexuality. Such as? My asking if imposing his own "sexual uncertainties" on to characters in his plays makes those characters "misrepresent broader realities, less disturbed lives than his own, perhaps". To which Frank could only reply, basically, "That's a fair point and I do ask myself continually am I doing that." Clearly, the closet still was Frank's favourite room. At least during interviews. "I did declare myself, but not in print," he responds. "And I do believe that in my plays of the Nineties – particularly *The Bird Sanctuary* and *Dolly West's Kitchen* – my homosexuality is more clear than ever before. Though in the earlier plays it definitely is more coded. And often the key issue. Whereas in the later work it's just another part of the play.' (Joe Jackson, 'The Healing Touch').

4. Joe Vaněk suggests that *Innocence* was marked 'by a refusal to be frozen by anachronism – *Innocence* did not belong to a specific period' as the design incorporated Victorian fires, fifties chairs and a lot of 'modern junk' into an 'ostensibly Renaissance setting, thus ensuring that the play was seen not merely as a museum piece' (Derek West, 'Joe Vaněk in Conversation with Derek West', p. 26).

5. In later plays like *The Breadman* and in *Dolly West's Kitchen*, McGuinness returns to his home place of Buncrana. The former deals with the guilt of The Sinner Courtney and his near madness in the aftermath of his brother's drowning. These incidents are the backdrop to the presence of those fleeing from the Northern Irish troubles and not finding the hospitality in Donegal for which the Irish are supposedly renowned.

6. According to McGuinness' 'And, of course, from that experience he wrote *The Conditions of the Working Class,* which is probably one of the key-texts that influence twentieth-century history'. (Kurdi, 'An Interview with frank McGuinness' p. 120).

7. Spenser's *The Faerie Queene* honours his virgin Queen, Elizabeth.

8. Joseph Long, 'Frank McGuinness in Conversation with Joseph Long', pp. 298–307.

9. I am conscious that slippage between English and British is a constant in the discussion, and this seems to reflect what the plays themselves do.

10. Helen Lojek, *Contexts for Frank McGuinness's Drama*, p. 102.

11. Elsewhere I argue, 'They talk, they act, they accuse and they pervert expectations and norms. But there are gender differences. What the female characters, whether heterosexual, homosexual or bisexual, seldom have, however, is access to the same levels of sexual desire . . . Clearly, female sexual desire is not as licensed like that of Caravaggio in *Innocence* or Gabriel and Conrad in *Gates of Gold*. Only Mary and Lizzie Burns can be considered as sexually expressive or assured. Also notable is the inclusion of many women that either have lost children or can't have them. There are few women with living offspring, which taps into a different anxiety.' See Eamonn Jordan, 'Meta-physicality: Women Characters in the Plays of Frank McGuinness', p. 142.

15 TOM Mac INTYRE

Daniel Shea

The Great Hunger; Sheep's Milk on the Boil; Good Evening, Mr Collins; The Gallant John-Joe; What Happened Bridgie Cleary

Introduction

Tom Mac Intyre's kind of theatre, at least in Ireland, is its own category, and Tom Mac Intyre the writer adheres to what can only be called a vision, a calling that only few hear and follow. For the reader coming for the first time to his work there is much to stumble over. Even admirers sometimes will make a pause at the menagerie of Irish and foreign vocabulary, at the antics of houyhnhnms, shape-shifters, dwarves and fairies in remote places, or at word choice like 'farewell lactic Slopes of Innocence, / welcome vales awash with cuntal juice' (*ABC*, p. 3) and 'Jesus stabs Ireland in the epididymal canal' (*Lovely Sweeney*, p. 46). But Mac Intyre has always drawn audiences because he writes with so much at stake for himself and because this shows in both the risks and the risqué in his career. In a theatre culture all but ignorant of dance and physical theatre Mac Intyre has helped extend the reach of both; for a society once loath even to talk about sexuality Mac Intyre has staged a girl's first period (in *Snow White*) and the father's male desire for the sex of his daughter (in *Dance for Your Daddy*); and to a country whose folklore attests to an avid imagination regarding the doings of the fairies Mac Intyre has fostered through his work what he terms 'the spirit magic'.[1]

Born in Bailieborough, County Cavan, on 10 December 1931, Tom Mac Intyre grew up in the small-town Ireland of mid-century, where the middle-class family and the Catholic Church held individual emotional and intellectual development in check, but also where folkways and the bits and pieces of a dying Gaelic culture harboured the resources which could subvert the conservative communal structure if somebody just tapped them. Mac Intyre has bent the landscape, the dialect, the folklore and the storytelling of the Midlands to his creative ends, and an oeuvre of poetry, short stories and, most notably, plays stem from this Irish source and from his unique style.

After the novel *The Charollais* in 1969 and the publication of new and selected short stories in 1970, he wrote a book-length investigative report on a 1970 political scandal involving the IRA and translated seventeenth- and eighteenth-century Irish poems before turning to the theatre. His first effort, *Eye Winker, Tom Tinker*, was staged by the Abbey in 1972 and, Mac Intyre has recalled, was found by one reviewer to be 'disgracefully conventional'[2] – an astounding critique in retrospect on Mac Intyre's subsequent home out on the fringe of mainstream Irish theatre. From here, Mac Intyre's stated aim has been to break with conventional theatre as widely practised, up to just recently, in Ireland.

During the 1970s (since drama schools in Ireland were first established in the mid-1980s) the usual route for anyone looking to do theatre differently was either via the Continent or the US. Mac Intyre had been to both places. Besides immersing himself in the study of dance and theatre from Vsevolod Meyerhold onwards, he admired the work of Pina Bausch, Merce Cunningham and Tadeusz Kantor. Collaboration with students at an Ohio college on the production of his *Deer Crossing* in spring 1978 carried over into the formation of Calck Hook Dance Theatre. In April of the following year Calck Hook was in Paris producing Mac Intyre's *Doobally/Black Way* (the town name Dooballagh translates as 'black pass, black road') to public and critical acclaim, but on transferring in October to the Dublin Theatre Festival the play was ill-received, and on its second night police had to remove protesting members of the audience.[3] By 1983, when the Abbey staged Mac Intyre's next production, *The Great Hunger*, he was 'at once both loved and hated' in Dublin.[4]

Although the number of performing venues and styles open to Irish theatre practitioners has, specifically since 1985, increased threefold,[5] by the early 1980s Ireland had only a few people capable of executing a professional production of a play like *The Great Hunger*. Physical and dance theatre demand collaboration, and few great works of the genres can be attributed to just one person. Theatre like this, which 'depends entirely on an intersection of energies to ignite the work',[6] takes risks which theatre that focuses on plot and dialogue does not, but it also can achieve things other theatre can't.

The Great Hunger as well as Mac Intyre's other, as yet unpublished collaborations at the Abbey's studio theatre, the Peacock, until the end of the 1980s (i.e., *The Bearded Lady, Rise Up Lovely Sweeney, Dance for Your Daddy* and *Snow White*) are the plays that most characterise public and critical opinion of his work. The theatrical idiom perfected during the productions and tours of these years has come to be known as Theatre of the Image. The appropriateness of 'Theatre of the Image' as a descriptor of Mac Intyre's plays lies not in its reference to pictures (i.e. images), but in its reference to the mental faculty which makes pictures (i.e. the imagination). Today, with the widespread use of image files and digital-photo applications, Theatre of the Image is misleading because, while connoting 'snapshot', it is meant to describe 'gestures, signals, objects, sounds, spatial relationships, pacing' on the stage.[7] Alan Read's *Theatre and Everyday Life*, a groundbreaking study on the image in theatre, removes notions of metaphor and symbolism from what we normally consider imagery of the stage in order to present a theatre image that is at once discursive (i.e. consisting of text and speech) and sensual (i.e. consisting of visual, auditory and olfactory input).

The salient effect which Theatre of the Image has on a performance is to order speech, the dominant component in conventional play productions and drama texts, not *above* but *beside* the other means of performance. Against the conventional relation of much dialogue to little description, the scripts of Mac Intyre's imagistic plays run for pages with few or no spoken lines. Also, Theatre of the Image taps an energy of the theatre often regarded as little more than the adjunct to normal entertainment practice: the audience. At a Mac Intyre play, those attending either respond to what's going on by playing their parts in the collaboration which is the performance or they don't connect and, as runs the line in his poem 'At the Theatre', 'leave at the interval' (*Glance*, p. 20).

Patrick Mason has spoken of Mac Intyre's 'capacity to surprise'[8] the theatregoer, and the past fifteen years have also held other surprises from him. From 1998 to 1999 he adapted Irish and English literature for Taibhdhearc na Gaillimhe, the Irish-language theatre in Galway,[9] and so reversed the age-old pattern of dominance whereby Irish literature and drama had been translated for the English-language stage.[10] In 1996, he collaborated with Irish Modern Dance Theatre on his piece *You Must Tell the Bees*, and his 2003 novel *Story of a Girl* showed him writing in a genre he hadn't attempted since 1969. In his eightieth year, his most recent play, *Only an Apple*, is being staged at the Peacock.

The Plays

The Great Hunger (1983)

Through the mid-1980s, in Ireland and abroad, *The Great Hunger* caused a considerable furore, both delighted and incensed. After opening at the Peacock in May 1983, *The Great Hunger* went back into rehearsal, was extensively revised, and then toured internationally. Some stops were welcoming, as in 1986 at the Edinburgh Fringe, when the play took a Fringe First Award; some were hostile, as in 1988 in New York and Philadelphia, where the fraternal organisation the Ancient Order of Hibernians complained that this was 'not the *real* Abbey at all'.[11] Also in Ireland, public opinion was divided over the impressions which were being made of the Irish, especially at the most talked-about stops of the 1988 tour, Leningrad and Moscow.[12]

Mac Intyre's *The Great Hunger* was so lauded and reviled not because it was theatre and dance and mime in one show – that kind of performance had been going on for well over fifty years and, anyway, had been one of the major influences on Mac Intyre's work in the first place. Instead, the play became such a controversy because it was one of the first occasions of Irish material being treated and Irish artists performing in physical theatre.[13] But *The Great Hunger* deserves more recognition than of just having been one of the first. In it a refined and demanding work of its type pioneered and, at the same time, challenged the field. The images of farmers bent over potato drills, of the tabernacle housing mystery, of collection boxes wielded with aplomb, of the matriarchal effigy struck, in particular, Irish audiences.[14]

The play *The Great Hunger* represents an acute challenge for the critic trying to recount its plot and analyse its structure. Irish writer and theatre practitioner Dermot Healy has remarked that Mac Intyre's plays are 'beyond paraphrasing',[15] and although this is less true of his productions since 1994, it accurately describes his Peacock work during the 1980s. A reasonable account of the story of the play would begin with the death or departure of Maguire's father (a nonentity in the action) and Maguire's subsequent inheritance of the farm. Where the action picks up is with Maguire's decision not to marry but to support his mother and sister. When his mother dies, he is beyond marriageable age, and from her he inherits more of the same frustration and desolation that he has experienced all his life. Maguire's death, foreshadowed in scene 21, is depicted as a time hardly distinguishable from his life. The idea to stage Patrick Kavanagh's 1942 poem 'The Great Hunger', which Mac Intyre remembers being talked about since the 1960s,[16] was probably inspired by the speaker's invitation to 'wait and watch the tragedy to the last curtain' (I) when, following 'Applause, applause', the spectacle of Maguire's life ends in 'Silence, silence' (XIV).[17] The poem has, besides, about five delineated characters and a strong storyline, so that with little alteration it could provide the material for a dramatic production. But Mac Intyre approached it differently. As a note heading the 1983 script of *The Great Hunger* explains:

> It has not been the aim to put Patrick Kavanagh's poem on the stage; rather, attending closely to it, to convey theatrically its central themes and supporting motifs. The language of the play is taken exclusively from the poem; the images are either taken from the poem or have evident roots there.[18]

The major themes of sexual, emotional and spiritual dearth, which the titles of both poem and play actually refer to,[19] are conveyed by fewer than a hundred lines from a poem of over seven hundred, so the images have to carry the greater part of the adaptation.

The poem is rich in imagery, and in it are found the men scarecrows (I and XIV; sc. 2), Maguire masturbating over the coals (V; sc. 3), ecstasy at green-leaved branches (III; sc. 5), ploughing (III; sc. 9), pub guests 'propping up' each other with their company (XI; sc. 10), and Maguire pawing the ground 'with the awkward grace of an animal nosing about for a clean place to die' (XIV; sc. 21). Besides such discerning selection of images from the poem, the play successfully translates poetry for the stage because the images are created with the same economy in theatrical terms as are the metaphors in phrasal terms. The play adapts, then, not just in choosing and arranging the material of the poem, but also in forging a theatrical style for what had known only literary expression.

What the audience of *The Great Hunger* sees on the stage are the pivots of Maguire's world, and what they watch are the menial jobs of his day and the shaping events of his life. All this is presented not realistically, but expressively. The audience should not, for example, be disturbed by Maguire's mother being a wooden statue, but they should recognise in the interrelation between actor and prop a definitive side to Maguire's psyche. The effect such transferences at the levels of both structure and performance will have on an audience is to reformulate outward things and occurrences as expressions of Maguire's inner life. For this to succeed not only must the functions of speech and figure be bent towards expression through performance, but also space and, by analogy, time must be restructured so as to convey the material in fitting images.

Space in the play is a fluid dimension, crystallising only at the three meaningful locations in the peasant's life: the field, the kitchen and the church. Time in both the poem and the play is conceived of in cyclical terms. At the opening of the play, Maguire enters in a dream, awakens to act out the reality of his life and, at the ending, lies down in the cemetery again to slumber. This structuring of space and time provides the optimal backdrop on which to project archetypal images and to portray Maguire's psyche. A prime example is scene 13.

Maguire, '*Sitting on a wooden gate*', can see the tussling between Agnes and Malone for sexual control but cannot be seen by them. But this is no simple voyeurism because the '*Two centres of simultaneous action*' (p. 39), as the Nebentext directs, interrelate and interfere in complex ways to reflect on the personality of Maguire. He is the blatant witness to things he will not see, but there is actually nothing for Maguire to see because Agnes and Malone part as they had met: celibate. Although this alone would be a sore enough reminder that the only kissing going on in Maguire's world happens when he overcomes every human instinct to kiss his mother's corpse, Maguire will still watch them through the lattice of the gate, hanging upside down, his legs in a V, jigging alternately each foot – in short, clowning to deflect his tension over sins no one is committing.

Sheep's Milk on the Boil (1994)

Sheep's Milk on the Boil retains the dance and visual elements of Theatre of the Image, but while lending more substance to plot and, a corollary of this, transforming the incantatory poetry of a *Great Hunger* into idiomatic dialogue expressive of individual personalities. In structuralist terminology, speech in Theatre of the Image stands in a complementary relation to the non-verbal information of a production, as in expressionist theatre,[20] while in a play like *Sheep's Milk on the Boil* verbal and non-verbal information both reflect and complement one another. Precisely these relations account for the individual figures of Mac Intyre's later plays, in contrast to the types of his Theatre of the Image. Also, in imagistic plays the action phases are juxtaposed because the actions and events rise, peak and fall separately and connect to one another primarily through common themes, verbal repetition or shared movement, gestures and props. *Sheep's Milk on the Boil*, in contrast, builds suspense, explains events and describes figures through dramatic exposition, proceeds to the resolution of a conflict – in short, it has a plot.

The play opens with Biddy starting to doubt Matt's faithfulness when he returns from the mainland, but his odd behaviour, the audience sees, is because of the mirror he has brought back and wants to keep only for himself. Two troupes of fairies intervene ostensibly to resolve the conflict, the Visitor on Biddy's behalf and the Inspector of Wrack on Matt's behalf, but mischief seems their first intent. Matt's and Biddy's fight escalates, not least because the fairies try to seduce them both, until Matt finally reveals the mirror to Biddy. This only drives Matt and Biddy further apart, so they enter the woods and spend a wild night with the fairies. Matt is repelled, but Biddy attracted by the experience so that, when the fairies on departing try one last time for each, Biddy goes and Matt, calling her back, stays behind.

Sheep's Milk on the Boil may draw its material from the fairy lore of Ireland, but it builds on the themes of emotional inhibition and sexual mores as they also occur in Synge's *The Playboy of the Western World* (1907). The points of contact between the two plays begin already with the playwrights' express sources and purposes. In his 1907 preface to the play, J. M. Synge argues that, since in Ireland

> the imagination of the people, and the language they use, is rich and living, it is possible for a writer to be rich and copious in his words, and at the same time to give the reality, which is the root of all poetry, in a comprehensive and natural form.[21]

Mac Intyre's own views on language are the following: the midlands idiom – in his words 'a quite extraordinary mix of late medieval, Elizabethan, Scots, and a throbbing, eloquent, plangent undertone of the recently lost Gaeilge'[22] – is the linguistic reservoir from which he draws a great part of his grammar and vocabulary. Young writers in Ireland today must make use of the wealth of linguistic expressiveness unique to the Irish, that mixture of native and foreign languages which has given them their own tongue, Irish English.[23] The tremendous artistic advantage to be garnered from this position is the same that Synge finds in the 'rich and living' language of the people: the freedom to crack the syntax and inflate the words of English in ways that outside the setting of rural Ireland would seem bombastic and ridiculous.

Mac Intyre seeks such freedom not just in the way the Irish speak, but also in the way they move. Long before any reading or travel introduced him to dance and physical theatre, Mac Intyre was impressed by the performance which was fair day in his home town Bailieborough.[24] Coupling Irish speech with Irish physicality, Mac Intyre gives form to that reality which Synge identifies as 'the root of all poetry', and so 'the imagination of the people' or, as one might write today, the Irish collective unconscious provides the ultimate source for and receives creative expression from speech and movement on the stages of *The Playboy of the Western World* and *Sheep's Milk on the Boil*.

These two plays are, in themselves, similar on many heads. In neither are libido and sex covered over in any way, so that Pegeen's fears alone at night have the faces of 'the harvest boys', 'the ten tinkers', and 'the thousand militia' (p. 76); Christy's hiding places in the bogs are familiar as 'where you'd see young, limber girls, and fine, prancing women making laughter with the men'; and Matt's and Biddy's inhibitions are assailed by the eroticism, the perversity and the hurt of sexual relations with the fairies in the wood at night:

A nest of spiceries
Vagrant kisses, wayward juices
shadows put to many uses . . .
Fits and seizures melt your garments
stir your limbs and ripe endowments
Farewell reins, farewell halters
strut your stuff for further orders
Prosper Jack, prosper Jill
foot the bill tomorrow morning . . . (p. 101)

Both plays have settings on the western coast and figures whose communities have sparse contacts to the outside world. Finally, and most importantly, the plays have structurally identical endings at which one figure regrets not having pursued her or his partner but can't find the courage to.

The enigmatic title *Sheep's Milk on the Boil* Mac Intyre has explained as being, in Irish folklore, the response to a question: 'What frightens men?' Answer: 'Sheep's milk on the boil.' For Mac Intyre the milk stands for 'the wave of the female fecundity, fertility', so its boiling is the sign that the peak is being reached.[25] Olwen Fouéré, who played the Inspector, has described how her costumes expressed the 'heightened female sexuality' which her figure embodies, and she has compared playing the Inspector to living 'all the fantasies you've ever had about playing all the female icons over the years that you've seen in the movies'.[26] Fouéré's insight into the personality of the Inspector draws attention to the archetype of femininity at the base of this figure and behind her relationship to Matt.

Pursuing the function, typical of Mac Intyre, by which a figure's unconscious is projected on to denizens of the other world, I correlate the Inspector with the anima Matt represses and the Visitor with the animus Biddy is beginning to unleash. These correlations can be extended to *The Playboy of the Western World* so that Matt and Biddy stand in direct relation, respectively, to Pegeen and Christy. Biddy is able to leave behind jealousy and Christy vanity because they consciously reflect on themselves, that is, on where they are, who they are with, and how all this is determining who, at the moment, they are. Christy finds his way out of that stifling Mayo village by subduing his father – murder, in the end, isn't necessary – and, thus, mounting the possibility of his actually becoming the playboy everyone has taken him for. Biddy's success in self-awareness is best measured against Matt's failure. While he, in his 'dotesomes' (p. 110), will regret having stayed back and chosen the settled life over life on the road, she will thrive because (to quote the speaker of Mac Intyre's 'Pot Black' pleading with a woman to accompany him on the same track) she has overcome 'the fear of danger to encounter the danger of fear' (*Yes*, p. 73).

Good Evening, Mr Collins (1995)

Mac Intyre's *Good Evening, Mr Collins* met with acclaim and success, not least because again, as in *The Great Hunger*, material or history very familiar to Irish audiences was re-expressed in unlooked-for form.[27] *Good Evening, Mr Collins* first played on the Peacock stage from 5 October 1995 as part of the Dublin Theatre Festival. It was then re-rehearsed and revised to open in 1996 again at the Peacock. A national tour followed. So *Sheep's Milk on the Boil* and *Good Evening, Mr Collins* played back to back at the same venue, and this concentration of Mac Intyre's attention and efforts is evident in two varied treatments of the same problem: what does the man do who is frightened by the feminine inside?

Marina Carr, in her programme note to the 1996 production, applauds the decision to have one actress play the parts of all three women because this doubling performs the crux of Collins's problem not with women, but with woman. These women figures in one actress represent, Carr writes, 'the vital connection between Collins and his fate'.[28] It would appear a bad decision, on the other hand, to have Collins always acting in full consciousness of his assassination as well as to skip this potentially dramatic event for the seemingly anti-climactic lying-in-state in City Hall. But this structuring of figure and plot are really just the rigorous consequence of the play's take on Collins's end: while his fate lies all the while in his hands, Collins remains incapable of seizing it because he cannot face the feminine, whether as projected on to others or inside himself.

Good Evening, Mr Collins is the play of Mac Intyre's recent work that most resembles, from a structural standpoint, the Peacock collaborations with Hickey and Mason. The plot, unlike that of *Sheep's Milk on the Boil,* is subservient to the images expressing Collins's personality, nor does a dramatic figure, as in *What Happened Bridgie Cleary*, dominate the action.

The historical background to *Good Evening, Mr Collins* is the last five years of Michael Collins's life when, rising to various positions of leadership during the fight against England and in the administration of the new state, he made for himself bitter foes and devoted supporters. The action picks up with the figure's counter-intelligence campaign before the War of Independence, and while some scenes can be chronologically pinpointed, such as 1.8 at Dublin's Gresham Hotel during Christmas 1920 and 2.8 at Dublin City Hall during the final days of August 1922, other scenes lie outside all historical or biographical reckoning to function instead as sites where Collins's inner troubles are played out on the set.

Such non-realistic scenes are further marked through the dialogue.

The referential and appellative functions of language, for example, are overridden by an expressive, poetic idiom that recalls the verse of Maguire or other figures of Mac Intyre's imagistic theatre. Episodic in structure, the action passes from historical fact to a mimed tennis match (1.3), a nightmarish dance (1.6), and imaginary meetings between Collins and Dev at which they play the parts, respectively, of pupil and teacher (1.4), of husband and voyeur (2.3), and of Commander-in-Chief and priest (2.6). By the time Collins visits his own lying-in-state (2.8), the audience has grown accustomed to relating other people and outward events to inner states of emotion. In this way, ambushes, raids and purges become a significative wartime backdrop to war of another order: Collins's war on the female sex. Collins's relationships to women are his obsession and become, as he increasingly and painfully realises (in 1.7 and 2.5), his downfall. He is incapable either of coming to grips with the women in his life or – which in the logic of this play amounts to the same thing – of standing midwife to the labour of a nation.

The Gallant John-Joe (2001)

Another collaborative project from Mac Intyre and Hickey, *The Gallant John-Joe* was produced by Skehana Theatre Company and performed for the first time on 22 January 2001 in the hotel and restaurant McGrory's of Culdaff, County Donegal. It then went on tour in Ireland and abroad. The play belongs to a theatrical form which is best described either as the one-person show or as the staged narrative and which, through work during the late 1980s and the 1990s by Sebastian Barry, Dermot Bolger, Marie Jones, Conor McPherson, Mark O'Rowe and Enda Walsh, among others, has quickly become an Irish favourite.

The story behind the figure of John-Joe is this. Father of three girls and widower, John-Joe Concannon will not be deterred from identifying the father of his youngest's, Jacinta's, unborn child, and he suspects everyone from hypnotist Dallan Devine to the owner of a fish-and-chips shop where Jacinta once worked. His behaviour, which from the impression he makes seems typical of him, causes Jacinta to admit herself into a mental hospital where it's then revealed that the pregnancy has been her fantasy. Acting on the belief that his original prime suspect is to blame now for Jacinta's mental illness, John-Joe murders the shop owner, a Chinese immigrant. Because of a violent outburst at the hospital, John-Joe is barred from seeing his daughter, and he ends his story convinced that he has played the 'escape-goat' to the double standards of a small town's prudery (p. 87).

One of the biggest challenges to understanding staged narratives is determining time and place of the delivery as well as identifying the addressee(s). It is safe to conclude from the 'Dirty brown lino', which defines the playing area, as well as from the Chinese lantern, which must be his trophy of the murder, that John-Joe's performance takes place in the kitchen where he also spends, anyway, most days. Another challenge of this theatrical form is sifting through the information garnered from the speaker to pick out what is worth believing. John-Joe's account of what actually happened (i.e. false pregnancy, murder, institutionalisation) must be taken for fact, but his role in all this is near opposite to how he perceives it. For instance, his Joycean Malapropism 'escape-goat' describes him in a way he does not intend (a satyr fleeing the site of a rape) but refers in its correct form, *scapegoat*, to his murder victim, the foreigner who bears away the wrongs of the native community.

The play's language, for all its vivid idiomatic turns and expressiveness of character, cannot carry the weight of reference and allusion, for example, to Jesus Christ as can a stark Mac Intyre image like Maguire on the gate, upside down, legs a V (*Great Hunger*, sc. 13). Much is revealed about Mac Intyre's kind of theatre when it is in the description of a gesture that one of the most striking moments of the performance is found: '*He views the black invisible load, hovering in the vicinity . . . lets it be*' (p. 84). In this image resides every attempt of the speech to portray John-Joe as the defiant victim who plods on to unforeseeable triumph (as references to Christ and Sisyphus demonstrate). It is a testament to Mac Intyre's drive to innovate theatre that the theatrically adventurous form of the staged narrative looks, next to his best plays, conventional.

What Happened Bridgie Cleary (2005)

After nearly ten years away, Tom Mac Intyre returned to the Peacock stage with *What Happened Bridgie Cleary*. This production has also continued his and Hickey's most recent period of collaboration stretching from Hickey's direction of *Sheep's Milk on the Boil* to his reading of *Don Murphy* at the 2006 Dublin Theatre Festival.[29]

The story of Bridget Cleary is just the right kind of material for Mac Intyre because, as the speaker of his poem 'Bridgie Cleary' explains the attraction of such stories, it has

> the stir o' company
> ye can't see, it spakes of other
> dominions not that far
> distant (*ABC*, p. 21)

This is the same material from which *Sheep's Milk on the Boil* is written. In Mac Intyre, dream-worlds, fairies and the afterlife often refer, more prosaically, to the repression and abreaction of the libido or, simply, the interplay between the conscious and unconscious components of our personalities. So *What Happened Bridgie Cleary*, which takes place in an afterworld of the fairies' making, has that probing both of the physical in the spiritual and of the spiritual in the physical which has produced the figures, with their conflicts and their ends, of all Mac Intyre's major poems, prose and plays.

What Happened Bridgie Cleary and *Sheep's Milk on the Boil* also share a heavy Irish English idiom in which the remnants of Gaeilge persist. Already in the title *What Happened Bridgie Cleary* does the linguistic idiom become apparent, and also significant. What at first might seem a question ('What happened, Bridgie Cleary?') turns out to be, on account of the dialectical use of *happen* without preposition, a statement ('What happened to Bridgie Cleary'). And precisely this is the matter the play takes on to express.

The story of Bridgie Cleary (based on fact, as Mac Intyre acknowledges in the published text) might be said to begin with the fairies who may have entered Bridgie's life through the strange occurrences in her childhood or through her bond with her mother or through the fairy fort which supposedly had been located on her and Mikey's house plot on the side of Slievenamon, County Tipperary. In any case, Bridgie and Mikey married (according to historical record, in August 1887), but she had affairs with the landed gentleman William Simpson and with a man whom she fell in love with and whom she planned to leave Ireland with, namely Phildy Reddan. Likely out of jealous rage, but ostensibly out of fear Bridgie was actually a changeling, Mikey and the neighbours burned her (according to historical record, in March 1895), and Mikey served a prison sentence before emigrating to Canada. This entire story precedes the action because the play is set in the afterworld where Bridgie, Mikey, and William find themselves together to atone ostensibly for the sins each has committed against the other, but really for the sins each has committed against her- or himself.

What actually happened to Bridgie Cleary was not the false accusation or the abhorrent burning, but her own failure to act on her love to Phildy. Bridgie wants it known that her story is a 'Love Story' (p. 93) and that, for this very reason, she sinned by failing to unfold that story to its end. The petition she makes at the mock re-enactment of her and Mikey's wedding could stand in as a Mac Intyre eulogy for all those who lose their nerve and buckle under the weight of the fate allotted them:

I want prayers in special for them that *nearly* breaks outa the shell, the trembly, the timid, that's often forgot about. Bridgie Cleary knows them all right – she knows them. (*To audience*) An' haven't youse, haven't youse all met them? The freckened wans that gets almos' all-the-way outa the shell an' then, for some rayzon – does the light hurt their eyes? courage fail them? some deloother occur? – for some rayzon they scrunch up, *frog in a frost*, sink inta quiet. (p. 88)

Summary

Good writing, that is, writing from the unconscious, is in Mac Intyre's words the end of a 'spirit journey'.[30] In the creative phase, the writer's psychological well-being is really in danger because he is forcing the portals of symbolic thought and feeling, and these only the initiate may pass. The writing emerging from this intensely introspective and emotionally taxing work is personal while being also universal. It is as if Mac Intyre digs so deep that he is mining the collective veins of the human or, more specifically, Irish unconscious. So it is that with his writing, psychoanalytic and archetypal approaches bring great interpretative returns.

Mac Intyre aligns himself with the artistic views and writing of William Butler Yeats and Patrick Kavanagh, who represent, in his opinion, a minority tradition in Irish literature.[31] He is indignant at the fact that, in his estimate, some nine-tenths of Irish theatre is 'hopelessly secular'.[32] 'Don't ask me to go to the theatre or read the novel or read the poem,' he demands,

> that hasn't that classic note of Irish literature from the year dot: the creak of the door between the two worlds, the whisper that . . . the haunting whisper, the echoing whisper that exists in the corridor between the two worlds. That is the Irish voice at its best. That's what I seek to articulate, whether it's in theatre, in fiction or in poetry. In theatre, to play with that in terms of the physical, to try and express the spirit magic through the magic of the body, that's one of the beautiful challenges.[33]

As says the speaker of his poem 'Lancelot du Lac', Mac Intyre writes 'about love – what else? – and death' (*Stories*, p. 38). Likewise, Mac Intyre's favourite situation, clearly traceable from *The Great Hunger* to *What Happened Bridgie Cleary*, is individual free will overcoming or, more often, failing to overcome various forms of subjugation, from societal to interpersonal, from violent to numinous.

Primary Sources

Works by Tom Mac Intyre

Good Evening, Mr Collins; The Dazzling Dark: New Irish Plays, introd. Frank McGuinness (London: Faber and Faber, 1996), pp. 173–230.

The Great Hunger and *The Gallant John-Joe* (Dublin: Lilliput Press, 2002).

Sheep's Milk on the Boil. New Plays from the Abbey Theatre 1993–1995, ed. Christopher Fitz-Simon and Sanford Sternlicht (Syracuse, NY: Syracuse UP, 1995), pp. 71–110.

What Happened Bridgie Cleary (Dublin: New Island, 2005).

Secondary Sources

Arts Show, The, RTÉ Radio, Radio 1, Dublin, August 2008 <http://www.rte.ie /arts/2008/0811/theartsshow.html>.

Carr, Marina, 'The Bandit Pen', programme note for *Good Evening, Mr Collins* (Dublin: Peacock Theatre, 1996).

Denman, Peter, 'Form and Fiction in the Stories of Tom Mac Intyre', *Études Irlandaises*, Vol. 4 (1975), pp. 87–94.

Etherton, Michael, *Contemporary Irish Dramatists*, Macmillan Modern Dramatists, (Houndmills: Macmillan, 1989), pp. 45–7.

Friel, Brian, *Essays, Diaries, Interviews 1964–1999*, ed. and introd. by Christopher Murray (London: Faber and Faber, 1999).

Göler, Hans von, *Streets Apart from Abbey Street: The Search for an Alternative National Theatre in Ireland Since 1980*, Prospekte: Studien zum Theater 5 (Trier: Wissenschaftlicher Verlag Trier, 2000).

Grene, Nicholas, 'Tom Mac Intyre', in Dennis Kennedy (ed.), *The Oxford Encyclopedia of Theatre and Performance* (Oxford: Oxford UP, 2003), pp. 780–1.

Healy, Dermot, 'Let the Hare Sit', *Theatre Ireland*, Vol. 11 (1985), pp. 9–10.

Heaney, Seamus, 'Introduction', *The Harper's Turn* (Dublin: Gallery Press, 1982), pp. 8–9.

Hogan, Robert, 'Mac Intyre, Tom (1931–), Man of Letters', in *Dictionary of Irish Literature*, ed. by Robert Hogan (Westport, CT: Greenwood Press, 1996), pp. 772–4.

Holmquist, Katherine, 'In the Beginning Was . . . the Image', *Theatre Ireland*, Vol. 6 (1984), pp. 150–2.

Hosey, Seamus, 'The Abbey in Russia', *Theatre Ireland*, Vol. 15 (1988), pp. 14–17.

Hurley, Vincent, '*The Great Hunger*: A Reading', in *The Great Hunger: Poem into Play*, Essays and Texts in Cultural History 2 (Mullingar: Lilliput Press, 1988), pp. 73–82.

Ireland, the Arts Council, *Views of Theatre in Ireland 1995: Report of the Arts Council Theatre Review* (Dublin: Arts Council, 1995).

Kelleher, Margaret and Philip O'Leary (eds), *The Cambridge History of Irish Literature*, Vol. 2 (Cambridge: Cambridge UP, 2006).

Llewellyn-Jones, Margaret, *Contemporary Irish Drama and Cultural Identity* (Bristol: Intellect Books, 2002), pp. 26–9.

Mac Intyre, Tom, 'Afterword', *Good Evening, Mr Collins. The Dazzling Dark: New Irish Plays* (London: Faber and Faber, 1996), pp. 231–3.

—, 'No Young Bums: Why Don't Young People Go to the Theatre?', *Irish Stage and Screen*, Vol. 1 (1989); p. 26.

—, *The Great Hunger: Poem into Play*, Essays and Texts in Cultural History 2 (Mullingar: Lilliput Press, 1988).

Mahoney, Christina Hunt, *Contemporary Irish Literature: Transforming Tradition* (New York: St Martin's Press, 1998), pp. 156–9.

Mason, Patrick, 'Director's Note', in *The Great Hunger: Poem into Play*, Essays and Texts in Cultural History 2 (Mullingar: Lilliput Press, 1988), pp. 69–70.

McGuinness, Frank, 'Introduction: Masks', *The Dazzling Dark: New Irish Plays* (London: Faber and Faber, 1996), pp. ix–xii.

Meyer-Dinkgräfe, Daniel (ed.), *Who's Who in Contemporary World Theatre* (London: Routledge, 2000), pp. 183–4.

Morash, Christopher, *A History of Irish Theatre 1601–2000* (Cambridge: Cambridge UP, 2002), pp. 257–9.

Mulrooney, Deirdre, *Irish Moves: An Illustrated History of Dance and Physical Theatre in Ireland* (Dublin: Liffey Press, 2006), pp. 173–88.

—, 'Tom Mac Intyre's Text-ure', in Eamonn Jordan (ed.), *Theatre Stuff: Critical Essays on Contemporary Irish Theatre* (Dublin: Carysfort Press, 2000), pp. 187–93.

Murray, Christopher, *Twentieth Century Irish Drama: Mirror up to Nation* (Manchester: Manchester UP, 1997), pp. 231–8.

Nice Moves, presented by Deirdre Mulrooney, RTÉ Radio, Radio 1, Dublin, May 2004 <http://www.rte.ie/radio1/nicemoves/ 1012995.html>.

Ó Conaire, Pradaic, 'The Woman on Whom God Laid His Hand', *The Finest Stories of Pádraic Ó Conaire* (Swords: Poolbeg, 1982), pp. 11–24. Reprinted in Seamus Deane (ed.), *The Field Day Anthology of Irish Writing*, Vol. 3 (Derry: Field Day Publications, 1991), pp. 832–7. Trans. of 'An Bhean ar Leag Dia Lámh Uirthi', 1913.

O'Toole, Fintan, 'Tom Mac Intyre', in Colin Chambers (ed.), *Continuum Companion to Twentieth Century Theatre* (London: Continuum, 2002), p. 465.

Pfister, Manfred, *The Theory and Analysis of Drama*, trans. by John Halliday, European Studies in English Literature (Cambridge: Cambridge UP, 1988).

Playwrights in Profile – Series 1, presented by Sean Rocks, RTÉ Radio, Radio 1, Dublin, February–April 2007 <http://www.rte.ie/ radio1/playwrights/1160140.html>.

Rattlebag, RTÉ Radio, Radio 1, Dublin, August 2006 <http://www.rte.ie/news/2006/0817/rattlebag.html>.

Read, Alan, *Theatre and Everyday Life: An Ethics of Performance* (London: Routledge, 1993).

Sternlicht, Sanford, *A Reader's Guide to Modern Irish Drama* (Syracuse, NY: Syracuse UP, 1998), pp. 130–1.

Sweeney, Bernadette, *Performing the Body in Irish Theatre* (Houndmills: Palgrave Macmillan, 2008).

—, 'Tom Mac Intyre', in *Dictionary of Literary Biography*, Vol. 245, (Detroit, MI: Thomson Gale, 2001).

Synge, J. M., *The Playboy of the Western World*, in John P. Harrington (ed.), *Modern Irish Drama*, Norton Critical Editions (New York: Norton, 1991), pp. 73–118.

—, 'Preface', *The Playboy of the Western World*, in John P. Harrington (ed.), *Modern Irish Drama*, Norton Critical Editions (New York: Norton, 1991), pp. 451–2.

Welch, Robert (ed.), 'Tom Mac Intyre', in The Oxford Companion to Irish Literature (Oxford: Clarendon Press, 1996), p. 339.

Notes

1. *Nice Moves*, presented by Deirdre Mulrooney, RTÉ Radio.
2. *Playwrights in Profile – Series 1*, presented by Sean Rocks, RTÉ Radio.
3. Bernadette Sweeney, 'Tom Mac Intyre', p. 253.
4. Christopher Murray, *Twentieth Century Irish Drama: Mirror up to Nation*, p. 233.
5. Ireland, the Arts Council, *Views of Theatre in Ireland 1995: Report of the Arts Council Theatre Review*, p. 70.
6. Deirdre Mulrooney, 'Tom Mac Intyre's Text-ure', p. 188.
7. Katherine Holmquist, 'In the Beginning Was . . . the Image', p. 151.
8. *Playwrights in Profile*, op. cit.
9. Sweeney, 'Tom Mac Intyre's Text-we', p. 251.
10. Mulrooney, 'Tom Mac Intyres, p. 191.
11. Quoted in Margaret Kelleher, *The Cambridge History of Irish Literature*, p. 632.
12. Sweeney, 'Tom Mac Intyre', pp. 254–5; Seamus Hosey, 'The Abbey in Russia', p. 15.
13. Murray, op. cit., p. 232; Bernadette Sweeney, *Performing the Body in Irish Theatre*, p. 50.
14. Cf. Hans von Göler, *Streets Apart from Abbey Street: The Search for an Alternative National Theatre in Ireland Since 1980*, p. 36.
15. Quoted in Mulrooney, 'Tom Mac Intyre's Text-we', p. 191.
16. *Playwrights in Profile*, op. cit.
17. Cf. Sweeney, *Performing*, p. 58.
18. Unpublished script for *The Great Hunger*, n. p.
19. Sweeney, *Performing*, p. 70.
20. Manfred Pfister, *The Theory and Analysis of Drama*, pp. 44–9.
21. J. M. Synge, 'Preface', p. 451.
22. *Playwrights in Profile*, op. cit.

23. *Rattlebag*, RTÉ Radio.
24. *Playwrights in Profile*, op. cit.
25. Ibid.
26. Ibid.
27. Sweeney, 'Tom Mac Intyre', p. 257.
28. Marina Carr, 'The Bandit Pen'.
29. *Rattlebag*, op. cit.
30. Ibid.; *Playwrights in Profile*. op. cit.
31. *Nice Moves*, op. cit.
32. *Playwrights in Profile*, op. cit.
33. *Nice Moves*, op. cit.

16 CONOR McPHERSON

Clare Wallace

Rum and Vodka; The Good Thief; This Lime Tree Bower; St. Nicholas; The Weir; Dublin Carol; Come On Over; Shining City; The Seafarer

Introduction

Conor McPherson came to prominence as a playwright in the late 1990s and currently ranks among the most successful of a new generation of writers in Ireland. Born in Dublin in 1971 and raised on the Northside of the city, McPherson's background is decidedly middle-class, urban and, moderately, Catholic. His involvement with theatre developed when he was a student at University College Dublin. As a member of the university 'dramsoc' he wrote and produced a number of his own plays including *Taking Stock* (1989), *Michelle Pfeiffer* (1990), *Scenes Federal* (1991) and *Inventing Fortune's Wheel* (1991). Later, while completing an MA in philosophy at UCD, he co-founded the Fly by Night Theatre Company which produced *Rum and Vodka* (1994) in several small venues in Dublin. In 1994 McPherson and Kevin Hely, the last remaining members of the Fly by Night group, produced *The Light of Jesus* in the City Arts Centre in Dublin. Though the two-week run was unsuccessful, in October that same year the play was revived under a revised title, *The Good Thief*, at the Dublin Theatre Festival, where it won the Stewart Parker Award.[1] McPherson's fortunes continued to improve in 1995; *This Lime Tree Bower* had a very successful premiere and run in Dublin Fringe Festival and then transferred to the Bush Theatre in London in 1996, where he also became writer-in-residence. The play gathered several awards between 1995 and 1996 including the George Devine Award for Best New Play. McPherson's major breakthrough, however, occurred in 1997 when both *St. Nicholas* and *The Weir* had their premieres in London and *The Weir* secured the Olivier Award for Best Play. The latter work, in particular, has been phenomenally popular, with productions in New York and across Europe. His subsequent work for theatre includes screenplays for *I Went Down* (1997), *Saltwater*, an adaptation of *This Lime Tree Bower* (2001), and *The Actors* (2003) – the latter two films he also directed – plus a version of *Endgame* (2001) for the Beckett on Film project. Finally, an important dimension to McPherson's theatre practice is that apart from *The Weir* and *Dublin Carol*, he has directed the opening productions of all his own plays to date.

The Plays

The contours of McPherson's dramaturgy are discernible even from his earliest published work. One of its most prominent and oft-discussed features is his repeated use of extended monologue. Of the ten plays currently in print, six are constructed around the device of monologue, while two comprise significant portions of uninterrupted storytelling or confession. A survey of the plays reveals not only McPherson's honing of the monologue and the micro-narrative, but also his growing skill in the naturalistic portrayal of character and an attentiveness to the rhythms and nuances of everyday speech.

Rum and Vodka (1994)

The first of these plays, *Rum and Vodka*, is an anecdotal monologue for a solo performer. As the narrative progresses it gathers momentum as a tale of drunken bravado and degradation. The unnamed narrator relates a weekend-long drinking session, during which he loses his job, is unfaithful to his wife and generally debases himself. A clerk in the voting registration department of the city corporation, at the age of twenty-four he has a wife, two small children and a burgeoning alcohol addiction. The trigger to his alcohol problem seems to be the realisation that 'this was as good as things were going to get' (p. 248) and his consequent sense of frustration with his life. The play is structured simply in two parts: in the first the narrator describes himself, his family and friends, and the outward trajectory of his weekend binge; in the second he charts his circuitous route home. Chronology and unity of character are maintained throughout. Notably, the narrator is the first of McPherson's ambivalent protagonists, simultaneously comic, pitiable and reprehensible – a type identifiable in all of his plays – and the monologue wavers uncomfortably between the normally mutually exclusive purposes of boasting and confessing. The facetious self-deprecating humour of the protagonist is darkened by his callous attitude to his wife and children. One striking dimension to the work is the way in which it echoes James Joyce's story 'Counterparts'. The instances of thematic citation between the two narratives are multiple. Farrington in 'Counterparts', like the unnamed speaker of McPherson's play, is a clerk in a Dublin office. His insatiable thirst similarly jeopardises his job. Like the protagonist of *Rum and Vodka*, Farrington seems to live only for drink and idle, opinionated pub talk. Both briefly lust after women from another 'world' – for Farrington the theatrical lady in the yellow gloves he sees in Mulligan's pub, in *Rum and Vodka* the student, Myfanwy, whom he first spots in the Stag's Head and with whom he spends the night. While Farrington returns home humiliated, disgruntled and, finally, viciously beats one of his children, the protagonist of *Rum and Vodka* eventually returns to sit in his daughters' room to contemplate their unbearable innocence and his intolerably ordinary life. Both narratives are characterised by a similar sense of alcoholic paralysis and hopelessness.

The Good Thief (1994)

Written as one unbroken monologue, *The Good Thief* is a more dynamic, if generic, tale of failure. The narrative is furnished with the requisite components of a contemporary crime story – love interest, betrayal and divided loyalties, violence, escape, capture and so on. The play's narrator, again anonymous, is a 'paid thug' (p. 199) for a crime boss who has just started a relationship with the narrator's former girlfriend. He tells the story of a botched assignment to threaten a businessman into paying protection fees. The narrator is involved in a shoot-out at the businessman's home in which three people are killed. Double-crossed by his former associates, he kidnaps the man's wife and daughter. Perhaps somewhat improbably, he establishes a tentatively friendly relationship with Mrs Mitchell and Niamh, his victims. They flee to Sligo, to hide out with a friend of the narrator. His boss, however, soon catches up with him and has the woman, the child and his friend's family killed. After spending ten years in prison, the narrator leaves the country. He concludes his story, as it began, thinking of his old girlfriend, the source of much of his frustration and confusion, still in a state of moral atrophy and isolation.

This Lime Tree Bower (1995)

Although both *Rum and Vodka* and *The Good Thief* are relatively one-dimensional narrative exercises, they incorporate basic techniques, devices and motifs that are developed with more sophistication in McPherson's subsequent work. Thus, *This Lime Tree Bower* can be seen in part to return to the alcohol-soaked, yet curiously lucid, narrators of the earlier plays and a core set of moral dilemmas, but both these elements are realised in a theatrically richer fashion. Like his early work, the play is composed of blocks of monologue and directions as to set design are absent. However, the ensemble monologue structure facilitates multiple points of view. The technique, a common one in works of fiction, as it is used here gives rise to a mosaic of observations and stories that ultimately fit together as a coherent whole.

The play is structured around three characters, each of whom tells stories about recent events in their lives: Joe, a teenage schoolboy; Frank, his brother, who works for their father in their chip shop/restaurant; and Ray, their sister's boyfriend, who is a philosophy lecturer. Joe's stories centre upon a boy he admires in school and his confused efforts to impress him. The climax of Joe's narrative occurs when, returning from a disco, he witnesses his friend, Damien, raping a drunken girl they are supposed to be safely escorting home. Later when a criminal investigation begins Damien attempts to blame Joe. Frank supplies details about his relationship with their father and the family business. He relates his frustration with how his father has been swindled by the local city councillor and bookmaker. He decides to solve his father's problem by carrying out an armed robbery of the bookie's shop. The heist is a success only because Ray accidentally drives past and offers him a lift just as he is about to be caught. Ray's stories develop around several events: an ill-advised drunken one-night stand with one of his students, a visit by a world-famous professor to the Philosophy Department, and his involvement with the robbery.

The rhythm of the play is established by the fixed order of delivery – first Joe speaks, then Ray and Frank; the play as a whole is framed by Joe's speeches. Tension is built through crests in each of the speaker's stories. A timely interval is scheduled after the first six monologues, at a crisis point in the tale of the robbery. The remainder of the play consists of four monologues. This contains a further two climactic points: Joe's witnessing of the rape and Ray's projectile vomiting at the final Konigsberg lecture. Although stage directions indicate that the characters are aware of each other, the monologue format is broken only once. This momentary exchange between Frank and Ray disrupts the speakers' isolation and foregrounds the performative nature of their narratives, which is further underscored at the play's conclusion. Joe expresses surprise at their story's happy ending, introducing the question of its plausibility in the shape of a coda – 'So in the end it was like things started off good, and just got better. Is that cheating? I don't know. It's hard to say' (p. 193).

In contrast to the bleaker material of the earlier plays, *This Lime Tree Bower* is laden with playfully deployed intertexts. Mischievous philosophical references are planted throughout. So for instance, Ray's academic specialisation is overtly divorced from his cynical and dissolute onstage persona. His claim to superiority over Joe and Frank on the basis of his 'philosophical training', equips him with the insight that they should do 'absolutely nothing' (p. 176) following the robbery. The visit by the famous philosopher Wolfgang Konigsberg who has, for decades, been honing his theory of language as an organic entity is a pocket of further tongue-in-cheek cleverness. While the professor is a fiction, his name alludes to Immanuel Kant – significantly McPherson studied moral philosophy and wrote an MA thesis on utilitarianism. Kant, 'the sage of Königsberg', reputedly never left his place of birth, in contrast to the ancient, peripatetic Professor Konigsberg of the play. In addition, it might be argued that Kant's three *Critiques*, of Pure Reason, Practical Reason and of Judgement, inform the dramatisation of questions of experience, judgement, morality and perception. Konigsberg's theory holds that language is now dying and that lack of sincerity is one of the signs (p. 178). Indeed, Ray's narrative might be taken as a demonstration of just such linguistic decadence or postmodern deterioration. The irony of Konigsberg's assertion that language is dying is enhanced by the fact that he himself prohibits communication by 'insist[ing] on giving his papers with no discussion' (p. 177), that is to say, he insists upon monologue.

St. Nicholas (1997)

With *St. Nicholas* McPherson returns to the solo monologue format, but blends it with the comic irony of *This Lime Tree Bower*. The play, commissioned by the Bush Theatre, features a single speaker, a debauched and cynical theatre critic in his late fifties. Until this point, while each of the plays has been addressed to the auditorium, none of the speakers has crossed into direct address of the audience or self-reflexive commentary on the nature of the narrative being presented. In *St. Nicholas* the speaker does just that, browbeating and, at times, berating the audience. Though it swerves abruptly into the fantastical, the narrative of the play is simple enough – jaded with his sordid existence as a journalist and his failure to write creatively, the protagonist, besotted with the lead actress in a production of *Salome*, follows her to London, where he lies, humiliates himself and then, after a drinking binge, finds himself a new life sharing a residence with a group of vampires. The vampires provide him with food and lodgings and, in return, he procures for them parties of victims who suffer little more than a severe hangover and no memory of the previous evening. Meanwhile, the protagonist spends his free time in an attic room attempting to write and conversing with his host, William, about art and literature. After some time he grows tired of this arrangement, comes to despise his hosts, and summons the will to leave. The monologue concludes with the speaker's plans to return to his old life with his new story, and a final barrage of querulous questions for the audience about the nature of reality.

At the crux of *St. Nicholas* is a form of narrative crisis. The speaker is well aware of his parasitical status and is jealous of those who can be, like the actress Helen, unself-consciously creative. Repeatedly, he bemoans the fact that he has 'no ideas for a story' (p. 81). As Scott T. Cummings describes, the narrator as critic feeds, like the vampire, upon others – upon their artistic endeavours, and upon their fear of his power. Moreover, his role as storyteller may be equated with the role he fulfils for the vampire household – drawing in victims/listeners, exploiting their sympathy and feeding upon their credulity.[2] The narrator also plays upon the construction of identity through storytelling and the arbitrariness of these micro-narratives that function not because they reveal a profound or universal truth, but as a process of self-performance. Furthermore, the play openly tackles questions of credulity and theatricality, as McPherson's Author's Note to the text also makes clear. The issues of judgement and credibility are frequently raised throughout the play by the speaker himself. After appealing to the audience's common sense, he abruptly interrupts his own story, and appears to drop the pretence of character, to refute audience scepticism:

> Mm. There's always going to be a smugness about you listening to this. As we all take part in this convention. And you will say, 'These vampires are not very believable, are they?' And you are entitled. (p. 108)

This is followed by criticism of their lazy reliance on conventions and received knowledge. To score his point he notes,

> We may know that the earth goes round the sun. And we may know that this is due to 'gravity'. But not one of us knows why

there is gravity. So don't sit there and cast judgement on the credibility of what I say, when you don't even know why you aren't floating off your seats. (p. 109)

Undoubtedly the issues of belief and incredulity are themes scattered across many of McPherson's works, yet none of his other plays poses the direct challenges of *St. Nicholas*, which highlights the monologue's potential to break the fourth wall.

The Weir (1997)

The Weir, McPherson's best-known play, is the first of his published works to use dialogue, though significantly action is minimal, and storytelling is the drama's engine. Set in a typical rural Irish pub, *The Weir* follows the course of a single evening and adheres to the unities of time and place, employs a conventional, firmly naturalistic approach to setting and incorporates regular stage directions. Conversation among the characters is low-key and formulaic, rarely wandering far from the safety of pub chit-chat. However, as the evening wears on they begin to tell stories and the play slips back into the now familiar mode of (partial) monologue. Prompted by the businessman Finbar, Jack, an ageing mechanic, begins with a story of fairies which apparently took place in the house Valerie has just occupied. Finbar follows this yarn with a description of an experience with a Ouija board. Jim, an odd-job man, then recounts how years previously he met the ghost of a man for whom he had just dug a grave. Valerie, a Dubliner, concludes the tales of the supernatural by telling of how her young daughter died and how she thought she had spoken to the dead child on the telephone. Finally, before they leave the pub, Jack narrates how he missed his chance to marry and was comforted by a stranger.

Each of the narratives in generically differing forms deals with an inexplicable or unaccountable event; each subtly raises the matter of believability while simultaneously contributing to the empathetic storytelling the play also delivers. As the characters settle down to tell stories of the supernatural in the pub, it should be obvious that no proof of their experiences is possible. The effects of their stories, however, are tangible – each is variously disclaimed or reflected upon with disbelief by the characters of the play in ways that anticipate likely audience reactions to such narratives. Unsurprisingly, most critics and reviewers have stressed the strong current of empathy in *The Weir*. The communion of storytelling is noted by both Gerald C. Wood and Cummings. Wood goes so far as to state that 'by the end of the play, the empathy and kindness that is established among the characters in *The Weir* gain religious resonance'.[3] Yet (re)assurance is coupled with doubt. As Eamonn Jordan argues, a provocative ambivalence with respect to the assumed authenticity of the pastoral mode is perceptible.[4] While *The Weir* might initially seem to pay sincere homage to the Irish penchant for yarns and pints, McPherson's playfulness emerges at a formal level. Dominic Dromgoole describes the play as a 'clever confection of different traditions of drama',[5] noting the shadows of Synge, O'Casey, Friel, Murphy and Billy Roche. Indeed, it abounds in signs of what is broadly perceived as the traditional Irish drama – a naturalistic pub setting, lonely old men, whimsical bachelors, boastful local businessmen, rural isolation, alcohol and storytelling. Into this is blended a handful of contemporary references, and a self-conscious sense of modern-day doubt, to temper the formal echoes.

Dublin Carol (2000)

McPherson's next work, *Dublin Carol*, continues in the naturalistic vein of *The Weir*, but returns to and extends some aspects of characterisation sketched in the early plays. In many respects, *Dublin Carol* offers an image of the protagonist of *Rum and Vodka* thirty years on (as US reviewer Diane Synder has also remarked), and it is a grim prospect. Set in an undertaker's office located on the Northside of the city on Christmas Eve, the play, rich with a morbid and at times painfully poignant humour, features three characters: John, a semi-reformed alcoholic; Mark, nephew of John's employer Noel, the undertaker; and Mary, John's daughter, whom he has not seen in a decade. The action falls neatly into three parts that chart the events of the morning, early and late afternoon in the undertaker's office, where John also lives. McPherson masterfully balances the pathetic, the selfish and the appallingly callous elements to John's character. He is lonely and desperate for auditors; however, in contrast to the portrayal of alcohol abusers in the preceding work, McPherson deliberately refuses the character 'the freedom of monologue'. Rather, the other characters 'ask him to be accountable',[6] yet they do so in a manner that is far from simply judgemental. Tolerance and, against all the odds, the possibility of redemption are among the central themes of the play.

In the opening scene, John attempts to engage Mark in conversation, offering tea and humorous small talk to forestall his departure. Mark has just assisted John at a funeral, but is impatient to leave. Eventually, John begins to talk of how Mark's uncle saved him from utter destitution by offering him a job and a fresh start that, ironically, keeps him in constant contact with mortality. The aptly named Noel proves to be John's earthly saviour, rescuing him from the extremes of alcoholism. The fact that Noel is now seriously ill evidently leaves John feeling vulnerable again. Predictably, given the setting, the conversation winds back to the topic of death, the worst and best deaths John has attended.

The connection with John's closing observations in part one and the arrival of Mary that afternoon emerge gradually. Mary brings news of the imminent death of Helen, her mother and John's estranged wife. The pathetic, but likeable, image of John now crumbles as their conversation summons the demons of the past to reveal the cruelty with which he has treated all those who cared for him. In spite of everything, Mary declares simply that she loves him, but she still challenges his explanations for his self-destructive addiction to alcohol. She begs him to come to the hospital that evening and to consider doing Helen's funeral. Both propositions fill him with dread.

In the final scene Mark returns to get paid for the morning's work. He too has had an upsetting afternoon, having attempted to break up with his girlfriend. Both John and Mark have attempted to dull the pain of their failures by drinking alone, though they continue for a while to do so together. Mark, with good reason, angrily rebuffs John's attempt to advise him on relationships. Their roles, in this respect, are then reversed when John tells him that Helen is dying. Mark advises him to visit her and John accepts his opinion.

The play is framed with references to Christmas and inevitably the significance of the date tunes expectations of some momentous event on the horizon. Yet this prospect is handled with a good deal of quiet irony. Introductory stage directions describe the decorations as '*terribly scrawny*' consisting of '*a few fairy lights [. . .] a foot-high plastic [. . .] tree on one of the desks [and] a little advent calendar with just a few doors left to open*' (p. 79). These paltry reminders of the seasonal festivities are rendered even more incongruous as the nature of the office is revealed.

Come On Over (2001)

Come On Over premiered as part of an evening of one-act plays at the Gate Theatre in 2001. A monologue confession piece for a male and female performer, it adopts a number of more experimental, non-naturalistic devices that are uncharacteristic of McPherson's work as a whole, and that ultimately seem more gratuitous than effective. The protagonists enter wearing sackcloth hoods, with eye and mouth holes; they are accompanied by a group of children, also equipped with hoods and discordantly playing recorders. McPherson justified his hooding of the characters as an attempt to create a 'purgatorial kind of space' that '[v]isually [. . .] conjures images of being hostage, dead, or executed'.[7] However, he goes on to admit that the story is an 'ordinary' one.[8] Matthew, a Catholic priest, and Margaret, his girlfriend before he joined the Jesuits, speak of their pasts and of Matthew's return to Ireland from Africa. The themes of faith, lost love and the motif of self-excoriating confession are, as is evident in the plays discussed so far, recognisable elements to McPherson's dramaturgy; their realisation in this play, however, is fragmented and somewhat formally confused, and the piece has not been subsequently produced.

Shining City (2004)

Shining City brings McPherson back to familiar territory, both thematically and formally. A naturalistic setting with conventional dialogue delineates the shape of the drama, while locating the action in a therapist's office facilitates some tracts of monologue and suggests echoes of Tom Murphy's *The Gigli Concert*. The motifs of inexplicable phenomena and the present haunted by the past are forcefully reintroduced across the play's five scenes, which span a period of ten months. The roles of priest and confessing sinner are transferred to those of therapist and patient, resulting in the modification of the Catholic practice of confession, atonement and absolution. Although God seems to be but a void concept for the principal characters, the church remains in the background, signalled in the play by the occasional sound of 'distant church bells' (p. 7). Such a belief system, however, fails to provide any comfort or explanation of the traumatic experience described.

Ian, a former priest, is counselling John, who has recently lost his wife in a car accident. John is not only burdened with remorse over the way he treated his wife just before her death, but is paralysed with terror because he is convinced he has seen her ghost. It soon becomes obvious that Ian's life is perhaps in a worse state of confusion than that of his patient. Having 'turn[ed] [his] back on the church' (p. 22), he now wants to free himself of his partner, Neasa, and their baby, despite the sacrifices she has made to enable him to start a new life. Later, his uncertainty is illustrated when he has a sexual encounter in his office with a man who is a prostitute. Meanwhile, John begins to tell his life story, confessing the ways in which he emotionally wounded his wife and betrayed their trust. Ian offers him a tolerant and unobtrusive hearing. Consequently, John clears his conscience and exorcises his ghost. Ian helps to haul John from the lowest depths of depression and away from a sense that the world is totally inexplicable and terrifying. Concurrently, Ian seems to be sinking into a mire of denial and dishonesty. These opposing trajectories are signalled by the transfer of the ghost from John to Ian. Unaware of Ian's private life or the ominous nature of what he is saying, John observes towards the end of the play: 'you don't believe in ghosts anyway, Ian. You've got it sussed' (p. 63). In response, Ian remarks to John '[w]e just know nothing really' (p. 64). Indeed, as if to prove Ian's statement, in an unexpected final plot twist, moments after John leaves, Mari's ghost appears, providing the play with a shocking closing image.

The Seafarer (2006)

The Seafarer, McPherson's most recent work, provides a plot with neat closure and sprinkled with religious allusions and once more makes use of the symbolic significance of Christmas Eve. The play follows a textbook climactic dramatic structure – the plot begins late in the story and is tightly woven on the basis of causal logic, the action is condensed, conflicts are pre-established, and the scene and characters are restricted. The all-male cast of characters are, to varying degrees, hopeless cases and, as such, are identifiable McPherson types. Consumption of alcohol and a card game furnish the play's action. Sharky, a heavy drinker trying to reform, his blind older brother Richard, and their companions, Ivan and Nicky, spend the evening with a mysterious stranger, Mr Lockhart. The secret of Lockhart's identity is not long kept, for by the end of the first of the play's two acts, he reveals himself to be the devil come for Sharky's soul. Lockhart's visit involves a raking over of the sins and errors of the past. He reminds Sharky of an incident twenty-five years previously when they met in jail and played cards. While drunk, Sharky had viciously beaten to death a vagrant man, but because he won their game of poker, Lockhart 'set [him] free' (p. 46). He has now come for another game. The Faustian allusions here are obvious.

The play's title reference to the Anglo-Saxon poem, The Seafarer – an extract of which serves as a preface to the play – summons further associations. Sharky has drifted from job to job all his life, including working on fishing boats; he has lost each job and wrecked his marriage, presumably because of his drinking and violent demeanour when under the influence. His efforts to stop drinking are mocked continuously by Richard, and finally, when the prospect of everlasting hell (portrayed by Mr Lockhart as a tiny coffin under 'a vast, icy, pitch-black sea' [p. 77]), seems imminent, he steels himself with poteen.

However, if Sharky is the obvious correlative seafaring figure, arguably the household of card players is more broadly a ship of fools, at sea in the world. This impression is reinforced by the setting – the house is near the coast, the living room where the characters congregate is a submerged space (a hold perhaps?), and as the evening wears on a storm builds outside. Richard, a cantankerous drunk, ironically derives great enjoyment from terrorising the winos in the lane behind the house. Ivan, who also has a serious drinking problem, has already spent one drunken evening at Richard's house at the beginning of the play. When he tries to return home later his wife throws him out. During the card game, Ivan acts as Richard's assistant, in a thinly veiled play on the blind leading the blind. If Ivan seems a merely comical, but harmless, figure of drunken fun, darker tones are brought forth when Mr Lockhart questions him about an accident he caused while drunk that cost the lives of two families. Even the devil himself seems a little tossed on the sea of poteen.

A climax is reached when Mr Lockhart wins the final card game and prepares to take Sharky 'through the hole in the wall' (p. 48). At the last minute the sinner is spared when Ivan finally finds his glasses and realises that he and Richard had the winning hand after all. The light under the picture of the Sacred Heart, broken at the opening of the play, flickers on as the devil departs and Richard decides that they should go to Mass, because the monks brew their own beer.

Summary

In their tales, McPherson's ambivalent storytellers lay claim to no monumental significance, mythic references or universal applicability, although, as will be discussed below, some critics have attributed an ethical purpose to these acts of narration.

In each play reality is constructed in a discursive manner privileging linguistic over physical elements; it is, as McPherson himself puts it, the words that are to do the work rather than the spectacle of the stage design or the characters' actions.[9] Nevertheless, experimental or avant-garde tendencies are largely absent – with the slight and flawed exception of *Come On Over*. Undoubtedly, his monologue plays disrupt the pretence of a naturalistic theatre of illusion, but crucially other fundamentally naturalistic elements remain firmly in place – language never spirals off into modernist or postmodernist free fall but is clearly determined by narrative purpose and causality; character is coherent and unified; and the world beyond the theatre is recognisable and geographically specific.

Alcoholism, the unknown or supernatural, failure and masculinity (in crisis or confusion) constitute the thematic compass points of McPherson's work since the mid-1990s. Pertinently, McPherson nearly died in 2001 as a result of heavy drinking and has subsequently given up alcohol, but his familiarity with the alcoholic's experience – both in comic and tragic terms – is writ large across the majority of the plays discussed above.

The reception of McPherson's work ranges from the ecstatic to the lukewarm. *The Weir*, especially, won many tributes from London critics when it opened at the Royal Court in 1997 and was generally seen as a testament to the poetic skills of Irish dramatists. It is arguable that his work was seen, in the 1990s at least, as a welcome antidote to In-Yer-Face theatre, a return to a more comfortable and pleasurable experience of theatre, reliant upon linguistic nuances rather than spectacle and violent sensation. Others (in particular American and, sometimes, Irish reviewers) have drawn attention to the short-story qualities of his plays, commenting, with somewhat less enthusiasm, on their 'plain-spoken and methodical' qualities and their inherent anti-theatricality.[10]

In spite of being claimed in 1999 as Ireland's latest 'literary giant',[11] McPherson's drama has certainly not generated scholarly debate comparable to that surrounding his close contemporaries Martin McDonagh or Marina Carr. The most extensive survey of McPherson's work currently in print is Gerald C. Wood's monograph, *Conor McPherson: Imagining Mischief* (2003). In Wood's opinion, McPherson's achievement is 'dedramatisation in favour of the story itself'.[12] The goal of this 'mischievous theatre' of straight storytelling is 'reflection inspired by reason'.[13] Consequently, actors and audiences are 'liberated from theatrical conventions' but not responsibility.[14]

Other responses may be grouped according to varying sets of common concerns. A number have highlighted the plays' contribution to an Irish storytelling tradition or considered their 'narrative imperative'.[15] Another hub of critical interest is the depiction of masculinity in the plays.

Recently, Kevin Kerrane has reviewed the 'structural elegance' of *The Weir*, a play that is also insightfully revisited by Eamonn Jordan in 'Pastoral Exhibits: Narrating Authenticities in Conor McPherson's *The Weir*'. Also attentive to the role of the pastoral and black pastoral in contemporary Irish drama, Nicholas Grene contrasts the approaches of Martin McDonagh and McPherson in 'Ireland in Two Minds: Martin McDonagh and Conor McPherson'.

McPherson in many respects seems to fit harmoniously within what are generally regarded as the traditions of Irish theatre. His concern with storytelling, attentiveness to the subtle rhythms and idiomatic expressions of everyday (Dublin) speech, and the leitmotif of a present haunted by the past might be considered features of this context. If his exploration of the monologue form has set his work apart from that of some of his contemporaries and predecessors, it remains to be seen whether he will return to this device. McPherson's significance lies in his blending of recognisable traditions with a contemporary sense of the ordinary, the urban and the secular dogged by the metaphysical and the inexplicable. In this, his work is certainly not marked by a self-consciousness about national identity that could be said to characterise the work of a previous generation of Irish playwrights, but can be aligned with a new sense of Irish identity at the close of the twentieth century. In *State of Play: Playwrights on Playwriting* McPherson claims that he

> had never set out to write consciously about [his] own country [even though his] work seemed to suggest Irish issues to certain critics. [Rather] all [he] was trying to do was to write plays that hold your attention, make you laugh and hopefully

engender a sense of community between the work and the audience.[16]

This is an ambition to which McPherson has indubitably remained constant and one that will likely lead to his recognition as a major Irish playwright in years to come.

Primary Sources

Works by Conor McPherson

Dublin Carol (London: Nick Hern, 2000).

McPherson: Four Plays [*This Lime Tree Bower, St. Nicholas, Rum and Vodka, The Good Thief*] (London: Nick Hern, 1999).

Plays: Two [*The Weir, Dublin Carol, Port Authority, Come on Over*] (London: Nick Hern, 2004).

Port Authority (London: Nick Hern, 2001).

The Seafarer (London: Nick Hern, 2006).

The Weir (London: Nick Hern, 1998).

Secondary Sources

Adams, Tim, 'So There's These Three Irishmen . . .', *Observer*, 4 February 2001 <http://observer.guardian.co.uk/theatre/story/ 0,,530394,00.html>.

Anon., 'Did Critics Toast Conor McPherson's The Seafarer at the National?' <http://london.broadway.com/blog/id/3003973/Did CriticsToastConorMcPherson%27sTheSeafarerattheNational?>

Cummings, Scott T., 'Homo Fabulator: The Narrative Imperative in Conor McPherson's Plays', in Eamonn Jordan (ed.), *Theatre Stuff: Critical Essays on Contemporary Irish Theatre* (Dublin: Carysfort Press, 2000), pp. 303–12.

Dromgoole, Dominic, *The Full Room* (London: Methuen, 2002), pp. 186–9.

Edgar, David (ed.), *State of Play: Playwrights on Playwriting* (London: Faber and Faber, 1999), pp. 99–103.

Franks, Alan, 'Ireland's Sober Voice', *The Times*, 11 December 1999.

Grene, Nicholas, 'Ireland in Two Minds: Martin McDonagh and Conor McPherson', *The Yearbook of English Studies*, Vol. 35, No. 1 (2005), pp. 298–311.

Gutman, Les, 'Review of *This Lime Tree Bower* by Conor McPherson', *CurtainUp Magazine*, 24 May 1999 <http://www.curtainup.com /limetree.html>.

Jordan, Eamonn, 'Pastoral Exhibits: Narrating Authenticities in Conor McPherson's *The Weir*', *Irish University Review*, Vol. 34, No. 2 (2004), pp. 351–68.

Kerrane, Kevin, 'The Structural Elegance of Conor McPherson's *The Weir*', *New Hibernia Review*, Vol. 10, No. 4 (2006), pp. 105–21.

McGinley, Nick, 'Three Short Plays', RTÉ Entertainment, 10 November 2001 <http://www.rte.ie/arts/2001/1011/3shortplays.html>.

McPherson, Conor, 'If You're an Irish Playwright, Come to London', *New Statesman*, 20 February 1998.

—, 'Old Ireland Bad, New Ireland Good', *Irish Times*, 30 December 1999, p. 12.

Moroney, Mic, 'The Twisted Mirror: Landscapes, Mindscapes, Politics and Language on the Irish Stage', in Dermot Bolger (ed.), *Druids, Dudes and Beauty Queens* (Dublin: New Island, 2001), pp. 250–75.

Singleton, Brian, 'Am I Talking to Myself?', *Irish Times*, 19 April 2001 <http://scripts.ireland.com/search/highlight.plx?TextRes= Conor. . ./fea2.html>.

—, 'Am I Talking to Myself? Men, Masculinities and Monologue in Contemporary Irish Theatre', in Clare Wallace (ed.), *Monologues: Theatre, Performance, Subjectivity* (Prague: Litteraria Pragensia, 2006), pp. 260–77.

Snyder, Diane, 'In Dublin's Fair City . . .', *Theatermania.com*, 19 February 2003, <http://www.theatermania.com/new-york /news/02-2003/in-dublins-fair-city_3125.html>.

Taylor, James C., 'Conor McPherson: One-Man Show', *The Simon* (Fall 1999) <http://www.thesimon.com/magazine/articles/old_ issues/0064_conor_mcpherson_oneman_show.html>.

Wallace, Clare, 'A Micronarrative Imperative – Conor McPherson's Monologue Dramas', *Irish Studies Review*, Vol. 14, No. 1 (2006), pp. 1–10.

—, 'Conor McPherson: Solitary Micronarratives', in her *Suspect Cultures: Narrative, Identity and Citation in 1990s New Drama* (Prague: Litteraria Pragensia, 2006), pp. 39–84.

White, Victoria, 'Telling Stories in the Dark', *Irish Times*, 2 July 1998.

Wood, Gerald C., *Conor McPherson: Imagining Mischief* (Dublin: Hiffey, 2003).

Notes

1. See Conor McPherson, 'Afterword: An Interview with Carol Vander', *Plays: Two*, pp. 210–11, for McPherson's comical description of the play's first run and its later transformation.

2. Scott T. Cummings, 'Homo Fabulator: The Narrative Imperative in Conor McPherson's Plays', p. 308.

3. Gerald C. Wood, *Conor McPherson: Imagining Mischief*, p. 49.

4. See Eamonn Jordan, 'Pastoral Exhibits: Narrating Authenticities in Conor McPherson's *The Weir*', pp. 351–68.

5. Dominic Dromgoole, *The Full Room*, pp. 188–9.
6. Mc Pherson quoted in Wood, op. cit., p. 136.
7. Ibid. p. 130.
8. Ibid.
9. Compare Tim Adams, 'So There's These Three Irishmen. . .'.
10. Les Gutman, 'Review of *This Lime Tree Bower* by Conor McPherson'. See also Wood, op. cit.
11. Alan Franks, 'Ireland's Sober Voice'.
12. Wood, op. cit., p. 2.
13. Ibid., p. 4.
14. Ibid.
15. See Cummings, op. cit.
16. Mic Moroney, 'The Twisted Mirror: Landscapes, Mindscapes, Politics and Language on the Irish Stage', p. 269.

17 GARY MITCHELL

Paul Devlin

In a Little World of Our Own; Tearing the Loom; As the Beast Sleeps; Trust; The Force of Change; Loyal Women

Introduction

As a playwright from a Protestant working-class background, Gary Mitchell's body of work is critically acclaimed because it is seen as having given unusual access to loyalist communities in Northern Ireland during a period when many people in these communities have felt their way of life to be under threat. Mitchell, who grew up in Rathcoole, a sprawling housing estate on the edges of north Belfast, has obsessively dramatised how the political negotiations leading to the signing of the Good Friday Agreement (GFA) reverberate at community level in Protestant working-class districts in Northern Ireland. His later works especially explore the impact of economic, structural and symbolic changes enacted in Northern Ireland under the GFA and have been widely received as possessing the 'ringing tones of authenticity on a divided community' during a politically volatile period.[1]

Mitchell, born in 1965, left school at sixteen with little in the way of formal educational qualifications and subsequently spent eight years unemployed.[2] The relative economic deprivation of Rathcoole in the 1980s, combined with his own upbringing in 'a family of active loyalism',[3] meant that like many of his peers he came into close contact with paramilitary activity in his formative years:

> I grew up completely loyalist, completely Unionist, completely Protestant . . . I believed it all. I was very frightened of this Catholic monster that was raping my community and

trying to kill us all. I tried to involve myself in the UDA[4] and find out where the UVF[5] was. I tried to play my part, I wanted to bring the war to them. I did some bad stuff to some people to prove myself but I was racked with guilt.[6]

As an adult, however, Mitchell questioned his assumptions about the Catholic population of Northern Ireland and the role of loyalist paramilitaries in his community. He later got a job with the Northern Irish Civil Service, where he 'made a point of meeting some Catholics'[7] and began to write plays.

Despite his success as a playwright Mitchell continued to live with his wife and family in the working-class district of Rathcoole. After a number of threats to his life, however, he finally left the estate for a nearby middle-class area. By then Mitchell's controversial work had attracted the attention of hardliner loyalist paramilitaries. In November 2005 Mitchell's Glengormly home was attacked, his car petrol bombed, and the homes of his uncle and niece simultaneously attacked by gangs of masked loyalists [8] His extended family, with the exception of his elderly grandmother, were ordered under threat of their lives to leave Rathcoole and told not to return. Mitchell subsequently went into hiding and has not returned to live in Rathcoole since the attack in 2005.

The Plays

In a Little World of Our Own (1991)

Mitchell's first play, *The World, the Flesh and the Devil*, was broadcast on BBC Radio Four and won the BBC Radio Drama Young Playwrights' Festival in 1991. This was followed by his first stage play, *Independent Voice*, produced by Belfast's then most prominent new writing theatre company, Tinderbox, in 1993 and later for BBC Radio Four in 1994; for which it won the Stewart Parker Award for a BBC Radio Drama. Several stage plays followed, but Mitchell's breakthrough work came when the Abbey Theatre in Dublin agreed to produce *In a Little World of Our Own* in February 1997, which proved to be very successful and established Mitchell as a remarkable new theatrical voice in contemporary Irish and British theatre. *Little World* is a play in four acts in which Ray, a UDA thug, rapes and mistakenly kills a young Catholic girl he was trying to stop from rejecting the advances of his learning disabled brother, Richard. Ray's brutal methods are exposed as out of step in contemporary Belfast and in the end he is killed by the local UDA he once loyally served.

Tearing the Loom (1998) and As the Beast Sleeps (1998)

In 1998 Mitchell was commissioned to write *Tearing the Loom* for the Lyric Theatre in Belfast and in June of the same year the Abbey staged his new play, *As the Beast Sleeps* (*ABS*), which brought Mitchell continued commercial and critical success. Set during the United Irish Rebellion of 1798, *Tearing* tells the story of a Protestant weaver family who are split by the events of the revolution. Richard, a proud weaver-poet, wants to stay out of the fight but he finds his family drawn into events as they unfold. David, his son, is anti-rebellion, while his headstrong daughter, Ruth, is a pro-rebellion activist. As the play hurtles towards its bloody conclusion, the family is torn apart and eventually both David and Robert are killed. In the closing moments Ruth too dies by committing suicide and martyring herself. Mitchell's early historical drama contains the beginning of a definite class-based analysis of the events it describes and their dramatic exploration clearly aims to allow the dire consequences of a rebellion that set neighbours and families against each other to resonate in the contemporary world of its staging.

ABS returns to present-day Ulster, but here loyalties are shown to be equally divided. Kyle and his loyalist gang find that in the wake of recent political developments, their style of direct action to support the loyalist cause is no longer required. Politicians have turned to 'talk' and left UDA hard men, like Freddie, Kyle's close friend and gang member, with nothing to do and nowhere to go. Kyle's wife Sandra is sick of having no money since Kyle has stopped doing 'jobs' for the UDA. Meanwhile, some of Kyle's other gang members have stepped out of line and been barred from their local UDA club. The UDA leadership instruct Kyle to organise a punishment squad to deal with dissenters, to which he reluctantly agrees. But Freddie is caught robbing the club and Kyle is forced to bring him in to find out who was his accomplice. When Freddie refuses to co-operate, he is beaten to within an inch of his life. In a final twist Kyle realises that the person Freddie was protecting by refusing to reveal their identity, his accomplice in the robbery, was Sandra, Kyle's disaffected wife.

ABS, which premiered shortly after the signing of the GFA, offers a heavily semiotised snapshot of this moment of transition. Kyle and Sandra's partially decorated home, and the notable absence of their child visually and thematically describes a failed alliance. The 'Club' where Kyle and his men drink, in the midst of an expensive and difficult refurbishment, is a thickly drawn theatrical metaphor for 'the state of the nation' amid the realisation of the GFA. The play's central dynamic is in part generated from Kyle's attempts to find a place for himself and his recently dispossessed and now unneeded loyalist gang: 'All we want is, obviously to be let back in – all of us . . . what I think would suit everybody would be if we could have a private area' (*ABS*, pp. 46–7).

Trust (1999)

In 1998 Mitchell was invited to become playwright-in-residence at the Royal National Theatre in London, during which time his play *Trust* was produced at the Royal Court Jerwood Theatre Upstairs in March 1999. *Trust* looks at the relationship between UDA godfather Geordie and his wife Margaret as they carry out their daily paramilitary business activities alongside the demands of raising their teenage son, Jake. When it emerges that Jake is being bullied by some local boys and Geordie fails to act, Margaret takes matters into her own hands and tries to use their UDA contacts to put pressure on the boys to leave Jake alone. Things quickly get out of hand, however, when a boy is badly hurt and Jake is arrested. When yet again Geordie doesn't act to save his son, Margaret decides to turn super-grass in order to buy her son out of youth offenders' prison.

The Force of Change (2000)

In 1995, a year after the IRA's ceasefire, the Patten Commission began a public consultation process designed to assess public opinion regarding the changes needed within the Royal Ulster Constabulary (RUC) that would enable the two majority traditions in Northern Ireland to support any future police force. The implementation of the results of the Patten Report, which included recommendations to change the name of the RUC to the Police Service of Northern Ireland (PSNI) in 2001, became a condition of the GFA. *Force*, staged in 1999, traverses these hugely significant shifts in Northern Ireland's recent history. Produced at the Royal Court Theatre Upstairs in April 2000, *Force* received the George Devine Award and the Evening Standard Award for best new play. Mitchell sets the drama in the holding cells of a fictional RUC station amid the pressures being brought to bear on the organisation to change in light of recommendations following the GFA. Caroline, an officious career-minded officer, has got a limited amount of time left to crack her UDA suspect, Stanley, if she is to make her bid for promotion within the force. But some of Caroline's colleagues are determined to see her fail. Bill, Mitchell's alienated and bigoted RUC man, is especially eager to impede Caroline: partly because he dislikes her and the new developments within the RUC she represents, but also because he has been colluding with Stanley and the UDA for a number of years and Caroline's investigation threatens to expose him. Bill's collusion with Stanley is exposed as unworkable in the emerging ethics and procedures played out in Mitchell's liminal *mise en scène*.

Loyal Women (2003)

Mitchell returned to the Royal Court in 2003 when his play *Loyal Women* was staged in the Jerwood Downstairs Theatre in November. Here Mitchell turns his attention to the Women's UDA (WUDA), where Brenda and Gail are asked by the UDA leadership to deal with a local girl who has been seeing a Catholic teenager in the Rathcoole estate. Brenda, who is known to have killed someone years earlier, has changed since her reckless days as a young WUDA volunteer and is increasingly open to negotiated rather than violent solutions. Gail, however, and her henchwomen Heather, prefer to solve things using older, brutal methods. When Brenda fails to extract a promise from the young girl that she will stop seeing the Catholic boy, Heather, Gail and Jenny, Brenda's gormless young daughter, tar and feather her in a brutal closing scene. Brenda recants her involvement with the organisation and the play ends with an extremely uneasy truce between Brenda and Gail. Mitchell's plays contain a number of variations on the dramatic rendering of intransigence versus progressivism. Bill and David in *Force*, for example, represent a politically moderate incarnation of the device, but we might equally look to Ray drawn in opposition to Walter in *Little World*, or most obviously of all Kyle set in dramatic contrast to Freddie in *ABS*. In *Loyal Women* Brenda and Gail demonstrate a more recent development, as Mitchell sees it, in Protestant working-class political thinking. Gail's violence seems outdated when pitched against Brenda's keen negotiation skills and, although both women are active members the WUDA, as Hutchinson notes, Brenda's tactics are those favoured by the UDA leadership.[9] Brenda has changed but Gail hasn't. Gail is a strong arm to be exercised only when absolutely necessary, but Brenda's personal journey from violence to negotiation is a more useful and marketable reflection of the public image the now more media-savvy UDA would like to project.[10]

Summary

The immediacy of the subject material Mitchell's work dramatises has meant that when premiered his plays attract considerable media attention and he has been adopted by the press both in England and Ireland as 'the chronicler of the Protestant experience in Northern Ireland'.[11] Mitchell himself is aware that as a Protestant working-class writer from the North, in the 1990s he was something of a rarity in the discourses then inflecting contemporary Irish theatre.

> Protestants don't write plays, you see. You must be a Catholic
> or a Catholic sympathiser, or a homosexual to do that. No one
> in our community does that because playwriting is a silly
> pretend thing.[12]

He conceives of his work as a necessary corrective to the stereotyping
of his community in the media and a challenge to a pervasive and
reductive analysis of that community. It is the self-promotion of his
insider status and the perception of Mitchell as a working-class
documentarian of an intransigent and violent version of Ulster
loyalism that has also framed the critical reception of his stage plays.[13]
While Mitchell's work remains relatively under-explored from an
academic perspective, those critics who have provided a sustained
analysis of his plays have at least partially redressed what Gerald Dawe
has described as 'the cultural resistance and uncertainty which still
exists in Ireland, and indeed elsewhere, when writing bearing upon
northern Protestant experience is addressed'.[14]

It is important, however, to stress that while Mitchell's socio-
political background makes him something of an oddity in Irish
theatre, his is not a sole voice in Irish theatre history. Reviews,
critiques and indeed Mitchell's own comments often seem to overstate
his 'unique' position as a Protestant, working-class, and Northern
playwright. From this perspective, while Mitchell's status as an
important cultural commentator on contemporary loyalism in
Northern Ireland is not in dispute, it is important to locate his work
in a discernible, if fragmented, tradition of Northern, Protestant
working-class playwrights. Wallace McDowell, for example, is correct
to suggest that Mitchell's working-class credentials set him somewhat
apart from the similarly dissenting voices of other Protestant middle-
class Northern playwrights such as Stewart Parker or Graham Reid.[15]
But Mitchell's ethno-class affiliations and the critique his work
engages with echo the material circumstances and thematic preoccupations of other Protestant working-class writers such as Thomas
Carnduff in the 1930s/1940s and Sam Thompson in the 1960s.

Mitchell's work has not always been received favourably in
Northern Ireland, least of all by the very community he chooses to

write about. He struggled to find success as a playwright in his native city at the beginning of his career. For example, he had originally conceived *The World, the Flesh and the Devil* as a stage play and, although the play was produced for radio, a stage version of it was never mounted. Later *Little World* was turned down by the Lyric Theatre in Belfast before he had offered it to the Abbey because of its potentially contentious subject material and because of its local loyalist community setting. Mitchell, however, has remained committed to documenting the changes within his community during the peace process. When success did come, and perhaps because that success had come via a Dublin premiere, Mitchell was received with apathy and sometimes suspicion in Belfast's loyalist communities. The growing recognition that his work was not simply engaged in a theatrical celebration of Protestant working-class Belfast meant that others were keen to express their irritation to him at having their districts framed in any negative way to outsiders.[16]

In recent years Mitchell's work has become much less visible and the appetite for his narratives of discontent seems to have somewhat diminished. He has not had a London premiere since *Loyal Women* in 2003, and, although Mitchell is completing a number of film scripts, his turn to screen writing has as yet not had the kind of success one might expect:

> BBC Northern Ireland told me I wouldn't be working with them any more unless I wrote about the peace process and it would have to be positive. So I told them, 'No, you won't be working with me.' How could I write a positive drama about the peace process when terrorists are blowing up my car?[17]

Mitchell's work is animated by a sustained and nuanced exploration of the fragmentation of contemporary Ulster loyalist identity. The divisions explored by Mitchell have a long historical gestation. The terms unionist and loyalist, for example, were at one point used interchangeably,[18] but in the past two decades these terms have become increasingly distinct. While unionism remains defined by its central commitment to a continuing economic union with

Great Britain and the political structures guaranteeing that union, loyalism, as James McAuley suggests,

> may be expressed in terms of strong declarations of devotion to the British Crown and flag and a strong feeling of 'belonging' to the six counties of Northern Ireland [but has not] hindered Loyalists from coming into direct confrontation with representatives of the UK state or its security forces. Underpinning loyalism, therefore, is the notion [. . .] that the relationship between loyalism and the British state is essentially *contractual* [emphasis added].[19]

The manner in which the term loyalist is popularly used to define those individuals and groups who are willing to use physical force against the perceived enemies of Ulster tends to homogenise the multiple groupings operating under this particular banner. In part this marks one aspect of the success of organisations such as the UDA and UVF and their ability to provide 'an important channel both for articulating social grievances and for reproducing sectarian ideology within the Protestant working class'.[20] As Brian Graham points out, however, loyalism 'is not a coherent ideology'[21] and beneath the apparent unity of anti-republican sentiment, there are many forms of loyalty at play.

A proclivity to schism has made the need for a unifying ethic all the more pressing both within and among loyalist paramilitary groups. Popular unionist campaigns designed to resist any changes that might be interpreted as potential stepping stones into a united Ireland are memorable for the apparent simplicity of their rhetoric – 'Ulster Says No!' or the even more direct and effective 'Never!', for example. Mitchell's plays dramatise how, in the heady changes following the GFA, dissimilarities of vision among these sometimes allied, sometimes competing factions are exposed at ground level. *ABS*, in particular, represents in microcosm the transitions occurring within loyalism as the GFA came to be ratified.[22]

Mitchell's play telegraphs a number of the difficulties currently faced by Protestant working-class districts across Northern Ireland.

Many economically deprived communities have struggled with an absence of cohesion and perceived security since the contingencies of a negotiated peace settlement and the transformed nature of paramilitary activity in their areas, ironically, seem to have removed them. Mitchell's work documents the impact of such changes and offers a series of blunt theatrical images in opposition to the pervasive official discourses of peace proffered by the media in the wake of the GFA. Mitchell's characters often long for the past and the security of a less complicated *weltanschauung*. Ray, in *Little World* for example, hankers after the 'old days, the old ways' (p. 7), a time when, he believes, his particular style of rough justice was respected. Bill, in *Force*, laments the changing nature of the police force: 'As far as I was concerned I joined a Protestant police force to protect the Protestant people of Ulster against the IRA' (p. 48). In *ABS* this general desire distils into a more precise and urgent necessity. Freddie articulates the felt need for the comfort of a returned zero-sum analysis amid the complexities of Belfast at the turn of the new millennium:

> Fuck politics, fuck talking, fuck all that shit . . . Taigs hate us and we hate them. That's the way it is and that's the way it's going to stay. They were fighting like fuck because we were on top. Now we have to do the same. (p. 81)

Larry too, in *ABS*, senses the mood of change. He tells Alec that when he thinks of the 'old days' he sees them in 'black and white' when: 'The Prods were the good guys and the taigs were the baddies. Simple as that' (p. 20). His nostalgia for simpler times stands in fatal contrast to Alec's ability to grasp the complexity of 'the world in blinding Technicolor' (p. 20). More than Freddie even, Larry is yesterday's man doing yesterday's job.

The disposition of this analysis continues and extends in Mitchell's later plays. In *Force*, for example, the thematic emphasis lies on the impact of structural change. Bill's 'Protestant Police force to protect a Protestant people' (*Force*, p. 48) is an anachronism reminiscent of Lord Craigavon's 'Protestant Parliament for a Protestant people'. David, Bill's young inheritor, however, vehemently rejects the gangsterism of Stanley and the UDA. 'I learned more about the Stanley Browns of this world just growing up in Rathcoole' (*Force*, p. 67), he tells Caroline. Later, face to face with the UDA leader, his opposition bears the strength and confidence of lived experience:

> When I look into your eyes I see a reflection of every IRA man you claimed to be protecting us from. I see old men closing their shops and going home penniless because you took their profit and more. I see old ladies cowering in fear trying to forget what they witnessed in case you or your cronies come back to make them forget permanently. (*Force*, p. 74)

In overview, Mitchell's stage plays can be read as following a thematic trajectory that begins by questioning the assumptions of violent loyalism and has now reached a point where his work often challenges the legitimacy of those organisations created to carry out acts of supposedly pro-state terrorism. In *Little World* Ray, despite his violence, is presented as human and caring in his relationship with his learning disabled brother. Even Freddie in *ABS* remains recognisably human, funny and likable in the right circumstances. In these early plays Mitchell's position often remains deliberately ambiguous. *ABS*, however, also marks a turning point in Mitchell's dramaturgy. While audiences are permitted moments where they might relate to Freddie and his situation, the play's construction and its foregrounding of Kyle's dilemma clearly asks sympathy for his position in their final analysis. In *Trust* Geordie is betrayed by his wife-turned-supergrass, Margaret, when he elects to protect the UDA rather than his son. Margaret's dissidence is later echoed in Brenda's newly constituted loyalty list (*Loyal Women*, p. 85) and her ultimate decision to leave the Women's UDA at the close of *Loyal Women*.[23]

Mitchell's work, then, viewed in this way might be usefully conceived of as increasingly involved in a post-unionist loyalist discourse. McAuley argues that the UDA represented a significant development in Protestant working-class politics in the early 1970s when it had within its emergent discourses the seeds of a radical departure that favoured a class-based analysis of the loyalist position in

Ulster over the apparent logic of sectarianism.[24] Mitchell's work draws a great deal of its potency from its grounding in the complexities of contemporary Northern Irish Protestantism's identity crisis. Mitchell's thematic preoccupations clearly locate his work amid the post-unionist discourse. From this perspective his plays chart the loss of consent within the Protestant working classes of Northern Ireland for some of the central tenets of mainstream unionism: a loss based on a perceptible sense of class differences within unionism.

> **Alec** I've seen too many bad Prods. Our own leaders, I couldn't support them. I just never felt like they represented me – or us. It was as though they lived in a different world and when you look at their lifestyle, let me tell you, you wouldn't be too far wrong. They're either very rich or very Christian [. . .] (*ABS*, p. 20)

Similarly, Kyle's ethno-politics have a definite economic dimension. He tells Freddie that 'Things have been going bad with us, Freddie, with everybody, ever since this fucking process started and we were told to stop doing what we do and all the money stopped coming in' (*ABS*, p. 63). Inclusion in a post-GFA and a politically rearranged Northern Ireland means not just a place at the table, but also a job and food on that table. Across the performances under discussion here, there is a keen sense of sectarianism compounded by economic poverty and intensifying class cleavages.

Mitchell's position in this discourse can be described in Gramscian terms as that of the organic intellectual.[25] He has stressed the importance of remaining connected to his class:

> It is important for me to stay here [Rathcoole, before he was intimidated out] and keep in touch with the people I'm in touch with. If you are not aware of how things are changing, you'll lose the detail and you'll write a lot of nonsense.[26]

Moreover, Mitchell's work resonates with Dario Fo's descriptors of work in the Gramscian mode, which he sees as aiming to 'create (or help create) public opinion, ferment dialectics, and pose problems'.[27] Mitchell's experiences as a playwright bear testimony to the difficulty of addressing such complex and volatile issues in as public an art form as theatre.

The contexts for the premieres of Mitchell's plays, all of which have been premiered outside of Protestant working-class communities, have meant that they have been open to the criticism that they are remarkable largely because they offer Irish and English middle-class audiences a commoditised version of loyalism. Maguire, for example, suggests 'There is a danger for Mitchell that, in the contexts in which his work is staged, audiences are able to engage in a voyeurism inflected with the distance of class and political identity.'[28] Like other working-class writers who have written for mainstream theatres and largely middle-class audiences, Mitchell's work risks mattering least to those he writes about.[29] Typically such writers are praised for the authenticity of their representations of working-class life and the privileged access afforded audiences because the playwright is perceived as writing from the 'inside' and from their own personal experiences.[30]

That Mitchell has overwhelmingly chosen to work in a realist form has also left his plays open to charges of aesthetic conservatism.[31] Realism has proved an extremely popular and resilient form for twentieth-century Northern Irish theatre makers. From the plays of St John Ervine in the early 1900s, through the many playwrights writing for the Ulster Group Theatre in the 1940s–60s, to the more recent use of the form by John Boyd at the Lyric in the 1970s, for example, and later Martin Lynch at the Lyric in the 1980s, realist plays have remained artistically viable and commercially desirable. There have, of course, been numerous playwrights who have sought and explored alternative forms of dramatic expression. For many playwrights after a decade of conflict the complexities of the Troubles became more pronounced and they sought what they perceived as more complex theatrical responses than those afforded by the realist mode. The stylistic experimentation of Brian Friel's *Freedom of the City*, or Stewart Parker's *Northern Star*, to name just two examples, attempted to find aesthetically inventive and historically inclusive dramatic models. At a time when a political settlement seemed an impossibility, many playwrights shifted the emphasis of their work away from the urgencies of realism to the disruption of metatheatrics as they sought for in theatrical invention what Parker would later famously refer to as a 'working model of wholeness' in drama that could fill the void left by the perceived failure of politics.

However, by the mid-1990s the peace process had started to gather momentum and, despite deep and widespread cynicism, it began to feel as if a deal might be imminent in Northern Ireland. In these seemingly accelerated contexts it seems critically short-sighted to read the production of Mitchell's realist plays as *only* aesthetically regressive or as *only* examples of working-class misery made palatable for middle-class theatrical consumption. Rather, conceived of as an example of glimpse theatre, a play like *ABS* might be assessed in relation to the heavily mediatised events surrounding its production. In this case, staged just after the signing of the GFA, the realism of Mitchell's play in reception is galvanised and made vital by events in many ways extraneous to the text but intrinsically linked to the performative moment of transmission. Offering audiences a glimpse into the previously unseen world of loyalism, at this precise point, arguably vitalised Mitchell's work and *re*-vitalised his use of realism as a form in such particular circumstances.

The manner of representation, then, is crucial. Ulster loyalists have often been negatively portrayed and stereotyped in the media. Mitchell himself has criticised such representations.[32] Loyalist paramilitaries in particular have been stereotyped as psychopaths, bloodthirsty, and lacking in political acumen. On the face of it, Mitchell's liberal and graphic use of violence, and the apparent mindlessness of some of his characters, seems to support such stereotyping. While some of his plays undoubtedly do stray into theatrical cliché, however, others deal in much more subtle and complex characterisations to powerful effect. Ray and Freddie will serve here are examples of Mitchell's more adeptly realised representatives of contemporary loyalism.

In a BBC Radio Ulster broadcast, Mitchell told an esteemed panel of guests: 'I think that everybody has the capacity to commit violent crimes. And maybe they haven't found it within themselves, but it's there; it's an animal thing that's within everyone.'[33] For Mitchell, loyalist violence is a part of Protestant working-class experience. Men like Ray have responded to a particular set of material circumstances in a manner that he may not agree with, but he can understand. Ray's actions have purpose and logic:

> **Ray** The world is a violent place. We know that better than anybody. Whether it's dealing with the IRA or dealing with petty theft or glue sniffing. Whatever, namby-pamby ways don't get results . . . See, I'm not just talking about beating people up. Doing people over. I'm talking about common sense. (*Little World*, pp. 3–4)

His commonsense remark is reminiscent of Gramsci's conception of the same phrase: the set of contradictory motivations that Gramsci suggests govern our everyday ideological orientation.[34] Ray is a contradictory product of his environment, capable of both gentleness and terrible violence. Mitchell's attempts to give Ray, the 'monster', a recognisable human face are, perhaps, somewhat theatrically awkward in this early play. Dramatically, Ray's 'nice side' feels overly structured; his bad/good sides arguably too neatly separated. In Freddie, however, Mitchell finds a more interesting contradiction. Despite his apparent psychopathic violence, Freddie is far from mindless. He understands the value of appearing to be psychopathic. In scene five, he recounts the story of his bar-room brawl the night before. The stage directions read: '**Freddie** *enjoys telling the story, complete with all the actions from his point of view.* **Sandra** *clearly enjoys it too*' (p. 52).

The thrill of performing the psychopath clearly appeals to him. Later, when Kyle tells him he is a 'crazy bastard' he takes it as a compliment: 'Don't try to butter me up' (p. 59). Like the comfort and simplicity of the zero-sum analysis he wants to return to, performing the psycho has value in these dangerous, transitional times. Terrorism, by its nature, is performative. Schmid points out that terrorism was originally defined as 'Propaganda by Deed' and that it enacts 'in an important sense, symbolic violence'.[35] Terrorism relies on an audience to receive the performance of the act of violence to engender the requisite sense of terror. Freddie understands the power of perception and the need to maintain an image. His violence, or rather the threat of violence he presents, is largely performative. In fact, he has far more violence visited upon him than he dishes out. But he is an important reminder to audiences alive to threats of such violence that loyalism understands the currency, symbolic and actual, of violence in political struggle. Freddie is an interesting attempt by Mitchell to represent the difficulties of changing long-standing beliefs and patterns of common sense within contemporary loyalism.

Mitchell's plays work best in specific moments as politicised thrillers offering middle-class and other similarly distanced audiences provocative glimpses into the subaltern world of loyalist Belfast. The sitcom-like realism of *Little World* was energised in reception because we had never been on these particular loyalist sofas before. But this could have easily been a one-hit wonder for Mitchell, were it not for his creative and ethical commitment to documenting the contemporaneous experiences of his community. When he does this, when his plays feel as if they might have been written that morning, Mitchell's realist dramas are vital socio-cultural events. *ABS* and *Force* are the clearest examples of this. But when he is out of step with this Mitchell's plays also suggest a limited degree of technique. His characters can appear underdeveloped and repetitive; his plots un-vital and uninventive. For the Protestant working class of Northern Ireland, Mitchell's plays are an important and public articulation of the changes occurring within their community and are part of a much wider discourse emerging there.

Primary Sources

As the Beast Sleeps (London: Nick Hern, 2001).
The Force of Change (London: Nick Hern, 2000).
Holding Cell (Belfast: Tinderbox Theatre Company, 2000).
In a Little World of Our Own (London: Nick Hern, 1998).
Loyal Women (London: Nick Hern, 2003).

Tearing the Loom (London: Nick Hern, 1998).
Trust (London: Nick Hern, 1999).

Secondary Sources

Anon., 'Embracing the Challenge', *Irish Times*, 9 June 1998.

Anon., 'Where are All Our Playwrights Going?', *Irish Times*, 2 May 2000.

Anon., 'Processed Peace', *Time Out*, 12 September 2001.

Anon., 'Balancing Act', *Guardian*, 5 April 2003.

The Book Club, BBC Radio Ulster, n.d. <http://www.bbc.co.uk/northernireland/radioulster/bookprogramme/feature_144190.shtml> (accessed 16 April 2009).

Bowcott, Owen, 'Never Say Never Again? Plan for Paisley Biopic,' *Guardian*, 22 March 2007.

Chrisafis, Angelique, 'Loyalist Paramilitaries Drive Playwright from His Home', *Guardian*, 12 December 2005.

Cornell, Jennifer, 'Recontextualising the Conflict: Northern Ireland, Television Drama, and the Politics of Validation', in J. Harrington and E. J. Mitchell (eds), *Politics and Performance in Contemporary Northern Ireland* (Amherst: University of Massachusetts Press, 1999), pp. 197–218.

Coyle, Jane, 'Mapping the Hard Road', *Irish Times*, 8 February 1997.

Dawe, Gerald, 'A Hard Act: Stewart Parker's *Pentecost*', in Eberhard Bort (ed.), *The State of Play: Irish Theatre in the Nineties*, CDE-Studies, Vol. 1 (Trier: WVT, 1996), pp. 65–74.

'First Minister Welcomes News of Loyalist Decommissioning', *Belfast Telegraph*, 27 June 2009.

Fo, Dario, 'Some Aspects of Popular Theatre', *New Theatre Quarterly*, Vol. 1, No. 2 (1985), pp. 131–7.

Fricker, Karen, 'A World Apart: A Protestant Playwright Evokes the Unromantic Ireland', *American Theatre*, Vol. 16, No. 6 (1999), pp. 54–7.

Gardner, Lyn, 'The Force of Change', *Guardian*, 10 November 2000.

Gibbons, Fiachra, 'Truth and Nail', *Guardian*, 10 April 2000.

Global Review of Ethnopolitics, Vol. 3, No. 1 (2003), Special Issue: Northern Ireland.

Graham, Brian, 'The Past in the Present: The Shaping of Identity in Loyalist Ulster', *Terrorism and Political Violence*, Vol. 3, No. 3 (2004), pp. 483–500.

Hennessey, Thomas, *A History of Northern Ireland 1920–1996* (Dublin: Gill and Macmillan, 1997).

Hutchinson, Wesley, 'Engendering Change in the UDA: Gary Mitchell's Loyal Women', *Estudios Irlandeses* (2005), pp. 67–76.

—, 'Gary Mitchell's "Talk Process"', *ÉA*, Vol. 56, No. 2 (2003), pp. 206–18.

Jarman, Neil, 'From War to Peace? Changing Patterns of Violence in Northern Ireland, 1990–2003', *Terrorism and Political Violence*, Vol. 16, No. 3 (2004), pp. 420–38.

Maguire, Thomas, *Making Theatre in Northern Ireland: Through and Beyond the Troubles* (Exeter: University of Exeter Press, 2006).

McAuley, James, '"Just Fighting to Survive": Loyalist Paramilitary Politics and the Progressive Unionist Party', *Terrorism and Political Violence*, Vol. 16, No. 3 (2004), pp. 522–43.

—, *The Politics of Identity: Protestant Working Class Politics and Culture in Belfast* (Aldershot: Avebury Press, 1994).

McDonald, Henry, 'Paisley Biopic Hits Crash Crunch', *Observer*, 22 June 2008.

—, 'Playwright Hits Back Against Intimidation', *Observer*, 29 January 2006.

McDowell, Wallace, 'Staging the Debate: Loyalist-Britishness and Masculinities in the Plays of Gary Mitchell', *Studies in Ethnicity and Nationalism*, Vol. 9, No. 1 (2009), pp. 89–110.

McEvoy, Kieran, Peter Shirlow and Karen McElrath, 'Resistance, Transition and Exclusion: Politically Motivated Ex-Prisoners and Conflict Transformation in Northern Ireland', *Terrorism and Political Violence*, Vol. 16, No. 3 (2004), pp. 646–70.

McGrath, John, *A Good Night Out* (London: Methuen, 1981).

McKay, Susan, 'Writer's Drama Becomes Reality', *Irish Times*, 20 December 2005.

—, '"You Can Make Your Wee Film But No Cameras": Unionism in 2005', *Field Day Review*, Vol. 2 (2006), pp. 154–67.

—, 'Tough Characters to Tackle', *Irish Times*, 2 August 2006.

Mouffe, Chantal, 'Hegemony and Ideology in Gramsci', in Chantal Mouffe (ed.), *Gramsci and Marxist Theory* (London/Boston, MA/Henley: Routledge and Kegan Paul, 1979), pp. 168–204.

Nun, José and Cartier, William, 'Elements for a Theory of Democracy: Gramsci and Common Sense', *Boundary 2*, Vol. 14, No. 3 (1986), pp. 197–229.

Parker, Stewart, *Dramatis Personae* (Belfast: John Malone Memorial Committee, 1986).

Patten, Chris, *The Report of the Independent Commission on Policing for Northern Ireland* <www.nio.gov.uk/a_new_beginning_in_ policing_in_northern_ireland.pdf> (accessed 21 August 2009).

Ransome, Paul, *Antonio Gramsci: A New Introduction* (Hemel Hempstead: Harvester Wheatsheaf, 1992).

Russell, Richard Rankin, '"Loyal to the Truth": Gary Mitchell's Aesthetic Loyalism in *As the Beast Sleeps* and *The Force of Change*', *Modern Drama*, Vol. 48, No. 1 (2005), p. 186.

Schmid, Alex P., 'Frameworks for Conceptualizing Terrorism', *Terrorism and Political Violence*, Vol. 16, No. 2 (2004), pp. 197–221.

Shirlow, Peter and Mark, McGovern, (eds.) *Who are the People? Unionism, Protestantism and Loyalism in Northern Ireland* (London: Pluto Press, 1997).

Terrorism and Political Violence, Vol. 16, No. 3 (2004), special issue: Northern Ireland.

'UDA Statement in Full', *Belfast Telegraph*, 27 June 2009.

Notes

1. 'Where are All Our Playwrights Going?', *Irish Times*, 2 May 2000.
2. Fiachra Gibbons, 'Truth and Nail'.
3. Mitchell quoted in Jane Coyle, 'Mapping the Hard Road'.
4. The Ulster Defence Association, Northern Ireland's largest loyalist paramilitary organisation.
5. The Ulster Volunteer Force, also a large loyalist paramilitary organisation.
6. Gibbons, op. cit.
7. Ibid.
8. The attacks were widely reported in the press. See, for example, Susan McKay's 'Writer's Drama Becomes a Reality'.
9. Wesley Hutchinson, 'Engendering Change', p. 71.
10. Ibid., p. 72.
11. Lyn Gardner, 'The Force of Change'. Reviews of any number of Mitchell's plays featured in the *Irish Times* share a similar conception of Mitchell as the unofficial historian of contemporary Ulster loyalism.
12. Quoted in Gibbons, op. cit.
13. For example, Richard Rankin Russell writes that Mitchell is 'an unblinking chronicler who understands their [Ulster loyalists'] plight yet is able to critique it' (' "Loyal to the Truth" ', p. 86); whereas Hutchinson reads Mitchell's work as specifically 'providing a unique insight into the closed world of loyalist paramilitarianism', 'Gary Mitchell's "Talk Process" ', p. 206).
14. Gerald Dawe, 'A Hard Act', p. 65.
15. Wallace McDowell, 'Staging the Debate', p. 93.
16. Mitchell recalls: 'I get knocked within my own community because I don't write romantic Protestant plays [. . .]. I'm writing about the realities of our situation.' See Karen Fricker, 'A World Apart', p. 56.
17. Henry McDonald, 'Playwright Hits Back Against Intimidation'.
18. Thomas Hennessey, *A History of Northern Ireland*, p. 202.
19. James McAuley, ' "Just Fighting to Survive" ', pp. 524–5.
20. James McAuley, *The Politics of Identity*, p. 82.
21. Brian Graham, 'The Past in the Present', p. 484.
22. Kieran McEvoy *et al.*, 'Resistance', pp. 653–4.
23. Mitchell continues and hardens this critique of loyalist paramilitary organisations in *Remnants of Fear* (unpublished), which controversially premiered at the Feil an Phobail (West Belfast Festival) in August 2006.
24. McAuley, *The Politics of Identity*, pp. 86–7.
25. Paul Ransome, *Antonio Gramsci*, Chapter 7.
26. Susan McKay, ' "You Can Make Your Wee Film" ', p. 156.
27. Fo, 'Some Aspects of Popular Theatre', p. 134.

28. Thomas Maguire, *Making Theatre in Northern Ireland*, p. 157.

29. Interestingly, many of Mitchell's works have of course opened at the Royal Court Theatre in London, which, John McGrath suggests, has a long history of presenting 'no more than the elaboration of a theatrical technique for tuning working-class experience into satisfying thrills for the bourgeoisie'. John McGrath, *A Good Night Out*, p. 11.

30. We might, for example, cite examples such as John Osborne or Jim Cartwright in the British theatre, Clifford Odets in the USA, or Sean O'Casey and Sam Thompson in the Irish tradition. Mitchell's work has commonly been received in such terms.

31. For a useful and concise description of the key questions surrounding the deployment of the realist form in contemporary Northern Irish theatre, see Maguire, op. cit., pp. 22–5.

32. See Fricker, op. cit.

33. Quoted in Russell, op. cit., p. 187.

34. For a discussion of Gramsci's conception of 'common sense', see José Nun and William Cartier, 'Elements for a Theory of Democracy'.

35. Alex P. Schmid, 'Frameworks for Conceptualizing Terrosism', pp. 205, 211.

18 TOM MURPHY

Gerold Sedlmayr

A Whistle in the Dark; Famine; The Morning after Optimism; The Sanctuary Lamp; The Blue Macushla; The Gigli Concert; Bailegangaire; Too Late for Logic; The Patriot Game; The House; Alice Trilogy

Introduction

In 1935, Thomas Bernard Murphy was born in Tuam, County Galway, the youngest of ten children. His father Jack, a carpenter, went to work in Birmingham, where he stayed for the rest of his working life. One by one, Tom's brothers followed. It is no surprise therefore that '[h]is work is full of brothers and parents who are absent and who yet haunt the imaginations of his protagonists'.[1] In 1955, he started training at Ringsend Technical School to become a metalwork teacher, worked in this profession in a town near Tuam, and resigned roughly five years later to embark on a career as a playwright. With his first full-length play, *A Whistle in the Dark*, being harshly rejected in Ireland, first and foremost by the then-managing director of the Abbey Theatre, Ernest Blythe, he turned to London in 1962. There, the play became a hit at Stratford East and, later, in the West End, yet Murphy was unable to follow up on it. In 1970, he returned to his home country, where success, let alone appreciation, came about only hesitatingly. Certainly, the fact that the Abbey had reopened under new management in 1966 made it easier for Murphy to gain a foothold in Ireland. However, although he was a member of the Board of Directors at the Abbey from 1972 to 1983, at least in the 1970s times were still rough. Nevertheless, Tom Murphy, who now lives in Dublin, has managed to establish himself in the long run as one of the most important and most sophisticated Irish playwrights, both in his own country and internationally.

The Plays

A Whistle in the Dark (1961)

A Whistle in the Dark, Tom Murphy's highly important first play, premiered at Joan Littlewood's Theatre Royal, Stratford East. In a complex way, it deals with the issues of emigration, family and the clash between old and new.

Four of the Carney brothers live in Coventry, England. They had emigrated from an impoverished County Mayo roughly a decade before. Whereas Michael is the only one married and working in a 'sound' job, the others lead lives dominated by violence, earning money by way of pimping and corruption. The play is set in Michael's house, where the other brothers have lodged themselves for a few weeks already, recklessly abusing Michael and Betty's hospitality.

The action ensues when the Carneys' father, Dada, together with his youngest son Des, comes to visit. Dada is a patriarch, representing the law and the sanctity of the family, and is idolised by every son except for Michael. He is worshipped as a hero, a model fighter presumably looked up to by people at home. However, when a fight with the rivalling Irish clan of the Mulryans draws near, he makes a quick getaway: in the course of the play, it becomes clear that he is nothing but a sham hero. The play's tragic character, though, is Michael. Although trying to be the opposite of his father, he eventually ends up as his double: a coward who compensates for his frustration by hitting his wife (p. 76). Events culminate during a heated argument when he strikes Des with a broken bottle and kills him (p. 86). The living room – symbolic for the private and unifying space of the family – hence turns out to be a place of death and dissolution.

Though it is set in England, Murphy in this drama angrily analyses what still rampant emigration means to Ireland and its people. He shows that emigration is a motor which keeps in motion and accelerates a vicious cycle of self-betrayal and self-destruction. Notions of the country as a green and fertile land housing a large but intimate family of heroes-cum-farmers-cum-poets, spread by the Irish Revivalists and cemented as the ideological basis of Free State and independent Ireland, are unmasked as illusory.

Famine (1968)

Famine, a play in twelve scenes, is set in and around the fictitious village of Glanconor and covers the time between autumn 1846 and spring 1847.

Murphy here recounts the lot of a small village community during the Great Famine, concentrating especially on the family of the Connors. As before, he draws attention to individuals trapped by dire circumstances, yet this time, by touching Irish history at one of its sorest points, he attempts to lay bare some of the roots of the hardships the Ireland of his own day suffers. The unavoidable breakdown of the village and family communities in the play mirrors the large-scale disintegration of the national community. The causes are multiple: the Famine is, indeed, a natural catastrophe, but its devastating effects are decisively intensified by the colonial administration's mismanagement, yet also by the communities' tendency to undermine themselves.

Most importantly, Murphy does not assume the position of an authoritative moral observer; instead, he abstains from identifying goodies or baddies; (historical) guilt, he seems to say, can never be allotted in an unambiguous way.

The Morning After Optimism (1971)

After having introduced fantastic elements in *A Crucial Week in the Life of a Grocer's Assistant* by presenting the protagonist John Joe's dreams on stage, Murphy in another play wholly abstains from his earlier biting realism. *The Morning After Optimism* is a surreal play dealing with two couples of confused lovers chasing each other in a forest, and so is strongly reminiscent of Shakespeare's *A Midsummer Night's Dream*. One couple consists of the middle-aged pimp James and his girlfriend Rosie, a thirty-seven-year-old '*dated whore*' (p. 5). The other couple are Edmund and Anastasia, two beautiful young people who function as the embodiments of the older couple's lost ideals and desires.

On the one hand, Murphy surely makes fun of the naïveté youthful dreamers are caught up in. What the play explores, though, is the difficulty of accepting the loss of one's dreams when growing old, as immature as they may be. *The Morning After Optimism* is a parable about the fall from youthful innocence, allegorising the pain which that fall causes.

The play's 'psychological concern', as Fintan O'Toole has shown, 'reflects the inner history'[2] of Ireland in that it fiercely deconstructs the still persistent Revivalist myths of a pre-colonial Golden Age. Apart from that, *The Morning After Optimism* represents a sharp break with the inherited language of the Irish theatre. After this, 'there could be no going back to the kitchen'.[3]

The Sanctuary Lamp (1976)

The Sanctuary Lamp is set in a Catholic church and covers one late afternoon as well as the ensuing night. Harry Stone, a down-and-out in his forties, is hired as a church clerk by a sympathetic elderly priest, Monsignor, despite Harry being a 'half-lapsed Jew' (p. 141). One of his main tasks is to tend the sanctuary lamp, '[s]ignifying the constant presence' (p. 106) of God. As Harry reckons that the candle will have to be replaced at 3 a.m., he stays in the church overnight. There he stumbles upon the sixteen-year-old Maudie, who has run away from her grandparents and now hides in the church. Later on, Harry's old friend and colleague Francisco also turns up and joins them. Throughout this meditative, gloomy and highly atmospheric conversation play, Murphy gradually discloses the stories of these three characters. Harry has to come to terms with the deaths of his daughter Teresa and his wife Olga. The same goes for Francisco, who had an affair with Olga. Similarly, Maudie is haunted by the death of her baby child, Stephen. Hence, what all of them are doing in the church is looking for forgiveness.

Again and again, directly and indirectly, the sanctuary lamp and what it stands for returns to the centre of attention. The play, however, deals not so much with the old question of theodicy, but with the problem of how to establish an intimate relation with a God who has been more and more dehumanised and removed by the Church. The spirit of Jesus, Murphy insinuates, may have been locked in the sanctuary lamp by the Church, but its light still shines forth and it does so in the earthly here and now. A transcendental God is not needed, because Jesus is 'Man, total man' (p. 155).

The Blue Macushla (1980)

While parodying American gangster movies and, more generally, the Americanisation of Ireland during the 1960s and 1970s, *The Blue Macushla* is both a gripping action drama and a subtly political play. Eddie O'Hara is the owner of the Blue Macushla, a successful nightclub in Dublin. The problem is that Eddie, who comes from a poor and underprivileged background, scraped together the money for his establishment through criminal activities. Its financial foundation came from a smuggling job he once did with his friend Danny Mountjoy. While Danny, back then, was caught by the police and locked up – without blowing the whistle on Eddie – the latter managed to escape and invest the money in the club. Now Danny, after five years in prison, suddenly turns up and, to Eddie's dismay, 'thinks he's in for half' (p. 180). The other, more severe, of Eddie's difficulties is that he is being blackmailed by a nationalist 'splinter o' a splinter group' (p. 188), which has found out that he raided a bank some months before in order to pay off his debts.

The Blue Macushla, which ends in a veritable showdown, is concerned with what an underprivileged background can make of a human being: Eddie keeps exploiting those people who are attached to him and is even prepared to kill an innocent person in order to save his club and his status as a successful businessman. However, there are also criminals of a different, nastier sort, especially the nationalist organisation and their boss, No. 1, who commit the worst crimes under the hypocritical cloak of patriotism. Murphy's most subtle political point, though, is made at the very end, when the piano player Pete, who turns out to be a Special Branch agent, reveals that it was he who betrayed Eddie's bank job to No. 1's group and thus willingly victimised him in order to get to them. On top of that, it becomes clear how corrupt even the government and the 'establishment' are when Pete covers up the responsible minister's involvement in the nationalist organisation's doings.

The Gigli Concert (1983)

The dramatis personae of the *The Gigli Concert* consist of only three characters: JPW King, Mona and the Irish Man. The '*English, upper-middle-class*' JPW is a '*DYNAMATOLOGIST*' (p. 165), a sort of esoteric psychologist adhering to the teachings of his guru 'Steve'. However, he has long been abandoned by the organisation, has had, throughout his 'career', no more than two clients all in all – including the Irish Man – and is generally in a state of decline.

When the play opens, the Irish Man, who is unwilling to reveal his name, unexpectedly comes to consult JPW. The Irish Man is a very successful building contractor who, however, has 'come to a standstill' (p. 172). He suffers from a severe depression, taking his anger out mainly on his wife and son. His illness, on top of that, has taken a peculiar form: he constantly listens to records of the famous Italian tenor Beniamino Gigli (1890–1957). The crux is that JPW and the Irish Man, although distinct like Faust and Mephistopheles,[4] seem basically to suffer from the same ailment. Both, at different points, utter the same desperate question: 'How am I going to get through today?' (pp. 166, 173). The main similarity, surely, consists of the fact that JPW also lives a lie, that he also, like the Irish Man, is unable to come to grips with who he is in this 'poxy everyday world' (p. 203). Hence, the boundaries between analyst and patient become more and more blurred, and even at times reversed.

After the departure of Mona, JPW's mistress who has cancer, and after having to release the recovered Irish Man, JPW obviously realises how lonely and lost he in fact is and tries to kill himself with sleeping pills. Like Faust, he makes a pact with those 'down there' (p. 239), and, in a 'great apocalyptic gesture',[5] while plunging into the abyss, suddenly manages to sing like Gigli. Thereby, he is healed, becomes one with himself and the world, and wakes up on a beautiful, hope-bringing morning. Instead of damnation, his revolt leads to salvation.

Bailegangaire (1985)

Called by Nicholas Grene 'the most extraordinary play to have come out of Ireland in the last twenty-five years',[6] *Bailegangaire*, like *The Gigli Concert*, features only three characters: Mommo, an old and senile woman, and her granddaughters Mary and Dolly. Set in the country kitchen of an old thatched house, it depicts a Sunday evening in 1984. Mary, a forty-one-year-old spinster, whose birthday it is, lives there and nurses Mommo, although the latter does not – or does not want to – recognise her. Dolly comes over for a visit. Each of the three characters has her own story, which is revealed in the course of the play, with Mommo's being the central one: it is the story of 'how the place called Bochtán [. . .] came by its new appellation, Bailegangaire, the place without laughter' (p. 92). This story Mommo tells 'night after night' (p. 101), yet without ever having finished it. This night, though, with Mary subtly pushing her on, she eventually does.

Briefly summarised, this is it: about forty years ago, shortly before Christmas, a 'stranger', Seamus O'Toole, and his wife (Mommo, in fact), unable to take their normal route home from a market, end up in the village of Bochtán. While their three grandchildren (Mary, Dolly and their brother Tom) are waiting at home, they cannot continue their journey and stay in John Mahony's pub. After a while, the stranger challenges the local Seamus Costello to a 'laughing competition' (p. 128), but the night ends in disaster. Unwilling to accept defeat – the winner shall be 'he who laughs last' (p. 162) – Costello, drawing on his final reserves, suddenly swoons and dies. A second catastrophe quickly follows: when the couple finally reach their home, they realise that their youngest grandchild Tom had poured paraffin on the fire in order to keep it burning, but it exploded and killed him. Two days afterwards, Mommo's husband also passes away.

Since then, these events have continually burdened Mommo. 'She's guilty' (p. 142), as Dolly says, without knowing exactly why. However, the sisters have their own burdens to carry. Dolly is unhappily married to a violent husband and currently pregnant from some other man. Mary, in order to assume Mommo's care from Dolly so that Dolly could marry, gave up her career as a nurse in London only to return to a deserted country area with a grandmother who refuses to recognise her. Eventually, however, the play, with all the necessary confessions made, ends on a conciliatory note. The 'brand-new baby' (p. 170), which Mary (the name hence becomes significant) will accept from Dolly and pass off as her own, is like the little baby Jesus, signifying hope and a new life. It is Mary's birthday indeed.

Thus, *Bailegangaire* is a Christmas story. Like many of Murphy's plays, it celebrates the human will to survive and carry on in a world full of adversity. Read against the long tradition of Irish storytelling, it also draws attention to the fact that the possibility of survival and the potential to decipher your (personal, local, national) identity is hugely dependent on the ability to have a grip on your own (hi)story, a story which inevitably and existentially is tangled up with the stories of others, especially your family, as well as the story of the place called 'home'. The past is a 'strange auld world' (p. 155), but it is necessary to become familiar with it in order to be familiar with the here and now.

Too Late for Logic (1989)

At the centre of *Too Late for Logic* is middle-aged Christopher, a professor of philosophy, whose career is finally about to set off in grand style, he having been invited to give a televised lecture on Schopenhauer. A successful man, one would believe, were there not a complicated and depressing private life he is hardly able to cope with. When the play opens, we see him isolated on stage, with a gun in his hand. Figure-like shadows close in on him, '*like a group talking sadly at a grave-side*' (p. 3), whom he implores to believe that he is not guilty of anything: 'I'll prove it! Let's go back a few days, backtrack a little' (p. 3). Accordingly, similar to Murphy's technique in *The Blue Macushla*, the subsequent action takes the form of a flashback, describing a circular structure. The action we are about to witness concerns the events following the death of Christopher's sister-in-law Cornelia and the effect this has on the family.

Too Late for Logic is a very demanding and intricately wrought existential play. To put it bluntly, it fathoms the way in which the world – and with it one's being in this world – acquires meaning.

Leaving aside the question whether the shot which finally – and unintentionally – is loosed from Christopher's gun, kills him or not,[7] it is important to notice that the main action takes place within Christopher's mind – it is his memory we see on stage – thus re-enacting Schopenhauer's dictum that 'The world is my idea' (p. 12). However, it is Christopher's family, the products, so to speak, of the *blind* will to procreate, that he cannot control and keep at a distance with his intellect. His attempt to completely *live* in the abstract world of philosophical knowledge ironically separates him from love and life, especially the life he created: his daughter Petra and son Jack. He thus becomes a sort of living dead. As his daughter angrily says: 'You nothing!' (p. 46). Yet, calmed by a message Cornelia left behind ('Death is nothing at all', p. 68), Christopher at last, in a play which also thematises the inability to communicate, manages to talk with his wife, connect with his daughter, and optimistically accept the fatality of existence: 'Nothing is what's happened here' (p. 74).

The Patriot Game (1991)

The Patriot Game, the original version of which was composed as a television play commissioned by the BBC in 1965, is a documentary drama, depicting the events leading up to and constituting the 1916 rising. Beginning with the formations of Eoin MacNeill's Irish Volunteers and its subgroup, the Irish Republican Brotherhood, led by Patrick Pearse, as well as James Connolly's Irish Citizen Army, it presents the faction fights among the rebels, the perspective of the representatives of the British administration, and the opinions of the common people, in order to finally stage the disastrous and bloody course of the rising itself.

Most conspicuous about the play is its meta-historical aspect. From the beginning, Murphy makes it plain that history can never be presented in its indisputable facticity, but is always being interpreted from a certain contingent point of view. As in *Bailegangaire*, Murphy hence draws attention to the difficulty of getting the hang of history, although precisely this would be indispensable in order to locate one's own historical identity. As the narrator laments, 'you wouldn't [even] know where to start the story' (p. 93), let alone finish it. So, especially in the end, the narrator's authority (and with it, any narrator's authority) is seriously questioned when the other actors simply refuse to heed her call to close the play, and go on, despite her protests, to stage the shooting of the rebel leaders.

On the one hand, then, Murphy's play is an honest attempt to explain and thereby demythologise this delicate phase in Irish national history: it ironically and frankly portrays the egotisms, petty quarrels, ignorance and empty rhetoric of the historical protagonists, who more often than not decided over the heads of the common people and willingly accepted catastrophe. On the other hand, Murphy draws attention to the fact that history comes down to us in the form of a narration, composed by a subjectively structuring consciousness, so that it is always necessary, when judging history, to also question its narrator as well as the narrative conventions to which he or she is adhering.

The House (2000)

The House is set in the Ireland of the 1950s. Due to financial problems, the de Burca family – sickly Mrs de Burca and her three daughters Marie, Louise and Susanne, who are in their thirties – have to sell their mansion, Woodland House, a 'private residence on over three acres' (p. 78). Shortly before the auction takes place, the town's emigrants come home from abroad for their yearly sojourn. One of them is the orphan Christy, who practically grew up with the de Burcas and now plans to buy the house himself. During a clandestine meeting with Susanne, they start an argument about this and he accidentally kills her. While telling nobody else, he secretly confesses what he did to Mrs de Burca, whereupon she soon dies of the shock. Burdened with his bad conscience, we see him witness the remaining sisters move out of their childhood home in the end: he has got the house indeed, but lost the family.

In this drama, Murphy re-creates the atmosphere of an uneasy time in which emigration had reached one of its peaks: the 1950s were a period of severe unrest and homelessness in Ireland. The major problem seems to be that emigration, on a psychological level, produces a particular sort of severance which cannot be mended any more, particularly when the place that is left cannot come up to the standard of a 'home'.

Alice Trilogy (2005)

Three stages in the life of Alice are highlighted in the *Alice Trilogy. In the Apiary* is set in 1980: Alice is twenty-five; *By the Gasworks Wall* is set in 1995: Alice is forty; *At the Airport* is set in 2005: Alice is fifty.

In *In the Apiary*, we see Alice in her attic, secretly drinking whiskey, taking tranquillisers, and on the brink of losing her mind: throughout, she conducts a conversation with her personified mirror image, Al. What the fragmented and sometimes confused dialogue reveals is that Alice leads a very unhappy existence. Married to 'Solid Bill' (p. 18), an up-and-coming banker, and having three children already, her life is caught in the constraints of being a housewife.

Fifteen years later, she meets an ex-boyfriend from her youth, Jimmy, who meanwhile has become a famous TV personality. Although their conversation is honest and even tender at first, Jimmy suddenly becomes aggressive so that Alice rejects his offer to make a new start with him.

In the last part, Alice sits with Bill in an airport restaurant. They wait for their youngest son's coffin to be unloaded off a plane: William, her 'pet' (p. 57), has died in an accident while in the USA. The scene, indeed the play, is largely taken up by Alice's interior monologue: *'we are encountering this place through* **Alice***'s odd mental state'* (p. 52).

In the *Alice Trilogy*, Murphy very pessimistically depicts the state of humanity in its existential forlornness. Alice, despite (or maybe because of) her family's middle-class affluence ('new house, nice estate, [. . .] Decent car', p. 14), is not in 'wonderland', but rather in 'horrorland': 'Life is inescapably harsh, cruel, self-centred, ugly, sordid, mean. [. . .] And humankind is vile' (p. 56). Her former dreams have turned into nightmares, also because Alice has unlearned how to dream: '"You haven't been practising," said the White Queen'

(p. 57). Looking at the dreariness of her existence, however, one is forced to ask: how could she have?

Summary

Although the issues which Murphy covers in the large body of his work are multitudinous, some themes recur again and again, varied and mutually reinforced as though part of a fugue.

One of these, and maybe the most conspicuous, is the theme of 'family', burdened with all the meanings Irish history and culture have laid on the term. From *A Whistle in the Dark* up to the *Alice Trilogy*, the notion of an incomplete and often self-destructive family has been a central concern: 'nowhere in Murphy's work are there happy families. His families are broken by violence, loss, cruelty, by the inability of men and women to cross the divide of the sexes.'[8] They are defined by absences, mainly the ghosts of the dead, whose memory and legacy haunt and torture the living. However, there are also all-too-powerful, self-imposing and thereby limiting living presences, be they fathers (like Dada in *A Whistle in the Dark*), mothers (like Mother in *A Crucial Week in the Life of a Grocer's Assistant*), brothers or sisters. Thus, Murphy's families are always in a state of imbalance, which is expressed through physical and, more often, psychological violence, eating away the substance of togetherness. Only rarely, especially in later plays like *Bailegangaire*, is reconciliation made possible.

Speaking of ghosts, another important theme is the impact of the past – the meaning of historical continuity and change – in a private as well as a public sense, with both aspects being constantly interwoven. In his earlier plays, Murphy makes palpable the strains arising in the 1960s within a complicated field of tensions. It was a period in which the idealistic, post-independence attempts to construct Ireland as 'a land whose countryside would be bright with cosy homesteads'[9] and the mood accompanying its actual stagnation in the repressive and conservative period between the 1930s and 1950s were suddenly inverted: jolted out of its dreams of self-sufficiency and past glory, Ireland awoke into a modern industrial world. With its sudden opening to foreign capital, old tribal notions such as that of the holiness of the extended family or the Everyman figure of the hero-farmer were slowly and painfully forced to give way. *A Whistle in the Dark*'s Dada, fantasising about being the chieftain of a warrior clan and demanding unflinching loyalty while stubbornly ignoring the social realities and the new rules an industrial society imposes, drives his family into disaster.

Murphy, though, not only casts his view towards recent history in order to explain the present, but also farther back. In *Famine*, set during the Great Famine in the nineteenth-century, he explores the roots of contemporary Ireland's emotional, mental and economic starvation. In *The Patriot Game*, to name another example of a history play, Murphy directly confronts the Easter Rising and its legacy. Yet even *The Morning After Optimism*, seemingly detached from reality, may be read as 'a playing out through a personal psychic history of the recent history of a nation';[10] the same goes for *Bailegangaire*. Indeed, precisely because the private and the public are mutually independent, the past with Murphy is always a psychologically defined site, where the 'repression of guilt, anger, shame, and sorrow emerges as the most potent binding force [. . .]. Consequently, variations of the return of these repressed emotions figure as the cathartic effect which make change possible.'[11]

Another, yet obviously related major aspect of Murphy's drama is that it is a drama of outsiders. Joe and Frank in *On the Outside* are not only physically prevented from entering the dancehall; they are generally excluded from the economic boost their country goes through and the opportunities opened up in the process. In an Ireland ruled by reckless and sly businessmen, *gombeen* men like Mickey Ford, Liam Brady (*Conversations on a Homecoming*), or John Mahony (*A Thief of a Christmas*), the economically deprived are in constant danger of slipping even further down the social ladder. The down-and-outs in *The Sanctuary Lamp*, Harry and Francisco, are a case in point. Murphy's outsiders, however, are not only on the sidelines in economic terms; as the increasing depiction of isolated middle-class characters in his later plays indicates, exclusion is always also a psychological matter, its reasons being manifold. Often, Murphy's characters are weighted down and pushed into loneliness by their memories, by some incident in their past, like Harry and Maudie in *The Sanctuary Lamp*, Mommo in *Bailegangaire*, or Vera in *The Wake*. Christopher in *Too Late for Logic*, elevating philosophical knowledge above everything else, actively and knowingly secludes himself from life, while Alice in the *Alice Trilogy* is helplessly compelled into seclusion by the imprisoning and suffocating effects of middle-class ideology.

Murphy's characters throughout are searchers: they search for themselves and for a place to call home. The fact that they are torn apart psychically, that they are longing for wholeness, mostly without success, is frequently emphasised by adding a second character who personifies what has been lost, who is the other, missing, even dialectically opposed, half that is craved, although often merely unconsciously: James and Edmund in *The Morning After Optimism*, JPW and the Irish Man in *The Gigli Concert*, or Michael and Tom in *Conversations on a Homecoming*.

That the achievement of wholeness as well as the discovery of a home, in most cases at least, are unattainable goals within the existing ideological frameworks and mentalities,[12] is spelt out, among other things, by Murphy's anti-Catholicism, evident mostly in the mature plays, such as *The Sanctuary Lamp* or *The Gigli Concert*.[13] As Murphy says, 'there is *no deus ex machina* in our times, in modern drama, to descend and resolve our problems; all the Gods can provide is a venue, which is an empty church'.[14]

This does not mean that his plays are firmly grounded in a realist, anti-metaphysical tradition. On the contrary, even *A Whistle in the Dark*, which on the surface appears to be a wholly naturalistic play, turns out to have 'mythic dimensions'.[15] As Fintan O'Toole has shown, Murphy's plays are informed by a 'politics of magic',[16] which is rendered visible in the dream sequences of *A Crucial Week*, the fantastic surrealism of *The Morning After Optimism*, or the strange doubling of Alice in *In the Apiary*. Its more subtle points become evident when taking into account the many intertextual references Murphy employs in order to provide significant subtexts: *The Sanctuary Lamp* is a condensed version of Aeschylus's *Oresteia* (458 BCE), with all its intricate negotiations of morality, the relationship between humans and the gods, and the pain of loss; *The Gigli Concert* is deeply informed by the metaphysical concerns of *Faust*.

Hence, precisely because Murphy never presents only one world on stage, but many which comment on each other and thus reveal new perspectives – the world of the past and the world of the present, of myth and of 'reality', of the individual and the communal self, of the sacred and of the profane – his plays are never unambiguous. Although always on the side of the outsiders, the voiceless, the forgotten, he is 'no moralist. In his theatre, virtue and vice are relative and historical, reactions to time and circumstance.'[17] Murphy's drama, which makes a theatre less of action than of words, is deeply philosophical throughout. One feature of Murphy's philosophical dialectics is his frequent employment of music. Music is habitually used to supply the reality of pure language and even the performativity of the stage with another level of expressiveness. By way of Schubert's 'Notturno' at the beginning and end of *Bailegangaire*, Peggy's enchanting rendering of 'All in the April Evening' at the close of *Conversations on a Homecoming*, or the constant presence of Beniamino Gigli's arias in *The Gigli Concert*, Murphy underpins both the theatrical action and his characters' dialogues with another kind of language which is harder to conceptualise, but is none the less sometimes fuller in meaning. What is more, by stimulating his theatre with music, language itself, however fragmented or violent, is urged to emphasise its harmonious qualities: 'words are treated as musical material and sound and rhythm are primordial'.[18]

Tom Murphy's entire work, in conclusion, may thus indeed be seen as one huge and intricately wrought fugue, a virtuoso creation which makes its composer one of the most accomplished playwrights Ireland has to offer.

Primary Sources

Works by Tom Murphy

Alice Trilogy: In the Apiary, By the Gasworks Wall, At the Airport (London: Methuen, 2005).
The Cherry Orchard (adapted from Anton Chekhov) (London: Methuen, 2004).

The Drunkard (Dublin: Carysfort, 2004).

The House (London: Methuen, 2000).

The Orphans (Newark, DE: Proscenium, 1974).

Plays 1: Famine, The Patriot Game, The Blue Macushla (London: Methuen, 1997).

Plays 2: Conversations on a Homecoming, Bailegangaire, A Thief of a Christmas (London: Methuen, 1993).

Plays 3: The Morning After Optimism, The Sanctuary Lamp, The Gigli Concert (London: Methuen, 1994).

Plays 4: A Whistle in the Dark, A Crucial Week in the Life of a Grocer's Assistant, On the Outside, On the Inside (London: Methuen, 1997).

She Stoops to Folly (London: Methuen, 2001).

Too Late for Logic (London: Methuen, 2001).

The Wake (London: Methuen, 1999).

Secondary Sources

Achilles, Jochen, 'The Change of Paradigms and the Return of the Repressed in Tom Murphy's Drama', in Giuseppe Serpillo and Donatella Badin (eds), *The Classical World and the Mediterranean* (Cagliari: Tema, 1996), pp. 79–86.

Arrowsmith, Aidan, '"To Fly by Those Nets": Violence and Identity in Tom Murphy's *A Whistle in the Dark*', *Irish University Review*, Vol. 34, No. 2 (2004), pp. 315–31.

Bertha, Csilla, 'Poetically Dwelling: The Mythic and the Historical in Tom Murphy's *The House*', *Hungarian Journal of English and American Studies*, Vol. 7, No. 1 (2001), pp. 213–26.

Cave, Richard Allen, 'Tom Murphy: Acts of Faith in a Godless World', in James Acheson (ed.), *British and Irish Drama Since 1960* (New York: St Martin's Press, 1993), pp. 88–102.

Fogarty, Anne, 'Tom Murphy in Conversation with Anne Fogarty', in Lilian Chambers *et al.* (eds), *Theatre Talk: Voices of Irish Theatre Practitioners* (Dublin: Carysfort, 2001), pp. 355–64.

Gleitman, Claire, 'Clever Blokes and Thick Lads: The Collapsing Tribe in Tom Murphy's *A Whistle in the Dark*', *Modern Drama*, Vol. 42, No. 3 (1999), pp. 315–25.

Grene, Nicholas, 'Murphy's Ireland: *Bailegangaire*', in Vincent Newey and Ann Thompson (eds), *Literature and Nationalism* (Liverpool: Liverpool UP, 1991), pp. 239–53.

— (ed.), *Talking About Tom Murphy* (Dublin: Carysfort, 2002).

—, 'Tom Murphy and the Children of Loss', in Shaun Richards (ed.), *The Cambridge Companion to Twentieth-Century Irish Drama* (Cambridge: Cambridge UP, 2004), pp. 204–17.

—, 'Tom Murphy: Famine and Dearth', in George Cusack and Sarah Gross (eds), *Hungry Words: Images of Famine in the Irish Canon* (Dublin: Irish Academic, 2005), pp. 245–62.

Henderson, Lynda, 'Tom Murphy: The Artist as Informer', in Jacqueline Genet and Elisabeth Hellegouarc'h (eds), *Studies on the Contemporary Irish Theatre* (Caen: Centre des Publications de l'Université de Caen, 1991), pp. 35–46.

—, 'Men, Women and the Life of the Spirit in Tom Murphy's Plays', in Jacqueline Genet and Wynne Hellegouarc'h (eds), *Irish Writers and Their Creative Process* (Gerrards Cross: Colin Smythe, 1996), pp. 87–99.

Kurdi, Maria, 'An Interview with Tom Murphy', *Irish Studies Review*, Vol. 12, No. 2 (2004), pp. 233–40.

Lanters, José, 'Schopenhauer with Hindsight: Tom Murphy's *Too Late for Logic*', *Hungarian Journal of English and American Studies*, Vol. 2, No. 2 (1996), pp. 87–95.

Maxwell, Desmond, 'New Lamps for Old: The Theatre of Tom Murphy', *Theatre Research International*, Vol. 15, No.1 (1990), pp. 57–66.

Morash, Chris, 'Murphy, History and Society', in Nicholas Grene (ed.), *Talking About Tom Murphy* (Dublin: Carysfort, 2002), pp. 17–30.

Murphy, Tom, 'The Creative Process', in Jacqueline Genet and Wynne Hellegouarc'h (eds), *Irish Writers and Their Creative Process* (Gerrards Cross: Colin Smythe, 1996), pp. 78–86.

O'Leary, Joseph, 'Looping the Loop with Tom Murphy: Anticlericalism as Double Bind', *Studies*, Vol. 81, No. 321 (1992), pp. 41–8.

O'Toole, Fintan, *Tom Murphy: The Politics of Magic*, expanded edn (London: Nick Hern Books, 1994).

Poulain, Alexandra, 'Fable and Vision: *The Morning After Optimism* and *The Sanctuary Lamp*', in Nicholas Grene (ed.), *Talking About Tom Murphy* (Dublin: Carysfort, 2002), pp. 41–56.

Richards, Shaun, 'Refiguring Lost Narratives – Prefiguring New Ones: The Theatre of Tom Murphy', *Canadian Journal of Irish Studies*, Vol. 15, No. 1 (1989), pp. 80–100.

Richards, Shaun, '"Spirits That Have Become Mean and Broken": Tom Murphy and the Famine of Modern Ireland', in Mary Luckhurst (ed.), *A Companion to Modern British and Irish Drama, 1880–2005* (Malden, MA: Blackwell, 2006), pp. 466–75.

Roche, Billy, 'Tom Murphy and the Continuous Past', *Princeton University Library Chronicle*, Vol. 68, Nos 1–2 (2007), pp. 620–31.

Russell, Richard Rankin, 'Tom Murphy's *Bailegangaire* as Comedy of Redemption', *Journal of Dramatic Theory and Criticism*, Vol. 21, No. 2 (2007), pp. 79–99.

Notes

1. Fintan O'Toole, *The Politics of Magic*, p. 26.
2. Ibid., p. 95.
3. Ibid., p. 111.
4. Ibid., pp. 208–27.

5. Ibid., p. 213.
6. Nicholas Grene, 'Murphy's Ireland', p. 239.
7. See José Lanters, 'Schopenhauer with Hindsight', pp. 93–4.
8. O'Toole, op. cit., p. 189.
9. Eamon de Valera.
10. O'Toole, op. cit., p. 109.
11. Jochen Achilles, 'The Change of Paradigms', p. 79.
12. It should, however, be emphasised, as Shaun Richards does, that Murphy 'evaluate[s] past and present against a future which [at least] contains the *possibility* of redemption' (p. 96; my emphasis).
13. See e.g. Joseph O'Leary, 'Looping the Loop'.
14. Maria Kurdi, 'An Interview', p. 237.
15. O'Toole, op. cit., p. 78.
16. Ibid., p. 80.
17. Ibid., p. 65.
18. Alexandra Poulain, 'Fable and Vision', p. 55.

19 DONAL O'KELLY

Patrick Lonergan

Bat The Father Rabbit The Son; The Dogs; Asylum! Asylum!; Catalpa; Judas of the Gallarus; Jimmy Joyced!; The Cambria; Operation Easter

Introduction

Donal O'Kelly is an actor, producer, playwright and activist who was born in Dublin in 1958. He is admired for his willingness to tackle provocative themes, and respected as a writer of plays that combine lyricism with formal inventiveness. O'Kelly has performed in most of his own plays, often playing multiple roles simultaneously.

After graduating from school in the mid-1970s, he joined the Irish Civil Service, where he worked as a computer programmer. He quit this job at the age of twenty-one, becoming active politically and in the theatre.

His first major success was the solo show *Bat the Father, Rabbit the Son*. It was soon followed by a series of plays that considered themes such as familial relationships, human rights and Ireland's history. In 1993, he co-founded Calypso Theatre Company, a Dublin-based group with the remit of pushing 'the boundaries of theatrical creativity while producing distinctive work that challenges injustice and social exclusion in today's rapidly changing world'.[1] The company asserted a belief that has informed the development of O'Kelly's career in its entirety: that theatre 'can be a crucial catalyst for change in society'.[2] The company's first three plays, all written by O'Kelly, were *Hughie on the Wires* (1993), which was about El Salvador; *Trickledown Town* (1994), which was about the International Monetary Fund's involvement in Jamaica; and *The Business of Blood* (1995), which was about the international arms trade.

In 2000, Donal O'Kelly Productions was established: most of his recent plays have therefore been self-produced. He continues to present new work regularly, usually writing, directing and performing in his own works, which tour regularly throughout Ireland and abroad.

O'Kelly is also a respected actor on screen and stage. He is probably best known for his appearance in such films as *I Went Down* (1998), *Bloom* (2003) and, in particular, the screen adaptation of Roddy Doyle's novel *The Van* (1996). He is a member of Aosdána, Ireland's council of artists, and is Associate Director of Afri, a group that campaigns and publishes on human rights, peace and justice issues.

The Plays

Bat the Father, Rabbit the Son (1988)

Bat the Father, Rabbit the Son was produced by Rough Magic theatre company at the Dublin Theatre Festival in 1988. The play considers a number of themes that would later dominate O'Kelly's works. It focuses on a successful businessman who is attempting to come to terms with his past. In particular, he is preoccupied with his relationship with his father, Bat, who fought in the 1916 Easter Rebellion by Irish nationalists against the British occupation of the country. O'Kelly's play is therefore one of the first to explore the impact of rapid enrichment and upward mobility upon an emerging class of urban Irish businessmen. By focusing on this phenomenon five years before the Celtic Tiger period of rapid economic expansion began, O'Kelly demonstrated both his prescience and his insight into the workings of Irish society. His consideration of the legacies of Irish nationalism, and his obvious love of Dublin city, are also evident, showing how he is indebted both politically and aesthetically to Sean O'Casey.

Central to the play's success is a technique that is found in most of O'Kelly's works: the use of a voyage as a metaphor for a character's development. Rabbit's journey is not just physical, but emotional –

allowing him to reconnect both with his father and his own sense of Irish history. The play therefore aims to heal fissures in 1980s Irish society – fissures that were caused by the impact of the Troubles on attitudes within the Republic of Ireland towards the Easter Rising, and by the economic problems that blighted the country at that time.

As in many of his other plays, O'Kelly achieved formal unity and thematic coherence using both the body and the word. Playing the roles of Bat and the Rabbit, he used his own physical presence on stage to mark the divisions, and ultimately the coming together, of both characters. *Bat* showed how O'Kelly's work is conceived both as literature and performance: he invests as much meaning in the gesture onstage as he does in the word on the page. The play later received a Stewart Parker Award.

The Dogs (1992)

O'Kelly turned to writing for an ensemble with his next Rough Magic production, *The Dogs*, a play for five actors which appeared at Project Arts Centre during the 1992 Dublin Theatre Festival. The play seems to offer an initially familiar plot: a family has gathered for Christmas dinner, and must overcome a series of disasters to reach agreement with each other. These circumstances are familiar to Irish playgoers from the many light-hearted seasonal comedies by such dramatists as Sam Cree, Bernard Farrell, Jim O'Hanlon and Marie Jones – but O'Kelly offers a decidedly new perspective on that tired old theme.

The play presents the Macken family, each member of whom is played naturalistically by one actor. Yet each performer also doubles in a non-naturalistic role, with (for example) the performer playing the family's mother also acting as a robin, while the actor playing the father also plays a rat. This role doubling introduced elements of pantomime into the original performance, which had the effect of emphasising the play's yuletide setting – but it also destabilised audiences' expectations. By emphasising how familial roles are not innate but performed, and by showing the difference between appearance and reality, O'Kelly allowed important themes to emerge, such as the family's attempts to come to terms with the son's homosexuality and the daughter's single parenthood. It is worth recalling in this context that both themes remained controversial on the Irish stage in 1992. Homosexual acts were illegal in Ireland until 1994, and plays that dealt explicitly with gay characters or themes were often greeted with hostility or indifference. Single-parent families in Ireland were also socially marginalised. Roddy Doyle's *The Snapper* (1991) was one of the first mainstream attempts to normalise the phenomenon of single parenthood within Irish culture, and O'Kelly's play soon followed. So *The Dogs* may be seen as evidence of O'Kelly's willingness to risk unpopularity by tackling important political themes, be they societal or interpersonal. Also evident is his ability to enrich and renew popular theatrical forms – a feature of many of his later works, which draw on such apparently exhausted forms as music hall, stand-up comedy and melodrama.

Asylum! Asylum! (1994)

The blend of personal and societal responsibilities was also a feature of *Asylum! Asylum!* which appeared at the Peacock Theatre in 1994. The play centres on a Ugandan refugee called Joseph Omara, who has applied for political asylum in Ireland. His deportation at the end of the play arises first because the Irish authorities refuse to believe that his life will be in danger if he is sent home and second due to the self-interest of many of the characters, who are too preoccupied with bureaucracy or self-advancement to take Omara seriously. O'Kelly thus reveals that Irish racism should not be dismissed as something that arises from the crude operations of the legal system: it also occurs because of the choices that individuals make – and fail to make.

The play establishes a number of strategies that recur in Irish dramas about multiculturalism. O'Kelly plays interestingly with different usages of the words 'civilised' and 'natural', with the audience being invited to consider the health of a society that treats refugees not as people but as problems to be solved. He also brings his two leading characters – the Ugandan hero and a white Irish woman – into a relationship with each other and, by giving them the names Joseph and Mary, reminds his audience that the Holy Family were also 'refugees' of sorts. Most importantly, the play presents Joseph not as a cipher for the working-through of Irish characters' racist tendencies, but as a fully developed individual who is deserving of both respect and sympathy.

This work, together with O'Kelly's unpublished 1997 play *Farawayan*, are among the more sophisticated plays in the growing genre of Irish multicultural theatre – and, again, they prove how prescient O'Kelly is. When *Asylum* was premiered, the total number of Africans living in Ireland was only about 4,800. That figure increased to 26,500 in 2002, and in 2006 was estimated to exceed 50,000. This increase (1,000 per cent in ten years) has resulted in a debate about race and Irishness that at times has been lively, and at times deeply divisive and embittered. It's notable that much of that debate focuses on issues that O'Kelly first raised (and resolved) in *Asylum! Asylum!*

Catalpa (1995)

Catalpa is O'Kelly's most respected (and perhaps his most popular) play. Originally staged in Waterford with the title *Catalpa – The Movie*, it has gone on to become one of O'Kelly's most successful plays, being revived (without the subtitle) at Dublin's Gate Theatre in March 1997 before touring internationally. It takes its title from the celebrated rescue of Fenian prisoners (a group of militant Irish nationalists, active mainly during the second half of the nineteenth century) who had been transported to Australia by the British government during the 1870s. That rescue was dramatic in a number of ways, with the rescue ship (named the *Catalpa*) suffering a variety of mishaps along the way: the desertion of its crew, the loss of its navigation equipment and near shipwreck on several occasions.

Wisely, O'Kelly does not restage these events naturalistically but instead has them narrated by a failed screenwriter named Matthew Kidd. It has been Kidd's long-standing ambition to have the story of the *Catalpa* filmed, but he has received one rejection letter after another from the studios. The play involves his use of found objects in his apartment (such as sheets and furniture) as props in a determined 'pitch' to an imaginary film producer. So the audience is not watching a play or a film, but seeing a lone performer enact the story of the *Catalpa*, using only his own body, voice and some randomly selected objects to convey the narrative. It is one of the play's great strengths that it is inspired by the protagonist's desire to have a story filmed, but ends by showing conclusively that live performance can express just as much as (and perhaps more than) a high-budget Hollywood movie. The description of the Catalpa's journey thus operates as a metaphor for Kidd's own journey, away from his presuppositions about the relative merits of cinema and drama, and towards a celebration of the theatrical.

Writing in the published script of the play, O'Kelly states that the

> theatrical challenge is to flick images into the audience's heads, to stimulate their imaginations so that they will see the *Catalpa* at sea[;] they will see and hear and feel and smell the Atlantic swell, the whale blubber, the scorched Australian shore. (p. 10)

This will not be achieved by props or special effects, he states, but with the language in the script:

> the images described, the bits of dialogue, the words used, the sounds, with movement, gesture, energy, stillness, with music sometimes, with lighting and the use of a few selected props. (p. 10)

The function of these different techniques is to inspire a response from what O'Kelly calls the 'the most important instrument of all: the audience's imagination' (p. 10).

This statement is a significant corrective to prevailing views on contemporary Irish plays, especially those written for one performer. Such plays became unusually popular among Irish writers during the 1990s, being strongly associated with a trio of young male authors who emerged in the middle of the decade – Conor McPherson, Mark O'Rowe and Enda Walsh, who excelled at writing monologues, involving the narration of a story to an audience by a lone performer. The primary criticism levelled against such plays was that they were anti-theatrical, since they tended to involve direct communication between an actor and the audience. It was further suggested that this mode of production turned audiences into passive consumers of information. Instead of observing action as they would in a naturalistic play, there were instead receiving one person's interpretation of events, as if that view was authoritative. *Catalpa* in contrast shows how plays featuring one actor who directly addresses the audience can be decidedly theatrical.

Judas of the Gallarus (1999)

O'Kelly's next play, *Judas of the Gallarus*, appeared at the Peacock Theatre in 1999. Unlike *Catalpa*, *Judas* is a naturalistic play for a cast of five. It is set in 1923 during the closing days of the Irish Civil War, in a remote part of County Kerry, on Ireland's south-west coast. The action takes place in the eponymous gallarus, a ninth-century oratory in the Dingle peninsula that overlooks the sea. Still standing today, the gallarus is noted for its stone architecture and for the many superstitions associated with it, which claim that sinners can be redeemed by exiting it through its tiny window. The action therefore takes place in a real-world setting that has strong symbolical associations.

In the play, a Scottish man called Jock McPeak has been fighting in the Irish Civil War, and hopes to escape the country by boat (a situation that recalls the plot of *Catalpa*). In the first of many nods to Sean O'Casey, O'Kelly has Jock meet a young woman called Noreen (a diminutive of Nora, the name of one of O'Casey's most famous characters), whose presence in the gallarus intensifies the play's treatment of themes of betrayal and rivalry – themes that lead ultimately to a tragic ending.

The play has been misjudged in some ways: its appearance at the Abbey occurred at a time when that theatre was regularly criticised for the poor quality of its new writing. In part, those criticisms arose because many of the young Irish writers then making an impact internationally – such as Martin McDonagh, Conor McPherson and

Enda Walsh – had not been produced at the Abbey (indeed, both McDonagh and McPherson had plays rejected by the theatre). The international success of those writers, coupled with the ensuing criticism of the Abbey, placed an impossible level of expectation on new plays at the theatre.

O'Kelly had also become a victim of his own success, to a certain extent: in the months prior to the opening of *Judas*, *Catalpa* had enjoyed a long run at Andrew's Lane Theatre, a commercial theatre in Dublin. The success of that run led audiences to expect another lively one-man show. What they got instead was a naturalistic play set in a gallarus, a space so cramped that the actors' movement was extremely restricted. *Judas* is not among O'Kelly's best works, perhaps because it didn't feature O'Kelly himself. But its treatment of themes of redemption – and its allusions to earlier Irish plays – make it a rich play that rewards careful reading.

Shortly after the premiere of *Judas*, O'Kelly founded his own production company, with which he revised and revived many of his earlier works, touring them both nationally and internationally. He achieved a notable success in 2002 when his unpublished *The Hand* appeared at the Dublin Theatre Festival.

Jimmy Joyced! (2004)

O'Kelly's next major production appeared in 2004, when his *Jimmy Joyced!* appeared at Bewley's Café Theatre Dublin, a venue primarily dedicated to producing short lunchtime plays. As the name suggests, the play was written to coincide with the centenary of Bloomsday, the fictional date in 1904 upon which the events of James Joyce's *Ulysses* (1922) take place. O'Kelly's play occupied an unusual place in Irish culture that year, in that it managed to combine a celebration of Joyce's achievement with a polite scepticism about the citywide celebrations of the Bloomsday Centenary, and the ensuing commodification of Joyce by the marketing industry, academia and tourism. The play's central character is JJ Staines, a stallholder at the now defunct market in Portobello, Dublin. O'Kelly cautions Irish audiences about their culture's fetishisation of all things Joycean by showing Staines's obsession with hoarding material objects that are associated with Joyce's life – but which, O'Kelly shows, add little to our appreciation of Joyce's art. This case is made by Staines's narration of the early life of Joyce, which is presented from a perspective that will be familiar to O'Kelly's audiences: that of a familial conflict between son and father – in this case, the young Joyce and his father John.

At a time when Irish culture generally was exalting Joyce, O'Kelly instead humanises him, while still doing justice to the excellence (and the difficulty) of his works. The story of Joyce's youth is presented in the familiar narrative form of a young man experiencing a clash between duty and desire: between the obligation to remain in Ireland, and the wish to elope abroad in the company of Nora Barnacle. Yet the play also deploys a quasi-Joycean approach to language, making use of non-verbal sounds, puns and neologisms to communicate the plot. What emerges most clearly is O'Kelly's linguistic inventiveness, which emulates that of Joyce himself. Also clear is the extent to which both writers are dependent on the physical and psychic landscape of Dublin for inspiration.

The Cambria (2005)

The Cambria followed in 2005. Written for two actors who must perform eleven characters between them, it is both musical and poetic. It draws together many of the strands from O'Kelly's earlier career. Like *Catalpa*, it is set on a boat, and uses the device of having a literal voyage become a metaphor for transformation. And like *Asylum! Asylum!* it focuses on an asylum-seeker as a way of encouraging its audience to explore broader issues about social justice.

It recounts how escaped slave Frederick Douglass fled the US for Ireland after his famous autobiography was published in 1845. His passage across the Atlantic was on a ship called *The Cambria* (hence the title). Upon arrival in Ireland, Douglass was given a hero's welcome, largely thanks to Daniel O'Connell, the Irish nationalist leader who achieved Catholic Emancipation in the United Kingdom, and who spent much of his political career campaigning against American slavery.

O'Kelly enacts an imagined version of Douglass's crossing of the Atlantic, showing his interactions with other passengers and crew members. The majority of these characters are standard melodramatic types. These include the ineffectual but ultimately heroic Captain Judkins, a likeable rogue called Juddy who, when Douglass's identity is revealed to the passengers, states that he is 'just doing his job' while locking Douglass in chains; Cecily, a feisty damsel from the northern US, who demands that Douglass be freed; the evil southerner Dodd, who is the cause of all this trouble; and Dodd's adorable daughter Matilda. The action is framed by a story about a contemporary asylum-seeker in Dublin, sending a clear message: Ireland accepted one of the world's great thinkers when he was an asylum-seeker, and should be careful about rejecting more recent arrivals.

The play therefore reminds Irish audiences of an important aspect of the country's history, which is rightly celebrated. It might be suggested, however, that this history is also oversimplified. O'Connell may have welcomed Douglass to Ireland, but he lost support from Irish-Americans for doing so: up to (and after) the US Civil War, Irish-Americans were regarded as highly racist, and the same was true of many people living in Ireland itself. *The Cambria* thus presents a utopian view of history, which diminishes slightly the play's political impact.

Also problematic is that this story is told in melodramatic form, a mode of writing that dominates Irish dramatic treatments of race since the 1990s. The problem of racism is rarely analysed or treated with any complexity on the Irish stage – instead, it is usually just a lever in a melodramatic plot. The genuinely racist are punished, the ignorant learn a lesson, and order is always restored – as has been seen in such Irish plays as *Done Up Like a Kipper* (Ken Harmon, 2002), Roddy Doyle's *Guess Who's Coming to the Dinner* (2001), Charlie O'Neill's *Hurl* (2003), Jim O'Hanlon's *The Buddhist of Castleknock* (2002) and others. Dodd, who is little more than a pantomime villain, personifies racism in *The Cambria*: he gets his come-uppance at the end of the play, and racism is no more, it seems. The play's messages about freedom are mostly conveyed by the symbolic release of Matilda's doll, a strategy that might be seen as infantilising the character of Douglass while trivialising his plight. Even the selections from Douglass's writings appear to have been chosen for their sensational rather than their intellectual impact. Furthermore, the play leaves unanswered many serious questions. What does it mean for the white O'Kelly to play an African-American liberator? Is O'Kelly's conflation of the contemporary asylum-seeker and Douglass fair to both?

Operation Easter (2006)

The framing technique of using the present to consider the past reappears in O'Kelly's most ambitious play to date, *Operation Easter*, another work which (like *Jimmy Joyced!*) takes a largely appreciative but occasionally sceptical look at the commemoration of an Irish anniversary – in this case, the ninetieth anniversary of the 1916 Easter Rising. The play is characterised by an interest in a condition that O'Kelly terms 'histrialysis' – or historical paralysis. His suggestion is that Irish culture has yet to come to terms with the fact that the birth of the Irish nation in 1916 involved an armed rebellion that was both undemocratic and violent, a legacy which, he believes, must be faced if Ireland is to move forward.

That need was made urgent by ongoing debates at the time of the play's premiere about the Easter Rising and its legacy. The Irish government had staged a commemoration of the Rising in Dublin in Easter 2005 for the first time since the outbreak of the Northern Irish Troubles – a move that was widely perceived as a rather cynical attempt by the governing Fianna Fáil party to retrieve the Rising's symbolism, which had been appropriated by the IRA and Sinn Fein. That commemoration was well attended, but there was some ambivalence about it in the media. Simultaneously, concerns were expressed about the 2005 proposal to demolish a building on Dublin's Moore Street: this was the site where the leaders of the Rising had surrendered, and many believed that the building must be preserved. This situation was further complicated by the changing status of Moore Street itself: long a symbol of Dublin working-class culture thanks to its colourful open-air fruit market, the area is now seen as symbolising Dublin's nascent multiculturalism, featuring as it does large numbers of shops that cater to the city's African, Asian and eastern European populations. In short, where in the past O'Kelly had anticipated issues of social importance before they arose, with *Operation Easter* he was entering firmly into three ongoing public debates: the commemoration of the Rising, the preservation of a building associated with it, and the increased multiculturalism of Ireland.

The action of the play opens in present-day Moore Street, before going back to 1916. Just as *The Cambria* forces a consideration of contemporary responsibilities by analysing the reception of Douglass in Ireland in the late 1840s, the technique is used here to draw a parallel between the Republican sentiments of the 1916 Proclamation of Independence, and the deepening inequalities in Ireland in 2006. By setting the play in a location seen as emblematic of Ireland's changing demography, O'Kelly asks audiences to consider whether the objectives of the Rising have been fulfilled. The bulk of the ensuing action dramatises the events of the Easter Rising, with a cast of thirty-five recounting events from the perspective of the Rising's leaders, their enemies and Dublin's citizenry.

The play's original production was particularly notable, however, in being performed in Kilmainham Gaol, the Dublin prison (now a museum) where the leaders of the Easter Rising were held before their execution. By reminding his audience that many of the characters in his play were killed in the building where the action was being performed, O'Kelly provided a sombre reminder that the Rising was conducted not by mythological figures, but by real people whose motivations must primarily be understood in personal rather than political terms.

Summary

The central technique in most of O'Kelly's plays is the use of the voyage. These voyages can be metaphorical, spiritual or emotional. They include literal journeys by sea, such as those presented in *Catalpa* and *The Cambria*. They include a focus on people who have travelled to Ireland from abroad, as in *Asylum! Asylum!*. And many of O'Kelly's plays involve a voyage from the present to the past, as in *Operation Easter* and *Jimmy Joyced!*, with the juxtaposition of the two time-periods used to challenge audiences' assumptions about how much Ireland has progressed.

Just as the plays involve movement in a thematic sense, they are also heavily dependent upon physical movement – on O'Kelly's skills as a performer. Much of the impact of his works arises from his ability to portray multiple roles (as in *Catalpa* and *Bat the Father, Rabbit the Son*), or his willingness to use techniques such as role doubling in the plays that he has written for ensembles (as in *The Dogs*). The kinetic energy of a Donal O'Kelly play makes it visually arresting but, by showing how one person may embody different characters, O'Kelly also reveals much about the construction of identity. This technique was used to most notable effect in *The Cambria*, in which the white O'Kelly played the escaped African American slave Frederick Douglass: at a time when Ireland was debating issues of racial and ethnic difference, O'Kelly showed how these apparent differences can be blurred through performance. A similar process is used in O'Kelly's doubling of characters from the present and past in many of his plays, which challenge audiences' sense of the linear development of Irish history.

The notion of 'histrialysis' outlined in *Operation Easter* can be seen as a critical element of O'Kelly's development as a writer, allowing us to understand how his aesthetic is informed by the belief that Ireland suffers from 'historical paralysis' or, put simply, an unwillingness to face certain issues from the past. Adopting what could be termed a revisionist approach, O'Kelly reinterrogates many of the myths around Irish nationalism, while retrieving important but forgotten stories. Through the use of the figure of Daniel O'Connell, he links Catholic Emancipation with the US Civil War, and then leads audiences to consider the plight of contemporary refugees in Ireland in *The Cambria*. He shows a keen awareness of the human – and the humane – characteristics of many of the figures involved in Irish nationalism in both *Catalpa* and *Operation Easter*. O'Kelly's treatment of Irish history is almost unique in Irish theatre: he bypasses the Troubles in Northern Ireland to consider instead the impact of Republican violence from the nineteenth and early twentieth century upon the cultural and political life of the Republic of Ireland today. Within the Irish tradition, only Sebastian Barry dedicates substantial attention to such themes.

This curiosity about history is closely related to O'Kelly's interest in human rights and social justice. He is just as keen to ensure that Ireland meet its moral responsibilities in the present as he is determined that the country accept its past. There are recurrent suggestions in his work that the Republican values asserted in the Easter Rising could be used to form a more just social order today. His work with Calypso Theatre Company has been important in this regard, but the key play for an understanding of O'Kelly's attitude towards this issue is *Asylum! Asylum!*. The construction of that drama shows how his work is always informed by an ethical dimension and by rigorous research. Yet the play is in no sense didactic; rather, the audience is placed in a situation of being forced to evaluate the performance of Omara, a technique that stimulates their imagination, promotes agency, and reminds them of their responsibilities. Like so many of O'Kelly's works, *Asylum!* is about performance, making clear that the determination of whether Omara may stay in Ireland is being made on the basis of his success in persuading the authorities of the credibility of his story. In other words, he will be allowed to stay in Ireland if he can *perform* his life story convincingly. The audience too must evaluate the stories that all of the characters tell, which contain idiosyncrasies and apparent contradictions, and which raise difficult questions about whether our actions can be excused on the basis of the impact of past events upon the construction of our personalities. By drawing a parallel between two state institutions – the Abbey Theatre and the Irish justice system – O'Kelly elevates the status of the theatre while showing the problems with the legal system. Theatre thus emerges as a space in which serious moral determinations can and must be made, while the Irish justice system is shown to be an institution where decisions are formulated casually and arbitrarily – and often on the basis of the impact that a 'performer' has on his or her audience. This is an excellent example of the strength of all of O'Kelly's work, which always invests authority in performance, and trusts audiences to act when they leave the theatre themselves.

Given that he has had a high profile within Ireland since 1988, it is surprising that very little critical scholarship on O'Kelly's work exists. A number of possible reasons for this oversight may be considered.

The most likely is that, because so much of his work depends upon his own skills as a performer – and his use of non-verbal communication, sound and theatricality – the strength of his plays is not immediately evident on the page. For example, explaining her decision not to include him in her survey of contemporary Irish literature, Christina Hunt Mahony praises O'Kelly, but says of *Catalpa* that 'such a play must not be read; in fact, reading its "dialogue" from the page is a thoroughly frustrating experience for the reader unable to see a production'.[3] Almost all of the existing criticism of O'Kelly's works focuses on *Asylum! Asylum!* which, in many ways, is his most conventional play, featuring naturalistic action as well as easily understood themes. Articles by Mária Kurdi, Paul Murphy and Heiner Zimmermann dedicate detailed attention to this play, articulating its politics while relating it to the Irish dramatic tradition and contemporary social developments within the country.

Yet, as Victor Merriman shows, recent developments in Irish theatre scholarship mean that there is no longer any excuse for the continued neglect of O'Kelly's work on the basis of its not being easily 'readable'. Indeed, the Irish theatre community's respect for O'Kelly's talent as a performer has often overshadowed their awareness of his skills as a literary craftsman – his ability to create what he calls 'word tunes', verbal constructions which acquire meaning not through language but through pitch and tone, counterpoint and harmony. As contributor to *Yeats is Dead!* – a comic novel written by fifteen Irish writers to support Amnesty International – O'Kelly also showed that he is a fine writer of fiction. His essays for publications such as *Irish Theatre Magazine* and his public talks for the City Arts Centre show that he is also a fine critic.

O'Kelly has himself speculated about the reasons for his not receiving much critical attention, suggesting that perhaps the political content of his plays may be an obstacle. There is certainly a tendency among Irish audiences to react dismissively to the subject matter of some of O'Kelly's plays. Referring to the 1994 and 1997 productions of *Asylum! Asylum!* Victor Merriman states that 'the typical comment which greeted [the play] in 1994 was "interesting play . . . couldn't happen here" '. For the 1997 production – at a time when audiences were realising that such things could and did happen in Ireland, the response of audiences was

'I don't like being told what to think'.[4] O'Kelly himself acknowledges that the political content of his plays may be a barrier for some. 'It turns off 90 per cent of your potential audience,' he told Joe Humphreys in the *Irish Times*. 'But,' he adds positively,

> I am who I am. Entertainment is my number-one goal, because people are buying a ticket for entertainment. But my part of the contract is to deliver my opinions – in as crafted a way as possible, of course.[5]

Primary Sources

Works by Donal O'Kelly

The Cambria (Dublin: Irish Playography, 2006).
Catalpa (London: Nick Hern, 1997).
Far from the Land [*Bat the Father, Rabbit the Son*] (London: Methuen, 1998).
Freshly Brewed: Twelve Short Plays from Bewley's Cafe Theatre [*Jimmy Joyced!*] (Dublin: Stinging Fly, 2008).
Judas of the Gallarus (London: Methuen, 1999).
Operation Easter (Dublin: Irish Playography, 2006).
New Plays from the Abbey Theatre [*Asylum! Asylum!*] (Utica, NY: Syracuse U P, 1996).
Rough Magic: First Plays [*The Dogs*] (Dublin: New Island, 1999).

Secondary Sources

Humphreys, Joe, 'Flying the Red Flag', *Irish Times*, Magazine Section, 12 March 2005, p. 8.
Kurdi, Mária, 'New Strangers in the House? Immigrants and Natives in Donal O'Kelly's *Asylum! Asylum!* and John Barrett's *Borrowed Robes*', *Hungarian Journal of English and American Studies*, Vol. 5, No. 1 (1999), pp. 225–39.
Mahony, Christina Hunt, *Contemporary Irish Literature: Transforming Tradition* (London: Palgrave, 1999).
Merriman, Victor, 'Besides the Obvious: Postcolonial Criticism, Drama, and Civil Society', *Modern Drama*, Vol. 47, No. 4 (2004), pp. 624–35.
—, 'Songs of Possible Worlds: Nation, Representation and Citizenship in the Work of Calypso Productions', in Eamonn Jordan (ed.), *Theatre Stuff* (Dublin: Carysfort Press, 2001), pp. 280–91.

Murphy, Paul, '"Inside the Immigrant Mind": Nostalgic versus Nomadic Subjectivities in Late Twentieth-Century Irish Drama', *Australasian Drama Studies*, Vol. 43 (2003), pp. 128–47.

O'Kelly, Donal, 'Strangers in a Strange Land', *Irish Theatre Magazine*, Vol. 1, No. 1 (1998), pp. 10–13.

—, 'Who Am I', *Engaging Theatre Performance* (Dublin: City Arts Centre, 2002), n. p.

—, *Yeats is Dead!* (London: Jonathan Cape, 2001).

White, Victoria 'Desperately Seeking Asylum', *Irish Times*, 26 July 1994, p. 10.

Zimmermann, Heiner, 'European Xenophobia and Ireland: A Postcolonial View: Donal O'Kelly: *Asylum! Asylum!*', in Bernhard Reitz (ed.), *Race and Religion in Contemporary Theatre and Drama in English* (Trier: Wissenschaftlicher Verlag Trier, 1999), pp. 65–76.

Notes

1. Mission statement on Calypso's website, <http://www.calypso.ie>.
2. Ibid.
3. Christina Hunt Mahony, *Contemporary Irish Literature* p. 30.
4. Victor Merriman, 'Songs of Possible Worlds', p. 290.
5. Joe Humphreys, 'Flying the Red Flag'.

20 MARK O'ROWE

Michael Raab

The Aspidistra Code; From Both Hips; Howie the Rookie; Made in China; Crestfall; Terminus

Introduction

Mark O'Rowe was born in Dublin in 1970 and started to write at the age of twenty-four 'for something to do'.[1] At first he wanted to get into films, which was hardly surprising as The Square cinema was just two minutes away from his parents' place in Tallaght, Dublin, where he still lived at the time. He went to the pictures practically every afternoon and sometimes saw the same film repeatedly: 'I wanted to write one myself. But I sort of knew that if I wrote a play, it would be easier to find somebody to put it on.'[2] Not exactly a fan of French *auteurisme*, for him the bloodier the film the better. And the regular visits to The Square were far from enough:

> Video came out when I was about thirteen. So I grew up on video nasties, cannibal movies and kung-fu flicks – *I Spit on Your Grave* and all that stuff. Really we only watched them for the goriness of the special effects. *Nightmare in a Damaged Brain* was so chopped to pieces by the censors that we would have to sit there and imagine what happened in the cut-out bits. I suppose they got our brains going.[3]

When he heard about a competition for young playwrights he tried his luck:

> I'd only seen about two plays in my life. I knew nothing about theatre. I knew nobody in any of those kind of arts. I wrote

The Aspidistra Code and sent it in. I got this call from Gerry Stembridge saying I was one of five winners. I hadn't a clue who he was.[4]

The text received a rehearsed reading arranged by Stembridge in 1995 at the Peacock Theatre, the Abbey's smaller auditorium. Despite getting printed by Nick Hern together with *From Both Hips*, it is O'Rowe's only play still awaiting a full production.

At least the contact with Stembridge led to a commission to write two youth theatre plays, *Sulk* and *Buzzin' to Bits*. It was a new experience for him to work to a deadline and a given formula: 'You've got to cast fourteen kids, they have to play their own age, they have to be kids. You have to divide it out equally enough.'[5] While gaining valuable experience and being paid for the first time, the two plays remained his only commissions, as he fears his texts might be interfered with in the process. *Rundown* also dates from 1996.[6] A year later, *Anna's Ankle* formed part of *Electroshock: A Theatre of Cruelty Season* by the Bedrock Theatre Company. In this Artaudian venture, O'Rowe featured together with Samuel Beckett, Heiner Müller and Edward Bond, Gavin Costick contributing the second new Irish play. *Anna's Ankle* showed a snuff video director's obsession with the eponymous heroine's foot, and Bedrock proudly posted a quote from the *Evening Herald* on their website: 'Degenerate . . . one of the most offensive pieces of work ever to be seen on the stage'.[7] Fishamble Theatre Company gave O'Rowe his full-length professional debut with *From Both Hips* in 1997. It marked the opening of the new Little Theatre in Tallaght, was shown at Project Arts Centre Dublin's temporary premises and transferred to The Tron in Glasgow. The dramatist later voiced serious reservations about the production, a disappointment not unconnected with his taking a break from writing for a year.[8]

When he started again, as always, he did not work to a preconceived plan: 'I have no ideas. I usually just sit down and start writing something. It sort of comes to me as I write.'[9] Following this ramshackle approach he is perfectly happy that 'there'd be half-finished plays left, right and centre'.[10] *Howie the Rookie* was written very quickly and in 1999 brought about O'Rowe's breakthrough, not only at home but also internationally. Produced by Mike Bradwell, artistic director of the Bush Theatre, the play helped the dramatist to conquer the London scene. It received a whole cluster of awards as well as touring extensively in Britain, Ireland and the US. Only in Dublin was the reaction muted; London and the Edinburgh Fringe were sell-outs. The play received the George Devine Award, the Rooney Prize for Irish Literature and the Irish Times/ESB Award for Best Play. It proved a difficult achievement to follow up on, and O'Rowe's next work, *Made in China*, in 2001 surprisingly received its world premiere at the Schauspielhaus Bochum where Patrick Schlösser had secured the rights after his successful German premiere of *Howie the Rookie* in Düsseldorf. Gerry Stembridge at the Peacock soon followed, but the play, despite being popular in Poland, did not have nearly the same impact as *Howie the Rookie*.

This was even more true of *Crestfall* (2003), O'Rowe's and director Garry Hynes's debut at the Gate, which – the efforts of a star-studded cast notwithstanding – provoked the dramatist's worst critical drubbing so far. That was mitigated, however, by the film *Intermission* (2003), starring Colin Farrell and based on a script written three years previously. The episodic structure owed a debt to Robert Altman's *Short Cuts* (1993). After getting the widest release since *Michael Collins* (1996), it became the highest-grossing Irish-backed film until then. No wonder that Mark O'Rowe wrote another script of his own, *Perrier's Bounty* (2008–09), as well as two adaptations of novels: Joseph O'Connor's *Star of the Sea* (book 2004, adaptation 2008) and Jonathan Trigell's *Boy A* (book 2004, adaptation 2007).[11] Nevertheless, he will not be lost completely to the theatre. In 2003 he edited *1 Henry IV* (c. 1597) for Jimmy Fay's production at the Peacock Theatre, initially whittling it down to seventy minutes. In the end the show had a two-hour running time, but the version was still too skeletal for many spectators. Together with Hilary Fannin he became writer-in-association at the Abbey a year later, the award money turning out to be a down payment for *Terminus*, which in 2007 marked O'Rowe's directorial debut, again at the Peacock Theatre.

The Plays

The Aspidistra Code (1995)

The play's protagonists Brendan and Sonia are heavily in debt. To help them against the psychopathic loan shark Drongo, Brendan's brother Joe has secured protection by another violent character, Crazy Horse. The latter has made it his mission to stand by the innocent without charging them. Drongo took the diametrically opposed career choice. When they both arrive on the scene, it turns out that they are old mates. Drongo is not the Australian hard man he claims to be, but actually called Fikey McFarlane; Crazy Horse used to be plain Alan Kilby. After swapping some childhood reminiscences, the situation seems to relax as Drongo casually dismisses the money problem: 'It's okay. This is a happy day, so . . .' (p. 159). But the tension rises again when he later claims Sonia misunderstood him and wants to take an allegedly expensive 'antique' chair she had planned to barter in the first place. Now she does not want to let it go and accuses Drongo of changing the rules. This very much riles him as his credo is: 'Rules are what keep society in shape, keep it from getting flabby. Rules are what prevent anarchy. Rules are the only thing preventing the extinction of the wallaby' (p. 149). Drongo offers to play Brendan at poker. If he wins, he will get the chair but still cancel the debt. The only snag is he'd want one of Brendan's precious aspidistras into the bargain. This poses a problem for its proud owner, as he had already lost one earlier against his neighbour Ronnie, while Sonia doesn't care about the plants and inadvertently selects the best specimen. Brendan, usually luckless at cards, wins for once but all of a sudden Drongo insists on two out of three games and claims: 'I wasn't sure of the rules' (p. 180). Brendan, Sonia, Joe and Ronnie put pressure on Crazy Horse to help them as Drongo's henchmen screech into the driveway. Crazy Horse then slips in some dog's piss and shoots Drongo in the chest, killing him. Armed with a second gun, he shoots Pebbles, the family dog, before going out through the front door to the sound of 'shouting, gunfire, and general chaos' (p. 184).

O'Rowe's debut is not much more than a proof of talent regarding dialogue with its moderate amount of humour mostly due to the two hard men and the running gag of Ronnie being called to the telephone by his intimidating wife, who sent her cowardly husband over to help by threatening the withdrawal of his conjugal rights for a month. The story is a small one and might be more suitable for a sitcom. Strictly obeying the rules of time, place and action, the structure remains conventional. Pointing ahead for O'Rowe, however, are Drongo and Crazy Horse as the first of his eccentric low life characters not exactly blessed in the IQ department.

From Both Hips (1997)

Paul has been accidentally shot in the hip by a policeman in pursuit of drug dealers. At the opening of the play his return from the hospital is imminent. His wife Adele and her sister Liz wait for him in a Dublin suburb. Adele has a problem with her nerves and before the incident asked her husband not to sleep with her any longer. Paul uses this request as his excuse for a fling with Theresa. The affair is exposed by Liz's attempt to inform Theresa that her dog is constitutionally unable to love her, one of a series of cod-psychological pieces of information taken from the local paper by the characters. Liz first suspects something when she asks Theresa over to deliver the supposedly shocking news in person. Theresa momentarily thinks Liz is referring to Paul and asks: 'Know about us? How come you knew?' (p. 49). For the moment she manages to wriggle out of the situation but after a drinking session with the two sisters she mentions that her flat has been burgled twice and lets slip the remark: 'When Paul's there . . .' (p. 85). Her lover in the meanwhile is in negotiations with Willy, the policeman who shot him. Even the latter's wife Irene knows that his new job with the Drugs Squad is not right for him, as he was better at just communicating with people instead of acting tougher than he is. He receives counselling against post-traumatic stress disorder and faces Paul's threat to expose to the press the fact that he wet himself after the shooting incident. To avoid this public humiliation, Willy offers to let Paul shoot him twice in retaliation and then forget about the whole thing. When they are just about to arrange their duel, Liz desperately shouts for her brother-in-law offstage, because Adele has a breakdown after Paul blurted out: 'You open your legs, that's all there is fuckin' to it. Is that so fucking hard?!!! I've got to go off with the dog lady' (p. 106). Before the final blackout he is left suspended with Liz calling his name and Willy almost simultaneously urging him to pull the trigger.

Like *The Aspidistra Code*, *From Both Hips*, set over one evening and the following morning, is rather conventionally structured. Susannah Clapp heard the voice of David Mamet in it as much as O'Rowe's own,[12] an influence he readily admits:

> He was the first playwright I read who had that sort of sensibility and that incredibly modern feel. His dialogue was so sharp, so enjoyable and so energetic, you could picture it. He writes about this world. It may be Chicago, but it could be Dublin. It's now.[13]

Paul's self-pity is convincingly done, but just as with Brendan and Sonia in the earlier play one does not really care about his predicament, nor for those of the other characters. Outlandish this time are not figures like Drongo or Crazy Horse but Willy's offer of a private tit for tat. Again the dialogue is competent and the opinions of the resident psychologists at the newspaper are funny, but reading *From Both Hips* there is hardly anything that prepares you for the sheer raw power of O'Rowe's breakthrough play.

Howie the Rookie (1999)

The text consists of two monologues by Howie and Rookie Lee (no relation) giving their version of two turbulent nights out in Dublin and mentioning a whole gallery of colourful other characters who do not appear on stage themselves. Howie is supposed to look after his younger brother Mousey while his parents are out, but prefers to track down Rookie with his mates and beat him up. Howie arranged that a neighbour would act as babysitter, but she does not pay attention properly, so Mousey is run over by a truck and killed. Rookie initially thinks that Howie is one of his enemies and is much surprised when he at first attacks him with the others, but on the next day helps him in two ways. He gives him a remedy against his itching skin and defends Rookie in a quarrel with the retarded son of one of his girlfriends after he vainly hoped to get a loan from her. Rookie needs the money to pay Ladyboy, because he accidentally knocked over a bucket containing his two precious fighting fish. In a brutal showdown Howie takes on Ladyboy at a party the same evening and loses his life, ironically not through his opponent, but through Peaches, who accuses him of having sexually exploited his overweight sister Avalanche. At the end Rookie informs Howie's parents about what has happened.

Andreas Rossmann summarises:

> Breathless, in a jumpy staccato, O'Rowe lets his characters talk and convey a richness of perceptions, moods and feelings challenging the apathy with which reality is suffered here. We got two people who talk for their life just as others run for it.[14]

With this play O'Rowe found a voice of his own. The language has immense speed, rhythm that would not be amiss in a rap musician, but also a strange poetry, and does not contain a single unnecessary word. By comparison, Conor McPherson's or Eugene O'Brien's monologues are softer, even sanitised. Jason Zinoman states in the *New York Times* that the play

> reeks of unpleasant smells wafting across the violent streets of working-class Dublin – terrible body odors, pungent ointments, bad breath and several instances of passing gas. This play stinks – and that is high praise.[15]

And Lyn Gardner draws a pertinent comparison to Rookie's situation: 'Mark O'Rowe writes as if he is itching all over. [. . .] It is a tragedy played out as a scabrous high comedy – the bleakest of scenarios conjured with the lightest of touches.'[16] The two monologues have a more theatrical quality than O'Rowe's 'proper' plays, *The Aspidistra Code* and *From Both Hips*. The audience can witness what happens to the two characters while they relate their stories and at the same time draw conclusions the pair is unable to see. They are convincingly individualised, Howie as the tough guy, Rookie as the better-looking ladies' man. According to Nick Curtis both have

> a scabrous disregard for political correctness. [. . .] The rather crude moral framework hardly makes you feel better about laughing so hard at the characters' hideous attitudes to women, gays and the disabled.[17]

But even he in the end felt drawn 'into a world of picaresque characters and brutal codes, against your better judgement'.[18] The question remains how the author himself sees his protagonists. Carole Woddis attests: 'O'Rowe's device exposes like no other the interior, cut-off quality of these intensely mythologized macho worlds with ultimately a surprising, tender honesty.'[19] And Sarah Hemming opines that the dramatist 'successfully demolishes the thugs' code and lifestyle'.[20] It is by no means clear, however, to what extent O'Rowe more or less endorses if not celebrates the two young men's thinking. Kate Bassett doesn't have a moral, but rather a structural problem and has various reservations:

> The climaxes of each monologue do feel slightly forced, and the Christian symbolism surrounding Howie – who feels contrition and ultimately preaches brotherly understanding – is slightly obtrusive. But it is interesting as a possible allegory of Ireland's religious wars and attempts at reconciliation.[21]

This is rather blatant over-interpretation. A meta-agenda like that would be completely alien to a writer as instinctive and visceral as Mark O'Rowe.

Made in China (2001)

After seeing *Howie the Rookie* Benedict Nightingale predicted: 'If this is a remotely representative picture of city life, the Irish Tourist Board would find it easier to sell the charms of Beirut or maybe no-go Moscow.'[22] But compared to O'Rowe's next play the two monologues seemed to cover relaxed evenings about town. The dramatist planned 'to write the antithesis'[23] of his previous piece. 'I wanted to write something that was really physical and much more theatrical. The whole mindset came from those notions of keeping the actors moving and keeping stuff happening.'[24] Mic Moroney in the *Guardian* summarises the action:

> It's set in the spare deluxe loft apartment of a sharply dressed hard-man, Hughie. He has become dangerously introverted while continuing to execute baseball-bat mutilations on behalf of his offstage boss, Puppacat. Hughie's gauche, skinhead sidekick Paddy gormlessly endures Hughie's sharp, philosophically avuncular put-downs. Their close relationship is murderously imperilled by Hughie's deputy-in-crime, Kilby, a wire-thin, combat-skilled psycho. Hughie's mother has been mown down in a car crash but Hughie baulks at Puppacat's gift of a grisly, teeth-extracting torture of the other driver. By not participating he is disobeying orders, so he is expelled from the gang and threatened with the less-than-divine judgment of the manically destructive Kilby.[25]

In the brutal climax of the play Kilby smashes Paddy's knees, Hughie whacks Kilby over the head with a baseball bat and leaves the flat, while Paddy can only crawl over to Kilby, unable to hit him again after the last words of the play 'Oh, no . . . no, fuck! Fuck! Fuck!' (p. 87). The thrice repeated final expletive is the text's most (over-)used word. O'Rowe in an interview with the director of the Dublin production, Gerry Stembridge, said:

> It's about three violent characters, or three characters who have a great capacity for violence. It's getting into the middle

of them and seeing how the rules play across each other . . . [. . .] I suppose, in the early plays like *The Aspidistra Code* or *From Both Hips*, you had violent characters seen from normal people's perspectives. It was with *Howie the Rookie* that I really had to question myself. It's not the kitchen sink element, the people in the house who are witnessing this. It's actually the people who commit. They're the people I'm interested in. [. . .] In *Made in China*, I don't think for a moment that the author or the director should ever tell the audience to judge these people. By asking people to judge it, you take them a step outside and you're looking down at these people. When I wrote this, I wanted us to be in there with them and, despite the fact that they're horrible people, to have an empathy with them.[26]

While in *Howie the Rookie* the audience maintains this empathy even in the most extreme situations, in *Made in China* the odds are weighed too strongly against the characters. This is due to their substandard intelligence as much as their language. The *Ruhr Nachrichten* objected: 'Not even crack-kids are talking in a code as restricted as that'[27] and pitied the three Bochum actors: 'Nobody believes them these idiots.'[28] According to a number of German critics the play looked like a cheap rearguard action at a time when the wave of new British 'in-yer-face' writing had petered out, and they insinuated O'Rowe simply wanted to up the ante in the sensationalism stakes. Admittedly the dramatist took great pains to show how much the three young men depend on command structures they are unable to fully understand, how they only imitate what they see in the cinema without leading lives of their own. But even in the heavily cut Bochum production, the dialogue quickly became repetitious. There is only a limited amount of variation available from four-letter words even for an author as gifted with language as O'Rowe, and *Made in China* is his most verbose work so far. Paradoxically it is also a less theatrical piece than *Howie the Rookie*.

Crestfall (2003)

For a long time Mark O'Rowe had been the most convincing proof for Mic Moroney's claim: 'The Dublinese sub-genre of Irish theatre has always been an unashamedly macho sport.'[29] No fairies up the garden path for him. Therefore it came as a surprise that the three characters in *Crestfall* were all women. They tell their story in monologue form and a in pared-down language with poetic elements. If this sounds like a return to the method of *Howie the Rookie* and a lesson learnt after *Made in China*, the subject matter is even more lurid than in the latter. Karen Fricker gives a concise summary:

> This is a play about motherhood: all three female characters are, or want to be, mothers, and the principal plot concerns the secret parentage of the hooker Olive's son. When Olive and her lover Inchy meet a gory end at the butt of husband Jungle's shotgun, the smack addict Tilly becomes a replacement mother for the child Poppin-eye. O'Rowe describes a society so calcified by violence that people are reduced to the most basic activities: having sex, killing and shooting up. But making the bonding of (surrogate) mother and child the play's final image is a conservative cop-out: aren't traditional roles part of the society that O'Rowe is going to such extremes to condemn? What is crucially missing here is humour: the tone is so serious that it is impossible to take the ludicrous events the play describes seriously.[30]

This absence of humour was very deliberate:

> With something like *Made in China*, it is very bleak from start to finish, we never get taken out of that darkness, and the humour is something to balance that, maybe make it something slightly more palatable. But this – no; I deliberately stayed away from having too much humour in it. There's a little bit, just as there is in any play, but it's definitely balanced by an immense sense of hope. It's very, very dark, it's darker than either of the

other two, but hopefully people will come out having been dragged through the mud and the shit, but hopefully uplifted.[31]

The dramatist dismissed humour as a 'safety net'[32] and overestimated the redemptive qualities of *Crestfall*. For too much of the play (which remains unpublished) he simply seemed to wallow in the violence and humiliation the three women undergo. The whole event reeked of misery tourism in the name of supposedly cutting-edge writing. Further productions in Scotland and New York were only partly able to dispel this impression.

Terminus (2007)

While up to this point he had written a new play every two years, it took O'Rowe four until his own production of *Terminus*. He had intimated that it would be 'lighter than my previous work'.[33] This was true formally, but not regarding the subject matter. *Terminus* is set in by now familiar O'Rowe nightmare territory and contains scenes of cartoonish violence but also elements of magical realism. Three characters, A, a woman in her forties, B, a woman in her twenties and C, a man in his thirties, all have long monologues interrupted only by brief sentences divided up between them. Colin Murphy summarises the stories A, B and C are telling:

> A woman falling to her death from a crane is rescued mid-flight by a winged creature made up entirely of worms. They fall in love, but are rudely interrupted by a posse of seven angels. The winged fellow is the soul of another, a psychopath who suffers from shyness, and who has sold his soul in return for a singing voice. This fellow is fleeing the scene of a grotesque sex murder in a speeding, stolen articulated lorry. Meanwhile, another woman is trying to save a former student, who is heavily pregnant, from a violent backstreet abortion to be performed by her thuggish lesbian lover. And all of this is narrated in rhyme.[34]

Alan O'Riordan called the dramatist 'something like the Guy Ritchie of Irish theatre'[35] and detected the influence of Flann O'Brien or Edgar Allan Poe:

> Rhythms like those in Poe's 'The Raven' propel the action, as do incessant – often ear-numbing – rhyming couplets. O'Rowe has never met a homonym or homophone he doesn't like. This can be wearisome: a river is inevitably a 'silver, sliver, slithering'; you can have too much of this rococo embellishment. But elsewhere, the rhythm has enough variation and the rhyme enough surprise to be impressive and add much to the moments of jet-black comedy.[36]

A typical sentence would be: 'And, without speaking, under no duress, nor awkwardness nor stress, we undress' (p. 15). Fintan O'Toole underlined the connection to 'the rapper's extempore flow':[37] 'The monologues are conducted through a maze of rhymes and rhythms, of assonances and alliterations, of off-beat metres and syncopations.'[38] O'Rowe's

> obvious ambition is to forge a kind of speech that is both artificial enough to acknowledge the unnatural context of the theatre and tough enough to have the demotic immediacy of an urgent conversation.[39]

Despite admiring O'Rowe's 'ability to move from the mundane to the fantastical, and from pathos to a final passage of outrageous and sublimely grotesque humour',[40] he concluded: 'Yet, as a theatrical experience, the play never matches the writing.'[41]

The strongest dissent came from Dermot Moore, who attacked the text as 'a manifestation of a particular kind of masturbatory male sexuality'[42] and accused the author of infantilism:

> This is a script that revels in sex, grotesque violence, a cold-blooded serial murderer separated from his soul on the run, women betrayed by their men, lesbianism, life after death,

Faustian pacts and worm-formed demons and angels. They are fantasy themes that any adolescent lad with half an imagination and a creepy obsession with gory fantasy fiction could come up with.[43]

For him O'Rowe's virtuoso writing was merely 'meretricious showy sub-Tarantino Dub loquaciousness'[44] and the production 'curiously undramatic, because all the action is reported, not enacted. The actors are disconnected, from each other and from us.'[45] While there are a few uncomfortable parallels to *Crestfall* in the writing, however, Helen Meany rightly recognised 'an emotional undertow that is new for O'Rowe'.[46] In particular she referred to B's 'litany of her life's most intense experiences, recited at the point of death [as] the most eloquent and powerful' passage.[47] Its lyricism and sheer rhythmic quality make it one of the most accomplished speeches O'Rowe has written up to now (p. 42f.).

Summary

In all his plays Mark O'Rowe's main topic is violence:

I don't think I'd ever say I want to deal with violence or do a study of violence, but I know it's what entertains me. In the end you write for an audience, but you write to please yourself as well in terms of what interests you. I love violence in its literary form, its cinematic form.[48]

His reference points are mostly cinematic, even down to the dramaturgy of the plays:

I've itchy feet in playwriting. I never want to linger too long on anything. I always want to move on. I find myself asking how can I do this as quickly as possible and get to the next story point. [. . .] Action has to be something kinetic, something hitting off something else to spark something. The history of cinema is filled with that sort of violence. It's what excites me and many people at the movies.[49]

The same applies to plot matters:

The darker stories turn me on. I like the feeling that things can turn bad at any time. I never sit down and deliberately plot a point of horror, but if I have a choice between a character being knocked down and killed in the next five minutes or falling in love, I'll usually go for them being run over.[50]

He respects David Mamet and Harold Pinter but nobody closer to home apart from a novelist like Cormac McCarthy:[51]

It means nothing to me, that whole writers' tradition. I've never felt part of it and I've never really wanted to be part of it. What actually happens, when you have a successful play like *Howie the Rookie*, people start making you, in a way, part of it. Although, with that kind of play, they kind of feel 'when he starts writing fifty-year-old characters in the bogs and talking about what it means to be Irish and the land, maybe we'll let him in then'. [. . .] The Irish literary tradition this is not meant to sound arrogant because I'm not talking about my own writing here, I'm talking about the kind of stuff I like – never impressed me that much. I'm much more of a fan of American literature, always have been.[52]

Therefore in reviews of *Howie the Rookie* not so much comparisons with the likes of James Joyce were pertinent, but rather those experiencing 'some bizarre world where Flann O'Brien meets John Wayne'[53] and particularly Paul Taylor's mentioning of Damon Runyon: 'There's the same absurd courtliness in their argot and nicknames, the same weird pedantry on points of honour.'[54]Among dramatists apart from Mamet and Pinter there is a relation to Neil LaBute who contributed what must be a contender for the most vacuous programme note of all time for *Crestfall*. After repeatedly admitting that he never saw a play by O'Rowe and only 'peeked' at the text of *Crestfall*, he proclaimed: 'Here is a voice that can now be spoken in the same room as Beckett and O'Casey and Synge'[55] – exactly the line of ancestors for whom O'Rowe does not care at all. What links him to the admittedly far smoother LaBute and somebody like Quentin Tarantino is the impression that as an author he somehow seems to get a kick out of the humiliation he inflicts on his characters. *Crestfall* in particular tries to rival the late Sarah Kane in the depiction of atrocities, but she would never have uttered that violence 'entertains' her. O'Rowe himself claims that the brutality in plays like Mark Ravenhill's *Shopping and Fucking* or Jez Butterworth's *Mojo* is 'shallow' and 'cartoonish' because not 'grounded in a very personal, human story'.[56] Unfortunately this is also true for *Made in China* and even more so for *Crestfall*. With the latter he claimed to have written a deeply humanitarian play 'basically about that small glimmer of goodness, trying to survive in a place that is completely soulless and lost'.[57] But Karen Fricker is right to say:

> While there are some beautiful passages in *Crestfall*, there is no sign of advance either in style, form or subject matter: he has merely turned up the dials on the brutal, scatological anthem he has been playing from the start.[58]

This may be partly due to the fact that O'Rowe abandoned his usual Dublin locations and imagined 'a place reminiscent of an apocalyptic frontier town in the Wild West, where normal relationships don't exist'.[59] In the resulting unspecified dystopian setting the violent acts seem to take place in a kind of void. O'Rowe explains this by strongly distancing himself from any attempt to see his work as social commentary:

> If Quentin Tarantino has two guys rob a jewellery store, no one says it's a commentary on poverty and desperation and alienation of the modern male. It's a fuckin' heist movie! It's as simple as that. These are the rules of the heist movie.[60]

His biggest aspiration is

> to push Irish theatre on to the next level. I'd like to be part of
> the thing that, in twenty years' time, made Irish theatre. I'd
> like it if I was part of that wave or whatever that turned it on
> its head.[61]

While this did not sound too boastful at the time of *Howie the Rookie*,
with *Made in China* and *Crestfall* O'Rowe had manoeuvred himself
into a cul-de-sac. *Terminus* wasn't a completely successful reversal
and revelled in some slasher-movie fantasies, demonstrating
O'Rowe's increasingly tiresome interest in video nasties. But despite
its fantastical elements it was set again in and around a recognisable
Dublin and showed a joy for language and a kind of bizarre humour
largely absent in *Crestfall*. Still, like Conor McPherson and Eugene
O'Brien, O'Rowe does not seem to get away from the monologue
structure as the basis for his writing. Fintan O'Toole rightly
summarises:

> Ironically, the problem is exactly the one that faced Irish
> writing a century ago, when poets wanted actors to stand still
> and deliver their beautifully wrought lines. That impulse had
> to be abandoned and poets such as Yeats had to look for new
> ways of using music, dance and design to give physical
> expression to their words. They realised that great theatre has
> to exist in two dimensions: words and action.[62]

Colin Murphy admitted as much and gave the most balanced verdict
on *Terminus* and Mark O'Rowe's current standing:

> Many will hate this play, or simply stay away, because of the
> grotesque violence (which climaxes in a literally spectacular
> disembowelment). O'Rowe's literary ambition is not matched
> by a theatrical one, and some will find the prospect of 105
> minutes watching three near-immobile characters talking at
> the audience to be dull. Both are valid objections. But there is

a brazen talent at work here, with a delirious indifference to theatrical convention and tradition. And that, for me, is a damn good reason to go.[63]

Primary Sources

From Both Hips: Two Plays (*From Both Hips* and *The Aspidistra Code*) (London: Nick Hern, 1999).
Howie the Rookie (London: Nick Hern, 1999).
Made in China (London: Nick Hern, 2001).
Terminus (London: Nick Hern, 2007).

Secondary Sources

Andrews, Rachel, 'On the Crest of a Wave', *Sunday Tribune*, 18 May 2003.
Bassett, Kate, 'A Fiercely Modern Vision of Ireland', *Daily Telegraph*, 26 February 1999.
Carty, Ciaran, 'From Stage to Screen', *Sunday Tribune*, 1 December 2002.
Clapp, Susannah, 'From Both Hips', *Observer*, 28 February 1999.
Crawley, Peter, 'High Rhymes and Low Crimes', *Irish Times*, 13 June 2007.
Cronin, Julie, 'Chinese Whispers', Gerry Stembridge in conversation with Mark O'Rowe, recorded by Julie Cronin in Dublin Corporation Arts Office, Parnell Square <http://nayd.ie/files/ Whispers.pdf>.
Curtis, Nick, 'Boys in Some Black Stuff', *Evening Standard*, 15 February 1999.
Fricker, Karen, 'Crestfall', *Guardian*, 24 May 2003.
Gardner, Lyn, 'Howie the Rookie', *Guardian*, 20 February 1999.
Gibbons, Fiachra, 'The Dark Stuff', *Guardian*, 24 November 2003.
Hemming, Sarah, 'Howie the Rookie', *Financial Times*, 4 March 1999.
Jones, Sarah, 'Delving into the Dark Side of Irish Life', *Scotland on Sunday*, 18 September 2005.
LaBute, Neil, 'So, Hats off Then to Mr. O'Rowe', Gate Theatre programme for *Crestfall*, p. 5.
Meany, Helen, 'Terminus', *Guardian*, 16 June 2007.
Moore, Dermod, 'Review: Terminus – Peacock Theatre' <http://bonhom.ie/2007/06/ review-terminus-peacock-theatre.html>.
Moroney, Mic, 'Made in China', *Guardian*, 12 April 2001.
Murphy, Colin, 'Theatre – Gripping, Grotesque and Deliriously Good', *Sunday Tribune*, 17 July 2007.
Murphy, Trish, 'That Glimmer of Hope', Mark O'Rowe in conversation with Trish Murphy <http://www.eventguide.ie/ articles. elive?session_id=1248242789662248& sku=030518143204>.

Nightingale, Benedict, 'Irish Eyes are Shiner', *The Times*, 16 February 1999.

O'Riordan, Alan, '"Ritchie" O'Rowe Revels in Rap, Rhythm and Rhyme', *Irish Independent*, 16 June 2007.

O'Toole, Fintan, 'Stage for Action as Well as Words', *Irish Times*, 23 June 2007.

PvD, 'Experiment Ameisenkolonie', *Ruhr Nachrichten*, 26 February 2001.

Rossmann, Andreas, 'Maulhelden der Westlichen Welt', *Frankfurter Allgemeine Zeitung*, 14 October 1999.

Taylor, Paul, 'Damon Runyon's Dubliners', *Independent*, 16 February 1999.

Woddis, Carole, 'Howie the Rookie', *Herald*, 17 February 1999.

Zinoman, Jason, 'Blood, Guts and Poetic Words on the Mean Streets of Dublin', *New York Times*, 25 May 2005.

Notes

1. Fiachra Gibbons, 'The Dark Stuff'.
2. Ciaran Carty, 'From Stage to Screen'.
3. Gibbons, op. cit.
4. Carty, op. cit.
5. Julie Cronin, 'Chinese Whispers'.
6. Revived by Purple Heart in 2003.
7. *Evening Herald* review<http://www.bedrockproductions.com/9/>reviews.html (21 August 2009), ellipsis there.
8. Interview with the author, 13 November 1999.
9. Carty, op. cit.
10. Cronin, op. cit.
11. First broadcast on Channel 4 and later released in the cinema.
12. Susannah Clapp, 'From Both Hips'.
13. Carty, op. cit.
14. Andreas Rossmann, 'Maulhelden der Westlichen Welt'.
15. Jason Zinomann, 'Blood, Guts and Poetic Words'.
16. Lyn Gardner, 'Howie the Rookie'.
17. Nick Curtis, 'Boys in Some Black Stuff'.
18. Ibid.
19. Carole Woddis, 'Howie the Rookie'.
20. Sarah Hemming, 'Howie the Rookie'.
21. Kate Bassett, 'A Fiercely Modern Vision of Ireland'.
22. Benedict Nightingale, 'Irish Eyes are Shiner'.
23. Cronin, op. cit.
24. Ibid.
25. Mic Moroney, 'Made in China'.

for almost a decade. He became an 'often acerbic but always compelling'[7] rock-music columnist for the *Irish Times* while writing plays for the theatre. In 1970, he edited *Over the Bridge*, Sam Thompson's classic (and controversial) play about sectarianism in the Belfast shipyards. In 1978, he moved to Edinburgh, and then on to London where he died from stomach cancer in 1988, having 'established himself as one of the most versatile and imaginative of the current generation of Irish writers for the theatre and television' as well as radio.[8]

His work received numerous prizes, among them the Evening Standard Drama Awards the Ewart Biggs Award and Harvey's Best Irish Play of the Year Award. A revival of *Pentecost* by Rough Magic in 1995 was voted Best Production at the Dublin Theatre Festival. In May 2008, nearly twenty years after Stewart Parker's death, the Lyric Theatre in Belfast and Dublin's Rough Magic Theatre Company commemorated that date – and the tenth anniversary of the signing of the Good Friday Agreement – with 'The Parker Project', featuring his first and last plays, *Spokesong* and *Pentecost*. And Queen's University Belfast organised, on the anniversary weekend at the beginning of November, a three-day conference – 'Stewart Parker: The Northern Star'. The playwright's memory is also kept alive through the Stewart Parker Trust Awards for the best new stage plays by Irish writers.

The Plays

Spokesong or The Common Wheel (1975)

Spokesong is set in a shabby Victorian bicycle shop in Belfast, threatened by the town developers' plans of driving motorways through the city and 'at risk from the "freelance" redevelopers of the IRA'.[9] Moving in and out of the past, the play, set 'in the early 1970s and the eighty years preceding them' (p. 3), intertwines the family history of Frank Stock, the inheritor of the bicycle shop, with the history of the bicycle itself, going back to John Boyd Dunlop, the Scottish veterinary surgeon who, while working in Belfast, 'invented the pneumatic tyre and started a different kind of revolution from those with which the city is more often associated'.[10]

Frank, who clings to his shop despite the twin threats of bulldozer and bomb, sees the bicycle as the future of transport in the city; he is a dreamer, a philosopher and a romantic at heart, slightly out of touch with the reality surrounding him. He falls in love with Daisy Bell, a school teacher, as his grandfather (who founded the shop after a fateful meeting with Dunlop) fell in love with the cycling suffragette Kitty. Matters are complicated by the return from London (where he had spent the previous five years) of his adopted brother Julian, who wants to sell the shop and also snatch Daisy from him.

Eventually, Daisy decides to stay, raises the money (by threatening to turn her father in, who is a murky figure in the loyalist workers' strike of 1974) to buy the shop, and takes over:

> God only knows how this hell-hole will ever redeem itself. But we'll start by dealing with the people the way they really are. In all their sweet reason as well as their depravity. (p. 70)

> *Spokesong* or *The Common Wheel* . . . is a beautifully lyrical play combining a passionate and sentimental history of the bicycle with an equally passionate but unsentimental tandem history of the troubles in Belfast.[11]

With the 'Trick Cyclist' as master of ceremonies, the songs by Jimmy Kennedy, *Spokesong*'s 'music-hall touches and self-conscious theatricality'[12] and its 'experimental shifts from realism to stylised vaudeville signalled the arrival of a huge playwriting talent'.[13] On the occasion of the Parker Project, where Lynne Parker's direction emphasised the environmental and communal message of the play, David Lewis commented: '*Spokesong*'s paean to the humble bicycle feels bang up to date – the idea that Belfast might one day have a free cycle scheme far less ludicrous now than it might have seemed in 1974.'[14] Jane Coyle concurred: 'In its spookily contemporary subject matter, it feels as though it could have been written yesterday'[15]

Catchpenny Twist (1977)

Three teachers, Roy, Martyn and Monagh, are dismissed from their jobs after being caught by the headmaster while fooling around after an end-of-term celebration. Roy and Martyn try their luck at songwriting, with Monagh as their singer. But in order to earn a few pounds, they write heroic ballads for the Republicans, and as a favour to a cousin of Roy's, 'a few comedy numbers' (p. 117) for loyalist drinking clubs. Result – two live bullets in the post.

They escape to Dublin, and then to London (mirroring Stewart Parker's own trajectory to Edinburgh and London), and one of their songs is chosen as the Irish entry to a European song contest in Luxembourg. It fails dismally. And while waiting for their flight, they open their fan mail and presents, and the final twist hits the songwriting 'band on the run':[16] the last parcel contains a letter bomb which goes off as Martyn picks at the tape of the package.

Staged at the Peacock Theatre in Dublin in 1977, *Catchpenny Twist* was, according to Philip Hobsbaum, 'based on the true story of a couple of Queen's University students who wrote a Eurovision song contest entry for their idol, the then famous singer Sandie Shaw',[17] referring to the songwriting partnership of Phil Coulter and Bill Martin.

For Parker's niece, the director Lynne Parker, Monagh, Roy and Martyn 'reflect a strong impulse on the part of a whole generation to flee the North's Troubles to seek a less complicated life in the civilised world. Wherever that might be.'[18] A 'charade' with music by Shaun Davey, *Catchpenny Twist* with its final image of Roy and Martyn 'on their knees, heads and faces covered in blood, groping about blindly', sticks out as Parker's most pessimistic perspective on the Northern 'comedy of terrors'. Parker, Andrew Parkin has argued, 'deliberately makes his victims Protestant and Catholic alike', their end symbolising the 'fragile image of national harmony.'[19] 'It is a brutal, sudden, and vicious play, capturing a mood of hopelessness and cynical stoicism that was not an uncommon reaction to the Troubles, north and south, in the 1970s,' wrote Robert Welch, adding: 'Its fluent stagecraft, moving deftly between registers of seriousness and levity, signalled the arrival of a major talent at the Abbey.'[20]

Kingdom Come (1978)

Kingdom Come: A Caribbean-Irish Musical Comedy (with music by Shaun Davey) saw its premiere at the King's Head Theatre in London in 1978 (four years later it was staged at the Lyric Theatre in Belfast). A madcap musical within a musical, set on a small Caribbean island called Macalla (Montserrat), it relates the story of Hugo Flood, an Anglo-Irish Wicklow man who was born in 1604 and died in 1690, after colonising the place. But it is also a critique 'of the Unionist establishment in Northern Ireland, American racism, British racialist attitudes toward immigrants within the UK, and imperialism generally'.[21]

It even suggests, through the explicitly Irish character O'Prey, that the Irish, given half a chance, were apt to try their own hand at the colonising game.[22] Marilynn Richtarik[23] pointed out that Parker was delighted with a Conor Cruise O'Brien review of the play in the *Observer*:

> It is indeed about the liberation of a people. But it is not about their liberation in the sense in which that term is used by those who use it most; quite the contrary. It is about the liberation of the people of Northern Ireland *from their supposed liberators* – the IRA in the case of the Catholics – and from their supposed defenders – the sectarian paramilitaries in the case of the Protestants.[24]

Nightshade (1980)

In *Nightshade*, first seen at the Abbey's Peacock stage in October 1980, Quinn, a mortician, also performs as an amateur magician, assisted by his odd-ball attractive but morbid tap-dancing daughter, Delia. Quinn's wife has disappeared; allegedly she is dead. The undertakers' staff go on strike, and the ensuing business difficulties lead to Quinn's breakdown. Not specific in its setting (although Lynne Parker argues persuasively that it has got to be Belfast), *Nightshade* 'tackles huge, elemental questions in a characteristically playful way'.[25] It is a hilarious mix of trickery, allegory and complexity, but with a darker message lying underneath:

Quinn's showmanship is duplicated in Parker's theatricality, but there is the crucial difference of intentions – between Quinn the magician who gives illusion that has the appearance of truth, and the playwright, Parker, who gives truth in the pleasant disguises of illusion.[26]

Lynne Parker calls *Nightshade* 'the most abstract' of Parker's plays, 'and the one he felt most satisfaction at having written':

> Ironically it appears to have little to do with politics, the Troubles or Ireland. Death is the great terror for most of us and it was a particular obsession of his. He chooses, of course, to deal with it in a very unsolemn manner, employing magic, wrestling, Jacob and the Angel, and the Sleeping Beauty to tell the story of a bereaved undertaker.[27]

Pratt's Fall (1983)

First performed at Glasgow's Tron theatre in January 1983, *Pratt's Fall* is set 'in the Map room of a major Metropolitan library', and various other locations which are conjured up in flashbacks. Godfrey Dudley is dressing for his wedding – it is ten minutes to twelve. But there is a ghost at the wedding: George Mahoney, who allegedly had discovered a map which proves that St Brendan discovered America more than 600 years before Columbus.

What unfolds is the story of how Mahoney uses his 'discovery' to seduce Map Curator Victoria Pratt. Pratt falls for him, until the dénouement at an International Brendan Map Conference. Victoria then sums up nicely what the play is about:

> You've got what you wanted. Amusement value, academic pratfalls, showing up the vanity of experts, whose horizons were so much less visionary than your own. (p. 331)

Pratt's Fall is a complex and witty play about authenticity and about faith, and their opposites, which could hold its own in comparisons with Frayn or Stoppard.[28]

Northern Star (1984)

Set in a half-finished and crumbling cottage on the slopes of Cave Hill above Belfast in the aftermath of the 1798 rising, *Northern Star* is 'an Irish "history play" like no other'.[29] It is the first of three plays conceived as a 'triptych', featuring 'three self-contained groups of figures' from each of the past three centuries. Here, Parker turns to the 'botched birth' of Irish Republicanism in the late eighteenth century, embodied in the failure of Henry Joy McCracken and the United Irishmen to create a secular, non-sectarian Ireland based on the principles of the French Revolution.

What fascinated Parker was that Republicanism was very much the product of radical Protestant thinking, heavily influenced by the Scottish Enlightenment. A relatively marginal figure like McCracken (who, towards the end of the uprising, was Northern commander of the insurgents) gives him the opportunity to tweak out these ironies and complexities of history. Taking its name from the United Irishmen's newspaper of the same name, founded in 1791, and its cue from the Seven Ages of Man,[30] the play covers the seven years of the United Irishmen leading up to and including the failed rising of '98, each of the ages presented in the unmistakable styles of Irish playwrights. In its series of pastiches, it also reflects Irish theatrical history from Farquhar and Sheridan to Behan and Beckett.

On his last night before he goes to the gallows, Henry Joy McCracken conjures up key moments of his life and of the development of the movement he helped found. In the first flashback, the Age of Innocence, a boisterous night in an alehouse on St Patrick's Day 1791, the Declaration and Resolution of the Society of United Irishmen is introduced, the lofty language counterpoised by the debate about the (abysmal) quality of the ale, a clear reference to George Farquhar's *The Beaux' Stratagem*. For the next phase, the Age of Idealism, Parker employs the patriotic melodrama of Dion Boucicault's *The Shaughraun* to dramatise the encounter between McCracken's Belfast idealism and the realities of land feuding and the opening rift between Protestant United Irishmen and Catholic Defenders.

Insincerity and levity mark the Age of Cleverness; Oscar Wilde's *Importance of Being Earnest* provides the pattern of repartee between Bunting and Wolfe Tone – the latter up from Dublin to rally the troops. The Age of Dialectic, featuring the intrusion of a Captain of Dragoons in search of McCracken, appropriately employs Shavian wit to discuss the case of the United Irishmen.

The Heroic Age marks the turning point from non-violent radicalism to McCracken's embrace of physical force, and the parting of the way between him and Jemmy Hope. In the style of John Millington Synge, Tone whips up a frenzy for the fight, like 'the only wonder of the Northern World' (p. 57). But the battle was already doomed, as the 'future ghost' Jemmy Hope explains: 'We hadn't the ghost of a chance' (p. 58).

The beginning of the end is delivered in the Age of Compromise, when betrayal and double-dealing enter the scene. McCracken is sworn into the Defenders by Gorman, a publican from Dublin, and his crony Croaker McFadden, perfect reincarnations of Sean O'Casey's Captain Boyle and Joxer Daly in *Juno and the Paycock*. And it ends in a brawl not unreminiscent of the 'Cyclops' scene in James Joyce's *Ulysses*.

The final flashback is set at Kilmainham gaol, where four prisoners comment, as in Brendan Behan's *The Quare Fellow*, on the fate of a condemned prisoner waiting for his execution. As Behan's characters, and not unlike Vladimir and Estragon in Samuel Beckett's *Waiting for Godot*, they while away the time with reminiscences and stories. As the day breaks, both in the prison and at the cottage, the doomed McCracken's soliloquy is Beckettian: 'To finish. Unless only to begin anew, there is of course that' (p. 78). But it also has echoes of *Hamlet*: 'All as in a dream, before the other dream unknown, perchance dreamless. Unknown' (p. 78).

Then, in a staccato scene we move right into contemporary 1980s Northern Ireland – in an interrogation accompanied by 'white noise' (pp. 78–80), the names of the leaders of the United Irishman rising are prised from the prisoners. In a final *coup de théâtre*, Parker allows McCracken a summing up, an 'exit line' which circumstances in reality denied him. At the beginning of the play, we had encountered him practising his speech under the gallows, a heroic oration in the style of Robert Emmet. Here now, we get a much more private *summa* of a failed hero, a failed movement, but also a prescient analysis of the consequences of that failure:

> We never made a nation. Our brainchild. Stillborn. Our own fault. We botched the birth. So what if the English do bequeath us to one another some day? What then? When there's nobody else to blame except ourselves? (p. 81)

Northern Star, Mark Phelan writes, 'is a masterpiece of modern Irish drama. A play that both contains – and critiques – the Irish theatrical canon.'[31] It has been successfully revived in Ireland but, by writing 'the intertextuality of his inheritance as Irish playwright into the terribly repeated and unfinished matrices of Irish history', Parker's 'density of Irish-specific quotation and allusion have prevented its finding audiences outside the country'.[32]

Heavenly Bodies (1986)

In 1890, in New York's Madison Square Theatre, a senior actor dismisses his class as he is feeling unwell. He is none other than Ireland's most successful nineteenth-century popular dramatist, actor and impresario (and theatre innovator), Dion Boucicault, who was deemed – despite all his melodramatic successes – but a marginal figure in the history of drama.

He meets the ghost of the song and dance man Johnny Patterson, recently deceased while singing his self-penned ditty 'Do Your Best for One Another', a song to promote Orange and Green harmony, in a circus in Tralee. In his attempt to save the circus from the riot his rendition had caused, he gets killed by the mob for his efforts. Patterson, for whom Boucicault has nothing but disdain, wants to lead him off into limbo, 'a dark and dacent corner of obscurity' (p. 93). But Boucicault insists that he is 'owed a place in posterity' (p. 93). His plea for immortality invokes the story of his life, scenes from his plays interwoven with his biography and historical events such as the Famine.

In the end, it is the wake scene from Boucicault's masterpiece, *The Shaughraun*, which by a whisker clinches immortality for him. This can be seen as a reflection on the impact this 'forgotten' Victorian has had on the theatre since. Parker shares with Boucicault his sense of theatricality and the 'delight in theatre's infinite possibilities of play'.[33]

Pentecost (1987)

Pentecost, Parker's last stage play, is set between February and May 1974, focusing on the Ulster Workers' Council Strike (14–29 May), which brought the province to a standstill and toppled the first attempt at a power-sharing executive following the Sunningdale Agreement.[34] It was Field Day's 1987 production, premiered at the Guildhall in Derry, 'the only Field Day play to deal directly with the Troubles'.[35]

Four troubled people in their late twenties and early thirties, two Catholic, two Protestant, have gathered in the house of a recently deceased Protestant woman. The house of Lily Mathews, respectable widow of Alfie Matthews, is the last occupied house in a late-Victorian east Belfast terrace, bang on the dividing line between the frontiers of the conflict, and threatened from urban redevelopment. Catholic Marian has chosen to live in the house, and only she is aware of a fifth presence – the ghost of Lily Matthews.

Marian is the estranged wife of Lenny, the inheritor of the house; Marian's evangelical friend Ruth, married to a wife-beating policeman, and Lenny's old college mate, the Protestant Peter, who has returned from Birmingham, make up the rest of the motley quartet washed up in Lily's house. Marian discovers Lily's diary, and as the play progresses, we learn more and more about her – born in 1900, as old as the century, about Alfie who fought in the First World War and came back impotent, about their lodger Alan Ferris, their child that was given away. First, Marian plans to preserve the house, keep everything as Lily had arranged it, even pass the property to the National Trust as a museum to a vanishing Belfast way of life. But the more she comes to terms with her own child, which died after just five months, the more she changes her mind.

She wants the house to live, to breathe. Lily's ghost must not be condemned 'to life indefinitely':

> I'm clearing most of this out. Keeping just the basics. What this house needs most is air and light. (p. 238).

We have reached Pentecost Sunday. The strike is over. Outside both sides celebrate, in Peter's words, the 'end of being forced to share the top table':

> . . . you'd think they'd given birth, actually created something for once, instead of battering it to death, yet again, the only kind of victory they ever credit, holding the good old fort, stamping the life out of anything that starts to creep forward . . . (p. 234)

What follows, Gerald Dawe has called 'an extraordinary moment in Irish theatre, and probably one of the most misunderstood scenes as well'.[36] Into the story breaks the Pentecost message, recited between Ruth and Peter, of how the Holy Spirit inspired the Lord's apostles:

> And they were all filled with the Holy Ghost, and began to speak with other tongues, as the Spirit gave them utterance. (p. 240)

Into the squabbling that resurfaces, Marian begins to talk about their lost child, Christopher, named thus because 'he was a kind of Christ to me, he brought love with him . . . the truth, and the life. He was a future' (p. 244). She first blamed him for choosing 'death in the cot rather than life in this town', blamed him, 'for all the pain'. But that, she now realises, was denying him:

> The christ in him. Which he had entrusted to my care, the ghost of him that I do still carry, as I carried his little body. The christ in him absorbed into the christ in me. We have got to love that in ourselves. In ourselves first and then in them. That's the only future there is. (p. 244)

It may be 'placing a strain on contemporary audiences' and mark 'a critical point in production' but, Christopher Murray argues, 'Marian's confession of her pain and anger at the loss of her child banishes hostility between self and world, "us" and "them", wife and husband, mother and the innocent dead'.[37] He quotes from *Dramatis Personae*, where Parker defined the challenge for the Northern playwright as finding 'a belief in the future and to express it with due defiance [. . .] to assert the primacy of the play-impulse over the deathwish'.[38]

Anthony Roche has called *Pentecost* 'Parker's most eloquently humane play, the one in which irony and whimsy give way to a passionate dramatizing of personal and cultural renewal',[39] while for Dawe *Pentecost* is a 'contemporary classic play, as central to Irish experience as *Translations, Double Cross, Bailegangaire* and *Observe the Sons of Ulster Marching Towards the Somme*'.[40]

Summary

A play which reinforces complacent assumptions, which confirms lazy preconceptions, which fails to combine emotional honesty with coherent analysis, which goes in short for the easy answer, is in my view actually harmful. And yet if ever a time and a place cried out for the solace and rigour and passionate rejoinder of great drama, it is here and now. There is a whole culture to be achieved. The politicians, visionless almost to a man, are withdrawing into their sectarian stockades. It falls to the artist to construct a working model of wholeness by means of which the society can begin to hold up its head in the world.[41]

This can be taken as Stewart Parker's credo. Throughout his short career he pursued, onstage, on television and on radio, this quest for a 'working model of wholeness'. It is the driving force behind his plays, fuelled by the 'multiple dualities' of his cultural and national background, but also by the experience of his own struggle with cancer and the loss of his leg.

Stylistic variety, experimentation and, above all, a sense of 'play' and conscious theatricality, drawing on popular entertainment such as variety and music hall, would be hallmarks of Parker's drama. He quotes with approval Johan Huizinga's contention, which echoes O'Casey's, that 'the whole of human life must be felt as a blend of tragedy and comedy',[42] with no clear distinction between play and seriousness onstage. Parker found inspiration in Dürrenmatt, Beckett and Behan, but also in O'Casey's later, experimental plays:

> What strikes me is that O'Casey was clearly moving towards two kinds of playwriting which have been conspicuous by their absence in Ireland – experimentalism, and politically committed work (in the socialist sense).[43]

The prime inspiration for the use of pastiche in *Northern Star* clearly came from James Joyce's 'Oxen of the Sun' chapter in *Ulysses*. Belfast's musical landscape is integral to much of Parker's writing – he has been called 'the Van Morrison of Irish theatre'.[44] And the incorporation of music and song emphasises, as in Brecht, the performance aspect of Parker's plays.[45]

The key for Parker's drama is, as Elmer Andrews has persuasively argued, that it is metaphoric, not realistic, thus providing a creative tension between actuality and potentiality. To realise this potential in play

> it must know itself to be play, to be figurative representation and not reality itself. Only by admitting the historical limits of understanding can it resist the claim to totalitarian knowledge and represent a view of history as an open-ended process of transformation.[46]

The most striking, and recurring, metaphors are the settings: the threatened bicycle shop holding out against destruction in *Spokesong*; the unfinished, crumbling cottage standing for the 'botched' revolution of 1798 in *Northern Star*; and the last inhabited 'parlour' house between the sectarian lines in *Pentecost*.

The majority of Parker's plays – *Spokesong, Pratt's Fall, Northern Star, Heavenly Bodies* – employ flashbacks as a structural device. These allow him to present, as in the 'ghost scenes' in *Pentecost*, diachronic depth in a contemporary time framework. The most interesting case of Parker's handling of time and history occurs in *Northern Star*. The flashbacks give McCracken the chance to assess his life and his achievements and failures. The wish for martyrdom makes way for disillusionment. In that, Parker's play is a close companion to Brian Friel's *Making History*. As McCracken feels himself condemned to be one of the ghosts in the ghost town of Belfast, due to his and the United Irishmen's failure 'to make it whole', Friel's Hugh O'Neill loses his battle against his biographer who will make his a heroic story, although he clearly sees himself as mistaken and a failure.

Parker's *Northern Star* shares with Frank McGuinness's *Observe the Sons of Ulster Marching Towards the Somme* the firm belief that there cannot be a solution to the Northern predicament without properly incorporating Protestant identities – best expressed in the figure of Jemmy Hope: 'Without the Protestants of the North, there'll never be a nation. Not without them as a part of it.' And McCracken's response: 'Not without them at the heart of it . . .' (p. 58).

Even during the darkest period of the Troubles, Parker could muster the optimism that theatre could be a means towards reconciling Catholics and Protestants in the North. While the happy ending of *Spokesong* seemed parodistically grafted upon the encroaching violent reality of Belfast, a music-hall rather than a real solution,[47] and *Catchpenny Twist, Nightshade* and *Pratt's Fall* show the darker sides of the abuse and perversion of the ludic, creative impulse,[48] where 'play' is used to deceive and escape rather than for an imaginative opening of possibilities, the final triptych of plays edges closer to resolution.

With the final scene of *Pentecost* Parker dared to present an image full of potential for a common future of the deeply divided communities, but also between the dead and the living. Exorcising Lily's ghost by merging with her, incorporating her, Marian embraces wholeness. 'Plays intend to achieve resolution,' Parker wrote, 'whilst ghosts appear to be stuck fast in the quest for vengeance.'[49]

Dealing 'properly' with history, in Parker's sense, means to show the openness of history in the making, the fact that events now in the past were once in the future. The flashbacks, thus, are more than mere recapitulation or stock-taking, they turn into a clear-out, assume qualities of a talking-cure,[50] but they also show history being constructed, mistakes being made, the potential for alternatives, the openness of the process. Such an understanding of history liberates, helps, to use the Joycean phrase, to awake from the nightmare of history.[51] The Irish President, Mary McAleese, reinforced the point at the presentation of the Stewart Parker Trust Awards in 2009:

> Stewart refused to adapt himself comfortably to the tribalism, to choose as Seamus Heaney has put it, 'one or other Ulster of the mind'. Instead he chose to introduce us to the deliberate 'misremembering of history', the ransacking of the past for reasons to continue to hate in the present and the wasted opportunities of that bleak landscape. Breaking open the hermetic seal on those jealously guarded histories was a courageous and necessary pathway to the reconciliation and peace that are still being constructed.[52]

Parker's hopes for reconciliation go beyond the uneasy peace the North has enjoyed after the Good Friday Agreement[53] 'and, as such, despite the apparent achievement of what he imagined, he can still challenge our complacency. There is more to peace, Stewart Parker tells us, than mere tolerance.'[54]

Multiplying dualities, Christian imagery, ghosts, 'wrestling with the past', in an innovative, experimental theatre, Stewart Parker's short twelve-year career on the stage, a cycle begun with *Spokesong* and 'completed with *Pentecost*',[55] constitutes an astonishing body of work, prescient and stimulating.

Primary Sources

Works by Stewart Parker

Dramatis Personae and Other Writings [edited by Gerald Dawe, Maria Johnston and Clare Wallace] (Prague: Litteraria Pragensia, 2008).

Kingdom Come [unpublished].

Paddy Dies (Kilcar: Summer Palace Press, 2004).

Plays: 1 [*Spokesong, Catchpenny Twist, Nightshade, Pratt's Fall*] (London: Methuen, 2000).

Plays: 2 [*Northern Star, Heavenly Bodies, Pentecost*] (London: Methuen, 2000).

Secondary Sources

Akenson, Don, *If the Irish Ran the World: Montserrat, 1630–1730* (Liverpool: Liverpool UP, 1997).

Anderson, Don, *14 May Days: The Inside Story of the Loyalist Strike of 1974* (Dublin: Gill & Macmillan, 1994).

Anon., 'On yer bike' [editorial], *Irish Times*, 12 September 2009.

Anon., 'Stewart Parker' [obituary], *Irish Times*, 3 November 1988.

Bort, Eberhard, 'Staging the Troubles: Civic Conflict and Drama in Northern Ireland', *Journal for the Study of British Cultures*, Vol. 2, No. 2 (1995), pp. 141–60.

—, 'Commemorating Ireland: Towards an Inclusive Culture of Commemoration? An Introduction', in Eberhard Bort (ed.), *Commemorating Ireland: History, Politics, Culture* (Dublin: Irish Academic Press, 2004), pp. 1–11.

—, 'Ireland', in Lars Eckstein (ed.), *English Literatures Across the Globe: A Companion* (München: Wilhelm Fink Verlag/UTB, 2007), pp. 328–52.

Brown, Terence, 'Awakening from the Nightmare of History: History and Contemporary Literature', in Terence Brown, *Ireland's Literature: Collected Essays* (Mullingar: Lilliput Press, 1988), pp. 243–56.

—, 'Let's Go to Graceland: The Drama of Stewart Parker', in Nicholas Allen and Aaron Kelly (eds), *The Cities of Belfast* (Dublin: Four Courts Press, 2003), pp. 117–26.

Coyle, Jane, 'Northern Star is Born in Belfast', *Irish News*, 15 November 1984.

—, 'Return of the United Irishmen', *Irish Times*, 7 November 1998.

—, 'Spokesong', *The Stage*, 7 May 2008.

Cropper, Martin, 'Heavenly Bodies', *The Times*, 24 April 1986.

Dawe, Gerald, 'A Hard Act: Stewart Parker's *Pentecost*', in Eberhard Bort (ed.), *The State of Play: Irish Theatre in the 'Nineties* (Trier: Wissenschaftlicher Verlag Trier, 1996), pp. 65–74.

—, *The Rest is History* (Newry: Abbey Press, 1998).

—, 'Stewart Parker in His Own Write', *Irish Times*, 28 November 2008.

Deacon, Nigel, *Stewart Parker Radio Plays* <http://web.ukonline.co.uk/suttonelms /sparker.html>.

Etherton, Michael, *Contemporary Irish Dramatists* (Basingstoke: Macmillan, 1989).

Gibbons, Luke and Kevin Whelan, 'In Conversation with Stephen Rea, 2 February 2001, Yale University', *Yale Journal of Criticism*, Vol. 15, No. 1 (2002), pp. 5–19.

Grene, Nicholas, *The Politics of Irish Drama* (Cambridge: Cambridge UP, 1999).

Harris, Claudia, 'Stewart Parker's Reinventing Theatre', in Eberhard Bort (ed.), *'Standing in Their Shifts Itself . . .': Irish Drama from Farquhar to Friel* (Bremen: European Society for Irish Studies, 1993), pp. 281–93.

Hobsbaum, Philip, 'Parker, (James) Stewart', in *Oxford Dictionary of National Biography (1984)*, <http://www.oxforddnb.com/view/ article/62957>.

—, 'The Belfast Group: A Recollection', *Éire-Ireland*, Vol. 32, No. 2/3 (1997), pp. 173–82.

Itzin, Catherine, 'Three New Plays', *Plays and Players*, Vol. 24, No. 3 (1976), pp. 32–3.

Kennedy-Andrews, Elmer, 'The Power of Play: Stewart Parker's Theatre', *Theatre Ireland*, Vol. 18 (1989), p. 24.

—, 'The Will to Freedom: Politics in the Theatre of Stewart Parker,' In Okifumi Komesu and Masaru Sekine (eds), *Irish Writers and Politics* (Gerrards Cross: Colin Smythe, 1990), pp. 237–69.

Lewis, David, 'Theatre Review: Spokesong/Pentecost' (2008) <www.culturenorthern ireland.org/article.aspx?art_id=215>.

Llewellyn-Jones, Margaret, *Contemporary Irish Drama and Cultural Identity* (Bristol: Intellect, 2002).

Maguire, Tom, *Making Theatre in Northern Ireland: Through and Beyond the Troubles* (Exeter: University of Exeter Press, 2006).

McAleese, Mary, 'Remarks by President McAleese at Stewart Parker Trust 20th Anniversary Award Ceremony, 20th April 2009' <www.president.ie/index.php?section=5&speech =640&lang=eng>.

McFadden, Grania, 'Feast of Parker to be Swerved on a Plath', *Belfast Telegraph*, 11 April 2008.

McKenna, Bernard, *Rupture, Representation, and the Refashioning of Identity in Drama from the North of Ireland, 1969–1994* (Westport, CT: Praeger, 2003).

McKittrick, David, 'The Enduring Scar of Sectarianism', *Independent*, 14 September 2009.

Meany, Helen, 'Spokesong', *Guardian*, 3 May 2008.

Murray, Christopher, *Twentieth-Century Irish Drama: Mirror up to Nation* (Manchester: Manchester UP, 1997).

Nowlan, David, 'Northern Star', *Irish Times*, 28 September 1985.

O'Brien, Conor Cruise, 'A Song of Disembafflement', *Observer*, 29 January 1978.

O'Riordan, Alan, '. . . the playwright who dared to be optimistic', *Irish Independent*, 10 May 2008.

Parker, Lynne , 'Introduction', in Stewart Parker, *Plays: 1 [Spokesong, Catchpenny Twist, Nightshade, Pratt's Fall]* (London: Methuen, 2000), pp. ix–xvii.

—, 'Catchpenny Twist – Programme Note' (Rough Magic, 2008) <www.culturenorthern ireland.org/article.aspx?art_id=2332>.

Parker, Stewart, Dramatis Personae: A John Malone Memorial Lecture (Belfast: Queen's University, 1986).

—, 'State of Play', Canadian Journal of Irish Studies, Vol. 7, No. 1 (1981), pp. 5–11.

—, 'Signposts', Theatre Ireland, 11 October 1985, pp. 27–29.

Parkin, Andrew, 'Metaphor as Dramatic Structure in Some Plays of Stewart Parker', in Masaru Sekine (ed.), Irish Writers and the Theatre (Gerrards Cross: Colin Smythe, 1986), pp. 135–50.

Paseta, Senia, Modern Ireland: A Very Short Introduction (Oxford: Oxford UP, 2003).

Patterson, Glenn, 'The Bard of Belfast', Guardian, 13 June 2008.

Phelan, Mark, 'Northern Star – Programme Note' (2008), <www.culturenorther nireland.org/article.aspx?art_id=2331>.

Rea, Stephen, 'Introduction', in Stewart Parker, Plays: 2 [Northern Star, Heavenly Bodies, Pentecost] (London: Methuen, 2000), pp. ix–xii.

Richards, Shaun, 'To Bind the Northern to the Southern Stars: Field Day in Derry and Dublin', in Claire Connolly (ed.), Theorizing Ireland (Basingstoke: Palgrave Macmillan, 2003), pp. 61–8.

Richtarik, Marilynn, 'Across the Water: Northern Irish Drama in London', The South Carolina Review, Vol. 33 No. 2 (2001), pp. 121–27.

—, 'Living in Interesting Times: Stewart Parker's Northern Star', in John P. Harrington and Elizabeth Mitchell (eds), Politics and Performance in Contemporary Northern Ireland. (Amherst: University of Massachusetts Press, 1999), pp. 7–28.

—, 'Stewart Parker at Queen's University Belfast', Irish Review, Vol. 29 (2002), pp. 58–69.

—, 'The Field Day Theatre Company', in Shaun Richards (ed.), The Cambridge Companion to Twentieth-Century Irish Drama (Cambridge: Cambridge UP, 2004), pp. 191–203.

Roche, Anthony, Contemporary Irish Drama (Dublin: Gill & Macmillan, 1994).

Rothstein, Mervyn, 'Stewart Parker, 47, a Playwright on Irish Troubles, Dies in London', New York Times, 4 November 1988.

Russell, Richard Rankin, 'Playing and Singing Toward Devolution: Stewart Parker's Ethical Aesthetics in Kingdom Come and Northern Star,' Irish University Review, Vol. 37, No. 2 (2007), pp. 366–94.

—, 'Exorcising the Ghosts of Conflict in Northern Ireland: Stewart Parker's The Iceberg and Pentecost', Éire-Ireland, Vol. 43, No. 3/4 (2007), pp. 42–58.

Satake, Akiko, 'The Seven Ages of Harry Joy McCracken: Stewart Parker's Northern Star as a History Play of the United Irishmen in 1798', in Eamonn Jordan (ed.), Theatre Stuff: Critical Essays on Contemporary Irish Theatre (Dublin: Carysfort Press, 2000), pp. 176–186.

Strain, Arthur, 'City on Threshold of Theatre Rebirth', BBC News online, 10 September 2009 <http://news.bbc.co.uk/1/hi/northern_ireland/8249027.stm>.

Walsh, Caroline, 'Loose Leaves', Irish Times, 31 May 2008.

Watt, Stephen, 'Late Nineteenth-Century Irish Theatre: Before the Abbey – and Beyond', in Shaun Richards (ed.), *The Cambridge Companion to Twentieth-Century Irish Drama* (Cambridge: Cambridge UP, 2004, pp. 18–32.)

Welch, Robert, The Abbey Theatre, 1899–1999; Farm and Pressure (Oxford: Oxford UP, 1999).

Notes

1. Mervyn Rothstein, 'Stewart Parker, 47, a Playwright on Irish Troubles, Dies in London'.
2. Stewart Parker, 'State of Play', p. 9.
3. Nigel Deacon, *Stewart Parker Radio Plays*.
4. See Parker's poem 'The Casualty Meditates upon His Journey' in Stewart Parker, *Paddy Dies*, p. 27.
5. See Marilynn Richtarik, 'Stewart Parker at Queen's University Belfast' and Philip Hobsbaum, 'The Belfast Group: A Recollection'.
6. See Richard Rankin Russell, 'Exorcising the Ghosts of Conflict in Northern Ireland'.
7. Gerald Dawe, 'Stewart Parker in His Own Write'.
8. Anon., 'Stewart Parker'.

9. Alan O'Riordan, '. . . the playwright who dared to be optimistic'.
10. Glen Patterson, 'The Bard of Belfast'.
11. Catherine Itzin, 'Three New Plays'.
12. Patterson, op. cit.
13. Helen Meany, 'Spokesong'.
14. David Lewis, 'Theatre Review: Spokesong/Pentecost'.
15. Jane Coyle, 'Spokesong'.
16. Lynne Parker, '*Catchpenny Twist* – Programme Note'.
17. Philip Hobsbaum, 'The Belfast Group: A Recollection'.
18. Coyle, 'Spokesong'.
19. Andrew Parkin, 'Metaphor as Dramatic Structure'.
20. Robert Welch, *The Abbey Theatre*, p. 206.
21. Richard Rankin Russell, 'Playing and Singing'.
22. See Robert Akenson, *If the Irish Ran the World*, p. 175 and Eberhard Bort, 'Ireland', p. 347.
23. See Marilynn Richtarik, 'Across the Water', p. 123.
24. Conor Cruise O'Brien, 'A Song of Disembafflement'.
25. Lynne Parker, 'Introduction', p. xii.
26. Elmer Kennedy-Andrews, 'The Will to Freedom', p. 247.
27. Lynne Parker, 'Introduction', p. xvi.

28. See Ibid. pp. x–xi.
29. Mark Phelan, '*Northern Star* – Programme Note'.
30. Jacques in Shakespeare's *As You Like It*: 'one man in his time plays many parts/ His acts being seven ages'.
31. Phelan, op. cit.
32. Nicholas Grene, *The Politics of Irish Drama*, p. 167.
33. Phelan, op. cit.
34. See Don Anderson, *14 May Days.*
35. Marilynn Richtarik, 'The Field Day Theatre Company', p. 199.
36. Gerald Dawe, 'A Hard Act', p. 71.
37. Christopher Murray, *Twentieth-Century Irish Drama*, p. 220.
38. Stewart Parker, *Dramatis Personae*, p. 20.
39. Anthony Roche, Contemparary Irish Drama, p. 228.
40. Dawe, 'A Hard Act', p. 65.
41. Stewart Parker, *Dramatis Personae*, pp. 18–19.
42. Ibid., p. 9.
43. Ibid, p. 8.
44. Grania McFadden, 'Feast of Parker to be Swerved on a Plath'.
45. See Terence Brown, 'Let's Go to Graceland'.
46. Elmer Kennedy-Andrews, 'The Will to Freedom', pp. 241–2.
47. See Michael Etherton, *Contemporary Irish Dramatists*, pp. 21–2.
48. See Kennedy-Andrews, 'The Will to Freedom', p. 249.
49. Stewart Parker, *Plays: 2*, p. xiii.
50. See Eberhard Bort, 'Commemorating Ireland', pp. 9–10.
51. See Terence Brown, 'Awakening from the Nightmare of History', p. 248.
52. Mary McAleese, 'Remarks by President McAleese'.
53. Even by 2009, more than ten years after the Good Friday Agreement, there were 1,500 sectarian incidents recorded annually in Northern Ireland (see David McKittrick, 'The Enduring Scar of Sectarianism'). 'The province needs more than just a political settlement,' argued an *Independent* editorial (14 September 2009).
54. O'Riordan, op. cit.
55. Lynne Parker, 'Introduction', p. x.

22 CHRISTINA REID

Christian Große

*Tea in a China Cup; Did You Hear the One about the Irishman?;
Joyriders; The Last of a Dyin' Race; My Name? Shall I Tell You My
Name?; The Belle of the Belfast City; Clowns*

Introduction

Along with Anne Devlin and the Charabanc Theatre Group,
Christina Reid belongs to the small but important group of Northern
Irish female dramatists.[1] Born in 1942 into a Protestant working-
class family in the Ardoyne in north Belfast, she was brought up to
distinguish between the 'acceptable' Protestant poverty and
'unacceptable' Catholic poverty and thus learned about the difference
between 'them' and 'us'.[2] Her family was politically utterly unionist;
her father was even head of an Orange lodge. Her mother's parents
lived in the other part of the city and Christina, together with her
mother, spent a lot of time there: her grandmother's house was the
location for many family parties, and it was the experience of these
meetings which influenced her in a positive way. The meetings
showed the Irish roots of the family: Christina's relatives told
beautiful stories – and thus fulfilled the true task of a '*sanchaí*' – and
provided them with a theatrical background, i.e. little performances
shown in the living room. These stories and performances stimulated
an interest in a mixture of 'local gossip, Irish folklore, and the
Hollywood movies'.[3] Other events which helped her develop further
interest in the dramatic world were the numerous shows in the Group
Theatre Belfast and the Opera House she attended together with her
mother, a ballet aficionado. The third childhood development which
finally led to her writing plays was a present from her family: as an
eleven-year-old girl, she was given a five-year diary and soon realised

that the most exciting stories were not those she experienced but the ones she made up around real events. A thematic source for her subsequent dramatic career was found in her numerous women-centred experiences during her childhood: the time she lived with her mother and grandmother was supplemented by her spending her holidays in Donaghadee with her aunts and cousins, where the men arrived only at the weekends.[4]

These numerous stimulating experiences notwithstanding, it was not until she was almost forty that Reid started her career as a professional dramatist. The reasons for this are manifold: despite her open mind and keen observational powers, she left school very early and started work in several jobs, including in a soft drink company, in the clothing business and public service. The working-class ethos of her family, which left little time for pleasure, further prevented her from starting to write earlier. She married young, had three daughters and thus concentrated on her life as housewife and mother. Around her mid-thirties, however, she returned to school, did her O- and A-levels and started a degree in English, Sociology and Russian Studies at Queen's University in London.[5] She did not finish this academic career, because during her education she continued writing and started to work for the Lyric Theatre; her university status thus served as a springboard: for the season 1983/84, she obtained the position of writer-in-residence at the Lyric and her first major play, *Tea in a China Cup*, which she co-directed, was premiered that year. From that time onwards, she could afford to dedicate herself to a full-time life as an author, since she was sponsored by Thames TV. This was indeed a decisive moment in her life because she was the only woman at the theatre at the time. Another famous Irish theatre, the Abbey in Dublin, staged only one play by a female author on the main stage between 1984 and 1989.[6] None of Reid's plays has been performed at a major house in the Republic to this day. In 1987, she moved to London with her daughters and in 1988, she became writer-in-residence at the Young Vic; there she premiered *My Name? Shall I Tell You My Name?* (1987) and a play for children, *Lords, Dukes and Earls* (1989). Apart from her work for the stage, she also writes for radio and television: *The Last of a Dyin' Race* and *My Name? Shall I Tell You My*

Name? were presented as BBC radio plays.[7] She has also adapted novels by Victor Hugo for the stage.

Asked about two important aspects in her life, her reasons for writing literature and her attitude towards Belfast, she gives two answers which could serve as a kind of paradigm for her work and career: her mother, before her early death at the age of fifty-eight, told her daughter not to forget the old stories and to tell them to her children, a request Reid has followed up to the present day; furthermore, while she actually lives in England, in her mind she lives in Belfast and London at the same time, torn between two cultures, which equally inspire and motivate her and which have proved to be equally important for her literary career.[8]

The Plays

Tea in a China Cup (1983)

Christina Reid's first major success is her play *Tea in a China Cup*. Many characteristic features of her later work can already be observed in this play.

She portrays three generations of Northern Irish Protestant female characters whose lives are formed either by the legacy or direct experience of wartime: Maisie, aunt and great-aunt; Grandmother, sister to Maisie and mother of Sarah; Sarah herself and her daughter Beth represent women who all went through or heard of the loss of men of their family in the First and Second World War, and throughout the Troubles they again need to defend their lives and possessions. The play uses the period of time between 1939 and 1972 as a frame, and illustrates the longevity of 'assumptions and stereotypes that keep Protestants and Catholics apart in Ireland even as their economic plight would logically seem to be the thing that should bring them together'.[9] Two central clichés are handed on from one generation to the next: the first is the seeming necessity to defend Protestantism, which is seen as clean and straightforward, against Catholicism, which is regarded as dirty and clumsy; one sign of this difference is the separation of Catholics and Protestants even in the cemetery of Belfast, as Beth discovers (pp. 6–7). This is also the reason why Maisie and Sarah are so proud of their set of china cups, which serves as a symbol of culture to them, and why they always try to keep up appearances, no matter how difficult circumstances really are. The second pillar of their ideology is the defence of Ulster as part of the English nation: in order to show the loyalty of the family, they have been sending family members – Grandfather in the oldest generation, Samuel in the Second World War, Sammy in the third generation as a member of the British Army – to fight for England, the assumed protective power of Ulster. Grandfather puts up three pictures showing the named characters, and he 'looks at the three photos with pride' (p. 43).

An interesting point regarding the interpretation of the play is made by Joanna Luft, when she states:

> She [Reid] demonstrates that the domestic sphere of the female characters parallels that of the Orange Order and is steeped in as much of the Irish Protestant politics of the day as is the official organization. [. . .] Reid investigates the gendered aspect of Northern Irish socializing processes and reveals how the perpetuation of social and political systems arises and is maintained in the private, traditionally female sphere of the house.[10]

Both institutions, the family – mainly dominated by women – and the political Protestant organisations, mainly male, follow the same goal and promote the stability of Ulster by making good Protestants out of their children. Examples of the parallelism between the two systems can be found in many places: at the beginning, Beth's offering of tea to her mother is accompanied by music of the Orange Order, the beginning of the second act is very similar, and the very end of the play mentions 'icons of "fine bone china and the Orangemen"'.[11] The tea-cup conversations influence the children inasmuch as they confront them with differences in behaviour between the two Christian confessions and promote Protestant dignity, pride and self-esteem, so that

Protestants are presented as the better part of mankind. Aspects not fitting this image, such as an adequate sexual education or female emancipation, are glossed over or explained misleadingly; this is the reason why Beth and Theresa marry the wrong husbands, fail in their marriages and discover themselves only later. Consquently, it is not only the traditional male discourse that is criticised by Reid but the female discourse as well:

> Through a gestic feminist criticism [the china tea cup set], Reid makes visible the extent to which domestic discourse is not private, but participates in and supports a political discourse of hostile oppositionality that secures [. . .] a conformity to a network of traditional values that sustain the practices of sectarian violence and gendered imbalances of power.[12]

Did You Hear the One About the Irishman? (1984)

'When an Irish person tells Irish jokes it's funny. If someone else does it, it is offensive.'[13] If stereotypes and traditional clichés about the Irish served as a part of the Protestant identity in *Tea in a China Cup*, they are examined more closely in *Did You Hear the One About the Irishman?*. At the centre of the play are Allison Clarke, a twenty-five-year-old Protestant woman, and Brian Rafferty, a twenty-nine-year-old working-class Catholic; both of them are in Long Kesh Prison in Belfast, according to Brian the only place – given the circumstances of Northern Ireland in 1987 – to bring the warring groups together on common ground, even if Protestants and Catholics are separated. The Romeo-and-Juliet-like couple try to come together by concentrating on the similarities of the two confessions, but their violence-soaked surroundings prevent them from fulfilling their conciliatory plans: both are killed at the end of the play by 'hands of their "tribes"'.[14] First produced on stage in 1985, this play won the Ulster Television Drama Award 1980, which made the Lyric Theatre aware of Christina Reid in the first place and thus laid one of the central foundation stones of her career. Even more than the previous play, this drama is a tightrope walk between comedy and tragedy: on the one hand, the comedian, who serves as an epic character in the play and 'tells jokes directly to the audience as if he is performing in a club' (p. 69), shows the absurdity of the persisting Irish conflict and tries to stimulate a more relaxed atmosphere; on the other hand, his ethnic jokes lead to anger and violence and thus the killing of the two protagonists:

> Their annihilation is a gesture on the part of those whose existence is verified by a continuation of the sectarian dispute. The play's parallel structure – scenes with the Catholic Raffertys following those with the Protestant Clarkes – [. . .] comment on a crisis numerous factions have an interest in maintaining.[15]

The prejudices and clichés on which the jokes are based are so much present in everyday Ireland that the danger of confusing them with reality is only too prevalent. Another example of this irrational atmosphere is provided by Allison's mother, who has objections towards Brian because he is a Catholic criminal but who does not mind Protestant terrorists (p. 75). Even though the play ends the same way as it started, the message is quite clear: 'The play leaves us with the same ethnic jokes with which it began but ultimately serves to show how such degrading humor leads to anger and ultimately to violence.'[16] The audience keeps the strong image of the comedian in mind, who cracks one joke too many about the Irish, which makes the Irishman believe he has to turn to the gun in order to gain more respect.[17]

Joyriders (1986)

Joyriders is one of Reid's most positively reviewed plays: it premiered in 1986 and toured several houses in England and Northern Ireland. According to McDonough the drama is striking in its social realism, as it presents the audience with a fictitious reality quite close to social reality.[18]

The play involves four Belfast youths with working-class backgrounds; all of them are on a training scheme to prevent them from becoming (more) violent members of society, a programme which is, even according to social worker Kate (an 'incurable optimist – p. 123 – and 'a shadow of a socialist' – p. 132), totally inadequate given the difficult circumstances of joblessness and poverty in which it takes place. The play investigates the reinforcement of political violence by the social violence of bad education and consequent bad job prospects. Each of the four youths is marked by the gloomy surroundings: Maureen is a girl of about sixteen, who grew up largely without parents and is deeply worried about her brother Johnnie, a joyrider and glue-sniffer (p. 101); she herself has no police record and feels quite comfortable in the programme. Arthur was accidentally shot by the British Army and the signs of this incident are still visible: his head is shaven, his face full of scars and he limps (p. 101); his past was quite violent but he wants to stop risking more crimes. Tommy also commits minor crimes but is more reflective than the others: he knows about his social status and neither supports the programme nor objects to it. Sandra is a bit blunted by this bad environment: she no longer reflects upon the reasons why people are killed in Northern Ireland, she just takes it as a fact (p. 118); furthermore, her language shows clear signs of brutalism. The only thing she is sure about is the fact that she does not have any prospects but will be caught by somebody in the end.

So, despite these characters representing a large part of contemporary Northern Irish youth, they are drawn as individuals and thus elicit a high degree of emotional identification from the audience. One trait of their characters will remain in the audience's mind: resilience. Maureen, whose biggest desire it is to find a job and live a life without poverty, and Arthur, who is constantly reasoning with Kate (p. 124f.), never lose hope completely, and all of them try to act as grown-ups with a vitality and humour which seem to serve as a kind of survival strategy.

A second pillar of the play's content is the imbalance of police control in the Northern Irish capital: joyriders are not only arrested but shot by the police, while the real danger of political or terrorist violence is not adequately checked. Criminals are executed, but the underlying causes of their illegal behaviour persist. This is the real tragedy of the play, because Maureen incidentally falls victim to a shooting by the British Army, and the baby in her womb, a possible hope for the future, is killed as well; it was not she who was targeted, she is an innocent victim.

The Last of a Dyin' Race (1986)

The Last of a Dyin' Race was originally written for the radio and later transferred to television. The play again presents a multi-generational view of a family, from the grandmother down to the grandchildren.

At the beginning of the play, Lizzie McCullough, mother of Joe and half-sister to Agnes, dies. As Joe is next of kin to her, he – or rather his more than dominant wife Sharon – organises the burial preparations. Sharon completely ignores the usual Irish tradition of honouring the deceased 'right and proper' (p. 49), which infuriates almost all of the rest of the family. Agnes, the half-sister, is not informed about the death of Elizabeth, but finds out about it, nevertheless. She, together with Sarah and Johnnie, starts a wake and takes possession of the undertaker's house to do so. Meanwhile, Sharon cleans up Lizzie's house, throwing away almost everything, as things from the past mean nothing to her: 'Your mother lived in the past. They all do around here' (p. 56). The conflict between the two parts of the family escalates as Agnes finds out that Joe and Sharon have given Lizzie's house back to the landlord: Agnes predicts that Lizzie's ghost will follow Sharon for ever in her life, a prophecy that seems to come true, at least inasmuch as Sharon suffers an emotional collapse before the burial when the hearse breaks down. As in so many other plays, the men do not come off well: Joe is too weak to assert himself over his wife, Agnes's father was never sober in his life and died drunk in a bar, and Sarah's husband Johnnie is accused thus by his son: 'Yer always promisin' my mother' (p. 54).

The central topic of the play is the importance of traditions – they unite the family – but also the necessity to overcome these traditions in order to experience a better future. When Dave sees the wake in the undertaker's house, he refers to the group as 'The Last of a Dyin' Race' (p. 57): the women around Agnes and Sarah want to keep up tradition and take the initiative of reinstituting the wake; the men participate in it quite voluntarily, it is Sharon who wants to put an end to being governed by the past. Even if her way of dealing with the death of a family member is too brutal for many of the play's characters, she none the less wants to rid herself of the past and feel free from its bonds.

My Name? Shall I Tell You My Name? (1989)

Originally performed as a radio play in 1987, *My Name? Shall I Tell You My Name?* was first put on stage in 1989 at the Dublin Theatre Festival. It is a deeply historical play, confronting the Troubles as a contemporary, postmodern phenomenon together with the cultural problems resulting from past wars and the confrontations underlying them. The starting point of the action is Ulster in the 1980s, but the play also refers to other places and periods: first, there is Andy, a ninety-five-year-old veteran of the First World War who survived the Battle of the Somme and now celebrates the seventieth anniversary of that event in a home for old people; he was a member of the Protestant paramilitary UDF, fought against the Anglo-Irish Agreement and for the separation of Northern Ireland from the Republic. His grand-daughter Andrea is in prison because she took part in a peace demonstration and remembers the 1960s, when Andy wanted to bring her up as a good Protestant girl and imbued her with his very traditional and patriarchal ideologies. As isolated as they are onstage, they do not share any values: Andrea tries to come to terms with her own and her grandfather's past and arrive at a reconciliation between the two. The interfigural conflict between the loyalty towards her family and her intention of not being overcome by the ideologies of the past cannot be resolved: grandfather and granddaughter stand opposite each other at the end of the play. It is memory of the past which holds Ireland back; the play illuminates a so-far marginalised position: that it is the conflicting memories of the First World War which, in part, led to the outbreak of the Troubles.

The play thus confronts audiences not only with the phenomenon of confessionalism and its resulting problems, but also with the question of gender. As Carla McDonough points out, Christina Reid, as well as Frank McGuinness, 'voiced marginalized attitudes not usually considered as relevant in historical narratives of "The Troubles".[19] According to her, it is the representations of the militancy inherited from the First World War, along with other kinds of cultural problems, which are the focus of this play.[20] Andy believes in the 'dominant ethic of male self-sacrifice'[21] and wanted to bring up Andrea according to his ideals of a traditional Irish woman; thus, it becomes obvious that the Troubles are not caused only by the conflict between the two confessions but also by a gendered ideology dictating what one should believe in.

The Belle of Belfast City (1989)

Just like *Tea in a China Cup*, *The Belle of Belfast City* is an extension of the traditional family play, portraying more than one generation. Christina Reid won the George Devine Award for this play.

Compared with *Tea in a China Cup*, *The Belle of Belfast City* takes a more complex and detailed look at the connection between tradition and change: the three generations of women represent three different attitudes towards this subject. Dolly, the seventy-seven-year-old mother of Vi and Rose, led a relatively unusual life for a woman, in the circumstances: according to her own statements she has never been a housewife, she was a music hall star, and she gave birth to Rose twenty-one years after Vi – which means that she was sexually active at an age normally considered unacceptable. Thus, Dolly is an advanced woman who paid little attention to traditional restrictions. The second generation is represented by her daughters Vi and Rose: the latter shares unconventional attitudes with her mother, having left Ireland to become a photographer and have a love affair with a black Baptist, the result of which is her illegitimate daughter Belle. Vi, much more than her sister, puts the family at the top of all her interests and wants to hold it together; furthermore, she is a unionist and opposes the Anglo-Irish Agreement because she thinks it gives too much power to the Catholics. Nevertheless, she turns out to be a person of moral integrity as she refuses to take part in the Protestant demonstrations following the Agreement and defends Belle against Jack's and Tom's racist behaviour towards her. Belle, then, is the third generation shown in the play: at the beginning, she is brought to Belfast for the first time in her life, which allows the spectator to see the abnormal and absurd situation in the capital, regarded as unremakable by the other characters, through her eyes. Belle is a very curious person and has a strong relationship to Dolly; she is full of self-confidence and enjoys life.[22]

The family panorama is completed by Dolly's nephew Jack, who – according to Rose – is 'well connected with the Protestant para-militaries here, and other right-wing organizations in the United Kingdom' (p. 199). Thus, he provides a sharp contrast to the almost apolitical Dolly, who has never put any importance on religion or nationality per se. His sister Janet, however, tries to overcome the barrier between the two confessions and marries a Catholic member of the almost all-Protestant RUC, Peter; after living in a celibate relationship for more than ten years, she goes to England, has a love affair and returns to her home country completely changed. She manages to separate from her husband and her brother and thus rejects the part she is expected to play according to Irish tradition; she is no longer wife and sister, but a woman in her own right: 'I'm tired of being the sister of a devil and the wife of a saint' (p. 189). Just as in *My Name*, it becomes obvious that patriarchy and male tradition are as much a reason for the Troubles as the conflict between the confessions. Janet's separation from her brother Jack is also a sign that there are tensions within the Protestant community; the confessional conflict is not only one between Catholics and Protestants. Janet is an example of the younger generation for whom history and family are still important but who tries to find new definitions for herself; she attempts to strike a balance between the past and the present and is willing to change in hope of a better future. Even if she is the only dynamic character in the play, she shares one trait with her more or less progressive female companions: 'Fanaticism, whether religious or political, is ultimately under attack in this play, which shows the women (sisters, daughters, mothers) working toward compromise and compassion above all else.'[23] The end of the play leaves the audience with a strong message, a message which calls for new ways of finding an Irish identity:

A song protesting Belfast sectarianism sung by a body with both Irish and African-American identity markers becomes a Brechtian gestus, a call to the audience to think critically about the historical conditions which have led to the constructions of identities in Ireland and around the world.[24]

Clowns (1996)

Clowns was written as a sequel to *Joyriders* and was performed in Richmond in 1996. Set in the same location as its predecessor, it features the same characters eight years later, the year of the IRA ceasefire. The central topic of the play is the difficulty of getting along with the peace process, a novel phenomenon for the Irish.

Sandra is the central character of the play. After Maureen's death in *Joyriders*, she leaves Belfast for England. This change of country does not, however, mean a change of the situation: the social and political surroundings in England are much more peaceful compared to what she has been used to in Belfast, but she cannot come to terms with her own, individual peace process. She keeps looking back, she can't forget what has happened to her in her life and so she contemplates revenge. She uses Maureen as a mask and plays her part on the English stage; in doing so, she confronts the Irish problem in general and Maureen's death in particular as a consequence of this problem; she needs the mask as protection against a history and reality too cruel for her. At the end, the imagined Maureen, Sandra's alter ego, forces her to give up the second identity and thus to stop dealing with the past and start welcoming the present. The problem of overcoming the past is thus again presented as a prerequisite for a better future. With this experience in her mind, she returns to Belfast, but it remains unclear whether she is suited for the new way of living.

Summary

Christina Reid's dramatic oeuvre is characterised by a number of constantly reappearing elements. A central topic is the omnipresence of the past. In each of her plays, characters are confronted with either the familial, national, religious or regional past: Reid's plays share this characteristic with those of many other contemporary and older dramatists and she goes back to the seventeenth century (1689 and the siege of Derry in *My Name? Shall I Tell You My Name?*) to explain the present situation. Esther Sullivan, in her essay on *Did You Hear the One About the Irishman?*, refers to just this aspect, which can be extended to all her plays:

> Whether in tragedy or comedy, *Did You Hear the One About the Irishman?* dramatically emphasizes the impossibility of referring to Ireland, Northern Ireland, Ulster, the South, the Free State, the Six Counties [. . .] without re-presenting the history, or histories, that have produced this 'situation'.[25]

This orientation to the past is the source of many conflicts because it leads to fanaticism and a distorted view of the present; as can be shown from the example of *Tea in a China Cup*, it is not only the male but also the female tradition which prevents Ireland from having a better future. But Reid presents a number of characters who try to come to terms with tradition and the past in order to find a way to a better future. No matter whether it is the couple in *Did You Hear the One About the Irishman?*; Andrea in *My Name? Shall I Tell You My Name?*, who still loves her grandfather, even if she does not share his values; Janet in *The Belle of Belfast City*; or Beth in *Tea in a China Cup*, who has a Catholic friend and who sells her husband's house at the end in order to move beyond the traditional ways,[26] Reid demonstrates that it is always the dynamic characters who manage to find a compromise in otherwise static surroundings.

In contrast to this, the male characters do not manage to find this compromise: Andy in *My Name? Shall I Tell You My Name?* or Jack in *The Belle of Belfast City* are perfect examples of the way men depend on the traditional concepts women try to overcome:

> The Irish male's obsession with history has given him a place to stand, a fortress of certainty: the stories of heroes, warriors,

and saints have created a sacred space in the world where men could feel free of the humiliations and trivialities of daily life imposed by their own or a conquering race or by the weight of economic necessity.[27]

The dynamic characters in Reid's plays are, in contrast to the majority of Irish plays to date, usually women, and the focus of the plays is always on women. This is no coincidence, as becomes obvious in a statement by Christina Reid herself: 'The majority of playwrights are men, and women in their plays tend to be presented only in relationship to one man; they are not explored in depth.'[28]

In all of Reid's plays it is the women who openly present their perspective on the situation in their home country, and thus she gives voice to a hitherto mute group. With reference to Gayatri Spivak, letting women talk about their experiences in Ireland is in accordance with the speaking of the subaltern as is demanded in post-colonial discourse. Reid presents a 'gendering of political discourse'[29] and thus fulfils an important task of the theatre, i.e. a complete cultural and national self-examination of the Irish situation, by adding a 'matrilineal narrative'[30] to the traditional patrilineal one. Moreover, by putting women at the centre of her plays, Christina Reid undermines a traditional trope of Irish realism, the so-called 'family memory play': instead of a male protagonist, who tells the audience about his childhood memories and thus assigns only a supportive part to the marginalised women, '[. . .] these dramas reflect how Carr and Reid have mastered a prominent dramatic form only to subvert it in ways that reveal Irish women's perspectives in contemporary Ireland'.[31] Many critics see in just this combination of traditional form and new content the reason for the success of her plays.

A third pillar of the content of Reid's plays is the mixture of the private and political spheres. In Northern Ireland, with its precarious situation, every action, even a seemingly private one such as the selection of a partner for marriage, is political, and public conflicts are often dealt with at home. Esther Sullivan quotes D. E. S. Maxwell on this aspect:

Maxwell [. . .] mentions [. . .] Reid and Charabanc as having produced 'plays where the brutalities of the warring factions are not directly the issue, [but] their assumptions pervade the daily run of domestic and social discourse'.[32]

The thesis of the mixture is also relevant to another aspect of Reid's art: the women try to get along with the economic difficulties and prejudices created or kept alive by the troubled situation. Thus, politics is not only important in terms of official ideology but also influences everyday life, and the change in perspective, the focus on the domestic sphere, shows that women are equally affected by a traditionally male agenda. The concentration on the domestic sphere leads to a devaluation of 'big history', which is presented only via its effects on the situation of the individual character; this, however, does not mean that history is unimportant, because Reid's plays are unthinkable without this background.

A problem connected with the aspects just mentioned is the question of identity. The change in focus from the male to the female sphere and the representation of the difficulties of women in coming to terms with a politically and socially patriarchicalised discourse mean that traditional female identity is called into question. This is, however, a positive aspect because some of the female characters loosen the bonds consequent upon being just mothers, sisters, wives, i.e. of being defined by their relationship to men, and thus lay the foundations for being just themselves. Sullivan also points out this aspect with reference not only to Reid's work:

[. . .] Northern dramatists such as Anne Devlin, Christina Reid, and Charabanc Theatre have produced an impressive bulk of work 'questioning the inherited norms of identity and relationships' directly or indirectly associated with the Troubles.[33]

The redefinition of the role of women is, however, necessary not only because of the political or historical context but also because of the fact that some women themselves tend to uphold the traditional values pressed on them. As becomes obvious in the case of Janet in *The Belle of Belfast City* or in *Tea in a China Cup*, it is the Protestant point of view of the older generation which keeps the younger from a better life unaffected by traditional conflicts. A good example of the traditional upbringing of children is Beth in *Tea in a China Cup*:

> The glorification of the Protestant past also demonstrates the inflexibleness that serves to destroy the very people it supposedly upholds. Beth's family's insistence upon 'keeping up appearances' keeps her in a bad marriage, covering up for her husband's 'gambling' in stocks, which she has learned is no different from from her father's betting on the dog races.[34]

As a consequence, only the changes and new identities of the dynamic female characters provide the ground for the better development of the next generation.

The new female identity can thus be regarded as part of a possible new Irish identity, which overthrows obsolete values, no matter whether they are traditionally male or female, public or private. So, the traditional concept of 'mother Ireland' could indeed be revitalised by women and the new Ireland one marked by the new and positive female image.

Reid's oeuvre is also characterised by a number of recurring dramatic techniques. A very important feature of many of her plays is a mixture of realism regarding content and anti-naturalism regarding the aesthetic production on stage. Reid changes between various points in time and settings to present a panorama of generations and thus underline her messages. She does so by juxtaposing various settings on the stage and by working with the fading of lights or voices as a indication as to which of the rooms the action is taking place in. The various settings are provided with only the most necessary props; the presentations of her plays on stage are thus not only anti-naturalist but also reductionist.

This leads to another technique frequently used by her: the encapsulation of different perspectives and levels of action. She often works with flashbacks and thus contributes to an aesthetic change of the traditional history play. This change necessitates, besides the use of lighting and sound, the employment of characters similar to epic characters, for example the Comedian in *Did You Hear the One About the Irishman?*, Belle in *Tea in a China Cup* or Beth in the same play. The epic characters sometimes, as in the case of Beth, deviate from the traditional concept in so far as they do not comment on the whole action but just on their own development; this does not, however, change the task of the epic characters, which is to give information to the audience essential to enable them to understand the play better. Belle, who stays in the present from an early stage, gives valuable comments on the situation in Belfast: she is an outsider – like many of the audience – and thus her perspective helps to define the situation as she sees it with different eyes, compared to the other characters.

Not as innovative as the two characteristics mentioned above but, rather, traditional is Reid's way of blending tragedy and comedy. As is typical of so many Irish authors before her, she does not only confront the audience with the violent and sad part of Irish reality but gives then the chance to find comic relief and thus relaxation. The humour she often uses stems from the politically and socially absurd situation: the two Christian confessions want to maintain their differences in order to vilify each other, but in fact they suffer from the shortcomings caused by just this act of maintaining.[35]

'I think labels diminish good art. I don't make political statements, I present words and images that are open to interpretation.'[36] Reid, as many other authors do when asked the to label their work, refuses a simple categorisation; but when one has a closer look at her work and rejects the statement that labelling diminishes good art, her position in contemporary Irish theatre is quite obvious.

Maxwell states that Reid writes political theatre without any political interest.[37] When reading her plays, the label of political theatre – in the sense that this is the one and only intention of her writing – is indeed wrong: it is true that plays examining the 'traditions, prejudices, and stereotypes that fuel political party lines'[38] can qualify as a kind of political theatre but another characteristic, a clearly identifiable didactic intention to sell this message to the audience as the most important part, is not as dominant as it should be for a clear definition of her work as 'political'.

Another label often attached to her plays is their characterisation as 'feminist plays'.[39] Reid changes the perspective and looks at traditional Irish topics from the female point of view; thus, she puts an emphasis on a social group so far neglected in Irish drama. She describes the struggle of women trying to get along with the bad situation caused by the male part of society and thus a characterisation of her work as 'female drama' is clearly correct. It is, however, difficult to see it as feminist drama because the social and political radicalism which is obvious in truly feminist plays is not present in Reid's work: the plays present more of a description of the social and political situation than an active fight against society, as bad as it is. This statement agrees with Reid's own comment when she says that '[she] write[s] about women as they are, not as feminism would want them to be'.[40]

Reid's work overturns the traditional concepts of the history and family play. By putting women at the centre of attention she leaves behind the concept of history as a truly male construction and shows not only the effects of history on women but also their active participation in the historic process. The extension of the family play to a multigenerational overview underlines the intensity of her message and shows that changes need to be brought about in order to achieve a better future for a troubled country.

With these characteristic features Reid has found her own place in contemporary Irish drama and, in the words of McDonough, 'will no doubt continue to be a strong female voice in Irish drama'.[41]

Primary Sources

Works by Christina Reid

The Last of a Dyin' Race, BBC: *Best Radio Plays of 1986* (London: Methuen, 1987), pp. 39–71.

Plays: 1: Tea in a China Cup, Did You Hear the One About the Irishman?, Joyriders, The Belle of Belfast City, My Name, Shall I Tell You My Name?, Clowns (London: Methuen, 1997).

Secondary Sources

Delgado, Maria M., 'Introduction', in Christina Reid, *Plays: 1* (London: Methuen, 1997), pp. vi–xxii.

Griffiths, Trevor and Margaret Llewellyn-Jones (eds), *British and Irish Women Dramatists Since 1958. A Critical Handbook* (Buckingham: Open UP, 1993).

Kurdi, Mária, 'Interview with Christina Reid', *ABEI Journal: The Brazilian Journal of Irish Studies*, Vol. 6 (2004), pp. 207–16.

Luft, Joanna, 'Brechtian *Gestus* and the Politics of Tea in Christina Reid's *Tea in a China Cup*', *Modern Drama*, Vol. 42, No. 2 (1999), pp. 214–22.

Maxwell, D. E. S., 'Northern Ireland Political Drama', *Modern Drama* Vol. 33 (1990), pp. 1–14.

McDonough, Carla J., 'Christina Reid (1942–)', in Bearnice Schrank *et al.* (eds), *Irish Playwrights, 1880–1995: A Research and Production Sourcebook* (Westport, CT: Greenwood, 1997), pp. 300–7.

—, '"I've Never Been Just Me": Rethinking Women's Position in the Plays of Christina Reid', in Stephen Watt *et al.* (eds), *A Century of Irish Drama: Widening the Stage* (Bloomington: Indiana UP, 2000), pp. 179–92.

Roll-Hansen, Diderik, 'Dramatic Strategy in Christina Reid's *Tea in a China Cup*', *Modern Drama*, Vol. 30, No. 3 (1987), pp. 389–95.

Sullivan, Esther Beth, 'What is "Left to a Woman of the House" When the Irish Situation Is Staged?', in Jeanne Colleran *et al.* (eds.), *Staging Resistance: Essays on Political Theatre* (Ann Arbor: University of Michigan Press, 1998), pp. 213–26.

Trotter, Mary, 'Translating Women into Irish Theatre History', in Stephen Watt *et al.* (eds), *A Century of Irish Drama: Widening the Stage* (Bloomington: Indiana UP, 2000), pp. 163–78.

Tylee, Claire, '"Name upon Name": Myth, Ritual and the Past in Recent Irish Plays Referring to the Great War', in Aránzazu Usandizaga *et al.* (eds), *Dressing Up for War: Transformations of Gender and Ganre in the Discourse and Literature of War* (Amsterdam: Rodopi, 2001), pp. 271–87.

Notes

1. See Mary Trotter, 'Translating Women', pp. 163–4.
2. Mária Kurdi, 'Interview', p. 207.
3. Ibid., p. 208.
4. See Carla McDonough, 'Christina Reid (1942–)', p. 300.
5. See Diderik Roll-Hansen, 'Dramatic Strategy', p. 390.
6. Ibid.
7. McDonough, 'Christina Reid (1942–)', p. 302.

8. See Kurdi, op. cit., p. 215.

9. McDonough, 'Christina Reid (1942–)', p. 302.

10. Joanna Luft, 'Brechtian *Gestus*', p. 214.

11. Ibid., p. 217.

12. Ibid., p. 221.

13. Kurdi, op. cit., p. 211.

14. Esther Beth Sullivan, 'What Is "Left to a Woman of the House"', p. 213.

15. See Maria M. Delgado, 'Introduction', p. xiii.

16. McDonough, 'Christina Reid (1942–)', p. 303.

17. Ibid.

18. Ibid., p. 304.

19. Carla McDonough, '"I've Never Been Just Me"', p. 179.

20. Ibid.

21. Ibid.

22. See Kurdi, op. cit., p. 212.

23. McDonough, 'Christina Reid (1942–)', p. 306.

24. Trotter, op. cit., pp. 175–6.

25. Sullivan, op. cit., p. 213.

26. See McDonough, 'Christina Reid (1942–)', p. 303.

27. McDonough, '"I've Never Been Just Me"', p. 183.

28. Ibid., p. 179.

29. Ibid., p. 184.

30. Trotter, op. cit., p. 173.

31. Ibid., p. 166.

32. Sullivan, op. cit., p. 222.

33. Ibid., p. 215.

34. McDonough, '"I've Never Been Just Me"', p. 184.

35. See McDonough, 'Christina Reid (1942–)', p. 301.

36. Ibid., p. 302.

37. See D. E. S. Maxwell, 'Northern Ireland Political Drama', p. 2.

38. McDonough, 'Christina Reid (1942–)', p. 302.

39. Ibid., p. 302.

40. Kurdi, op. cit., p. 208.

41. McDonough, 'Christina Reid (1942–)', p. 302.

23 J. GRAHAM REID

Jochen Achilles

The Death of Humpty Dumpty; The Closed Door Dorothy; The Hidden Curriculum; Remembrance; Billy; Ties of Blood

Introduction

Born in Belfast into a Protestant working-class family in 1945, Graham Reid earned an academic degree from Queens University in Belfast in 1976.[1] Later he became writer-in-residence at this institution. Reid worked as a teacher for some years but has been concentrating on his literary production since 1980. He has written a number of teleplays for the BBC. His works for the stage have predominantly been produced by the Peacock Theatre, the experimental offshoot of Dublin's Abbey Theatre. Some of Reid's works, such as the *Billy* plays, build up on one another and trace the stages of a character's development. All of his dramatic works investigate the effects of the political and military struggles between Catholics and Protestants, nationalists and unionists in the Northern Ireland of the 1970s and 1980s. Nevertheless, the goals and convictions of the various factions hardly take centre stage. Reid does not write plays in order to suggest or advocate any particular solution to the Northern Ireland conflict. His theatre is political in a way that is similar to Sean O'Casey's or Brendan Behan's. The political demands of the respective groupings and the violence used to assert their aims are measured against the impact these groups have on individual characters and their families. Reid's plays focus on the personal and existential consequences of living in a region ruled by violence. Into this interpersonal space, the struggles between para-military groups come tearing in like the blind and anonymous forces of fate. In this way, Reid's plays acquire a peculiar tension between regional and political specificity on the one hand, and universal existential issues on the other. Reid emphasises that he is principally interested in family problems, the ordinariness of which all human beings share. Against this specific background seemingly world-shaking, large-scale events appear as mere abstractions.[2] This does not mean, however, that Reid wants to shut out contemporary global problems entirely, as did, for instance, Thornton Wilder in *Our Town* (1938). Rather, he portrays individual human beings caught up in the conflict between their personal lives and the general political situation, between self-determination and other-directedness.[3]

The Plays

The Death of Humpty Dumpty (1979)

Reid's first and most widely received play, *The Death of Humpty Dumpty*, premiered 1979, at the Peacock Theatre. Its central character, Protestant history teacher George Samson, paralysed from the neck down after a terrorist assault, presents a brutal image of the injuries the Northern Ireland Troubles could inflict on the people who became entangled in them. Samson shares the fate of the wall-sitting, egg-shaped Humpty Dumpty character in the nursery rhyme, immortalised by Lewis Carroll in the sixth chapter of *Through the Looking-Glass* (1872) and heightened into a symbol of fallen humanity by James Joyce in *Finnegans Wake* (1939). Just as in the case of Humpty Dumpty, the King's, respectively the Queen's, army will never be able to bring George Samson back to his former state.[4] On the level of political allegory, George Samson's paralysis constitutes an assessment of the situation of Northern Ireland that is akin to Joyce's diagnosis of universal social and mental paralysis put forward in his short-story collection *Dubliners* (1914) half a century before. Similar to O'Casey's First World War play *The Silver Tassie* (1928), the irreducible existential situation of the lame and the crippled is at the centre of *The Death of Humpty Dumpty*, in which the Troubles in Northern Ireland have replaced the First World War background.

The universal significance of the issue is underscored by showing how, in hospital, Protestant middle-class intellectual George Samson makes friends with Gerry Doyle, a working-class man who is a paraplegic like himself. Doyle performs a complex function. He opens the play with a kind of prologue, in which he emphasises the equalising effects, across all social and religious divides, of his own and George's invalidity. Doyle's death in a traffic accident after his release from hospital marks the end of the first and the beginning of the second part of the two-act play. Yet in spite of his physical demise, Doyle's voice with its cynical commentary still has the last word in *The Death of Humpty Dumpty*.

Reid achieves this by making Doyle's voice the inner voice of George Samson in Act II. It gives utterance to Samson's thoughts and feelings, articulating the desperate and hopeless perspective of a man excluded from normal life. In terms of technique, this internalisation of Doyle as Samson's inner voice, which facilitates a dramatisation of the psychological consequences of Samson's paralysis, is reminiscent of Gar O'Donnell's split into a private and a public self in Brian Friel's early success, *Philadelphia, Here I Come!* (1964). On the one hand, this psychological technique of Reid's makes it possible to act out the ways in which hate, self-pity and aggression determine the emotional dynamics of George Samson. Samson tries to fight back against the ambivalent compassion he receives from his environment by the cynically destructive comments of Doyle's inner voice and the bullying behaviour that is fuelled by this attitude (p. 17). Later on, when Samson is permitted to spend the weekends at home with his family, he passes on the humiliation he has to bear by harassing his wife, his son and his daughter. Samson's physical deformation begins to induce mental deformation in his family (pp. 38, 54–5).

The Death of Humpty Dumpty also tries in other ways to reveal the interconnections between terrorist violence and mental dispositions. The whole play is interspersed with analogies of sexual and political repression and exploitation, 'the similarity between what is presented as the principal attributes of this violence and the natural attributes of male sexual identity'.[5] This is a theme that also dominates other plays by Reid, such as, for instance, *Dorothy*. In *The Death of Humpty*

Dumpty, it is foreshadowed from a historical perspective. Before the assault on George Samson that will bring about his paralysis, in a scene that documents an intact family life, he and his son David discuss the historical role of Irish MP John Redmond, who attempted to achieve a moderate solution for Ireland's independence within the framework of the British Empire. In a school composition, David takes up the opinion of Sean O'Casey, who regarded Redmond's conciliatory attitude towards the English colonial power as a form of political prostitution and expressed this by giving the only prostitute in *The Plough and the Stars* (1926), his play on the Easter Rising, Redmond's name (p. 9). Reid links the question of the right moral stance in the face of political oppression to the issue of sexual self-determination. In *The Death of Humpty Dumpty* this becomes clearly apparent, when George Samson, initially depicted as a happily married family man, proves to be a notorious philanderer. The scene subsequent to his debate with his son on John Redmond's selling-out shows Samson, who appeared as the concerned husband and father mere moments before, in a cosy post-coital chat with his young colleague Caroline Wilson. In a way, Caroline becomes George Samson's Delilah, for their assignation at the 'Giant's Ring' in the hills outside of Belfast results in his becoming an unwilling and unwanted witness to the machinations of a terrorist group. The men take down Samson's registration number and later shoot him in order to ensure his silence by his death. Ironically, this is just what they fail to accomplish. George can still think and speak, even though he is dead in every other respect.

Later on, Doyle emphasises the defeat a state like this means with regard to one's sexuality: 'You can talk, some social intercourse, but no sexual' (p. 15). The course of the play makes this abundantly clear when Caroline Wilson visits George Samson at his hospital bed and tells him that the teacher who has taken over Samson's position in the school's hierarchy has also become her lover and intends to marry her. As Doyle's voice comments, 'First they take over your Empire, and then they take your woman' (p. 45). Like territorial gains or losses, love affairs appear to be just another manifestation of power relations. The achievement of *The Death of Humpty Dumpty* does not least consist in showing the underlying pattern of power and rebellion, repression and outbreak, that dominates the political situation in Northern Ireland as a nearly ubiquitous structure, which not only informs institutions such as the educational and healthcare systems, but also the family. The hospital situation George Samson has to endure proves another potential system of oppression. Sister Thompson, the angelically humanitarian Ward Sister, is counterpointed by brutal and sadistic young male nurse Willy John, who brings the violence and terrorism of the streets into the hospital. The Ward Sister draws attention to this interconnection when she confronts Willy: 'You are like so many others in this bloody country. You're a bloody animal, limited in everything but your capacity for cruelty' (p. 35). In a similar manner, George Samson's injury in Northern Ireland's civil war, and the humiliations arising from it, leave their mark on his family. His son David can eventually think of no other recourse than to smother his father to death with a pillow. The metaphorical references of George Samson's fate to the irreparable fall of Humpty Dumpty and, above all, to an atavistic battle of the sexes over male dominance and emasculation, as represented by the biblical story of Samson and Delilah, lend a grim inevitability to Reid's play. His use of metaphor not only makes clear that the Troubles have encroached into all areas of life. It also raises the question whether the Troubles, in their turn, are not a form of acting out a dynamic of libidinous and aggressive instincts that must be considered an anthropological constant.

The Closed Door, Dorothy and The Hidden Curriculum (1980)

Reid's second play, *The Closed Door*, was also first shown at the Peacock Theatre, on 24 April 1980. Like *The Death of Humpty Dumpty*, it deals with the complex problems resulting from Northern Ireland's civil war, although it focuses on a different aspect. *The Closed Door* is not primarily about the sufferings of the victims of violence, but about the question of whether personal courage can contribute to a change in the situation. By presenting the extreme emotional states engendered by terrorist brutality, Reid makes it clear that, in spite of the all pervading sense of powerlessness, there remains some little room for individual decision, which might even grow to be a prime cause for fundamental change. In this play, however, the door referred to in the title remains closed. Any perspective of making a new moral start is strongly denied. It is only in his later works that Reid begins to adopt a more optimistic attitude.

Reid's next two plays, *Dorothy* and *The Hidden Curriculum*, were both performed for the first time in 1980, *Dorothy* at the Oscar Theatre during the Dublin Theatre Festival, and *The Hidden Curriculum* at the Peacock Theatre. Both plays elaborate on themes already present in *The Death of Humpty Dumpty* and *The Closed Door*. In *Dorothy*, it is the theme of the interrelation between sexual and political violence; in *The Hidden Curriculum*, it is the failure of the school system in the face of the political and social situation. Dorothy, the central character in the play of the same name, is an unusually attractive fifty-year-old woman, bored by her marriage to building contractor Charles Williams and looking for pleasure by testing her erotic magnetism in party flirtations. The Williams family seems to have succeeded in leaving behind the problems that shake Belfast. Although both Dorothy and her husband originally came from sordid circumstances, they have become prosperous and now live in a luxury bungalow on a hill, with a view of the city and the sea. Their spatial detachment permits Dorothy to watch the bombings down in the city as if they were a fireworks display (p. 54). Nevertheless, the violence from the city finally surges up into the residences of the affluent. The Northern Ireland conflict leaves no social class untouched, there is no buying one's way out of it. One weekend, when husband Charles and their grown-up son Douglas have gone off in the car, and bored Dorothy is sitting alone at home, Stephen Montgomery, a former fellow student of her son's, drops by for a visit. Stephen also sneaks two other men into the house, the dyspeptic terrorist Mike and his sidekick Andy, an utterly ruthless killer.

The play goes on to create a nightmarish atmosphere of horror, as feelings of social inferiority, the desire to seek retribution for previous injustice and sexual lust mingle to form a fatal amalgamation. Stephen uses the two terrorists to threaten Dorothy into submitting to his quasi-incestuous sexual desires, as he sees her as a mother-substitute. Andy and Mike are not primarily interested in sex but try to find a vent for their rage against all their social and financial betters and anyone who stands aloof from the Troubles. Andy's sadism derives from the brutal slaughter of his father, who, to make matters worse, was a bricklayer lorded over by building contractors like Dorothy's husband. In a similar fashion, Mike believes himself duty-bound to seek retribution for his mother, who works as a charwoman for upper-class ladies. The mounting rage and aggression of the three men is finally discharged as they rape Dorothy. Reid's play presents this vortex of destructive emotions as a vicious circle without escape. When Dorothy's husband Charles learns of the rape of his wife, he immediately plots revenge. He wants to reconquer his seemingly unassailable position on the hill beyond the social and religious lines of demarcation, from which Stephen, Mike and Andy have ousted the family by their assault on Dorothy (p. 92). Yet revenge fails. Andy and Mike hear about Charles's plans, and once again they manage to establish themselves as squatters in the house on the hill. The intermingling of violence and Northern Ireland domestic life proves to be ubiquitous.

The Hidden Curriculum casts light on the situation of west Belfast schools in the 1970s. On the one hand, the play features a teaching staff mostly made up of jaded veterans solely interested in their private lives, and a headmaster who is energetically pursuing his career and wants to present to the public as positive an image of his school as possible. On the other hand, Reid shows the desolate world of the pupils, whose lives are stunted by family catastrophes and political terror. He principally attempts to answer the question as to what kind of difference school education can make against this background. The interaction of two English teachers, Tony Cairns and David Dunn, with two former Protestant pupils on a visit to their old school, Tom Allen and Bill Boyd, highlights the functions of school education in troubled times. Unlike their colleagues, both teachers take a sincere interest in helping their pupils to cope with the problems in their lives. The approaches they use differ significantly, however. Intellectual Tony Cairns tries to establish a connection to the present-day situation of his pupils by introducing them to subjects like the War Poets of the First World War and by campaigning to have a course on Irish history added to the curriculum. David Dunn does not believe in methods and schemes and rather bases his impulse for reform on empathy. He speaks the language of his pupils, trying to imagine himself in their places and to help them on a day-to-day basis.

Through Allen and Boyd, the two former pupils, Tony Cairns in particular arrives at an awareness of the secret behind education in Ireland, the hidden curriculum that determines their lives much more drastically than any amount of schooling. 'Comprehension and the War Poets count for nothing out there' (p.132), Allen explains, and he adds:

> Look at me, do I look like a rich, influential member of the Protestant ascendancy? I've got nothing . . . I live in a slum . . . I can't get a job . . . I've no fancy car . . . my ma ran off with her fancyman . . . my sister got knocked up the shoot by a Brit . . . my brother's in jail . . . and my da's dying in agony. (p. 134)

David Dunn is convinced that problems that run this deep can by no means be cushioned by the teachings of the school system (p. 143). Tony Cairns, however, tries to help out another former pupil, who by now has become a mass murderer working as a hit man for a terrorist organisation, by going to see the criminal's father, who gave his son away to the police. At this point, the father, having turned police informer, is himself menaced by Allen and Boyd. Tony Cairns has to realise that his offer of help will, at best, merely jeopardise his own life, without making any difference at all. His attempts to initiate a radical reform of school structures are also thwarted by the narrow-mindedness and indifference of his colleagues as well as by the opportunism of the headmaster. Like the ending of Dorothy, the ending of The Hidden Curriculum can only acknowledge the apparently inescapable 'vicious circle' (p. 164) of violence.

Remembrance (1984)

Remembrance, which opened in October 1984 at the Belfast Lyric Theatre, is Reid's first play that not only outlines the vicious circle of violence but tries to break it. *Remembrance* introduces the second and, so far, last phase in Reid's writing. This second phase continues in his two television programmes, pursuing an attempt not only to diagnose the situation of Northern Ireland, but to alleviate it by showing a possible way out of the chaos. *Remembrance* is also Reid's first play to use elements of comedy so that humour plays more than just an occasional role. Different from Reid's previous works, the central metaphor in *Remembrance* is the image of bridge building across the graves of the victims of terrorism. The symbol for this bridging of the abyss is the bench in the cemetery on which former British soldier Bert Andrews and Theresa Donaghy, a Catholic Irish woman, meet and fall in love. Both are over sixty years old. Both are widowed and have lost a child to terrorist attacks. Bert's son, Sam, was shot by the IRA, Theresa's son, Peter, by a Protestant terror organisation. Their sons' graves are almost adjacent. This brings Bert and Theresa closer to each other. They begin to wonder whether, in the face of their advanced age and the religious and political chasm that separates them, their affection will be strong enough to fight for a future together.

The social prejudices and problems that stand in the way of their new life together appear to be personified in the family backgrounds of these mature lovers. In addition to being a womaniser and a drunkard, Bert's second son, Victor, is a loutish and brutal torture specialist with the police force of the Royal Ulster Constabulary (RUC). He has come back to live with his father after the separation from his wife Jenny, whom he betrayed systematically. Victor is thinking of emigrating to South Africa, whose apartheid rule has built up a demand for racist torturers even greater than Northern Ireland's Troubles. His *minima moralia* are summed up in statements like this: 'I might bash the odd head on the odd wall but I'll never blow an unarmed man's head off from three feet' (pp. 13–14). In spite of his many affairs, however, Victor also remains attached to his wife, who by now has taken up a kind of housekeeper's function in the Andrews household. Theresa is living with her daughter Joan, who worked as a nurse before the killing of her brother. Since then, she has felt partially guilty of his death, and only powerful sedatives keep her recurring fits of hysteria under control. Theresa's second daughter Deirdre is raising her three children as a single mother: her husband Joe is an IRA fighter, serving life imprisonment for the murders he committed.

Bert's and Theresa's attempts to explain their budding relationship to their children at first meet with mockery and a complete lack of understanding. During the course of the play, however, people other than Bert and Theresa end up meeting on the cemetery bench as well. Joan has a first talk with Bert, coming to trust him so much that she confesses why she believes herself to be partly responsible for the death of her brother Peter. Joan's sister Deirdre strikes up an acquaintance with Victor on the cemetery bench. Even though the brother of Protestant policeman Victor was slain by an IRA killer just like Deirdre's husband, both immediately feel a liking for one another. The ending of *Remembrance* remains open. Deirdre and her sister Joan move to England in order to make a new start. Victor appears to be serious about building a relationship with a new partner, but he also keeps making more-than-interested inquiries about Deirdre. Theresa and Bert exchange letters, telling each other how much they are looking forward to visiting the cemetery together in the coming spring. Here, Reid's overriding perspective is no longer the cycle of violence, the irrevocable fall of Humpty Dumpty, or the closed door, as in the previous plays. Reid rather tries to develop a perspective of sustaining the fragile bridgework that has been built as well as the hope that the Northern Ireland conflict and the casualties it has claimed will eventually all recede into history. Only painful memories will remain which do not necessarily prevent reconciliation for those who live on. Reid's subsequent teleplays reinforce this constructive aspect of his dramatic work.

Billy (1982–4)

Reid's three-part series of teleplays, *Too Late to Talk to Billy*, *A Matter of Choice for Billy*, and *A Coming to Terms for Billy* was aired on BBC between 1982 and 1984, starring Kenneth Branagh as the title character, before he embarked on his international career. At first glance, the series seems to be just another tableau of the dreary stasis of life in a Protestant working-class family in west Belfast. The father, Norman Martin, a dockhand, is an irascible and violent drunk. His wife, Janet, has never been a model of marital fidelity. When the play begins, she is hospitalised with terminal cancer. Lorna, the seventeen-year-old daughter, is acting as a surrogate mother for her sisters Ann and Maureen, who are still at school age, and for her eighteen-year-old brother Billy. Billy Martin is living in a state of war with his father Norman, trying to make up his mind whether he should accompany his middle-class girlfriend June to England, where she wants to go to university.

Using the cinematic devices of flashback and subjective camera, *Too Late to Talk to Billy*, the first part of the trilogy, draws the problems of communication and violence within the Martin family sphere out into the open. Loss of communication and missed opportunities to relate to one another characterise the Martins' family life, as the title of the play suggests. Particularly sad, because it is irremediable, is Norman's inability to speak with his dying wife again. When he eventually shows up at the hospital, Billy has a bitter greeting for him: 'You're too late to talk to her and too early for the funeral' (p. 52) Loss of communication, caused by severe injuries of an emotional and even physical nature, is not just a factor in the situation of the Martin family, but also in the entire Northern Ireland situation. Conversely, the domestic violence that Reid presents is a component of the public violence the play does not show.

As in *The Death of Humpty Dumpty*, Reid invokes the interplay of psychosexual and political self-definition. It is due to feelings of both sexual impotence and political powerlessness that violent flare-ups occur. Familial power and communication structures, and the latent or undisguised willingness to use physical force both coincide with and reinforce the Northern Ireland conflict. Reid's *Billy* plays derive their edge from this interaction of micro- and macrostructures, which merely appears to remain dormant, as the Northern Ireland conflict as such seems to be playing only a marginal role in them. And yet Reid manages to turn the saga of the Martin family into a political allegory. Reid is not content with merely diagnosing the disruption and disunity of the Northern Ireland situation. He also tries to contribute towards an improvement of the political conditions by putting forward suggestions for changing psychological and familial structures. Near the ending of *Too Late to Talk to Billy*, the Martin family seems about to break apart for good. Janet, the mother, has died. Norman, her husband, goes to England like so many other Irish men of his generation, having landed a job in Birmingham. Billy sees his father off at the ferry, where the two of them have a cautious and tentative reconciliation. Billy puts up his parents' wedding photograph in the living room, in order to evoke a promise of marital harmony that never became real for him and his siblings. In this bleak world, family harmony seems to be feasible only in the form of remembrance and yearning. And yet, the two subsequent *Billy* plays also develop a realistic perspective for the future that is no longer exclusively shaped by hatred and confrontation. In *A Matter of Choice for Billy*, the protagonist undergoes a change of character. Billy no longer has to wear himself out in ceaseless conflict with his father, and he meets Catholic Pauline Magill, a nurse, who gradually begins to gain influence over him. Billy eventually makes the right decision in the 'matter of choice' the play derives its title from. He refuses to let Pauline disappear like June, his former girlfriend, and goes to live with her, leaving his own family behind, since, in Northern Ireland, he can hardly dare marry her across the denominational divide. His new role as his girlfriend's responsible partner sets off a change in Billy.

A Coming to Terms for Billy, the last part of the sequence, develops this perspective of change further. Billy's father Norman is visiting his family with his new English wife Mavis, a former teacher. Apparently, she has managed to domesticate him and has considerably reduced his inclinations towards drinking and violence. The couple is staying with Pauline and Billy. One reason for their coming, among others, is their wish to take the youngest of the Martin children to England to raise them there under less tenuous political conditions. This, however, results in the final breakdown of the Martin family's original structure. Under the newly arisen circumstances, Billy's sister Lorna in particular must give up her ambition to replace her deceased mother and make the decision to live her own life, independent of her family. The old behavioural patterns prove to be tenacious, not to be shaken off easily. The scars of the past cannot be readily overlooked (p. 145). At the end of *A Coming to Terms for Billy*, Norman and Mavis return to England with Billy's younger sisters Ann and Maureen. Billy and Pauline will visit them in their new home. Billy puts the old wedding photograph of Norman and Janet back into a drawer (p. 171). He has made his peace with the traumatic aspects of his childhood and is now free to start over again. It is no longer the memory of the wounds he sustained in the past that determines his life, but the hope for a future in which his Protestantism and Pauline's Catholicism, their mutual rootedness in Northern Ireland, and Mavis's English background will not be irreconcilable any more. Ann and Maureen, at any rate, will stand for a new intercultural perspective.

With its background presences of Janet, the dying mother, and Uncle Andy, the invalid, the *Billy* sequence is reminiscent of George Samson's fate in *The Death of Humpty Dumpty*. Ann's difficulties at school look back on similar attempts at remedying educational problems in *The Death of Humpty Dumpty*, *The Closed Door* and especially in *The Hidden Curriculum*. Reid also analysed the interconnection between sexuality and violence before, most forcefully in *Dorothy*. And yet, with his teleplay trilogy about the Northern Irish Martin family made for an English television station, Reid achieves something new. He is no longer concentrating on a core motif, as in *The Death of Humpty Dumpty* and *The Closed Door*. Instead, he traces a development that brings his characters out of their stagnation. To a certain degree, this may be considered a concession to genre. But this is not the whole story: to a predominantly English audience, the Billy sequence provides an illustration of the Northern Ireland question that is much more complex than its ostensible packaging in a soap opera format would lead viewers to expect. Directing his focus on family relations enables Reid to accentuate those elementary psychological problems that keep grudges and traditional structures of violence alive even in the political sphere. The cracking-up of the essentially oedipal encrustations of Billy and Lorna through the efforts of the 'Women's Initiative' formed by Pauline and Mavis triggers a process of development that gains validity as a metaphor for an analogous process on the social level. As, figuratively, the Martins open themselves up to non-unionist influences, Northern Ireland society must do as well. This may require first impulses both from the Irish Republic as represented by Catholic Pauline, and from England, which has an agent in Mavis. However, this endeavour will succeed only if the fatal entanglement in the compulsive repetition of the violent attack-and-retaliation pattern that was overcome in the family is broken through in the public sphere as well.

Ties of Blood (1985)

Aired in November and December 1985, *Ties of Blood*, Reid's second programme for the BBC, runs to six episodes, showing aspects of the Northern Ireland conflict without any links provided by recurring characters or a common storyline. Like the *Billy* teleplays, these episodes utilise cinematic techniques such as flashbacks, close-ups, silent pans across the settings, and the juxtaposition of scenes as mutual commentary through fast intercutting. Unlike the *Billy* trilogy, however, *Ties of Blood* is not a family saga. Among other things, the programme is much more concerned with the role of the British Army and the motives that drive the actions of its soldiers. Reid, who at age fifteen ran away from home to join the British Army, may well have worked off his personal experience for the benefit of a British audience.[6] The appeal to give up nationalist solipsism and sectarian fanaticism that could already be felt in the *Billy* trilogy becomes more emphatic in *Ties of Blood*. And again, chiefly women are ready to try out intercultural advances and their psychological and political consequences. With its dominant theme of finding possible ways of transition from a nationalist and denominational to an intercultural definition of identity, Reid's drama contributes to a more comprehensive reorientation that has become more and more evident in Irish literature, both in the Republic and in the North. Brian Friel's groundbreaking play *Translations* (1981), Dermot Bolger's *In High Germany* (1990), and the *Field Day* pamphlets on nationalism, colonialism and literature by Terry Eagleton, Fredric Jameson and Edward Said belong to this trend.

Out of Tune and *Attachments*, the second and fourth episodes of *Ties of Blood*, explore the reasons of young soldiers to sign up for a tour of duty in Northern Ireland, and then set these subjective attitudes against the objective military situation. Both teleplays accordingly feature two contrasting plot lines, each juxtaposing the motivations and the morale of English soldiers with an incident in which a British soldier and, respectively, an officer of the Royal Ulster Constabulary (RUC) are seriously wounded in terrorist assaults, presumably launched by the IRA. Again, especially women address the problems of unclear loyalties and of love across the political and religious lines of demarcation. *McCabe's Wall* is the first and only one of the six episodes of *Ties of Blood* set in Northern Ireland's Catholic Republican milieu. In the environment of the McCabes, a Catholic family of farmers, two factions confront one another, with the agrarians and nationalist conservatives Liam, Declan and Grunter rallied around Sean McCabe, patriarch and *pater familias*, on one side and urban, England-oriented and cosmopolitan Trish, who exerts a growing influence on Sean's daughter Mary, on the other. The dynamics of *McCabe's Wall* derive from Mary McCabe's increasing sympathies for Trish's cosmopolitan outlook. A clear sign of the mood of departure from stifling rural ways is Mary's relationship with Will, a Welsh soldier in the British Army. At the end of *McCabe's Wall*, Reid finds persuasive symbolic images for the bridging of the gap that intercultural tolerance, as embodied in Mary and Will, can afford. After an accident, Sean McCabe has just finished repairing the damage to the wall around his farm, when it is destroyed again by British soldiers, this time beyond mending. Sean's endeavours to keep his daughter Mary locked inside the wall around his property prove to be in vain. The wall breaks down. When he learns of Mary's relationship with Will, the enemy soldier, he sends a sniper after his daughter's lover. On the beach, where Mary is taking a last walk before leaving her home for ever, the killer in vain waits for Will to join her. Disappointed, he lowers his gun, through the sights of which the viewer watches Mary continuing her walk on the beach (p. 55). The open sea that Mary looks out over remains a valid symbol for the new horizons beyond the Irish Sea for which she will set out together with Will. Sean is left behind on the wreckage of his wall, old and abandoned. Among the six episodes of *Ties of Blood*, *McCabe's Wall* becomes the most complex and the most convincing representation of a change in consciousness and emotion towards greater tolerance and acceptance of the other, which also seems to be bearing political fruit. In several ways, *Going Home*, the third episode of *Ties of Blood*, elaborates on the option of an intersubjective crossing of the boundaries that begins to emerge out of the union of Mary and Will in *McCabe's Wall*.

Invitation to a Party and *The Military Wing*, the two last instalments in the *Ties of Blood* series, differ from the preceding episodes in being increasingly driven by psychological interest. Both episodes deal with the emotional deformations that can be caused by the Northern Ireland conflict. *Invitation to a Party* depicts the fate of Marion, a young woman whose newly wed husband was shot to death by an English soldier on their wedding day. Marion eventually kills a British soldier, whom, in her confused state, she simultaneously identifies with both her husband and his murderer. As happens so frequently in the Northern Ireland conflict, the distinction between murderer and victim blurs. After the deed, Marion kills herself. The essential concern of this episode is the sudden shift from military to private violence that had been of interest to Reid as early as *The Death of Humpty Dumpty*. *The Military Wing*, the last episode of *Ties of Blood*, centres on nurse Yvonne Duncan, newly deployed to the military ward of a Belfast hospital, and her problematic involvement in both biculturalism and bisexuality.

Summary

In its entirety, Reid's dramatic output, tied as it is to the Troubles, provides fundamental insights into the interplay of religious, political, social and psychological factors that determine and help perpetuate the Northern Ireland conflict. Reid's dramatic style of realistic renditions of characters and settings heightened by unobtrusive symbolism is not experimental, but informative and well suited to the seriousness of his subject. The perspective of Reid's dramatic works changes from an emphasis on the inevitability of the Northern Irish cycle of violence to cautious suggestions as to how to break through this cycle. Like several other recent Irish dramatists, Reid is counting on the growth of intercultural tolerance and the concomitant dwindling of nationalist prejudice. This change in Reid's work sets in around 1984, with the cemetery bench in *Remembrance* becoming a site of reconciliation in full view of the graves of terrorism's victims. In his early plays, the dominant images are of irretrievable loss and total isolation – the hopeless fate of Humpty Dumpty or the closed door. By contrast, the multi-part teleplays of the mid-1980s, the *Billy* trilogy and *Ties of Blood*, introduce and affirm the possibility of bridging the abyss and of a reconciliation of the warring parties. This political perspective has grown stronger and more reliable in recent years. It seems to confirm the development of Reid's drama.[7]

Primary Sources

Works by Graham Reid

The Billy Plays: Too Late to Talk to Billy; A Matter of Choice for Billy; A Coming to Terms for Billy; Lorna (London: Faber and Faber, 1987).
The Death of Humpty-Dumpty (Dublin: Co-op Books, 1900).
The Plays of Graham Reid: Too Late to Talk to Billy; Dorothy; The Hidden Curriculum (Dublin: Co-op Books, 1982).
Remembrance (London: Faber and Faber, 1985).
Ties of Blood [*McCabe's Wall; Out of Tune; Going Home; Attachments; Invitation to a Party; The Military Wing*] (London: Faber and Faber, 1986).

Secondary Sources

Achilles, Jochen, J., 'Graham Reid', in Jochen Achilles and Rüdiger Imhof (eds), *Irische Dramatiker der Gegenwart* (Darmstadt: Wissenschaftliche Buchgesellschaft, 1996), pp. 96–112.
Bolger, Dermot, *In High Germany*, in *A Dublin Quartet* (London: Penguin, 1992), pp. 71–109.
Campbell, P, 'Graham Reid – Professional', *The Linen Hall Review*, Vol. 1, No. 2 (Summer 1984), pp. 4–7.

Carroll, Lewis, *The Annotated Alice: Alice's Adventures in Wonderland and Through the Looking-Glass*, intr. and ann. Martin Gardner (Harmondsworth: Penguin, 1970).

Deane, Seamus (ed.), *The Field Day Anthology of Irish Writing*, Vol. 3 (Derry: Field Day Publications, 1991).

Eagleton, Terry, *Nationalism: Irony and Commitment* (Derry: Field Day Theatre Company, 1988).

Etherton, Michael, *Contemporary Irish Dramatists* (London: Macmillan, 1989), pp. 33–8.

Fitzgibbon, Emelie, 'All Change: Contemporary Fashions in the Irish Theatre', in Masaru Sekine (ed.), *Irish Writers and the Theatre* (Totowa, NJ: Barnes and Noble, 1986), pp. 35–7.

Fitz-simon, Christopher, *The Irish Theatre* (London: Thames and Hudson, 1983), p. 201.

Henderson, Lynda, '"The Green Shoot": Transcendence and the Imagination in Contemporary Ulster Drama', in Gerald Dawe and Edna Longley (eds), *Across a Roaring Hill: The Protestant Imagination in Modern Ireland, Essays in Honour of John Hewitt* (Belfast: Blackstaff, 1985), pp. 212–13.

Jameson, Fredric, *Modernism and Imperialism* (Derry: Field Day Theatre Company, 1988).

Maxwell, D. E. S, *A Critical History of Modern Irish Drama, 1891–1980* (Cambridge: Cambridge UP, 1984), pp. 185–6.

Murray, Christopher, 'Recent Irish Drama', in Heinz Kosok (ed.), *Studies in Anglo-Irish Literature* (Bonn: Bouvier, 1982), pp. 439–43.

O'Toole, Fintan, 'Graham Reid's Heart of Darkness: The Cost of Living in Belfast', *Dublin*, 16–19 April 1982, pp. 15–16.

Pilkington, Lionel, 'Violence and Identity in Northern Ireland: Graham Reid's *The Death of Humpty Dumpty*', *Modern Drama*, Vol. 33, No. 1 (1990), pp. 15–29.

Roche, Anthony, *Contemporary Irish Drama: From Beckett to McGuinness* (Dublin: Gill & Macmillan, 1994).

Said, Edward W., *Yeats and Decolonization* (Derry: Field Day Theatre Company, 1988).

Notes

1. This essay is based on my previous article on Reid; see Jochen Achilles, 'Graham Reid'.
2. Lionel Pilkington, 'Violence and Identity in Northern Ireland', p. 17.
3. Christopher Murray, 'Recent Irish Drama', p. 441.
4. Lewis Carroll, *The Annotated Alice*, cf. 276.
5. Pilkington, op. cit., p. 22.
6. Michael Etherton, *Contemporary Irish Dramatists*, p. 33.
7. A few of Reid's more recent plays are not accessible, however. These are *Callers*, produced on the Peacock Stage of the Abbey Theatre, 3 October 1985; *Lengthening Shadows*, produced by the Point Fields Theatre Company and the Lyric Theatre Belfast, 7 September 1995 and *Love*, produced by the West Yorkshire Playhouse, Leeds, in 1995.

24 BILLY ROCHE

Peter Paul Schnierer

A Handful of Stars; Poor Beast in the Rain; Belfry; Amphibians; The Cavalcaders; On Such as We; Lay Me Down Softly

Introduction

Billy Roche was born in Wexford on 11 January 1949, the son of a publican. After leaving school, he supported himself with a variety of jobs on building sites and factories both in Wexford and in London. His public career began in the early 1970s; for most of that decade he toured Ireland as a singer and guitarist with the Roach Band, a pub-rock outfit he co-founded. He still lives in Wexford, and his plays are usually set in the town: his first three plays, *A Handful of Stars* (1988), *Poor Beast In the Rain* (1989) and *Belfry* (1991), are collectively known and published as *The Wexford Trilogy*. This was followed quickly by *Amphibians* (1992) and *The Cavalcaders* (1993); the former also set in 'Wexford, a small town in Ireland', the latter merely 'in a small town in Ireland'. Roche then concentrated on writing screen plays based on his own early theatre successes; the film *Trojan Eddie* (1996, public release 1997) is based on Roche's original script and certainly the biggest commercial success for a versatile man of literature who has sung, acted, produced, directed for the stage and the screen, and written a novel (*Tumbling Down*, 1986) and short stories (*Tales from Rainwater Pond*, 2006), which in turn have provided him with material for adaptations and dramatisations. When he returned to writing original full-length plays in 2001 with *On Such as We*, he no longer specified the setting; *Lay Me Down Softly* (2008), his latest play to date, finds its scene 'somewhere in Ireland'. The conflict between such rootedness in the local, even parochial, and the increasingly insistent demands of modernity arriving late in the backwaters of a backward-looking country is at the core of Roche's work.

The Plays

A Handful of Stars (1988)

Roche's first professionally produced play, *A Handful of Stars* is the first part of what came to be known as *The Wexford Trilogy*; it is nevertheless a self-contained play that merely shares some characteristics with the two plays to follow. Since these characteristics can be found in all of Roche's dramatic texts it makes little sense to isolate the *Trilogy* and treat it as a single coherent work. As far as it is sensible to draw attention to a parallel in Irish literature, Martin McDonagh's Leenane Trilogy, mainly held together by topography, may serve; Roche's plays certainly do not possess the kaleidoscopic completeness of O'Casey's Dublin Trilogy.

> *A Handful of Stars* was first performed at the Bush Theatre, London, in 1988. It is set in a scruffy pool hall. There is a pool table, a jukebox, a pot-bellied stove and a one-armed bandit. [. . .] Along one wall there is a long bench and a blackboard and a cue stand and all the usual paraphernalia that can be found in a club of this sort. (p. 2)

Similar stage directions begin his later plays, too. They are both precise and unspecific: 'the usual' and 'of this sort' indicate a generic setting, designed to convey a complex of signals which in turn can manipulate the audience's assumptions. We know what a pool hall is supposed to look like, we are shown one, thus we establish a horizon of expectations based on our knowledge of the sort of plot usually occurring in such settings: the return of the retired champion, the underdog taking on the ringer, playing for big stakes and whatever else billiard/pool films such as *The Hustler* (1961) have anchored in our memories. It is not the least of this play's charms that Roche makes good these implied promises while offering many little twists to them.

The Hustler's Eddie Felson character here is Jimmy Brady, a 'good-looking, tough boy of seventeen or so' (p. 2). His behaviour, brash, aggressive and given to excess, marks him as the adolescent outsider hero of many similar coming-of-age plays; ultimately, and in an Irish context, he is a revenant of Christy Mahon, Synge's *Playboy of the Western World* (1907); Jimmy, too, has problems with his father, an awkward courtship with a woman willing to sacrifice much for him, and a tendency towards self-aggrandisement that strikes those around him as histrionic. His self-image as 'the King of the Renegades' and his career in drunken brawling and petty robberies offer little to impress either his fellow-characters or the audience.

Jimmy, for all his centre-stage strutting, remains a rather flat character; Roche's dramatis personae throughout his work run the gamut from stock figure to enigmatic complexity. The former extreme in *A Handful of Stars* is marked by Swan, 'a wily detective' (p. 2), who is the stereotypical plodding Garda. Stapler, the 'auld fucker' of the following excerpt, is on the opposite end of the scale, as the stage directions describing his differentiated emotional responses make clear:

Stapler What's all this?

Jimmy I won this last night on a boxin' match. I backed a fella called Eddie Harpur. He was fightin' this auld fucker last night yeh know? He nearly killed him too. Broke his nose and everything.

Stapler *is tongue-tied with anger now. He pockets the pound note and makes to leave.*

I'm goin' to tell you one thing Stapler, it's a good job I didn't put me few bob on you last night, that's all. I'd have been up after you this mornin' to bate the back off yeh with a big hurl or somethin'.

Stapler *heads towards the back room, crestfallen.*

Hey Stapler.

Stapler (*in the doorway*): What?

Jimmy You should have ducked.

Stapler *is not amused.* (p. 26)

This passage, apart from carefully notating mood changes and showing Jimmy at his worst, also serves to further the theme of boxing. It makes an appearance in most Roche plays and becomes the subject matter of his most recent one, *Lay Me Down Softly*. Ultimately its significance lies not so much in purveying a thematically integrating symbol, but in Roche's concern with male rivalry and male bonding. *A Handful of Stars* has a cast of six men of different ages and just one girl, and in all of Roche's plays there are many more men than women, with longer, more dominant parts and longer monologues. Roche, in terms of gender balance in contemporary Irish drama, is about as far away from Anne Devlin as it is possible to get.

Poor Beast in the Rain (1989)

The second part of *The Wexford Trilogy*, also first performed at the Bush Theatre, London, is 'set in an old fashioned betting shop' (p. 68), where the proprietor Steven and his daughter Eileen run a tranquil operation for customers such as Georgie and Joe; the former a young lad with an eye on Eileen, the latter a man in his thirties who already lives more off his reminiscences than for any prospects. Two events coincide to jolt them a bit out of their daily routines: it is the weekend of the All Ireland hurling final, with the Wexford team playing away, and a character nicknamed Danger Doyle pays a quick return visit to the place of his youthful delinquent exploits with Joe, his womanising, and his eventual elopement with Eileen's mother, Steven's wife. In the end, Wexford have won, Eileen has left for London and her mother with Danger, and Georgie is a little wiser.

Poor Beast in the Rain is a typical second play. The pool hall of *A Handful of Stars* has become a betting shop, Jimmy has grown into Danger, the seventeen-year-old Linda here is modulated into Eileen, but the concerns of the play, with small-town boredom, juvenile delinquency, inept courting and the yearning to be somebody people remember structure both plays. When Roche describes the setting as cluttered with 'the usual stuff that can be found in a betting shop of this sort – pads and pencils and skewered dockets etc.' (p. 68), he almost verbatim repeats the corresponding stage direction of *A*

hands of a lesser playwright this tangle, just as the poetic justice ladled out liberally, might very quickly seem contrived; Roche manages to convey the impression of a closely knit community where no private move remains without public consequences and where any infringement of the rules of cohabitation will be sanctioned.

Roche's favourite themes are in evidence again but the strong local colour and the unusual outdoor scenes set this play apart from the others. The initiation motif works particularly well, since its doubling allows Roche to exploit both the atavistic force of a rite of passage and its comic potential in a world that has little time and regard for 'mere' ritual. Thus an initiate can meet his imminent branding with 'This better not hurt me' (p. 106), and Eagle goes to great lengths to make the night on the island comfortable for his son, newly constructed bed and comic books included; the only thing he inadvertently leaves behind is the ghetto blaster.

He and his son thus remain amphibian – not quite on *terra firma*, but not quite answering the call of the sea either; they are in-betweeners, topographically as well as socially and historically. If that is their choice, it is a wise one: the landmen are brutalised and without prospects; Maria Brennan, who haunts the play's interspersed narratives, chose the water and 'gave herself to the sea'. She, one of the many major offstage characters in Roche's drama, is yet another female suicide by drowning in contemporary drama in Ireland; why the motif has been used so often in the past twenty years is an intriguing question.

The Cavalcaders (1993)

This is Roche's first play to receive a professional production in Ireland, on the Abbey's Peacock stage, before its English premiere. While all of his earlier pieces used their small-scale setting to allow the characters to make points about the past, the present and the (lack of) future, *The Cavalcaders* is the first of his more recent plays concerned with formally interweaving the present with the past. It is set 'in the present day, flashing back to about seven years ago' (p. 10); even these flashbacks – which constitute most of the play – are full of stories, memories and conjurations of the past. There is almost no plot: four men, Terry, Rory, Ted and Josie, make up a quartet performing barbershop songs; two women, Breda and Nuala, join them in celebrations, love entanglements and reminiscences. We get to see Terry between the two women; others we only hear about. We see Josie courageously or innocently prepare for medical treatment – in the 'present' he is spoken of as dead. The shoemaker's workshop where the play is set is semi-functional in the past and about to be refurbished in the present; a piano is played, tuned, out of tune. There are petty treacheries and a good-humoured acceptance of life's unpleasantnesses. Songs and snatches of songs punctuate the play.

The randomness of the scenes, the permanently oscillating time scheme (for even in the 'past' there is no linearity from the first to the last flashback) and the absence of such dramatic near-necessities as suspense, causality or closure make this Roche's formally most ambitious and dramatically least satisfactory play. Particularly after the tightly plotted *Amphibians*, it marks a relapse to *Belfry* and the then current vogue of memory plays. Brian Friel's *Dancing at Lughnasa*, responsible for the spate of such texts in the early 1990s, achieved its focus through a single man's recollections and his earnest attempts at communicating them; the result is an unreliable narration that generates its charm by musing on its unreliability. Since such a focaliser, however flawed, is missing in Roche's play, the task of assembling the backstory is completely devolved on to the audience; the rewards for such reconstructive participation are, however, slight: no extraordinary story emerges. *The Cavalcaders* is not a bad play – Roche has not written one to date – but it certainly does not represent a major achievement. The author, perhaps for this reason, concentrated on screenplays and other performance-related work; the major text to emerge from that period is *Trojan Eddie* (1997).

On Such as We (2001)

Roche's longest play, again for the Abbey's Peacock stage, features three distinct but simultaneous settings: 'an old-fashioned barbershop' (p. 2), a hallway and a bedsit. The plot revolves around Oweney, the equally old-fashioned owner, his affair with the wife of his old school mate P.J., the assorted hangers-on and lodgers that populate the shop, and above all the attempts of P.J. to obtain Oweney's premises for development purposes by money, cajoling and violence. The final showdown between the two bare-fisted men, blood dripping on the Christmas snow, is a bravura piece of reported action. Oweney emerges as the winner of the bout; whether he will be able to stand his ground against the forces of modernisation remains unresolved.

On Such as We contains more and longer stage directions than Roche's other plays, and the word that recurs in them is 'sad'. The elegiac bass notes, never completely inaudible in his work, here dominate the composition, if this metaphor is permissible for a play so full of songs. The usual shop or club location again serves as a forum for (mainly male) attempts at fashioning a meaningful life, but these attempts end in stomach-aches, destroyed affections and pessimism. Visually, this downward slide is most effectively represented by the barbershop: after an attack by two thugs, its mirror is shattered, the bench is ripped out and 'The living quarters too are wrecked' (p. 86). Without any obvious parallel, the play evokes the tone of resignation at the end of Synge's *Riders to the Sea* (1904). Maurya's 'No man at all can be living forever, and we must be satisfied' echoes through Roche's play from the outset: 'May the Lord Have Mercy on Such as We'.

Lay Me Down Softly (2008)

Roche's most recent play, yet again for the Peacock Theatre, is also his most mature work. It tells the story of love, friendship and violence among the members of Delaney's Travelling Roadshow, a large fairground company that includes among its many attractions a rifle range, swing boats, a ghost train, a soothsayer, dodgems and, above all, the Academy, a boxing marquee where 'All comers' are offered a fight with the employees. The owner of Delaney's, Theo, rules his outfit with a mixture of roguish charm and outright brutality; when he suspects one of his men of having shaved off some of the takings, he breaks his jaw. His partner Lily, who is well capable of holding her own, and the (ex-)boxers Junior, Peadar and Dean complete the cast until Emer arrives; she is Theo's daughter from an earlier relationship. Against the background of Theo's dubious – and modestly successful – financial dealings, mostly involving betting on or against his own men, and the careful portrayal of life on the road, two main plot lines emerge, both involving Junior, the youngest of the boxers and the one with some semblance of a future before him. Dean, the least controlled of the fighters, administers a severe beating to a harmless, middle-aged challenger, only to find that his victim is uncle to Joey Dempsey, a professional welterweight boxer. Dempsey challenges Dean, wins and two days later fights Junior to a draw. Junior, meanwhile, has fallen in love with Emer, and after his big fight, bruised and cut, runs away with her and the day's takings. The last image of the play shows Peadar, who has helped them get away, sitting stoically and waiting for Theo's retribution.

Formally, this is another of Roche's well-made two-act pieces. The story is clear, suspenseful, interlaced with a rough – and male – humour that seems to emerge from the characters and lends them depth, definition and a slightly frenetic dignity. The imagery is never haphazard: the ubiquitous bandages, for instance, first of all are there to tie and tighten the pugilists' fists before the fight and to wrap up their injuries afterwards. But they also are a visual reminder of the prevalence of violence in the little world of Delaney's: characters are continually handling them, putting them on, away, into order. And Roche shows his craftsmanship in allowing the bandages, like the milk cartons, and the trains offstage, to acquire symbolic meaning: they speak of being tied down to a predictable life, of the need for help and ministering to this need, even of the rickety duct-tape nature of the boxer's certainties.

The most interesting formal feature of *Lay Me Down Softly* is its correlation of space and action: the entire play is set in and around the boxing ring, with no change in scenery other than a slackening and tautening of the ring's ropes – another instance of Roche's mature stage symbolism. But this ring remains a place of anticipation and recollection: all the fights occur between scenes, all the play's outward action, if that is the right word, happens off stage, and Peadar's terrible punishment will be administered after the last scene. We the audience are, as it were, only allowed to witness half the play and meet half the cast: Sadie the soothsayer, her lover Ernie, Joey Dempsey and his uncle, the crooked bookie, all these characters are essential but absent.

These absences first of all parallel and thus evoke the sense of nostalgia the play trades upon without surrendering to it: travelling roadshows may not be a 'forgotten world', as the programme to the Abbey's premiere claimed, but they certainly are fading away. In this sense the absence of so many theatrically attractive elements mirrors the disappearance of a form of popular entertainment; the play on this level works as an obituary. Yet all these absences are also the formal reflex of one of the play's themes: the wish to be elsewhere, to be away. Most of the characters speak of a past that was more stable than their present, and yet they all ended up in a travelling community; their talk is of getting out of that, too, but only Junior and Emer, the two outsiders in this company of outsiders, make the attempt. It takes another outsider's view, that of the spectator, to realise the layered irony of their escape: they try to reach the milk train, to get them to another place, but that other place will be just another Irish dairy village:

> **Junior** *picks up a milk bottle, which he sniffs and tastes like a wine expert.*
> **Junior** *Daisy Day* . . . Don't tell me: we're in the midlands, right? Just outside Bridgewater somewhere.
> **Emer** *sort of cheers and applauds.*
> Now if it was *Milkmaid* we'd be in Stoneyville.
> **Emer** What about Huntley Town?
> **Junior** Eh . . . *Fireside Dairies*? No, *Avondale*, though. Am I right?
> **Emer** Bang on.
> **Junior** *winks and taps his wily temple.*
> One way of knowin' where yeh are in the world at any point in time, I suppose.
> **Junior** I suppose. Good as any.
> **Emer** Mmn . . .

They chuckle and hold hands.
What about you, Peadar, how do you tell where you are in the
world from day to day?
Peadar I don't . . . I'm good and lost wherever I am. (p. 45f.)

'Good and lost wherever I am': that is the summary many Roche
characters would be happy to accept; Peadar's coming punishment at
the hands of Theo seems to be a small price to pay for such insight and
certainty of place.

Summary

Roche's plays have generally met with good, even eulogistic reviews;
the one characteristic few critics fail to mention is their 'humanity'. Of
course, the term is vague enough to cover most of drama, in Ireland
and elsewhere, but it nevertheless draws attention to Roche's many
fundamentally decent characters with their little acts of kindness, their
jokes, their liberality. Reviewers have also praised his transposition of
Wexford English into a stage language that speaks to audiences on
both sides of the Irish Sea. The theatres have recognised this; while
there are many playwrights with one or two professionally produced
plays, Roche's record is of another order entirely. To have one's first
three plays produced by London's Bush Theatre is rare indeed, and
the subsequent productions by the Royal Shakespeare Company
and the Abbey Theatre placed him centre stage in both Britain and
Ireland.

His steady success is primarily due to the sheer quality of his
dialogue; he offers excellent parts for actors keen to venture beyond the
psychological and linguistic drabness of in-yer-face theatre, whose rise
parallels that of Roche without any point of contact. In fact, Roche's
popularity with theatres and audiences alike may well be due to the fact
that his work firmly belongs to the mainstream of Irish drama with its
emphasis on the local, on stage realism, on 'authenticity'. National
themes are absent from his plays; the telling of stories, often not by
dramatic means but as tales recounted by characters, is not.

Billy Roche, in many ways, is as typical a contemporary Irish playwright as one can hope – or regret – to encounter: his plays are easily stageable two-act affairs with realistic settings, no fancy effects work, geared towards second-tier venues with limited casts. They are set in small-town Ireland, with Wexford as the dominant *pars pro toto*. The characters, mostly male and mostly at the less respectable end of society, grope for and sometimes achieve a little triumph – of being listened to, of solidarity, even of some degree of freedom. They are not interested in world affairs, and neither is their creator. Comfortable routine or disappointment has robbed them of a sense of purpose; their acts of resistance often turn into self-harm. They are either too young or too old, or too much concerned with the past and too little equipped for the future.

If this summary seems uncharitable it is none the less accurate; like most of his contemporaries, Roche would be out of his element writing about, say, global warming or heroism among the Barbary pirates. There is, however, a streak to his work that not only saves it from being merely of Wexford and specialist interest, but places him among the more important Irish dramatists. It is, paradoxically, the very parochialism of his characters and settings that gives him the opportunity to transcend these limitations and meditate, time and time again, on the nature of movement and stasis, the local and the far-off, the sense of belonging and the lust for uprootedness. In *Lay Me Down Softly* this conjoining of opposites is encapsulated perfectly in the symbol of the boxing ring in the marquee: a space that generates and delimits movement, in a temporary structure that is designed to be on the move and never changes, erected by a group of travellers who fear change. It may be too strong a claim to read and see Roche's plays as universal, but they are as close to a *theatrum mundi* as contemporary Irish drama is likely to get.

Primary Sources

Works by Billy Roche

The Cavalcaders and *Amphibians* (London: Nick Hern, 2001).
Lay Me Down Softly (London: Nick Hern, 2008).
On Such as We (London: Nick Hern, 2001).
Rain; *Belfry* (London: Nick Hern, 1992).
The Wexford Trilogy: A Handful of Stars; Poor Beast in the Rain; Trojan Eddie (London: Methuen, 1997).

Secondary Sources

'Billy Roche in Conversation with Conor McPherson', in Lilian Chambers, Ger FitzGibbon and Eamonn Jordan (eds), *Theatre Talk: Voices of Irish Theatre Practitioners* (Dublin: Carysfort Press, 2001), pp. 409–23.

Murray, Christopher, 'Billy Roche's Wexford Trilogy: Setting, Place, Critique', in Eamonn Jordan (ed.), *Theatre Stuff: Critical Essays on Contemporary Irish Theatre* (Dublin: Carysfort Press, 2000), pp. 209–23.

Wilcher, Robert, 'Billy Roche', in John Bull (ed.), *Dictionary of Literary Biography*, Vol. 33: *British and Irish Dramatists Since World War II: Second Series* (Detroit, MI: Bruccoli Clark Layman, 2001), pp. 240–4.

25 ENDA WALSH

Lisa Fitzpatrick

Disco Pigs; Bedbound; The Walworth Farce; The New Electric Ballroom; The Small Things

Introduction

'For what are we . . . if we are not our stories?' Dinny asks his sons in the closing scenes of *The Walworth Farce*. This is the question that Walsh, born in Dublin in 1967, poses in much of his work, exploring the creation of identity, family and community through language and storytelling. His strange dramatic worlds are inhabited by dysfunctional characters who create their own private languages, as in *Disco Pigs*; or their own myths that structure and limit their lives, as in *Bedbound*, *The Walworth Farce* and *The New Electric Ballroom*; or who struggle against the silencing of stories, as in *The Small Things*. These claustrophobic, paranoid worlds are often ripped asunder by violence, both diegetic and performed: in both *Disco Pigs* and *The Walworth Farce* the story reaches its conclusion through the enactment of violence on stage; in *Sucking Dublin* and *The Small Things* the violence is narrated, and in *The New Electric Ballroom* and *Bedbound* language is the medium of a psychological violence that demonstrates the truth of Dinny's words: we are our stories, and our stories shape our lives. Walsh's characters rarely escape theirs.

Walsh's early work was developed and produced with Corcadorca Theatre Company, an independent company based in Cork city. Together with Pat Kiernan, the company's Artistic Director, Walsh was a founding member and was for a time writer-in-residence. The company's approach to theatre-making emphasises taking performance out of theatre spaces and into the streets or other sites, the development of new writing, and an openness to international forms and styles of performance. It is one of the most consistently innovative companies currently working in Ireland. With Corcadorca, Walsh adapted *A Christmas Carol* for a promenade performance at Cork City Gaol in December 1994. There is very little information available on that production and the script was never published. His next production with Corcadorca Theatre Company was the unpublished *The Ginger Ale Boy* (1995), described by Fintan O'Toole in his review as exploring 'the bleak gulf between the outward show of fun and the innate intimations of cruelty, isolation and madness in the act of ventriloquism' (p. 153).

The Plays

Disco Pigs (1996)

Walsh's next production with Corcadorca was *Disco Pigs*, which was initially staged at the Triskel Arts Centre in Cork at midnight. The timing was chosen to work with the play's subject matter and setting: Ric Knowles describes it as a 'club drama',[1] referring to the situating of the action in the night-time city, largely in bars and clubs. The characters of Pig (male) and Runt (female) therefore blend into their surroundings, becoming only an exaggerated, violent version of the scene outside the theatre. The play is probably most renowned for its creation of a dialect, an almost incomprehensible patois that combines urban Cork with baby talk, animal noises and teenage slang. The play opens with Pig and Runt retelling the story of their births on the same day in the same hospital; as Runt exclaims, 'Owney one sec tween da girl an da boy! An us no brudder or sis or anyth!' (p. 164). They are each the first person the other sees in their hospital cribs, and they grow up together, initially developing their private language of snorts and grunts as part of a game. Runt explains, however:

> **Runt** We grow up a bit at a dime an all dat dime we silen when odders roun. No word or no-ting . . . An da hole a da estate dey talk at us. Look nasty yeah. But . . . we make a whirl

where Pig an Runt jar king an queen! . . . we make a whirl dat no one can live sept us 2. (p. 173)

Picturing themselves as a latter-day Bonny and Clyde, Pig and Runt develop a series of violent rituals that they play out across 'Pork Sity' at night. They intimidate bus drivers, attack clerks in off-licences to steal alcohol, and use Runt as bait to launch physical assaults on men in clubs. Runt chooses a victim, dances with him, kisses him, and then Pig attacks the man and beats him up. But on the night when the action takes place, Runt and Pig have just turned seventeen and, Runt remarks, 'all of a puddin, ders a real big differ-ence' (p. 173). That night Runt meets someone she likes, and to her horror Pig continues their game, attacking the man and beating him to death. Suddenly confronted with the horrific implosion of the Real into their play, Runt flees, abandoning Pig and finally breaking out of her linguistic isolation. The last words spoken on stage are Runt's, as she struggles with language: 'an I watch . . . da liddle quack quacks . . . I look . . . at the ducks . . . as they swim in the morning sun . . . in the great big . . . watery shite . . . that is the river Lee' (p. 188).

The play represents violence through language, the raucous poetry and harsh accents of the two characters heightening the acts they narrate. The speed and energy of the performance add to this effect. In a scene where Pig beats up the clerk in the off-licence, for example, the dialogue describes the action as follows:

Pig Free drink pretty please.
Runt No ney panic button, Foxy he panic. He say 'I can't Darren.' Pig he get da buzz in da ead he wanna fisty! . . .
Runt Took Pig ten mins smash all buddels in dat drink shap . . . He stamp na Foxy face. Da nose like tomato itgo squish n' drip drop. Foxy cried. (pp. 167–8)

The scene builds a sense of threat from Pig's initial impossible request with its mocking 'pretty please', through the repetition of 'panic', to the vivid descriptions of Pig's 'buzz in da ead' and Foxy's crushed nose as a squished, bleeding tomato. In production, the audience experiences the aural violence of Pig's strange, harsh speech, and has time to fear what he will do before the actor performs the stamping on Foxy's imaginary face. The pacing of the performance adds to the sense that things are out of control. The violence of Pig's movements, coupled with Runt's description of the broken nose 'itgo squish n' drip', and her likening of it to a squashed tomato, engages the imaginations of the audience. Because the action is not presented in a naturalistic style the consequences of the violence are never revealed, leaving the audience to the images in their own imaginations. Anthony Kubiak writes on the evocation of fear in the audience that 'the real pain inflicted on the body . . . can never become a sign, can never enter a system of information and exchange. It remains unsignifiable, unrepresentable.'[2] What the audience do not see is always more terrifying than the revelation of stage artifice that inevitably accompanies what they do see.

Bedbound (2000)

In many of his plays, Walsh returns to the idea of closed, private worlds such as that shared by Pig and Runt. He does not again use dialect as the isolating factor, however, replacing the barriers of language with physical, visual barriers such as the walls in his one-act play *Bedbound*. This play opens with a box visible on stage, before the front wall 'crashes to the ground' to reveal a filthy, small bed with two characters – Dad and Daughter – perched on it. The panicky claustrophobia of their relationship is given a physical expression in the set and in the frantic pace of their unceasing talk, in which they rehearse the events in their lives that have led them to this point. The Daughter contracted polio as a result of a childhood mishap, and the disease has deformed and disabled her once healthy body. Simultaneously, Dad experienced a humiliating business defeat that prompted his gradual withdrawal from the world. He moves from Dublin to his home town of Cork, tells people that his daughter is dead, and builds a room in his house to contain and hide her and her mother. The room shrinks and shrinks until it is the tiny space seen on stage, the size of a child's bed. Dad's psychological and emotional withdrawal, and his fixation with his daughter's illness, is communicated in Walsh's typically expressionistic style through the physical representation of his tiny, obsessive world.

The Walworth Farce (2006)

Walsh's characters often opt to avoid the rest of the world, burying themselves in fictions to hide from the grief and pain of life, which is expressed through the metaphors of words as methods of social control and limitation, and of stories as rigid expressions of identity and barriers to possibility. Family relationships are strongly implicated in this process: it is Dad in *Bedbound* who imposes physical restrictions on his daughter and wife; in *The Walworth Farce* Dinny isolates his two sons from the rest of the world and forces them to constantly perform an absurd fictional version of his emigration from Cork, and in *The New Electric Ballroom* two older sisters force the youngest to eschew all relationships, because they were once disappointed in love. Walsh has said in an interview with Jason Zinoman that 'I like family stories with characters who we find monstrous or grotesque but who we then begin to like'.[3] His characters tend to be oddly sympathetic, and in spite of the things they do they can arouse the compassion of the spectator. Dad in *Bedbound* is a tormented character, pitiful despite his appalling treatment of his daughter and wife. Dinny is a murderer who has destroyed the lives of his two sons, yet his refusal to confront the truth of his leaving Cork and his obsession with the daily competition to win the acting trophy is genuinely moving. The childishness of his ambition, and his repeated evocation of *The Waltons* as an image of his grotesque family, softens the spectator's response to his actions. The simplicity of what he wants in the midst of the horrors he has inflicted and his motivation as a mixture of love and selfishness make him an Everyman figure, albeit a grotesque version.

Dinny left Cork, we discover, because he murdered his brother Paddy and sister-in-law Vera with a kitchen knife. He fled to London, to Walworth Road, and his small sons were sent after him for reasons which are never explained. Sean speculates that he and Blake were sent by their mother 'Because she still loved you. Because what we had used to be so good in Ireland. Maybe she could forgive you. (*Slight pause*). Dad, I don't know why she sent us' (p. 59). Arriving in London, Dinny realises the full weight of his guilt, which distresses him so much that he retreats to the flat where the family still lives and never leaves it again. This story has become so embedded in his sons' minds that when he begins the narrative, Blake completes it:

> . . . the people . . . come out from houses and shops and they're after you. Their skin, it falls to the ground and their bodies running you down and wanting to tear you to shreds . . . they come up out of the ground . . . And they're all snapping teeth and grabbing hands they have. (pp. 31–2)

This horror film image of the outside world is the only one Blake knows. Even Sean, who goes every day for the groceries, is afraid of the world outside the flat. Apart from his trip to Tesco where he speaks to no one, the family sees only each other. Their days are spent replaying Dinny's story of how he became a brain surgeon, and how his brothers and sisters-in-law Eileen and Vera were killed with a poisoned chicken. They left him all their wealth with their dying breaths, so he went to London to 'build for [his wife and children] a castle to overlook the English scum'. Then disaster struck, in the form of the 'bad people' who emerge from the ground (p. 32), and Dinny's dream of a castle was never realised.

Thematically and dramaturgically, the play explores the representation of violence onstage. Dinny's play within a play is the story of his brothers' murder with poison – there are the inevitable echoes of *Hamlet* there – and they and their wives die onstage in a scene performed by Dinny's sons, with Blake in a wig performing the parts of the women. The characters die holding their stomachs and exclaiming about the pain, while making speeches that provide closure to their story of illicit love:

> **Sean** *as* **Peter** (*holding his stomach in pain*) I fear we've come undone, Vera. Our budding love affair cut short and a shame I'll never get to see you in the nip! . . .

[**Sean** *as* **Peter** *and* **Blake** *as* **Vera**] *both drop to their knees and hold hands.*
They collapse dead.
Blake *gets up and puts on* **Eileen**'*s wig.* (p. 81)

These deaths, which are self-consciously and explicitly performances and are revealed as such when Blake recostumes himself as another character, contrast sharply with the killing of Dinny and Blake in the final scenes of the play. The murder scene is violent: Blake '*fires the knife into* **Dinny**'*s back*', then '*pulls out the knife, turns* **Dinny** *towards him quickly and stabs him in the stomach hard*' (p. 83). Dinny gasps but speaks through his pain, commenting with pleasure on the realistic detail of the 'real' blood (p. 83). Unable to face life outside the apartment Blake tricks Sean into stabbing him too. Again, the stabbing takes place in full view of the audience.

The contrast between the farce, the sense of threat that builds throughout the play and the deaths of Dinny and Blake allows Walsh to explore a range of dramaturgical devices, though the evocation of a sense of threat is probably the most effective. This is created in a number of ways: first through Sean's obvious fear, which suggest he knows more than the audience does about what might happen; the tying up of Hayley; the male characters' tenuous grasp on reality; the presence of knives on stage, and Hayley's own silence and tears, which communicate her terror. Dinny's incorporation of Hayley into the family story does not seem to bode well, and in one frightening moment he smears her face with cream to make her appear white. The racial violence that this action suggests acts as a reminder of racist violence and terrorism in the 'real' world, reminding the audience of events outside the safe space of the theatre and disturbing the sense of watching something that is only a fiction.

The New Electric Ballroom (2008)

The most recent of Walsh's plays on the Irish stage is *The New Electric Ballroom*, which first played in August 2008 at the Town Hall Theatre in Galway. The play was first performed in 2004 in Munich, at the

Kammerspiele, and won *Theater Heute*'s prize for best foreign play in 2005. This play has often been described as a companion piece for *The Walworth Farce*, since it seems to explore the same material. Two sisters, Breda and Clara, hurt by the same man, prematurely retire from the world of romance and take refuge in their house by the sea. Their sister Ada, who is twenty years younger and so was born after their self-imposed incarceration, has been so misshapen by their stories that she has never been kissed. She works in a fish factory, 'canning the sea', where she takes care of the accounts. Her comfort with numbers is in stark contrast with her inability to deal with other people. The sisters' only visitor is Patsy the fishmonger who bursts on to the stage at three different points, providing a comical disruption to the action. On the day in question, however, Patsy is haunted by a strange dream which he tells to Ada. For a brief moment towards the end of the play they contemplate a life together, before the older sisters remind Patsy that there is no escaping the defining, limiting power of stories. They remind him that it is not possible to embrace new opportunities or to redefine oneself, and, defeated, he leaves. Ada's last hope for escape is thereby removed.

Although the narrative arc of the play is similar to that of *The Walworth Farce*, Walsh has publicly revised his opinion that the two plays are linked. Speaking to Mark Fisher he says:

> For the past couple of years I've been saying *New Electric Ballroom* must be a companion piece because I wrote the plays within the same three months . . . For ages I thought they must be companion pieces because they are both about theatre happening in a living room, both dealing with people using theatre as a form of torture or a weird therapy. But apart from that, their approach is very different.[4]

Indeed, a comparison of the two plays shows that *The Walworth Farce* explores the issue of violence in performance, as discussed above, while *The New Electric Ballroom* is concerned with 'the risk of falling in love and whether it's worth it . . . It is a quieter thing [than *The Walworth Farce*] that concentrates on the heart, loss and love.'[5] The tragedy of

Breda and Clara, one which they inflict on everyone close to them, is that they cannot risk falling in love. Having been hurt once, they perceive themselves as eternally marked in the eyes of their community, 'branded, marked and scarred by talk' (p. 35). Their sense of themselves is such that they cannot imagine their misfortune is not the topic of every conversation. Breda says,

> Mocking talk all week turning the streets narrower around us. Them nasty words crashing about from Monday to Friday and locking that front door behind us. What chance for the brokenhearted . . . to keep clean when people have the making of us? (p. 35)

Her words echo Dinny's question – what are we, if we are not our stories? Dressing themselves in rara skirts and sweaters as they did in their teenage years, making themselves up and rehearsing the moment of betrayal, they insist that a single story defines their lives. Later, again through experimentation with costume, they transform Patsy the fisherman into a handsome man in a suit, capable of contemplating a life with Ada. But ultimately, like the two older women, he cannot risk the pain and exposure: '. . . my heart tells me that the risk is far too great. It's too great, Ada! . . . My own heart's too scarred by days and nights alone' (p. 44).

One of the recurring concerns in Walsh's work is that of performance in relation to truth, and in relation to the power of performance to shape reality. *Disco Pigs* makes self-conscious reference to itself as a performance, both through the eschewal of naturalism and in the characters' habit of addressing the audience directly as 'soap-opera fans' and 'drama fans'. Many of his later plays are explicitly concerned with performance as well: Dinny's performance of the family history in Cork, or Breda and Clara's performance of their teenage selves, presents the audience with a metatheatrical representation of the past. Breda and Clara perceive themselves to be marked by their stories, but in fact it is the obsessive repetition in performance of their humiliation that fixes them in the past.

The efficacy of performance is at the heart of these plays, and the nature of theatre itself, which Walsh explores by playing with the functions of costume, make-up, props and set. Objects take on other functions: the wardrobe in the flat on the Walworth Road becomes multiple offstage spaces; the wigs that Sean and Blake whisk on and off their heads become performative markers of gender and character, and salami represents the chicken that the family ate for their last dinner together, many years earlier. In fact, the salami standing in for the chicken is not satisfactory, in Dinny's opinion. The situation has arisen because Sean has brought home the wrong shopping, which has also necessitated the substitution of Ryvita with cheese spread for cheese sandwiches. Dinny, angry, explains

> The story doesn't work if we don't have the facts and Ryvitas aren't the facts . . . they're not close to the facts . . . A Ryvita's just taking the piss, Sean. A Ryvita's a great leap of the imagination. (p. 13)

Tellingly, it is the spilling of his 'real' blood on stage when Blake fatally stabs him that pleases Dinny the most: 'Fuck it, that's some acting. Real blood' (p. 83). In celebration, he kisses his acting trophy.

The Small Things (2005)

The emphasis on the 'facts' and the need for truth in performance, the question of what 'truth' in performance might be, the efficacy of performance in shaping life and the world, are central concerns in Walsh's work. His fascination with words and the power of the spoken word are an aspect of that, and the defining, scarring, limiting and freeing potential of language recurs in his dramas. The play that precedes *The Walworth Farce* and *The New Electric Ballroom*, however, is one that explores the silencing of stories and the trauma of wordlessness. *The Small Things*, like Walsh's other work, is concerned with trauma, violence and the human capacity to survive.

The Small Things, which was produced by Paines Plough in 2005 at the Menier Chocolate Factory, has two characters, Man and

Woman. Throughout most of the play they appear to engage in a deceptively gentle dialogue of childhood memories: the first day at school, going swimming together, first kisses. The unsettling home-life experiences of the woman, and the strange and violent images that occasionally encroach into this safe space, gradually create a sense of unease. However, only as the play unfolds and the terrible trauma that the characters witnessed is revealed, does it become clear that they occupy different houses which face each other from either side of a mountain valley, and that they each believe the other is dead. They continue to speak about the 'small things' as a way of defying the devastation of their community, and of keeping each other alive in their memories and imaginations.

The story they reveal is a horrific tale of two men who terrorise their own community, and then the wider world. Woman's father develops an obsession with routine and order. He imposes this initially on his children through strict timetables, but he is further empowered when he meets the chip-shop man, who is obsessed with silence. They begin to slice off people's tongues and give them timetables to follow, insisting that these mutilated people walk in straight lines and complete counting tasks each day:

we talk about those ten people who've been silenced already. We watch them walk about the village with clipboards and stopwatches . . . I see a woman made to count her breaths in a single day making that number of breaths her marker for all her days. (pp. 21–22)

The thirst for power and influence is such, however, that the men scheme to silence the entire village. They gather everyone at the pool, and threaten to cut out the tongues of the children if the parents will not submit peacefully to the procedure. The parents comply, but the children are not saved. Their tongues are cut out too, and their bodies are tossed into the swimming pool. The Woman's story suggests that the women are taken into the forest to be raped, and that the old are executed:

I'm hid under my mother's coat. We're sat on the ground at the edge of the woods with all the other women. All of them made silent and one at a time taken to the woods . . . Shot bodies of old women thrown about the dead wood. (p. 29)

These images, common to other genocides, heighten the horror of the story, reminding the spectators of real-world atrocities and of the fragility of their own existence.

The story concludes. Only a few are spared, to spread the good news from village to village, and the Man is one of those. His guilt at his complicity now torments him, and he wears onstage the shoes of one of his child victims. The silent are eventually herded into the sea (p. 37), an image of mass annihilation that Pinter also uses to evoke the Holocaust in *Ashes to Ashes*. The Woman escapes, believing the Man to be dead. They arrive at their separate mountain tops: 'surely there's safety in the skies. And your face it guides me upwards. It takes me to where's safe,' Man says (p. 37). Woman says, 'And your face it guides me upwards and finds me this house and keeps me safe. It comforts me and opens my day and closes my night' (p. 38). Their overlapping dialogue, of which this is only one example, expresses their love and need for each other, and their longing for contact. Man says, 'And speak to you daily though you are surely dead, love. Life passes and memory repeats' (p. 38).

The drama explores and represents our human longing for contact and understanding, the need for what the characters call 'chit chat chit chat' (p. 10). In *The New Electric Ballroom* Breda repeatedly affirms that 'by their nature people are talkers' (p. 5). Though she and Clara see words as damaging and limiting, they obsessively complete their own narratives and use language to control their own small world. But while *The New Electric Ballroom* explores the power of fiction and performance to create or shape reality, in *The Small Things* the control of speech is identified as a priority for any dictatorship, and the drama centres on the ability of small numbers of fanatical individuals to distort and destroy entire populations.

Summary

While the thematic concerns with family, language and violence are shared by Walsh's contemporaries – Marina Carr, Conor McPherson and Martin McDonagh among others – his work has attracted comparatively little academic attention. What scholarly interest he has attracted has tended to examine his work in relation to the phenomenon of globalisation, as both Patrick Lonergan and Ric Knowles do in their respective discussions of *Disco Pigs*. This may be because, after the success of *Disco Pigs* in 1996, Walsh's work was staged in relatively small venues in Ireland, or overseas and in translation. It was not until Druid produced *The Walworth Farce* in 2006 that Walsh was once more on a main stage in Ireland. In contrast, the work of Carr, McPherson and McDonagh premieres at the Abbey and the Gate in Dublin, and the Royal Court and the National in London.

However, it is arguable that Walsh's work has not been staged at the major Irish and London theatres because it does not easily fit within the contemporary Irish repertoire or the scholarly narratives of contemporary Irish theatre. It tends towards expressionism, rather than the broadly naturalistic performance style of most Irish theatre. In general, though the language may reflect Walsh's fascination with Cork speech patterns and accents,[6] his darkly absurd characters in their strange worlds do not comment on or reflect Irish society. His fascination with stories and storytelling does not result in plays like McPherson's *The Weir*, or work that sits within a storytelling tradition. Rather, Walsh's work is concerned with the nature of performance itself, and the plays must be seen and studied in performance – the texts alone will not do. The tendency in Irish scholarship to privilege the literary over the performative is one reason for the delay in engaging with Walsh's work; however, the recent success of *The New Electric Ballroom* seems likely to result in increased academic interest.

Primary Sources

Works by Enda Walsh

Bedbound (London: Nick Hern Books, 2001).

Disco Pigs, in John Farleigh (ed.), *Far From the Land* (London: Methuen, 1998).

The New Electric Ballroom (London: Nick Hern Books, 2008).

The Small Things (London: Nick Hern Books, 2005).

The Walworth Farce (London: Nick Hern Books, 2007).

Secondary Sources

Fisher, Mark, 'Enda Walsh – Halcyon Daze', *Scotland on Sunday*, 10 August 2008 <http://scotlandonsunday.scotsman.com/sosreview/Enda-Walsh—Halcyon-daze.437 2930.jp>.

Fitzpatrick, P., 'Enda's Delirious Hunger for Moving On', *Sunday Independent*, 19 October 2008 <http://www.independent.ie/lifestyle/endas-delirious-hunger-for-moving-on-1503294.html>.

Knowles, Ric, *Reading the Material Theatre* (Cambridge: Cambridge UP, 2004), pp. 195–200.

Kubiak, Anthony, *Stages of Terror: Terrorism, Ideology and Coercion as Theatre History* (Bloomington and Indianapolis: Indiana University Press, 1991).

O'Toole, Fintan, 'The Ginger Ale Boy', in Julia Furay and Redmond O'Hanlon (eds), *Critical Moments* (Dublin: Carysfort Press, 2003).

Zinoman, Jason, 'Mr. Normal's Dysfunctional Irish Families', *New York Times*, 6 April 2008 <http://www.nytimes.com/2008/04/06/theater/06zino.html?_r=2&oref=slog in&ref=theater&pagewanted=print>.

Notes

1. Ric Knowles, *Reading the Material Theatre*, p. 195.
2. Anthony Kubiak, *Stages of Terror*, p. 21.
3. Jason Zinoman, 'Mr. Normal's Dysfunctional Irish Families'.
4. Mark Fisher, 'Enda Walsh – Halcyon Daze'.
5. Ibid.
6. See P. Fitzpatrick, 'Enda's Delirious Hunger for Moving On'.

INDEX